And the Road Below

by
John Westley

The blister-by-blister account of his
record breaking walk around the
coastline of the British Isles

Wealth I ask not, hope nor love,
Nor a friend to know me;
All I seek, the heaven above
And the road below me.

Robert Louis Stevenson
'The Vagabond' (*Songs of Travel*, 1886).

Meridian Books

Published 1994 by Meridian Books

© John Westley 1994

ISBN 1-869922-25-5

A catalogue record for this book is available from the British Library.

Meridian Books
40 Hadzor Road
Oldbury
Warley
West Midlands
B68 9LA

Printed in Great Britain by BPC Wheatons Ltd., Exeter.

Gullible Travels

(with apologies to William Cowper)

John Westley was a citizen
Of credit and aplomb;
Twenty years a postman he
Of Lower Edmonton.

Both lithe of form and fleet of foot,
His features aquiline.
Yet harboured he the urge to do
Deeds worthy and sublime.

His mother's health was failing fast,
And haunted by her plight,
John pondered long and hard and deep,
Far late into the night.

'Just how to serve dear mother's cause,
To aid such folk as she?'
Then waking smartly with a start:
'I'll walk for charity!'

'A sponsored walk I'll undertake,
Finances to secure,
To help allay such suffering,
Mayhap to find a cure!'

Ten thousand rugged miles he'd trek
With Britain's coast in view.
And just to make the figures up,
He'd throw in Ireland too ...

Sean Morven

Dedication

For Eileen –
Whose enthusiasm was infectious;
Whose potential boundless
– And the walk we never got 'round to.

Acknowledgements

In view of the sheer scale and duration of the Around the Isles project, a fair and comprehensive acknowledgement would, by its very nature, run to a veritable tome of *War and Peace* proportions. Thus, in the interest of brevity and expediency, I restrict my heartfelt appreciation to the following:

John Mole, walk co-ordinator (not forgetting his long suffering family), for his diplomacy and selfless dedication; William Cockburn, Royal Mail Chief Executive, my champion and sponsor respectively; Kathleen Mole, for her 'persuasive' telephone manner; Tamzin Mole, typist supreme; Bob and Steve of Basecamp; Therm-a-Rest Ltd; Microft Technology Ltd; Halifax Building Society (particularly Manager and staff of Turner's Hill Branch, Cheshunt); Mystic Meg, Astrologist Extraordinaire; B&I ferries; Mary and George, for their inspiration; Paul Austin of Ladbrookes; Ken Merrell, for his 'intoxicating' company; Bank of Scotland; members and supporters of the Multiple Sclerosis Society of Great Britain and Northern Ireland; *The Irish Times* and Aer Lingus, for coming to my rescue; John Walford, MS Society's General Secretary, for an elevating Thames-side oration; friends, family, and the good folk of Cheshunt, for a memorable 'Homecoming'.

To those mentioned above – as well as those lamentably overlooked (you know who you are!) – I hereby extend my eternal gratitude.

And what of all the rest?
For each one played their part:
Endeared themselves to me,
Won places in my heart.
Of all these caring souls,
I'll always live in praise
For those *slí na mara** days.

---

*   An obscure road sign proclamation in Ireland's *Gaeltacht* (Irish speaking) regions, *Slí na mara* (pronounced: Schlee na mara) lyrically indicates…'The way of the sea'.

About the Author

John Westley, reigning British Endurance Walking Champion, was born in Enfield, Middlesex in September 1952 – eighteen months after the family bookbindery (Westley & Co.) ceased production after 200 years. His education took place at St Mary's High School, Cheshunt, Hertfordshire ('Could do better') where he excelled at sport and art. To this day he holds the unique distinction of being the only chorister to be expelled from St Mary's church choir for 'talking in the ranks' – only to be reinstated later that same day. Apparently his soprano strains were indispensible!

On leaving school in the summer of '69 he became a telegram boy in North London – in his own words 'the best job in the world'. Throughout his subsequent twenty-two years loyal service to the Royal Mail he dabbled with mixed fortunes at devising board-games and the penning of short stories, poetry, stage musicals and television plays. Only when he began writing on the subject of his pet hobby, genealogy, did his literary output find a ready market.

John has agreed to donate half his royalties from sales of this book to the Multiple Sclerosis Society. This sum will be matched by an equal contribution from the publishers.

John Westley on Ben Nevis

The Multiple Sclerosis Society would like to acknowledge the generous support made available by John Westley and Meridian Books through the publication of *And the Road Below*.

The Multiple Sclerosis Society has the dual aims of encouraging and funding research to find the cause and cure of multiple sclerosis, and the provision of a welfare and support service for families, one member of which suffers with this condition.

Prologue

The following being unabridged extracts from my private journal – abruptly curtailed thereafter in a fit of remorse:

February 3rd 1988 'Black Wednesday. Utterly devastated. My worst fears confirmed. Mary (*author's mother*) has been positively diagnosed to be suffering from Multiple Sclerosis; a fact further corroborated by symptomatic loss of bladder control and failing vision. According to the Reader's Digest *Family Medical Adviser*, it is still possible for one so afflicted to live a long and comparatively active life. So I suppose there remains some reason for optimism? At this evening's (hospital) visit, Mary understandably looked tired and drawn, though true to form she remains magnificently brave. How can such tragedy befall one so selfless? One who actually gave away her few remaining pounds to the cash-strapped nurses without even a thought for her own financial welfare? Mary's faith was in a decidedly delicate state before this current bombshell; I daren't even consider its present standing. At times like this words simply fail one...'

February 14th 1988 'It would appear that the logical beneficiaries of my long-intended charity walk have been thrust tragically before my very eyes. Surely there is no need to look further afield than the nation's hapless host of Multiple Sclerosis sufferers?'

Two short years, one postponement, and myriad unacknowledged correspondence later, that lofty ideal was made manifest in the guise of *The Around The Isles Campaign In Aid Of Multiple Sclerosis*. Hereafter, duly invigorated with grievous inspiration, began the most singularly edifying – and often perilous – episode of my life to date ...

John Westley

With due regard to the climate of political upheaval in Northern Ireland, the names and professions of some of the Province's more colourful characters, along with the locale of certain incidents, have been suitably modified in order to render those individuals concerned a degree of anonymity.

1 Have boots, will travel

A journey of a thousand miles must begin with a single step.
Chinese proverb

Sunday, 5th August, 1990.

THE summer had been moderately good by British standards, without being spectacular. Between showers, Wimbledon fortnight had long since been and gone; while cricket's protracted county championship neared its traditional rain-sodden denouement. The first weekend in August, however, saw a dramatic transformation in the nations meteorological fortunes. As the temperature soared into the 80s, and sprinkler and hose-pipe bans became the order of the day, a shimmering heat-haze hovered over the length and breadth of our now parched and arid land ...

A waxen sun had been stoically disseminating heat for a good five hours by the time I vacated my fourth floor suite for the plush air-conditioned silence of the deserted corridor. The six weeks since receiving verification of my Royal Mail sponsorship had passed with Juggernaut-velocity, allowing little or no time to consider the full implications of my proposed undertaking, let alone gauge the extent of my inner resolution. A curiously discordant chime broke the spell of my fragile reverie, heralding the imminent arrival of one of two lifts. A brace of highly-polished metallic doors divided to reveal a corpulent payload of archetype American tourists, mirror 'shades' and camcorders to the fore, intent only upon 'doing' London. I joined the hearty company.

'Some backpack, huh!' exclaimed RayBans, shattering the fleeting quiet.

'Some sorta hike?' probed Blue-rinse, likewise eyeing my bulky impediment.

'Something like that,' was my polite yet curt reply, not wishing to court further discourse.

The very prospect of conversing with my own sunglass-borne reflection fuelled my welling disquiet. As we sluggishly decelerated, I glimpsed my three-D image in the multi-facets of the lift's mirrored interior. From the pristine whiteness of my T-shirt, boldly emblazoned with the 'Around the Isles' logo, to the viscous-sheen of my newly 'Nikwaxed' walking boots, I appeared – much to my chagrin – every inch the callow novice. My ensemble, so diligently assembled, felt at once constricting and capacious, and in general the source of much discomfort. Such was the weight of my rucksack (in excess of 40lb) upon my lithe form (less self-deprecating than 'thin') that even the most innocuous of tumbles would have left me marooned upon my back, limbs flailing, in a posture of beetle-like vulnerability. Was this whole thing really my idea? Just what had I let myself in for? Intoxicated by blind ambition, I'd surely bitten off more than even I could chew this time.

Our descent complete, the doors parted. Flushed from the lift like so much flotsam on a flood-tide of voracious colonials, I negotiated the foyer's obstacle course of departing guests and luggage in a state of inebriated abstraction. Though not yet 10 a.m. the stark contrast between the near frigidarium of the hotel's inner sanctum and the torrid heat of the sun-baked forecourt was of physical dimension. Girding my all too flaccid loins, I stepped from the intermediate sanctuary of the revolving door into full unremitting glare of sunshine, well-wishers and media alike ... resulting in instant sobriety.

Following a rousing countdown inaugurated by walk co-ordinator John 'Hacker' Mole, I departed promptly at 10 a.m., initially accompanied by balloon-toting friends and family. From the gravelled forecourt of the Tower-Thistle Hotel, the theory was to cross the Thames by way of the newly refurbished Tower Bridge, and thence to head east towards Kent, hugging the contours of the river where possible. Such was the theory. In actuality, no sooner had our conspicuous band reached the bridge's southern pier than my presence was urgently requested back at the start – by a late addition to the corps of press photographers, who overrode my better judgement with pleas of imminent dismissal should I fail to comply. Back at the start, some ten brief minutes after departing ('That was quick!'), my unscheduled return was both embarrassing and anti-climatic. Like attending one's own sparsely patronised wake, my presence was surplus to requirements. Certainly seeing Mary shaken and in tears did little for my morale. I eventually set out on the walk proper at 10.30 a.m., some half-hour behind schedule. All orientation was dependent upon a stockpile of some 140 odd Ordnance Survey maps, carried mercifully in manageable batches of six. I cast an appreciative glance to a sun-kissed Tower of London, home of the original Ordnance Survey some 200 yards and nearly 200 years distant.

Air temperature at Erith, Kent: 85F and rising.

Six and a half hours, 32 kilometres, numerous tourist attractions (*Cutty Sark*, National Nautical Museum, etc.), and several interesting characters later, I found myself in the hinterland of Dartford, Kent. Apart from one or two necessary technical adjustments, the equipment had acquitted itself well. As to my physical condition, the shoulders were inevitably the main source of discomfort (an absence of flesh!), the feet, conversely, were bearing up well.

And so to sleep, the Sleep of the Just – Just knackered!

Monday, 6th August. Tempered only by the welcome presence of a zephyr-like north-eastern breeze, the glorious sunshine remained my day long companion. With a view to escaping the urban sprawl, I set my sights on attaining the outer reaches of the Thames Estuary by nightfall.

Initially every joint, muscle and sinew in my body cried out in revolt. Though after an hours yomp (Falkland's jargon now being a part of everyday parlance) this subsided to an occasional mute grumble. My journal adequately reflects the temper of the moment as I passed within sight of the as yet incomplete, yet none the less impressive, Queen Elizabeth II Dartford-Thurrock Road Bridge: 'Must shed excess luggage!'

At Gravesend I joined the Saxon shore way – the first authentic stretch of off-road walking. With the Thames Estuary gliding effortlessly to my left and grass (be it tinder-dry) now underfoot, my journal bares witness to my nouveau elation: 'At last, that heady cocktail of saline enriched ozone is filling my nostrils!' A mood heightened by the sudden abundance of cormorants swimming, in flight, or merely sunning themselves in cruciform posture.

Following the supreme euphoria of my initial Thames-side peregrination, the afternoon deteriorated into a veritable slog beside a seemingly endless sea wall. Concrete, concrete everywhere! On Halstow marshes I spotted a pure white rabbit; a remarkable though ultimately doomed specimen – too conspicuous by half. Such examples of albinism I was latterly informed are most uncommon.

Around St. Mary's Bay a sizeable section of shoreway had been paved with opalescent granite chippings; most excruciating underfoot – akin to walking barefoot over gravel. Coinciding with the general onset of fatigue, I took a most undignified tumble, base over apex. As the talcum-like dust cloud cleared, I found myself pinned to the deck by my rucksack. Despite pain-wracked and bloodied knees and elbows, the utter indignity of it all prompted a bout of uncontrollable laughter. Surely if the road to Heaven is paved with gold, the road to Hell is paved with granite chippings!

I trudged the final few leg-weary kilometres into Allhallows-on-Sea – a regular one-horse-town (and the horse has bolted!) – in zombie mode. Having slogged in excess of 47 km, I was more than ready for bed. Alas, Allhallows lone hostelry was unable – or unwilling? – to oblige. With daylight rapidly fading, I scoured the remainder of the village in search of accommodation – in vain.

Retracing my footsteps through the now deserted village, I made my way by moonlight to the featureless sward of Allhallows Marsh. Though too dark to pitch a tent (my torch

THE LONGEST WALK ROUND THE COAST OF THE BRITISH ISLES WAS ONE OF 9,524 MILES (15,239 Km) MADE BY JOHN WESTLEY OF CHESHUNT, HERTS FROM AUG 5, 1990 TO SEPT 20, 1991, IN AID OF MULTIPLE SCLEROSIS.

The author as pictured by Dick Millington in the 'Daily Mail' Factfile

batteries being inexplicably flat), I managed to assemble an arrangement of sleeping, bivvy and survival bags into an almost inviting combination – 'almost' being the operative word.

A thoroughly miserable and sleepless evening ensued – spent alternately sweltering (when submerged beneath down and Gore-Tex) and shivering (having surfaced for air). I managed to divert my mind from the cold and all pervading dampness (a gossamer-ribbon of mist now veiled the length and breadth of the marsh) by surveying the myriad stars playing peek'a'boo behind the scudding clouds, and lamely trying to stare out the Man in the Moon.

A thoroughly inauspicious end to a largely inauspicious day. Oh, for the coastline proper!

Tuesday, 7th August. A blush of pink dusted the Eastern horizon. Following an evening of indescribable purgatory, I rose and struck bivvy ('camp' being too grand a term for such squalor) as soon as the pallid light of dawn permitted. Not wishing to outstay my unwelcome, I departed Allhallows Marsh, both spirits and attire thoroughly dampened and chilled to the bone, sustained only by a can of fruit cocktail – and utterly resolved to purchase a decent tin-opener.

Having completed the ten kilometres to Grain power station by 8 o'clock, even allowing for the numerous enforced detours, it was clear that I must have vacated Allhallows Marsh as early as 5 a.m. An enervating concept! Suffice it to say, after seven hours on the hoof and no sleep during the previous twenty eight, I was all in. At Hoo St. Werburgh (virtually a garrison town for Channel Tunnel employees) I called it a day.

Wednesday, 8th August. In view of the soaring temperature without, I donned a neckerchief to protect my already sunburnt nape. Despite my fair skin, I was well pleased with my overall acclimatisation and I bade farewell to Hoo St. Werburgh in high spirits, amazed at the recuperative power of a decent night's kip.

Following a morning fraught with further blocked and hopelessly overgrown footpaths, I crossed Bridge Reach shortly before 11am, the jagged molars of Rochester Castle soaring majestically to my right. Beneath the welcome shade of a cherry tree, I paused in the lee of Rochester Cathedral to savour a chilled can of Lucozade. Sheer nectar! My liquid intake having risen in direct correlation to the temperature abroad, I now required to drink every hour on the hour – without the slightest inclination to pass water!

Midday temperature at Chatham Dockyard: 90F and soaring.

Impatient now for the bucolic oases I knew to exist beyond the industrial blight of late, and dismayed at my pedestrian pursuit of same, I regained the Saxon shoreway beyond Bloors Wharf, determined to make some discernible headway. Shortly after this, on the barnacle goose thronged backwater above Ham Green, I developed an excruciating dull ache in my left shoulder – an inconvenience that was to plague the entire walk. Dismissing all thought of stress fracture from my mind (if not the pain itself) I struck out along the sea-blite fringed saltings to Lower Halstow. Famed in Roman times for the gathering of oysters from the nearby Halstow creek, Lower Halstow, another Kentish disaster, afforded nothing in the way of accommodation. A further evening alfresco loomed large. My only encounter in this otherwise ghost-village, with a shopkeeper whom I invited to sign my witness book (a prerequisite of *Guinness Book of Records* status), resulted in an offhand rebuff. Somewhat disheartened, I adopted the cross country section of the shoreway beyond Barksore. The stroke of 4 p.m. found me lying prostrate at the shady end of a sheep meadow at Funton and displaying all the classic symptoms of sunstroke: soaring temperature, exhaustion, headache, nausea, drowsiness, and a distinct absence of perspiration. Though clearly unable to proceed, the prospect of another evening beneath the stars, in the present circumstances, filled me with dread. The mind was willing, but the flesh was decidedly weak. Resigned now to holding my ground until physically removed, a passing tractor-borne shepherd, sympathetic to my plight, suggested I camp where I sat. Good man. Then so be it. In no fit state to prepare a hot meal, let alone eat it, I contented myself with a can of Seven-Up and a dose of paracetamol. Nearly two hours of earnest convalescence later, I committed the following rambling jottings to paper, inspired by the utter tranquillity of the golden moment:

"As I sit here now, my Ironman wristwatch (huh!) reports the time to be 5.30 p.m., and the world has suddenly come to life around me. No more the frenzied scurry of the 'Quest', at least for a few brief hours."

"The pear orchard beyond the fence upon which I now languorously lean is alive with rabbits. The sheep, in whose meadow I have taken up temporary (one hopes!) residence, graze ever nearer, in the certain knowledge that my quiescence and inertia present no threat. A distant cock crows. And there, above and beyond the drowsing sheep, a ragged flight of rooks wend their way homeward. I repose beneath a neglected fruit tree, blue with plums. Further along the shady canopy, greengages galore encumber many a taut bow. But none do I pick. My energy is all but spent. I rise momentarily to stretch my cramped muscles. And, by so doing, I witness a column of rabbits making their way between oblivious sheep. Watership Down lives! Have just been joined by the cutest mouse imaginable – a common dormouse, I believe. A hen pheasant, roguishly scurrying past within a few feet, clucks at me with malice. Mayhap I'm obstructing the route of her evening constitutional? A gentle cooling breeze ruffles the leaves above my head, and a dog fox can be heard barking just out of view. As I finish these notes my tent, now erect, awaits my occupation ."

Thursday, 9th August. Awoke to find my green 'Rip-stop' nylon tent the flavour of the month to my ovine meadow-mates (milk sheep are insatiably curious). The heat-stroke symptoms all but subsided, I set forth from Funton shortly before 8 o'clock; the temperature on my dual purpose thermometer-cum-mirror already nudging 70F.

Having bisected the barren sheep-shorn plain of Chetney Marshes, I followed the south-easterly course of Long Reach. By-passing Kings Ferry Bridge, for I was giving the Isle of Sheppey a wide berth, it not being a physical extension of mainland Britain, I was struck by the sheer volume of litter, a constant source of dismay.

The remaining throat-parching kilometres into Sittingbourne was completed along a meandering trackway ankle deep in coal dust. No doubt a by-product of Kemsley power station it mirrored the all pervasive properties of ethnic talcum powder. Running parallel to this latter portion of Saxon Shore Way, Milton Creek is further contaminated by the sewage treatment works to the north of town. Judging by the sickly pungent odour, it appeared to be discharging semi-treated effluent directly therein.

As the temperature touched 84F, I found myself mercilessly taunted by visions of ice-frosted glasses, effervescing with amber nectar, à la *Ice-Cold in Alex*! I made do with a chilled Coke.

Completing the next instalment of Saxon shore way (hereafter mentally prefixed 'damned') from Murston to Conyer Creek, I cut inland via Blacketts in search of bed, board and bath. The latter being perhaps the greater priority, as my bare feet – courtesy of the coal dust – appeared to be clad in black suede ankle socks.

At the La Cometa Motel/Restaurant, Teynham, I secured what mine host assured me to be the only vacancy in the entire Swale district. Hyperbole, no doubt, yet at £25 bed and breakfast it was far from cheap. But the prospect of soaking away my aches and pains in a piping Radox bath was worth the money alone. Duly bathed and changed, Ismail, the in-house chef, presented me with a mammoth dish of pasta. Free and gratis! And this, on top of a complementary ham and tomato sandwich at a creekside Sittingbourne pub, fully restored my erstwhile wavering faith in humankind.

Phoned home before turning in. Mary and George (*author's parents*) sound distinctly subdued. Careful to allay their concern, I made no mention of my recent indisposition.

Friday, 10th August. Undeterred by the already intense heat, my acclimatisation was now such that I was able to maintain a steady 6 kph no matter what the terrain.

At the otherwise sleepy hamlet of Conyer I paused to admire the flitting aerial ballet of pre-migratory sand martins. With all the twittering anticipation of holiday-bound school children, they gathered in serried ranks upon the fourfold telephone cables. Soon they would be following the sun to exotic climes. Whereas I…?

Undoubtedly one of the Southeast's prettiest towns, Faversham's pubs, it would appear, open on a flexitime basis. Which is most surprising considering the town boasts two breweries. Departing Faversham, my prodigious thirst unslaked, I rejoined the Saxon shoreway proper at the pylon-bestrode prairie of Nagden Marshes.

Ten kilometres to the east, Seasalter provided my first time-warp glimpse of the genuine British Holidaymaker: deck chair, braces, and the obligatory knotted hanky. Now I knew I was on the coast!

Strolled into Whitstable just after 4 p.m. The Western tip of the town, with its weather-boarded fisherman's cottages and rickety black-tarred boat sheds, is quite authentic; as for the remainder – bland.

Saturday, 11th August. Even at 9 a.m. the heat was only partially modified by a constant offshore breeze. Aware of my ability to run-off an injury, from my amateur football days, I was able to push through the pain barrier on a regular basis. Even with my feet in the most pitiful condition (I'd run out of Compeed skin protectors), I knew that before too long my body would mercifully release its own natural anaesthetic.

My arrival at Reculver seemed only to confirm my intense dislike of caravans; a dislike that grows even more vehement with every blighted panorama. Their impermanence and total lack of aesthetic qualities are positively vomit inducing.

Although largely unnecessary at this juncture, my mapmanship and general awareness was hourly improving. A skill that would no doubt prove its worth before the walk's end.

Throughout the south-east the landscape resembled a dust bowl. Crop fires – the unintentional variety – had become an everyday occurrence, with the clamour of speeding fire-tenders replacing the mewing gulls in audible ascendancy.

The temperature at 3 p.m. stood at 86F; my exposed flesh was simmering away nicely.

Arrived in Ramsgate at 5 p.m., after eight solid hours on the hoof. Taking no chances, I booked into the first guest house displaying a vacancy sign. While having a strip-wash – the shower refusing to co-operate – I noticed the diabolical state of my 'plates of meat'. Something chronic! Blood blisters, the lot. As for my overall person – equal proportions of sunburnt and anaemic flesh. Most alluring!

Sunday, 12th August. I suppose it was inevitable that the immutable law which decrees negative to exist foursquare beside positive should extend to guest houses. The fact that mine was situated on the main harbour-ward thoroughfare resulted in a night-long convoy of Continent-bound lorries, including the occasional monster juggernaut, whose shock wave vibrated the sash windows in their frames. On the plus side, the soothing caress of crisp cotton sheets was a positive boon to my sunburnt limbs

It was another morning of blazing sunshine – as indeed it had been at the start of the walk, one short week and 235 kilometres ago.

The southerly trek from Ramsgate to Sandwich was completed post-haste, pausing only for liquid refreshment in Pegwell Bay and Great Stonar. It was clear that if I was to keep my 3 p.m. rendezvous with John Mole I needed to follow the lead of Felix – keep on walking!

The most northerly of the (five) Cinque Ports, Sandwich – where I arrived just after 11 o'clock – is a most enchanting and historic old town of winding streets, medieval gateways, and olde worlde atmosphere aplenty. I sought out the local police station in order to gain an official endorsement in my witness book. Alas, as is often the case in this neck of the woods, it remains closed for all but two hours a day.

And so to Deal, where much of the frontage to the northern end of town is of architectural merit. The Kingsdown end, by comparison, is somewhat gross.

According to my journal: "The currant bun is burning my sunburn; blistering my blisters!"

Continuing south via The Leas, I rendezvous with the welcoming figure of John Mole at the foot of the imposing Dover Patrol Memorial. John was amazed at my turn of pace and comparative punctuality, I being only seconds overdue! Over a splendid alfresco repast, John briefed me as to future arrangements and events and managed to allay my feeling of isolation with all the latest gossip. All too soon the picnic was over; John returning to Berkshire, I continuing on to Dover. As a parting quip John assured me that he could see a topless bather on the French side of the Channel, which from nearby St. Margaret's Bay is only twenty-one miles distant. The shortest distance between our two countries.

Monday, 13th August. Minutes before 8 a.m. I was rudely awakened by the roar of wildly gunning engines, like a horde of Hell's Angels revving *en masse*. From my skylight vantage point I could see the first Hovercraft of the morning preparing for departure.

It was a shimmering heat haze of a morning, more reminiscent of Kentucky than Kent! Beyond Western Heights I gained a foretaste of the swardy roller coaster that is the North Downs Way.

For one usually so averse to sultry weather, my conditioning was all the more remarkable. Certainly my pace had faltered on occasions, but at no time had I seriously considered jacking it all in. Don't buckle, that's the thing. And this the hottest August on record!

Folkestone came and went: the volume of mature trees and ancient houses, preserved rather than modernised, was a positive bonus. Sandgate, by comparison, was all very tasteful, if archly Bohemian. Seabrook offered up the first overt naturist – one suspects not of British origin; too brazen by half.

On the odd occasion when the offshore breeze relented, wave upon wave of searing heat swept over me, without obvious ill-effect. I put my acclimatisation down, in part, to a dramatically increased liquid intake. On an average day I now quaffed 4-5 cans of soft drink (mainly Coke), a couple of pots of tea, the occasional pint, and at least a litre of vitamin C enriched fruit juice. Hythe – one of the original Cinque Ports – exuded a certain octogenarian charm: the type of resort where tourists are tolerated rather than encouraged.

Prompted by a battery of red flags flying over Hythe Military Firing Range, I detoured inland, regaining the coast proper at the northern limit of Dymchurch Wall: a massive sea wall that dates back to Roman times. And at the old Romney township of Dymchurch, with its triumvirate of warlike Martello towers, I gratefully curtailed the day's proceedings.

I spent a relaxing evening amid the antiquarian charm of Dr. Syn's Restaurant & Guest House; eponymously named in (dis)honour of the title character of the Russell Thorndyke novel: an eighteenth century smuggling melodrama with a Dymchurch/Romney backdrop. Boasting a *melange* of original features (low ceilings, black beams, leaded lights and creaking floorboards), all it lacked was a resident ghost. This period illusion was diminished only in part by an intermittent melodic whistle – the audible embodiment of the Romney, Hythe and Dymchurch Railway: at fifteen inches, one of the narrowest gauge tracks in Britain.

Tuesday, 14th August. For the second day in succession I was brusquely jolted from my slumber, on this occasion by the strident alarm call of a magpie intent upon haranguing an innocuous looking coal-black tom-cat. I watched this procession of world-weary moggie and gambling magpie until they were out of both eye and earshot. Even at such an ungodly hour (5 a.m.), it was clear, or rather unclear, that Dymchurch was shrouded in an all-enveloping blanket of fog, like the scene of a dry-ice machine run amok. The fog was equally dense when I ventured abroad some hours later. It was in fact a welcome addition, for it masked the towns few lurid sea front imperfections. What could aptly be termed: Meteorological censorship!

From Dymchurch I made a beeline for Dungeness – the largest shingle bank in the world – at the south-eastern tip of Denge Beach: a bleak flatland of shanty huts and hardy sea kale.

Littlestone-on-Sea, for some obscure reason, was largely peopled by Orthodox Jews. Their black frock coats, wide-brimmed hats and ringlets striking a discordant note with the scantily clad holiday makers.

Lacking the conviction of previous days, the sun finally broke through by midmorning, in a kind of half-hearted show of defiance to the fleeing fog bank.

After nine days of shoreline walking, I couldn't fail to be aware of the constant struggle between man and the sea. From the Thames Barrier to Dymchurch Wall man has constructed a bewildering array of obstacles by which to keep the ever encroaching sea at bay. Yet all the signs pointed to the overwhelming fact that we are ultimately fighting a losing battle: cliffs continue to crumble, sea walls are taken apart by each successive storm, dykes are breached, sand-dunes are subject to erosion. The final campaign of this protracted conflict? Grim prospect.

I followed the strength sapping shingle foreshore to Camber, crossing the county boundary in the process. I was now in East Sussex. The gently sloping bank was alternatively occupied by strong silent rod-fishermen and a series of cylindrical protuberances, bearing a striking resemblance to the abortive Iraqi Super Gun. Avoiding all soft and pliant sections – they merely absorb kinetic energy and impair forward momentum – I chose to walk beside the surf, the area of maximum compaction.

I arrived at Camber in a most sorry condition: wind-buffeted and leg-weary, I was all in. Barely 4 o'clock, and far too early to stop for the day, I pushed on to Rye, just over three kilometres distant.

I trudged into the town in no fit state to either adjudge or describe its undoubted and much lauded merits, other than that the central elevated section appeared to hold the monopoly of charm and character. Obtaining a berth for the night, I retired with haste.

My post walk regimen was simple: even on evenings when my presence was required elsewhere (functions, receptions, personal appearances), boot and foot care took precedence over all else. Having stuffed them with newspaper to absorb any perspiration or rain/sea water ingress, each boot was then Nikwaxed, using the index finger for maximum penetration. Running repairs apart, the sum total of my foot care amounted to occasional washing in warm and then cold water, liberal applications of Scholl foot powder, and clean Thorlo walking socks.

Wednesday, 15th August. I awoke to a morning of high wind and rain – the first of the walk. And it couldn't have come at a worse time. As I donned my virtually pristine weatherproofs, purpose bought for the walk, I felt a pang of regret at not having fully explored the town. By all accounts Rye is well worth closer inspection, comprising a fourteenth century gateway, narrow cobbled streets, and many fine medieval dwellings. Having grown used to the freedom and comfort of shorts and T-shirt, my weatherproofs felt hot and constricting by comparison. A discomfort magnified tenfold by a morning spent fighting the prevailing wind and sheeting rain, the latter accelerated to hailstorm velocity. Assuming a cross-country route of water-meadows liberally flecked with grazing sheep (apparently impervious to the hellish conditions), I regained the shoreline at Winchelsea Beach. This wasn't a day for sightseeing, this was a day for head-down, no nonsense tenacity.

At midday, during a brief window in the weather, I called into the Circle Shop, Fairlight, for the usual witness book endorsement. The village itself is forever consigned to my memory as a water-logged blur. Finding the component parts of a fine savoury lunch pressed upon me, in lieu of a donation, I seated myself on a bench overlooking Fairlight Cove. Without so much as a scotch egg consumed, the window in the weather promptly slammed shut. Victuals hurriedly stowed, I battered down the proverbial hatches and set a course for Hastings, by way of the magnificently rugged terrain of Hastings County Park: 520 acres of woodland, gorse covered glens and sandstone cliffs. At Lover's Seat, named in memory of a young girl who waited on this very spot for her fiancé to be rowed ashore, I stopped to answer a call of nature. Caught by a rogue gust, my urinary issue travelled all of fifty feet!

Fairlight Glen, just west of Lover's Seat, was a joy to behold, the most impressive natural phenomenon to date. Picture for one moment the symmetry of a near vertical sided gorge cloaked in alternating stratum of bracken and gorse. Abut this virtually inaccessible hollow to a rocky foreshore and you have a passable likeness of Fairlight Glen. The very ambience of the place conjures visions of smugglers plying the surf in their contraband laden craft.

And so to Hastings, a goal achieved at the expense of no little perspiration and bloody-mindedness on my part. By virtue of the precipitous sandstone cliffs that hem the old town both to the east and to the west, Hastings has retained its intimate scale – unlike the urban sprawl of many a coastal town. Open-hearted, warm, honest-to-goodness *bonhomie*, that is Hastings. A town with no side to it; a town for all the family; a town that has retained its integrity. Proof positive that a working town – with its forty-strong fleet of fishing boats and elongated net drying huts – can also be a resort town. Having dallied awhile in order to retrieve a couple of parcels at the Cambridge Road Central Post Office, I struck out for Bexhill at 2.30 p.m.

Thursday, 16th August. According to the Met Office we were in for a bright and breezy day. As it transpired, the 'breeze' increasingly assumed all the characteristics of a full-blown gale with every westward laboured step.

Call it paranoia, but when walking through the plush middle-class suburbs of Bexhill I felt distinctly out of place, a fish out of water, a stranger in a strange land. For this was off-road parking country, this was twitching curtain country; and I was the vagrant on the pedestrian-free boulevards of Beverly Hills, I was the kaffir in the whites only neighbourhood … call it paranoia?

Passing briskly through my teenage haunt of Norman's Bay and the chalet-land of Pevensey Bay, I covered the fifteen kilometres to Eastbourne in under three hours.

Following a lung-bursting introduction to the South Downs Way, I found myself atop the 534 ft. 'Beautiful Headland' of Beachy Head (from the Norman/French *Beau Chef*). Without my rucksack it would have been a breeze, with it – a laborious slog. Such was the strength of wind thereabouts that I was prompted to don my as yet unused 'Windshirt', a garment of close-meshed Pertex construction. And what a Christening! From Beachy Head to Cuckmere Haven across a sun-scorched sword of rolling downland, I was subject to the full frontal assault of blasting head wind and occasional squally shower. Much to my annoyance, it appeared that everybody bar myself was travelling from west to east and having a jolly time being blown down one slope and up the other side, whereas I had to fight for every tenuous foothold, every inch of headway. After six hours of punishingly slow progress I was beginning to suspect that the elements were conspiring against me. So much so, that at the exposed fishing hamlet of Birling Gap I actually heard myself cursing the wind for impeding my advance. Don't tell me that adversity breeds character – it sows the seed of a bitter and twisted dotage!

From Cuckmere Haven, beyond the white-faced Seven Sisters Cliffs, I followed the inland course of the Cuckmere River to Exceat Bridge, where I joined the Seaford-bound Vanguard way.

Upon the very threshold of the now popular resort town of Seaford, and still leaning into the prevailing wind in order to gain the slightest leeway, the sky blackened menacingly. And within minutes the clouds split asunder. For the next rain-sodden half-hour, accompanied by a sonorous duet of thunder and lightning, I trudged the woebegone streets in search of a suitable evening's billet. And thus, having already spent the afternoon scaling the extinct river valleys that divide the Seven Sisters and Birling Gap, I found myself climbing the little wooden hill to Bedfordshire.

Thought for the day: You know you've booked into a down-market hotel when your room doesn't include a Gideon Bible.

Friday, 17th August. Perhaps in retrospect I've been more than a little harsh criticism-wise on places I've encountered at the end of a long hard day. Seaford, I suppose, is no exception. However, seeing it bathed in sunshine and not wreathed in rain cloud gave the whole town a vital new complexion.

Physically speaking, I had no doubts as to my ability to complete the task at hand. Certainly no new infirmities had arisen. And those that existed formally were well on the mend. Now if only I could shake off the bouts of depression. Indeed, to date I don't think I'd 'completely' enjoyed a single day. Though individual moments had been worthwhile, ten days of broiling sun, followed by two of gale force wind and rain – my least favourite elemental combination – had hardly been conducive to peace of mind.

From Seaford I headed west, taking to the footpath where the Esplanade came to an abrupt end. After trekking inland to cross the River Ouse, at Newhaven, I took some time out to photograph the stately Dieppe-bound ferry. At times like that I longed for an S.L.R. camera with a wide-angle lens, instead of my weight-conscious idiot-proof, auto-zoom job.

Apart from the fine panoramic view from Castle Hall across the South Downs, the Ouse Valley and Seaford Bay, my undulating westward coastal route threw up little in the way of scintillating diversion. Certainly cliff erosion was very much in evidence. And Brighton's shopping paradise, the Lanes, were understaffed and over priced. Yet nothing could shake my black mood.

The day came to an inauspicious head when my promised Hove accommodation failed to materialise. And as if to add insult to injury, the chill-blast that had chivvied and pursued me for the last two days was forecast to continue for the foreseeable future. Oh, happy day!

Saturday, 18th August. Architecturally speaking, the walk so far had failed to live up to expectation. Apart from the occasional pocket of character or affluence, the coast appeared to be in a generally depressed state. This latter view was graphically illustrated in my passing from the comparative wealth of Hove to the urban decay of the neighbouring borough of Southwick. A vivid confirmation of the polarisation of housing stock.

In order to accommodate a 3 p.m. press call at Worthing Pier, my schedule for the day was limited to a mere 23 km.

On crossing the River Adur into Shoreham-by-Sea, the northern prospect was regally dominated by the imposing presence of Lancing College Chapel, a local landmark and monument to Gothic architecture. Completed in 1978 after more than a century in the building, it remains the most worthy erection for many a long kilometre. Following a leisurely circuit of Shoreham Beach, I continued my westerly passage via South Lancing.

My rucksack continued to be the bane of my life. A recurring dream was to rid myself of this infernal burden – a dream whose fulfilment remained some thirteen months distant.

And so to the biggest resort in West Sussex, Worthing, arriving just under an hour early for my pier-head press-call.

Considering the torture I'd put them through, it was nothing short of miraculous that my feet were in such fine fettle, their skin texture resembling that of a baby's bottom.

On the home front, Mary had been on the receiving end of a bouquet of flowers and an apology from a local newspaper which had reported her 'tragic demise'. In an earlier interview I had credited my inspiration to Mary having been 'struck down' with M.S. I meant, of course, 'laid low'. Oops!

But my abiding memory of Worthing will undoubtedly be the sand-flies – a veritable plague of the intrusive little monsters did their damnedest to put a damper on an exquisite sea front nosh-up laid on by Kathleen, John and Tim Mole, who had driven down from Maidenhead expressly – that and the lamentable non-appearance of the local press-corps!

Sunday, 19th August. My departure was delayed by the arrival of the Chairman of the Worthing M.S. Branch. At the behest of Mrs Robinson, my landlady and M.S. fund-raiser, he'd popped in to apologise for the town's 'poor showing' and shabby treatment at the hands of Worthing's 'gentleman' of the press. Furthermore, he promised to 'get things moving' further along the coast.

It was blowing a gale and raining without, gilding the pavements and gushing in torrents from faulty gutters. The chairman of Worthing M.S. accompanied me for the first saturating fifty yards – before seeking the sanctuary of his car. And thus it continued for the greater part of the day: I bent double in genuflect wind-defying posture, not seeing, just going through the motions on auto-pilot.

Adopting a strictly coastal route, I was accompanied between Worthing and Littlehampton by Margaret Clark, who was walking her dog (or vice versa). In spite of the atrocious conditions we maintained a spirited conversation. Pumping her on the subject of her native Ireland, I vowed to drop her a postcard as and when I arrived in her beloved Emerald Isle. She genuinely craved my seal of approval.

Middleton-on-Sea, easternmost satellite of Bognor Regis and location of a World War II seaplane base, provided the architectural high spot of the day, during a welcome respite from the rain. Generating an almost sinister air, the town resembled a Disneyland mock-up of the Idealised English Village: thatch, half-timber, manicured lawns. Even the shops, resplendent with Olde Worlde script, appeared vetted for suitability: ONE hairdresser, ONE patisserie, ONE delicatessen. No duplicates by order! Uniform ageing suggested the entire enterprise to have been erected *en masse* between the wars. The overall surreal impression was evocative of the fictional North American town of Stepford – minus the wives! (Indeed, citizens in general).

Monday, 20th August. The morning was golden-ripe with the first prolonged sunshine for five days. Stripped to my basic attire of shorts and tee-shirt, I strode to Pagham village, fuelled by the finest breakfast since Teynham.

Beyond the squat church of St. Thomas à Becket, Pagham, with its exquisite rose window, I passed a tractor ploughing-under a field of corn stubble (more ecologically responsible than burning), its undeviating course tracked by an attendant flock of gulls, as if tethered by an invisible thread.

Before me now lay Pagham Harbour, 1,000 acres of shingle beach and mud-flats, an impressive and strategically important nature reserve, being home to numerous species of flora and fauna, and also the over-wintering ground to some 4,000 brent-geese. A hovering host of cabbage white butterflies took my eye, caught on the humid breeze like so much animated confetti.

Due to the rising tide I was forced to seek an alternative route via Halsey's Farm, before regaining the public footpath at the sleepy backwater of Sidlesham. Despite its much vaunted 'skin-texture', my left foot (good title for a movie!) was giving me no end of gyp. A nagging pain just behind my little toe would butt in after an hours walking and stubbornly persist until I packed up for the day.

Taking the narrow footpath from Ferry House to the St. Wilfred's chapel-blessed hamlet of Church Norton, I ran the lacerating gauntlet of gorse and blackthorn. Most invigorating.

The low-lying headland of Selsey Bill appeared an idyllic location for a swim. With its steeply shelving shingle beach, the sea was most enticing – though the fact that every holidaymaker remained securely shore-bound suggested a treacherous undertow. I marvelled at a flight of common tern, plunging mob-handed upon their chosen food-source and barely breaking the surface of the water.

What began as a pleasurable day deteriorated into fiasco between Selsey Bill and Bracklesham. If only farmers would attend to the upkeep of footpaths on their land – or at the very least maintain the signposts. Any chance of reaching Chichester by nightfall was dashed by the frequent need to retrace my footsteps where footpaths came to a dead end or where right of way was obstructed by crops. On another instance a bridge across a dyke clearly displayed on my map, was nothing more than a pile of rotting timber. A curse on all inconsiderate landowners! Utterly thwarted, I threw in the proverbial towel at Birdham.

Tuesday, 21st August. Heading north along the A286, I took the Apuldram turnoff and there, across a crew-cut field of corn stubble, I espied the lofty eminence of Chichester Cathedral, which dates back to Norman times. All about me elder bushes were heavy-hung with their autumnal harvest; likewise blackberries were evident in rich profusion, though unlike the elders, were not yet ready for the picking.

There ensued a mind-numbing 10km yomp along the hard-shoulder of the A27 Chichester to Havant Road. Driven to the verge of motorway madness, the tedium was partially elevated by the anxious driver of an 'Age Concern' minibus who suggested I take a lift. I realise I must have looked somewhat the worse for wear… but 'Age Concern!'

I crossed the River Ems into Hampshire at precisely 1 p.m. Farewell Sussex and onto pastures new – hopefully well maintained and signposted. My roadway introduction to Hampshire was not a pleasant one. Adopting the Solent Way beyond Portsea Island, I derived some solace in sighting the distant floodlights of Fratton Park, home of Portsmouth F.C. I arrived in the city of Portsmouth (a status gained in 1926) with little or no expectation of what I might find, and lo and behold – Southsea! A positive revelation! A jewel in the maritime crown! None of the pretentiousness of Hove or brashness of Margate – but an abundance of charm, a sea front, a pier (South Parade), the D-Day museum – and 1,000 years of naval heritage to boot. What more could one desire? In short, the 'Resort City' of the South!

Wednesday, 22nd August. Even at 9 a.m. the day promised to be sultry – a promise most admirably kept. With no other practical pedestrian route open to me (apart from a gruelling inland detour), I had little option but to take to the embankment of the M275. As to the illegality of such a perambulatory indulgence, I can only claim that necessity swayed my better judgement.

Though a total bane to yours truly, motorway embankments are apparently the ideal habitat for grasshoppers – clouds of which fled my every footfall in locust proportions.

After several motorway-weary kilometres, and as many old fashioned looks from passing motorists (though thankfully no police), I descended the embankment and climbed a perimeter fence to freedom – the freedom of the good old A27. And good riddance to the M275!

Another sumptuously hot day was upon me, the third on the trot, and Porchester Castle – across the azure expanse of Portsmouth Harbour – was all but lost in the swirling heat-haze.

I took advantage of a vacant telephone box to acquaint Walk H.Q. with my position and status. Unable to satisfy the voracious appetite of the coin box, I found myself instead denouncing the scandalous profiteering of British Telecom.

What followed was a straightforward route march from point A to point B: point A being Porchester; Point B being Fareham. Neither town did I explore, nor have the remotest inclination to do so – heat fatigue has that effect on me.

From Fareham I headed south towards Gosport along the A32, taking to the grass verge between Bridgemary and Brockhurst. After kilometre upon kilometre of tarmac and concrete, the pliant turf came as a positive balm to my badly drawn feet.

Never have I seen so may bicycles at any one time. Why, Gosport – at the end of a working day – resembled High Street, China, in the rush hour! From the ferry port I could see the point of my morning departure. So near and yet so far!

Thursday, 23rd August. Gosport was cloaked in sea-mist – and all the better for it. My overall impression of Gosport, given the benefit of the new day, was that of a diluted version of Portsmouth. All the ingredients were present, though lacking the depth of character of its more illustrious neighbour. I crossed the Haslar Bridge to the Clayhill district where, through a forest of masts, I could see HM Submarine Museum. And there, breaching the mist like a grounded leviathan, the sombre hulk of HMS Alliance, one of the last WWII A-class submarines.

In open defiance of the current IRA offensive, each and every M.o.D. installation that I passed in the course of the day was bristling with newly installed razor-wire and armed sentries, even Haslar Royal Naval Hospital. Despite their obvious necessity, the outward casualness of these tooled-up youths contributed to the unreality of the situation and filled me with unease.

Having regained the Solent Way at Stokes Bay, the stroke of 10 a.m. saw me skirting the parish of Alverstoke. I had now been walking for an incredible eighteen days without break – yet they had passed with the brevity of a week. Activity, I realised, is all time consuming; whereas inactivity, enforced or otherwise, makes time drag *ad infinitum*.

Within the hour the sun broke through, burning off the last vestiges of mist – and all was suddenly right with the world. To the seaward, a gruffly bellowing foghorn foretold a different picture to the landward tranquillity. A total absence of wind suggested we were in for a heavenly, if sweltering day – if only it could always be so. This said, I was now perspiring freely and beginning to peel for the first time in years.

At the tiny harbour of Titchfield Haven, I joined a crowd who were avidly watching a circling shoal of mackerel and several specimen red mullet in their vain bid to find the narrow harbour exit.

Just after midday I gained my first sighting of the massive Fawley Oil Refinery, across Southampton Water. I wondered how such a huge installation would be able to maintain its present production levels in view of the looming Iraq-Kuwait crisis?

At 'Sea Breezes' caravan park, I was left without option but to take a lengthy inland detour. Even though the coastal frontage was clearly designated a public right of way, the powers that be had nevertheless taken it upon themselves to erect a substantial barricade.

Once more upon my chosen route, I was consigned to a protracted spell of shoreline walking at its most arduous – shingle. The Solent Way promptly threw up some fine examples of that Victorian delicacy, sea kale, and more plentiful and flourishing than their Dungeness counterparts.

With the college of Nautical Studies to my right, I entered the mouth of the River Hamble, location of the TV series *Howard's Way*. And it certainly lived up to its billing as one of Britain's most concentrated maritime centres. More yachts than you can shake a stick at! My northerly route to Bursledon followed the course of a tapering, foot-shredding causeway of gravel and flint chippings, with the Hamble flowing swiftly either side.

From Bursledon, Southampton – my destination for the day – was less than an hour away, and my mood was one of elation. The most thoroughly satisfying day to date. Despite the debilitating heat, my energy seemed boundless.

With most major towns or cities the pedestrian tends to slink in by a back road or footpath. In Southampton one enters, at least via Itchen Bridge, in the grand manner. And what a point of entry! What a view! The whole city was spread before me in Toytown relief. Southampton is basically a low level city, perhaps as a result of intense bombing during WWII, with a skyline punctuated by a welcome profusion of conical steeples. All cities should be thus endowed.

Friday, 24th August. As of yesterday, another misty start to the day, with heat wave conditions promised before long. I must admit that Southampton had already endeared itself to me – that is, apart from its horrendous traffic congestion. Considering the hammering it took at the hands of Jerry, the city was in remarkably good shape, the numerous manicured open spaces being an additional bonus. Whereas to enter or exit Portsmouth a car is a virtual prerequisite, Southampton, by contrast, boasts a network of pedestrian-cum-cycle tracks. Three cheers for Southampton!

I had heard great things about Hythe. But even taking into account the exclusivity of its marine development, Hythe struck me as an abject anticlimax. Even when I explored the inner precincts of town, with its tight little streets, my opinion remained one of 'much ado about nothing'.

Towards the outer environs of Hythe, I walked for a kilometre or more with an elderly gentleman who complimented me on my 'foin stroid'. He bore a remarkable likeness to my dear departed grandfather in feature, stature and mannerism. London born, he spoke with a bizarre composite Hampshire/Wiltshire brogue. Utilising the age old 'public house' mode of direction, he put me on the road to Beaulieu in a manner that would have warmed the cockles of my grandfather's heart.

In crossing the horizon-wide expanse of Beaulieu Heath, with its vibrant drifts of heather and gorse, my imagination peopled it with the spectres of long-dead highwaymen. Certainly in the depth of winter a more inhospitable locale I couldn't envisage. Whereas now, in the grip of a heat wave, the panorama was awash with myriad oases of pink and yellow upon a pony-cropped greensward.

On entering the picturesque and scrupulously litter-free village of Beaulieu (from the Norman-French *Beau Lieu* – beautiful place) I noticed that every driveway was equipped with a cattle grid – no doubt also to hinder the ingress of the ever curious and plentiful New Forest ponies. Apart from its more familiar attractions, Beaulieu possesses what must be the most characterful bus shelter in Britain. Complete with resident swallows, it resembles a mini-Barbican, being entirely stone built.

Where there are ponies there are inevitably flies. Where there is a proliferation of ponies flies materialise in sympathetic droves. Thus my memory of Beaulieu Heath will forever be.

Saturday, 25th August. In traversing Beaulieu Heath I spotted a cock Dartford warbler atop a gorse bush. Once spread throughout Southern England, this usually furtive bird is now restricted to Dorset and Hampshire. Between rafts of gorse and bracken, the pony-shorn turf

A footpath for Messiahs only! The Hamble River.

was peppered with marble-size puff balls, a singular delicacy when attaining the size of a large grapefruit.

This was the twentieth day of my trek and a sixth consecutive day of balmy weather. With the sun soaring relentlessly above the yard-arm, my flaking epidermis continued to peel by the square foot. Not a pretty sight!

With Bank Holiday Monday less than forty-eight hours away, the roads were chock-a-block with coastward bound traffic. In spite of an array of road signs advising to the contrary, I saw many cars passing at speed within inches of oblivious jay-walking ponies. Beware thoughtless motorists!

Having spent the greater part of the day upon roads, I entered the county of Dorset, Borough of Christchurch, around 2 p.m. My modest target for the day was the tiny village of Mudeford, situated to the east of Christchurch Harbour. Here I was greeted by John Mole and family, and Chris Rogers, District Postmaster of Bournemouth, who gave my undertaking his personal blessing. With the Bank Holiday virtually upon us, the placid waters of Christchurch Harbour and surrounding greensward were alive with the sight and sounds of holiday pursuits: sailing, wind-surfing, dog walking, Frisbee throwing, kite flying, swimming and paddling. And a grand time was had by all.

Sunday, 26th August. Another misty yet humid start, which bode well for the day ahead. By the time I reached Southbourne, a little after 9 a.m., that portend had come to pass with sweltering accuracy. To my certain knowledge, Southbourne's one legitimate claim to fame is its 'unique shell garden', which occupies the entire frontage of an otherwise unremarkable residence. The whole front plot is given over to an impressive tessellated mosaic of terraces and concrete statuary inlaid with shells from the seven seas! And one is left in no doubt as to its charitable status: 'Show your appreciation by leaving a donation', commands the sign.

The scimitar sweep of Poole Bay now lay before me, skirted by a reputed seven miles of uninterrupted promenade, sand, and tree-clad cliffs interspersed by valleys – the Chines. To seaward, the mist clung on with grim determination. To landward, the beaches and promenade were filling up nicely.

It was clear that I had hit the road far too early for my 2.30 p.m. reception, Poole being barely 12km away. I slowed down accordingly and took in the scenery. At Alum Chine I paused to partake some lunch, scotch eggs now being a firm favourite of mine. Also to kill some more time (never arrive early!). A few hundred yards offshore a power boat race was in full clamorous swing, each competitor having their own attendant helicopter in tow. Exhilarating for the participants – a catastrophe for marine life.

It was clear to all that the trend towards skimpy fluorescent swimwear merely succeeded in highlighting the imperfection rather than the perfection of the wearer. Clear to all, that is, bar the wearer. Likewise, unabashed topless bathers were now ten-a-penny.

From Poole Head, I circled the wide reaches of Poole Harbour and made for the prearranged liaison point – the forecourt of The Nelson Public House, Poole Quay.

In the event, welcomer in chief Lady Mayoress, Cllr. Anne Stribley, had rearranged her busy schedule to accommodate my arrival at the revised time of 2 p.m. Thus, far from being punctual to the minute – I found myself half an hour late. No matter. To my utter amazement on approaching the balloon-waving throng I actually received a hearty round of applause. Most gratifying! All went remarkably smoothly from thereon in: the press took their photos and asked their questions, and a highly fruitful collection took place. The collection's leading light and solicitor-in-chief was Marion Mole, mother of Walk Co-ordinator John Mole. Not only did her boundless energy belie her septuagenarian status, but her never-take-no-for-an-answer persistence put us all to shame. Awesome!

Prior to my belated coming, so I'm reliably informed, Cllr. Stribley, whose avowed objective is to see this notoriously volatile watering hole closed on the Sabbath, had remained serenely unruffled in the face of a hostile reception from The Nelson's regulars.

I complimented her upon her intricate gold and enamel chain of office. She replied that it wasn't very old – only two centuries, one link per mayor. An office, she confided, that had existed since the thirteenth century. "How fortunate the chain wasn't introduced then," I pointed out, "otherwise the present incumbent would resemble Marley's ghost!"

Monday, 27th August. It was another brilliant morning. My view across the liquid iridescence of Poole Harbour was dominated by the 500 acre bulk of Brownsea Island, famed for its colony of red squirrels and birthplace of the scouting movement. Poole and its hospitable citizens had been kind to me and my journal was likewise complimentary. Particularly noteworthy were the Quay and Old Town with their wealth of meticulously maintained Georgian properties.

Throughout the ensuing day I was subject to a barrage of honking horns and waved acknowledgements from passing motorists, even the occasional good humoured, though largely unintelligible, shouted comment. Clearly these people had witnessed by arrival in Poole the previous day. Such was the fragility of my state of mind that my resolve thrived upon personal recognition ("You're the chap walking round Britain!"), yet withered in its absence.

At Holton Heath my attention was drawn to a series of glinting sawdust-like excrescences beneath a honeysuckle-festooned hedgerow. On closer examination I identified these as the seething nests of Britain's largest ant, the wood ant. Past experience forewarned me that such close encounters could be of the painful kind.

At the church of St. Martin-on-the-Wall, Wareham, I photographed Eric Kennington's effigy of T. E. Lawrence, of whom the latter spent the last few years of his incident-packed life six miles away at Cloud's Hill Cottage. Here I was drawn into conversation with a most charming and persuasive elderly lady, the curator of this fine Saxon edifice. Within minutes I had purchased a booklet on Lawrence's life (I didn't need much persuading) written by a friend of a friend. She advised me to keep my eyes peeled for the little known movie, *Lawrence AND Arabia* – as opposed to David Lean's *Lawrence of Arabia*, which she maintains is somewhat inaccurate.

My theory for successful ultra-distance walking is simply a matter of retaining good habits, while discarding the bad. Good habits, however, are easily shed, bad habits not so. Indeed, this could quite easily be one's code for life.

Each day now, during my semi-regular 7-8 hour plus walking stint, I experience the full gamut of emotions. Parting with new found friends on a daily basis being a particular wrench. In fact I'm beginning to feel quite emotionally drained.

I finally escaped the tarmacadamed-monotony to the south of Newton Heath, where I took to the maze of forestry commission tracks. Here I caught sight of my first deer of the walk. Taken unawares by my sudden intrusion, I glimpsed the powder puff rump of a roe deer as it fled the dappled light of a forest glade.

Apart from an inability to accurately waymark their tracks, the Forestry Commission amply redeemed themselves by the welcome inclusion of a number of strategically located 'bat boxes'.

From the northern extremity of South Haven Point, I walked to the wooded village of Studland across the fine sandy beach that fringes Studland Bay.

Tuesday, 28th August. With the sun already beating down from a cloudless sky, I made my way to The Foreland by way of the Dorset coast path. In striding towards the alternatively known Handfast Point, I disturbed a flock of Canada geese who promptly ceased grazing the crop stubble and took flight in a ragged formation, trumpeting their disapproval.

I paused at the promontory of Ballard Point to fill my lungs with the saline updraft. My headache of the previous evening was easing now – though not quickly enough for my liking. The breathtaking view, however, more than compensated for such a transient malady. With distant Swanage radiating before me and the cliff dropping sheer at my feet, the universal sensation could be naught but elation.

At Swanage, I entered the eastern limit of Hardy's Wessex. Both shops and thoroughfares reflected this literary heritage: it was all 'Tess' this, 'Casterbridge' that and 'D'Urbervilles' the other!

Such was the acuteness of gradient above and beyond Peveril Point that I was forced to conclude that in such terrain one mile as the crow flies necessitated expending the energy to cover ten miles on the flat.

Being Mediterranean in climate and scenery, the Dorset coast path between Durlston Head and Anvil Point conjured images of the Lotus Eaters. From this point forth the agility and sure-footedness of mountain goats was essential. To my left, the spangled English Channel; to my right, parched bovine-abundant terraces; before me, the unremitting sun. And thus my destiny was sealed for the next five hours.

I derived considerable succour from the newly erected Royal Marines Memorial at West Hill: "Rest awhile and reflect that we who are living can enjoy the beauty of the sea and countryside." Most poignantly put, sir.

Beyond West Hill, and after nigh on six hours of continual climbing/descending, my erstwhile inexhaustible energy was all but spent. Every new ascent prompted an insurmountable psychological barrier. Indeed, my rude introduction to the Dorset coast path reduced the rigours of the South Downs Way to the status of a kiddies' nature ramble.

At Rope Lake Head, with spirits and vitality at an all time nadir, I offered up a silent prayer. Thereafter, partially restored, I resumed with new, if temporary vigour.

As I approached Clavell Tower, a nineteenth century folly overlooking the shingle sweep of Kimmeridge Bay, my haunting vision manifested itself anew in the guise of Idris ginger beer ... I could even hear the chink of ice-cubes on the frosted glass ... control yourself, man!

So much for the generosity of the folk of Kimmeridge Bay. My pleas for a glass of water fell upon deaf ears. "There's a shop in town – might be open," being the pick of a decidedly non-helpful bunch. Maybe my twenty four days growth put them off?

Before me now loomed Rings Hill. My resolution shot and all vestiges of energy leached away, defeat stared me in the face. I assaulted Rings Hill with the devil-may-care attitude of one relieved of responsibility – the responsibility to succeed. Yet even as I floundered on all fours within striking distance of the summit – I was snatched from the very jaws of ignominious defeat by a floral-clad apparition. Silhouetted against the setting sun, she plied me with Rowntree's Fruit Pastilles and a Cluster bar before departing ... unnamed ... mute. From the brow of Rings Hill I looked back for my ministering angel – and saw only a deserted slope falling away to Worbarrow Bay. And was the close proximity of 'Flowers Barrow' entirely coincidental?

On the outskirts of Lulworth Cove, common sense deserted me. Instead of sticking to the footpath up and over Bindon Hill, I opted for the 'easy' route across the Royal Armoured Corps firing range. All went swimmingly as I photographed the huge hill-mounted targets, burnt-out tanks (purchased from the Soviet Union at £10,000 a time for target practice), and even the odd 'live' shell. A plume of smoke on the horizon changed all that. Fear of being in the firing-line was promptly quashed as a Land Rover emerged from what transpired to be a dust cloud and veered towards me at breakneck speed. Left in no doubt as to my 'error', the driver (Paul C.) and his oppo escorted me from the danger area. Recently returned from a tour of duty in Northern Ireland (Long Kesh), Paul made light of my rucksack, informing me that 'grunts' (infantry) carry a 60lb pack, no sweat. Cold comfort indeed.

Enveloped by a bank of sea fog, I blindly descended a winding sheep-track to the welcoming haven of Lulworth Cove – and to dreams of my 'floral apparition'!

Wednesday, 29th August. At one time the mere concept of sleeping in a strange bed (let alone a tent!) filled me with revulsion – yet now I did just that on a nightly basis without qualm. And what's more I slept soundly. There's much to be said for honest toil.

In the wake of yesterday's mammoth ten hour yomp, I made a sedate start to the day. The sun was already going through its paces as I made for the natural amphitheatre of Lulworth Cove proper, so cruelly obscured the night before. Sadly I was not the only one with such ideas. Descending from my evening billet of West Lulworth, the milling throng resembled a post-football match crush.

Beyond the massive limestone portal of Durdle Door, I stood transfixed by the sight of jackdaws and gulls scattering from the deliberate flight-path of a lone patrolling raven, an occasional 'kronk-kronk' clearing all from its cliff-top route. No sooner had this harbinger of ill fortune taken its leave than a sea fog materialised about me, as if from the ether, and just as soon lifted. With vision restored, I made the acquaintance of David Tetlow, an assistant anaesthetist and former marine. This apparent contradiction of occupation, however, eluded him completely. Having developed an abject dislike for all things military during the intervening years (he once padlocked the gates of Aldermaston), he conceded that the Marine Corps at the very least had given him his fitness and an awareness of the need to retain it. Certainly he cut a fine dash in his straw Fedora, knee socks, shorts and smoked Granny glasses. As we walked, I more than holding my own against this patently fit individual, he exhausted his entire repertoire of jokes which revolved around popular song titles and their lyrics. A thoroughly amusing chap. We parted company at the Smuggler's Inn, Osmington Mills, he wishing to savour the remaining hours of this, the final day of his holiday, I detouring inland via the A353 to avoid a major cliff fall between Osmington Mills and Furzy Cliff. Rain clouds were massing ominously over Hardy's semi-fictional 'Isle of Slingers' as I crossed the causeway between Wyke Regis and the Isle of Portland. My intention was to complete a round-trip of the 'Island' before turning in. In the event I booked into the Beach House Hotel, prompted by the impending cloudburst. No sooner had I done so than the heavens opened. Discretion being the better part of valour, I retired gracefully.

Thursday, 30th August. The incessant coming and going of helicopters from HMS Osprey Air Station was particularly annoying. How the locals put up with it night after night I couldn't imagine. Not only did the hubbub continue until well after dark, but it resumed at first light the following morning. This inconvenience was only partially remedied by the introduction of ear plugs.

Relieved of my burdensome rucksack, I found a new lease of life. If only it could always be so. Armed only with my camera and Witness Book I set out upon a circuit of the 'Island'. All trace of yesterday's downpour had been succeeded by a bright spring-like morning. The air was astringent and invigorating. Even without my impediment, the climb from the low-lying northern tip of Fortuneswell to the aerial viewpoint of Verne Yeates was most prodigious. From this point the tableland cambered gently southward to the twitchers paradise of Portland Bill. Here I met sculptress Reiko Nireki. Temporarily based at the old lighthouse, she was in the process of completing a major stone figure, which will remain on display at the quarry Sculpture Park. And it wasn't only sculptors who exploited the pale native limestone. Examples of the mass utilisation of this abundant local resource were everywhere: kerb stones, flag stones, field divisions, dwellings, bus shelters, souvenirs (not forgetting Buckingham Palace and St. Paul's Cathedral).

With a good sixteen kilometres under my belt, I returned to my hotel somewhat later than the designated 10 a.m. 'all out' deadline, though nobody appeared the slightest bit miffed.

Once again rucksack encumbered, I finally took my ultimate leave of Fortuneswell a little before 10.30 a.m. From the steel grey of yesterday, The Fleet, seven and a half miles of land-locked brackish lagoon, had assumed a polar turquoise hue. Allied with a keen nip in the breeze, this was not a day for taking the plunge.

With the enchanting village of Abbotsbury and the far from enchanting ascent of Wears Hill behind me, I strode into Burton Bradstock (Best Kept Village in Dorset 1989) at 5 p.m., much relieved at completing the day's schedule.

Friday, 31st August. Rejoining the Dorset Coast path from the off, I was somewhat perturbed by the number of Bridport RDC signs which proclaimed: 'These cliffs are dangerous and liable to fall at any time.' I pressed on with due caution. From the elevation of Burton Cliff the caravan site at Burton Freshwater appeared almost idyllic. On closer examination, however, it resembled a veritable totter's encampment of mongrel dogs, bald types, scrap metal and mounds of household detritus.

Yet this wasn't the only optical illusion. The foreshortening effect between headlands resulted in a constant battle against flagging morale. For with each successive bay I rounded, numerous erstwhile unforeseen bays materialised before me, and my original distant goal remained precisely that.

Nestling amid the ample cleavage of Doghouse Hill and Golden Cap, Seatown (barring the ubiquitous caravans) was a gem of a village, all thatch and ochre-coloured stone.

My way was now summarily blocked by the gorse-garlanded sandstone eminence of the aptly named Golden Cap, at 626ft the highest cliff in Southern England. From Seatown to its very pinnacle, including full backpack, took a masterly twenty minutes. As I made my final heart-pounding surge to the summit, a sand lizard scurried across my path. A good omen I trust? Climb complete, I presented myself with a can of Sprite and a Topic bar as a reward for my labours. Such carrot and stick inducements were to become a permanent feature of my future motivation.

On entering the 'Rockhound' capital of Lyme Regis it began to rain – though only a shower. My ardour temporarily dampened, I paused to don my weatherproofs before continuing upon my way. Lyme Regis is an elegant town – even the deluge couldn't mask that fact. A maze of winding streets and colour-washed buildings, it is a joy to the eye – as well as to the palate: pasties and cream teas, to name but two gastronomic delights available hereabouts.

Just beyond Lyme I espied The Cobb through a chink in the oak scrub. A fourteenth century stone breakwater, it was prominently featured in the 1980 film *The French Lieutenant's Woman*.

As I crossed the county boundary into Devon the rain miraculously abated. At Ware I began a five mile stretch of the South Devon Coast Path which forewarns those contemplating the walk to allow themselves three and a half to four hours to complete this often arduous passage. Abundant with animal and plant life, it follows the course of the great landslide of Christmas Day 1839 along Downlands Cliffs, and is now a National Trust Nature Reserve. In deference to the clammy subtropical heat, I stopped after only a few yards to remove my sauna-like weatherproofs. For the next two and a quarter hours I would see neither sky nor sea, such was the density of the burgeoning forest canopy. The whole rain-forest ambience was further accentuated by the scent of putrefying forest debris activated by the rising humidity. If the Dorset Coast Path presented the stiffest physical and mental challenge to date, the South Devon Coast Path was fated to endear itself to me by virtue of my penchant for woodland walking. Content just to roll with the undulating swell of the root-studded byway, I let the ebb and flow of the rasping surf set the rhythm of my pace. Despite my seeming solitude, at no time did I feel alone or vulnerable. On the contrary, my oneness with the lush verdance of my surroundings elevated the entire experience to a spiritual plane. I could envisage undertaking such a walk of a Sunday morning and being, as a result, more in communion with God than could ever be achieved within the four walls of any purpose built erection. I realised my euphoria was wildly out of keeping with my long term predicament, yet such is the lot of all who consciously commune with nature.

Even allowing for the brief shower, this had to be the most rewarding day yet. Not only did I achieve my daily target with ease, but on emerging at the Seaton End of the LDP (Long Distance Path) – there, beside his car, was George Budden (*author's uncle*). Such was our intuitive synchronisation that after our combined journeys of 70km we had arrived at a prearranged location within seconds of each other. Deploying my rucksack in the boot, I was whisked off to be wined and dined by George and his wife, Olive, in Chard.

2   If it's Sunday it must be Saltash

Nothing awakens a reminiscence like an odour.
   Victor Hugo

Saturday, 1st September.

AVING overindulged the previous evening, I partook only a light breakfast before being transported back to Seaton. Within a few strides of my 10 a.m. departure my fragility was no more – such is the efficacy of deep breathing.

Thanks to John Mole's masterstroke of ingenuity I now had about my person several hundred 'Around the Isles' appeal cards. Compact, explicit and concise, they will enable me to broadcast my cause without a time consuming verbal explanation to each and every prospective donator. I hoped that the result would be a much needed influx of revenue.

With a humidity level comparable to the 'jungle' of Downland Cliff, midday saw me just short of the brow of Dunscombe Cliff, and saturated with perspiration. I strode the length of Sidmouth's deckchair-fringed esplanade in a welter of sweat and impatience (for the day's end). Its wealth of Georgian and Regency architecture, however, did not go unnoticed.

Beyond the River Sid my impetuosity met its match; for there, high above the richly wooded brownstone pinnacle of Peak Hill, a pair of buzzards sailed effortlessly on the balmy up-draught. I marvelled with open-mouthed admiration.

At Brandy Head, south of Landram Bay, I grasped the opportunity to disseminate a couple more appeal cards: one to a quartet that I was later to bump into again in Budleigh Salterton; and another to a bus driver who was convalescing after a multiple piles operation, "The driver's disease, innit."

Sunday, 2nd September. Beyond the precincts of Budleigh Salterton – where the painter Millais lived and created *The Boyhood of Raleigh* – already I was glistening with perspiration. As had been the case during much of the walk so far, the sun was doing its damnedest to remove yet another layer of skin from my frazzled person. Assuming a westward tack, I made for Exmouth by way of the steeply crumbling cliffs known as The Floors – a feat I was scheduled to fulfil yesterday.

From Exmouth I trekked north parallel with the River Exe to Countess Wear, the nearest pedestrian crossing point. Viewed from the bridge, the gravelly bedded Exe was alive with specimen fish – which I took to be trout, possibly rainbow.

My southward passage beside the meandering Exeter Canal was pure hell. As the sun continued to beat down, my erstwhile shoulder injury flared up with a vengeance. Even the introduction of a folded sock beneath the offending strap failed to quell the pain. By the time I reached the lively resort of Dawlish Warren I had once again taken to audibly cursing my misfortune.

The remainder of my journey to Dawlish remains somewhat of an angst-ridden blur, though I recall reflecting upon Exmouth's superabundance of sand and floral displays. However, even Exmouth's herbaceous adornments were overshadowed by those of Lympstone – 'Britain in Bloom' winner 1984-85.

Monday, 3rd September. A fine drizzle accompanied my 9 a.m. departure, yet I refrained from donning my weatherproofs until I reached the village of Holcombe, in the vain hope that it would pass over.

South of The Parson and Clerk headland, where Brunel's Dawlish-Teignmouth Railway Tunnel emerges from the Red Devonian Sandstone Cliffs, I made for the tall Victorian frontage of Teignmouth, buffeted by passing InterCity trains.

Leaving behind the fast flowing River Teign, I followed the Devon South Coast path to Torquay by way of Babbacombe Bay. Turning into Torquay's Union Street shopping centre I suffered an anxiety attack. Day upon day of near-solitude had left me ill-prepared for the seething scrum that greeted me. Such was my consternation, that I very nearly fled without getting my witness book endorsed. As it was, this townscape of hotels and guest houses bore scant resemblance to 'The Loveliest Sea Village in England' so beloved of Lord Tennyson.

With its pastel-hued houses ascending in terraces above the cosy inner harbour, gull-sentried quays and all pervading odour of fish, Brixham lived handsomely up to expectation. The perfect antidote to Torquay.

Tuesday, 4th September. Though bathed in sunshine, there was a distinct nip in the air as I made for the Devonshire Coast Path just north of Brixham's Coast Guard Station. Beyond the massive nineteenth century fortifications of Berry Head my southerly route proved largely uneventful if strikingly scenic, particularly the view from the 430ft Southdown Cliff.

On the wooded threshold of Kingswear, however, the morning came electrifyingly to life. Never have I seen such a proliferation of buzzards, evidently Britain's most common larger bird of prey. Each new creek and hillside revealed a pair of keen-sighted hunters wheeling silently aloft. A welcome feature that accompanied me all the way to Totnes.

Flanked on either side by a yacht-peppered Dartmouth Harbour and the southernmost section of the Torbay and Dartmouth Railway line, I enjoyed a leisurely stroll to Britannia Halt, where the blue and white liveried paddle-ferry was doing a brisk trade.

Cutting inland via the A379, I climbed to the commanding viewpoint of Hillhead. From here, with a minimal turn of the head, I could see Torquay, Paignton, Kingswear and beyond. The patchwork-quilt of Devon's rolling hills stretched before me, a vista only partially marred by the incongruous flagstone field divisions: a succession of vertical slabs arranged end to end like so many oversized anaemic dominoes.

I arrived at Totnes in the mid-afternoon. It was carnival week (2nd – 8th), and all was spick and span. The locals traditionally sport Tudor costumes every Tuesday from June to September, but none did I see. Perhaps the fact that the town's famous Eastgate landmark had gone up in flames the previous evening had put a dampener on the proceedings.

Wednesday, 5th September. I took my leave of Totnes already clad in my 'rainproofs'. And rain it did – sheeting in from the west and penetrating my shell garments with ease. Initially at a loss as to my optimum route, this was soon remedied by the lofty eminence of The Mount, a short-sharp-shock of a hill – from the brow of which I headed south along a hairpin switchback of country lanes; at some points barely a car's width wide.

Situated at the tri-confluence of River Wash, Bow Creek and Harbourne River, the rambling hamlet of Tuckenhay radiated the self-sufficient air of a closed society; a coterie of like-minded individuals bound by a common affluence. No offer of a friendly cuppa here. Even as I dodged the puddles, the glare of unseen disapproving eyes bore into me.

Four weeks on the road had honed my sense of smell to a fine degree. I could now differentiate between the excrement of cow, sheep, pig and horse by olfaction alone. Each has its own uniquely piquant odour. And, to my nose, not in the slightest bit offensive.

The northern end of Slapton Sands is overlooked by a granite monument erected by the US Army in appreciation of the local populace who gave up hearth and home during World War II to provide a realistic battle practice zone. Just short of Torcross stands a second monument: a Sherman tank. Recovered from the sea bed, it commemorates the 279 American servicemen who drowned off Slapton Sands when their landing-craft sank during practice for 'Operation Overlord', the D-Day offensive.

South of Torcross I came a cropper while descending to Sunnydale (a misnomer if ever there was one). This steep section of Devon South Coast Path was shod with a black igneous rock, polished by the feet of myriad pedestrians and lubricated by the rain. Sustaining a slight groin strain (I did the splits!) did me no good whatsoever. As I shambled up the steps beside the single row of cottages that constitute the village of Beesands the unmistakable aroma of coal fire transported me back some thirty years to my pre-smokeless zone childhood: winter evenings before a roaring blaze; roast chestnuts spluttering on the grate ...

Situated on a rocky outcrop above a beach of pale pink shingle, The Hallsands Hotel – my evening stop-over point – resembled the Bate's household from Hitchcock's *Psycho*; a mood enhanced by the rain, gloom and darkling clouds. Hallsands proper – or what's left of it – has neither a Hall nor sands. Most of the former fishing village was destroyed by the fatal combination of high tide and gales in January 1918. The hostelry in which I now resided was utilised as a temporary residence for those made homeless.

Thursday, 6th September. In the sunlight that greeted the new day, the hotel's air of menace had departed along with the deluge. After a glorious nights sleep in a huge hammock of a bed – comfortable as an old sweater – I promptly overslept.

Even the eerie silence of 'old' Hallsands could not diminish the magnificence of this spectacular bracken-clad coastline. Ravens Cove failed miserably to deliver the goods in regards its eponymous namesake. From the grassy slope of The Narrows, I watched a band of rooks mob a solitary buzzard – which contemptuously soared above and beyond their reach with barely a flap of its wings. Though noticeably absent during yesterday's precipitation, butterflies of every size and hue were now abroad in ever welling numbers, frantically making up for lost time.

Any hope I might have entertained of capturing the Devon thatched charm of South Pool on film was scuppered by the presence of a road gang re-surfacing the village's main thoroughfare. Though I did bide awhile with a fellow from the Ordnance Survey, as he painstakingly transposed his observations to a single three-quarter inch square. The omnipresent Devon-pink wash varied in tone from cottage to cottage. Yet to my eye the more pastel hue rang true.

Within the hour Salcombe presented me with its snooty side. The tourist information girl was more intent on shutting-up than finding me a billet, and at my first guest-house port-of-call the middle-aged landlady coldly looked me up and down before sending me on my way – despite a patently visible 'vacancies' sign.

Friday, 7th September. Like thousands of American troops before me, I took my leave of Salcombe with a sense of foreboding. Though, unlike my Normandy-bound predecessors, my concern was merely directed at the gathering rain clouds. With weather-eye duly cocked, I headed south to rejoin the coast path at the inexplicably named Stink Cove. Hope Cove, meantime, in the wake of Bolt Head and the richly wooded Bolt Tail headlands, proved most attractive, not least for its lack of blatant commercialism.

To the landward side of the wave-pierced Thurlestone Rock, the rain-pocked sand pitched me into a trough of depression. The combination of rain and sand is quite incongruous to my way of thinking; being evocative of many a miserable rain-ravaged holiday.

In crossing the River Avon to Aveton Gifford, I caught sight of a kingfisher as it departed in a blur of iridescence. A privilege that never fails to raise the spirits.

Regardless of the occasional setback, in the last few days I felt I was marching to the beat of a different drum: one of newly acquired method, of purpose, and of pre-ordained achievement – a state of mind that was sorely tested at Challaborough. All the charm and grace of a POW camp: dogs running amok, prefabricated concrete chalets, a perimeter fence – everything, in fact, bar the machine-gun posts! What a dive!

Saturday, 8th September. According to *Steven's Tide Tables* low tide on the nearby River Erme was 13.55 (2.3 ft). Fording the Erme could save me half a day's inland yomp to the nearest bridge. On the other hand, could I afford to hang about on the off-chance of finding a suitable crossing point? I plumped for the slow but sure 'around the cottages' route.

Having crossed the River Erme at Sequer's Bridge, I headed south to Halbeton, where the sight of a dead badger, a bloated travesty of a once magnificent beast, stopped me in my tracks. Such road-borne carnage was to haunt my entire journey.

Flies of all species had plagued my progress ever since Beaulieu Heath. On the summit of Beacon Hill, with its fine southerly prospect, their attention reached its zenith. No sooner had I put a Coke to my lips, than I was enveloped in a buzzing predatory swarm. I departed forthwith.

On the Ordnance Survey map, Cunnimall appeared to consist of a church and a couple of minor dwellings. The reality was a terrible let down. Certainly the aforementioned erections were in evidence – as indeed were several hundred caravans! Above Cannimall my route took me through a magnificent beech grove, a sight worth seeing in its own right. As with the hazels around Kingston, the fruits were lamentably out of reach. From Stoke Point to Mouthstone Point the rolling sheep-trimmed LDP sloped down to a laminated rocky foreshore that resembled rank upon serried rank of outsize roofing slates, awaiting only the attention of an equally outsize tiler. Nevertheless, this was ideal all-weather walking terrain.

Beyond the bulky islet of the Great Mew Stone, a wedge of powder-blue hove into view in the middle-distance. Thus Gara Point afforded me my first covetous sight of Cornwall – still one day and 50km away.

From the mouth of the River Yealm I followed the eastward course of a creek that flanked the extensive and mature National Trust Woodland. Before me now lay the very 'U' Noss Mayo: all wetsuits and Range Rovers. On the opposite bank, across a rapidly draining inlet of marooned yachts, was Newton Ferrers, a characterful village, with a backdrop of steeply rising woodland. Hereafter I struck out with a view to reaching Brixton by 5pm. I made it with 30 minutes to spare.

Sunday, 9th September. Despite a good night's sleep and an accompaniment of brilliant sunshine, I found it strangely difficult to regain my form of the last few days, though having regained the Devon South Coast Path at Warren Point, I did precisely that.

In my naivety I assumed, from their stationary seaward direction, that the target of the mercifully silent guns of the HMS *Cambridge* Gunnery School on Wembury Point was the Great Mew Stone. Not so opined a local yokel, "The target is usually towed behind an aircraft!" So there.

The Staddon Heights section of the LDP must rank (literally!) as the most flyblown area on the south coast. On the other hand, the view therefrom was highly impressive. As I paused to admire the cornflower-breadth of the yacht-dotted Plymouth Sound, my momentary abstraction was sundered by the massive report of a field gun (no doubt part of Plymouth's Battle of Britain celebrations). Preceded by an equally resonant – though less startling – verbal command, this voluminous duality reverberated around the contours of The Sound – drawing my gaze to distant Plymouth, now merely a ribbon of grey and white, with the occasional green oasis.

As for Plymouth proper, apart from the historic greensward of The Hoe and a superfluity of associate maritime attractions, I saw little to commend it. Not that I was entirely blind to Plymouth's undoubted charms, merely that I was totally infatuated with Noss Mayo, and in comparison all else paled into insignificance.

And so to the highlight of the day: Isambard Kingdom Brunel's Royal Albert (rail) Bridge. What scale! What symmetry! How something so vast, so advanced could have been constructed across such an inhospitable stretch of tidal water so many years ago (completed 1859) filled me with admiration for the genius of the man and the fortitude of his legion workers.

Crossing into Cornwall via the adjacent Tamar Road Bridge (1961) was like entering a foreign country: a bilingual sign bade me, 'Welcome to Cornwall/Kernow'. The stroke of 4.30 p.m. saw me standing on the Cornish Soil of Saltash (well, pavement actually). Accommodation-wise I struck lucky at the first attempt. Celtic hospitality was much in evidence as I was welcomed into the home of Mr and Mrs Haydon with all the warmth reserved for a returning long-lost son.

Monday, 10th September. My destination for the day was Milbrook, some forty-five sweat-inducing kilometres distant. Before taking leave of Saltash, I partook of a full English breakfast in the gregarious company of three female students, all of whom had stinking colds, of which I was understandably wary

As Mr Haydon saw me off from the elevated front step, the sun was already making its presence felt. No need for my wind-shirt today. Such was the clarity in fact, that Dartmoor was clearly visible to the north-east.

As I purposefully bestrode the A38 for Tideford I sensed an almost tangible change of atmosphere from the hyper-conservatism of Devon for the more egalitarian Cornwall. From time to time random photo opportunities again prompted me to bemoan my lack of a manual zoom lens, particularly so east of Landrake where I witnessed a buzzard stoop into an adjacent field before flying to a tree to devour its hapless victim.

By mid-day I had yet to catch so much of a glimpse of the ocean or the famed Cornwall Coast Path. Though far from ideal, road walking is one sure-fire method of eating up the kilometres.

On approaching Torpoint, with its twin royal naval shore bases of HMS *Fisgard* and HMS *Raleigh*, my route was strewn with a carpet of 'grounded' bees, wasps and butterflies; a combination of road victims and the imminent onset of autumn.

Reaching Millbrook by late afternoon I gained B&B accommodation at Bethany Cottage, home of Mrs Mavis Bailey. After a most exquisite evening repast, I opined that Cornish tap water was possibly the best in Britain. Mavis disagreed, declaring Scotland's drinking water to be 'Gods Champagne!'

Whereas I received regular postal-consignments of essential laundry items, before retiring for the evening I resolved to do some washing when the opportunity arose, having worn the same pair of Mountain-Equipment shorts for a constant thirty-seven days!

Tuesday, 11th September. Having joined the Cornish section of the LDP just south of Cremyll, I entered Mount Edgcumbe Country Park shortly after 10am. Home of the Mount Edgcumbe family from 1553 to 1987, it covers 865 lush acres of the Rane peninsular. From Barn Pool, the one time fortress and prison of Drake's Island hove into view at the end of an avenue of mature oaks, like a scaled-down Alcatraz. Invigorated as much by a sense of well-being as by my sumptuous surroundings, I positively charged through Mount Edgcumbe's rhododendron-banked deer park in a state of euphoria. Mind you, I invariably fire on all cylinders after a good meal or two – and Mavis Bailey's cuisine certainly fell into that category.

Overlooking Cawsand Bay, beyond the precincts of the Country Park, I met a most fascinating GP who took time to educate me as to the history of her village, Kingsand. Apparently a wall-mounted *fleur-de-lis* denoted the original Devon/Cornwall boundary, until it was decided that the River Tamar represented a more substantial and natural division.

Within sight of Kingsand I thought we'd been invaded by Wales. For much of the previous hour I'd exchanged fleeting pleasantries with straggling groups of determined-looking Welsh-speaking squaddies, alternately running and walking. Now faced with the main fatigue-clad body, a spokesman proudly informed me that they were Welsh Guards on backpacking manoeuvres, fresh from tackling the Pembrokeshire coast path. And gentlemen to a man!

The intimate scale of the twin village of Kingsand and Cawsand leave their more commercialised counterparts elsewhere in Cornwall for dead. This was the Cornwall of fuchsia-draped balconies, of colour-washed cottages – in short, the Cornwall of one's dreams.

Beyond the ruined chapel at Rame Head, ever-territorial Red Admiral butterflies appeared in wild profusion, either jealously patrolling their chosen domains or, having alighted, exuberantly displaying their vibrant colours. Richly scented honeysuckle was significantly plentiful hereabouts also, it being a prime butterfly food plant.

At Tregantle Cliff an inland detour was required to avoid an extensive military firing range. From the lofty viewpoint behind Tregantle Barracks – erected as a national monument in the wake of the Napoleonic wars – my route of the last two days was graphically spread before me: Plymouth, Devonport, Saltash, Torpoint... Meanwhile to the seaward, it was impossible to adjudge just where the sky terminated and where the ocean began, such was the monochrome haze.

Thoroughly satisfied with my introduction to the Cornish instalment of the South West Way I concluded the day at Downderry, an elongated strip of a village, hemmed by vertiginous slopes and the sea.

I, meanwhile, had left my heart in Kingsand.

Wednesday, 12th September. Following a frightful sleepless night (acutely sloping bed and interminable traffic noise), I finally dropped-off just as the dawn chorus began – at which point my landlady, Nancy Clarke, decided I required an unscheduled early morning call. A pleasant breakfast ensued, though hardly compensation for a lack of sleep. As with the students in Saltash, Nancy had a right stinker of a cold.

Having travelled less than fifty yards, I was very nearly mown-down by a negligent youth in a yellow Maxi: "Sorry mate, didn't notice you." Still somewhat shaken, I adopted the LDP beyond Downderry, and within minutes I was upon the neighbouring village of Seaton: notable for its grey sand and propensity to flooding. While retaining the coast path west of Seaton, I passed within yards of Murrayton Monkey Sanctuary, though with barely four kilometres under my belt I felt disinclined to be side-tracked – even by the lure of a colony of free-ranging Amazon Woolly monkeys.

With a plaintive accompaniment of foghorns, I paused briefly at the National Trust owned Bodigga Cliff to survey distant East and west Looe and the verdant hump of Looe Island – bombed during World War II by an enemy aircraft whose pilot mistook it for a British warship! Here too I exchanged pleasantries with a sprightly pensioner who was on the verge of having walked the entire South West Way. His sterling achievement set me up handsomely for the day's exertions.

With the notable exception of Abbotsbury, I had never seen such a concentration of swans as in Looe Harbour. This I noticed when crossing the ancient multi-arched bridge from east to west Looe; where I spent a subsequent half-hour in the distinguished company of the one-time personal PR Technician of ex-British Coal supremo, Ian McGregor. A former Burma-boy, he confirmed that my mind-over-matter walking doctrine matched his own when fleeing from the advancing Japanese Army. Though, heavens above!, our circumstances and motivation couldn't have been more different.

I had been eagerly looking forward to Polperro for some days. Jewel of Cornwall, some said. Bloody grockles paradise, others said. In reality it was a combination of the two: narrow streets (resident's cars only) radiating from a cramped little harbour; whitewashed cottages with lichen encrusted roofs the colour of Colman's mustard; and too many tourists by half.

I climbed the steep dirt-track out of Polperro determined to return – out of season. It was now late afternoon, and the veritable ghetto-blast of the day's heat had tangibly subsided. The resulting audio-vacuum was filled with the eerie intermittent chime of a lone seaward buoy. The remaining coast-path kilometres between Polperro and Polruan – my destination – were among the most arduous I'd faced for some days. I grasped every opportunity to divert my attention from my suffering by chatting and distributing appeal cards to anyone who would partake of either. It was very much a case of making hay while the sun shone. Rain-soaked cards, after all, lack the same 'appeal'.

Six weeks of intense people-watching had prompted the irrefutable conclusion that males, far from being the dominant sex, are in fact merely two dimensional when in their own company. Only in the civilising society of females do they become the well-behaved, courteous, fully rounded human beings I was to encounter in Polruan and beyond.

Thursday, 13th September. For someone who had never previously heard or seen a buzzard in the flesh, the last two weeks had been a banquet for the senses. As indeed were the undulating lanes between Polruan and Lostwithiel, with every break in the often dense canopy producing a plethora of new sightings and avian tongue.

My observations over the next two hours served only to confirm that my ideal home, should the opportunity arise, would be a secluded cottage along one of the West Country's myriad tree-fringed creeks. A close proximity to water and woodland being essential.

I met an elderly couple in Lostwithiel who recognised me from an article in MS News, their niece being a Multiple Sclerosis sufferer. Despite spending the last thirty years exiled in Liverpool, the duo had stoically hung onto their Cornish accents – Lostwithiel will forever be their heart's home.

Beyond Lostwithiel I made tracks for the tiny hamlet of Castle, from where the westerly prospect of Restormel district was dominated by an alabaster range of china clay heaps – the 'Cornish Alps'.

I reached Fowey (pronounced 'Foy') by early afternoon and made straight for the composite Post Office-cum-Tourist Information Centre, where I received my weekly parcel, a souvenir enamel brooch and a resounding *bon voyage* from the staff, who informed me that yesterday's Polperro – Polruan section of the LDP is the toughest in Cornwall.

At Coombe Hawne, south-west of the enigmatically named Readymoney Cove, a retired fisherman excitedly drew my attention to an elongated dark trace about a mile out to sea. To my naked eyes it resembled a huge animated oil-slick. My field-glasses confirmed the 'oil-slick' to be animated indeed – a veritable seething cauldron of mackerel in a feeding frenzy. According to the learned gentleman, this was the biggest shoal to frequent these waters since he was a boy. He went on to estimate the shoal to measure two miles by a quarter of a mile. Allied with the 'perfick' conditions and tide, he suspected the mackerel to be gorging themselves on plankton or krill, on which occasions they won't be tempted by any other foodstuff – hence the absence of line fishermen. As we parted company the shoal – as predicted – began likewise to break up.

The southern extremity of Gribbin Head was my next port of call, strikingly lorded over by the 84 ft high red and white mariner's 'daymark'. Thereafter resuming a northerly coastal tack, Polkerris and Par were poles apart in terms of scale, character and ambience. A case of 'from the sublime to the ridiculous'. As a last resort I repaired to Par's Snowlands Caravan Park. "Twelve pounds", intoned Mr Snow, "take it or leave it." I muttered something as to my charitable involvement. "Charity? Not my problem."

And thus I found myself installed in a grimy caravan, without even the comforting prospect of a full English breakfast to look forward to…

Friday, 14th September. I rose early, determined to put as much distance as possible between myself and Par, my overall impression of which was succinctly summed-up by a crude wooden sign erected above a particularly dog-soiled stretch of footpath by a discerning local wag: 'Shit Alley'.

Everything beyond the western perimeter fence of Par's china clay works (through which the LDP passes) was dusted with a coating of white, reminiscent of an especially heavy frost. A winter-scape illusion betrayed only by the soaring temperature.

Following the corrugated contours of Carlyon Bay, the Cornwall coast path was flanked on either side by a golf course and a sheltered, if sparsely populated Naturist beach. The few hardy devotees of the latter, all pendulous breasts and flaccid buttocks, appeared urgently intent upon securing occupancy of their favourite sun-trap hidey-holes. Verily 'The charge of the Cellulite Brigade'!

Within three kilometres of my Close Encounter of the Nudist Kind, I descended a grassy incline to the enthralling little working-port of Charleston, so named after local eighteenth century copper mine owner Charles Rashleigh. This was authentic Cornwall in aspic.

Birds of prey had long held a certain fascination for me. At Penare Point, to the north of Mevagissey, I was presented with the golden opportunity to examine at close quarters one of the swiftest avian hunters of all – the peregrine falcon. As it looped the loop high above Mevagissey Bay, local falconer Gavin explained how he was training it to hunt partridge – though it seemed more than taken by the suspiciously wheeling gulls.

Even in mid-September the confined streets of Mevagissey were seething with holidaymakers. Only the explosive intervention of a PR conscious coastguard who launched a maroon from the quay ("Makes their day") forestalled my immediate departure.

Portmellon by contrast was virtually deserted, though the harbour was surprisingly choppy. From here I made a beeline for Chapel Point along the cliff path. I recalled recently seeing the more characterful of Chapel Point's two dwellings on sale in *Country Life*. And a more exclusive locale I couldn't envisage. The only sign of life, however, was a mixed herd of cows drowsing upon the white sands of the adjacent Colona Beach.

The same cliff path led me to the unsullied charm of Gorran Haven – the perfect antidote to Par. Yet all was not plain sailing. In crossing a pasture to the north of the village the resident cows seemed strangely reluctant to make way. Only when in the very milling-midst of these usually timid creatures did I realise that the 'cows' were in fact young bulls – horns, testes, the works!

Such was the conspiracy of heat and punishing terrain leading to and beyond the bracken-clad Dodman Point, that all my old infirmities returned to plague me: raw back and hips, throbbing shoulder, etc. Just how I completed the final four kilometres to Portloe, four rancorous, bile-spitting kilometres, I do not know. Yet by the grace of God, and no little tenacity on my part – I did just that.

Saturday, 15th September. I awoke to the certain knowledge that if the weather turned cold before I took possession of my next laundry parcel I was in dead lumber. Since day one of the walk my weight had dropped by an incredible twenty-one pounds to a lean, mean, nine stone, a fact only brought home to me the night before when I tried on my one pair of long trousers. Bell tents, after all, aren't exactly the nattiest of evening wear! Even my watch strap, once tight, now flapped about my wrist like a hula-hoop.

It was another gloriously sunny morning, with only a hint of breeze. Yet the cliff path between Jacka Point and Gerrans Bay, for all its moody magnificence, was pure purgatory, as all the pains of yesterday promptly returned.

There are two Cornwalls, two Kernows; one, the rugged coastal Cornwall, home of the equally rugged fisher-folk who hold down more jobs than most people manage in a lifetime – a storm-battered Cornwall that puts on its Sunday best for the multitudinous tourists; and second, the genteel creek and river Cornwall where palm trees outnumber ravens and yachts outnumber fishing boats … St Mawes fell into the second category.

Sunday, 16th September. What a year for nature's bounteous gifts! The hedgerows were a positive riot of edible colour; blackberries, sloes, rosehips and elderberries, all in a state of pristine perfection. Surely the result of a wet spring and an Indian summer, and indicative of a severe winter to come.

Trethem Mill produced my second kingfisher of the walk. Beyond Trethem Mill I witnessed a large bird of prey standing in a field, alternatively furling and unfurling a pair of substantial wings in a semi-ritualistic manner. I took it to be the antics of a juvenile buzzard.

The weather throughout continued to be kind to me, though I refused to take it for granted that such would always be the case. Likewise I considered myself extremely fortunate to be meeting such interesting people, be it on a transient basis, and parting company before the *ennui* of familiarity had time to set in. For during such brief encounters conversation remained forever fresh and spontaneous, anecdotes amusing, and inquisitiveness squarely to the fore.

Before me now, probing southward like a variegated green finger, lay the largely deciduous Lamorran Wood, in these coniferous mono-culture days, a unique sight in itself. Deep, dark and mysterious – here the mighty oak was king. And long may it reign!

I entered Truro, Cornwall's administrative centre, via a housing estate, and was immediately depressed by the dilapidation and squalor that met my eyes: burnt-out cars, boarded-up windows, vacant-eyed taciturn youths. Guided by the lofty spire of Truro Cathedral, I fared little better in the town centre – where the Tourist Information Bureau was inexplicably closed. After an hour and a half of pavement pounding – and having drawn a total blank at the local cop shop – I struck gold accommodation-wise in the guise of the enigmatically titled 'Blue Haze' guest-house; an island of tranquillity in an ocean of disquiet.

Monday, 17th September. A stiffish breeze had chased away the bulk of the clouds from the sky, leaving in their wake a few fleecy islets. As I strode the A39 southwards, it was clear that I wasn't quite my old self. Though not sufficiently incommoded to jeopardise the walk, I remained light headed and detached, like an ongoing 'out of body experience'.

My aforesaid 'astral travel' came to a rude and abrupt halt at Perranarworth where I removed a dead cock robin from the road and laid it to rest beneath a hedgerow. Such a graceless end for one who brings such pleasure to us all via song and cheeky antics. Yet, in essence, surely all demise is undignified…

In the aftermath of the overnight downpour, blackberries and sloes, erstwhile in the full bloom of their ephemeral perfection, now bruised the roadside like so much superfluous litter. A dark stain is all that bore witness to their former immaculacy. Yet how many of us will leave so much as a stain as testament to our all too brief earthly passage? …Must shake this black mood!

I drifted through Falmouth as if in a dream, conscious only of a rapidly falling temperature and the crowds of shoppers. From Pendennis Point to Rosemullion Head I kept a vigilant seaward eye upon Falmouth Bay, yet failed to see Morgawr, Cornish for 'Sea Giant', which is said to frequent these waters.

At Parson's Beach I cut inland through the manicured graveyard of Mawnan Church, where I noticed a conspicuous incongruity in the comparative preservation of tombstones, the more recent of which (1850-1900) were virtually worn away and illegible. Yet the older pre-1850 examples were as sharp and well defined as the day they were erected. Why the discrepancy? Elementary! Whereas the recent additions were of a less robust stone construction, earlier specimens were made of the more durable solid slate.

Less than two short kilometres away was the unlikely sounding village of Mawnan Smith, my objective for the day.

Tuesday, 18th September. I quit Mawnan Smith in the knowledge that I had a fully fledged cold – courtesy, no doubt, of Nancy Clarke at Downderry. Despite feeling decidedly shivery throughout the previous evening, I warmed up nicely in the face of the legion hills that confronted me between Mawnan Smith and Gweek, famed for its Seal Sanctuary.

The skies above Gweek were alive with all manner of aircraft, no doubt originating from the nearby Culdrose Airfield. At Helford Passage I could well have taken the passenger ferry to Helford, and saved myself a twenty kilometre round trip of the Helford River in the process. However as such shortcuts were not part of my brief, I adhered instead to the labyrinthine network of minor roads that orbit the Helford River, before rejoining the Cornwall Coast Path at Gillan.

For much of the afternoon the brow of each successive hill afforded a tantalising glimpse of the distant Goonhilly Downs Satellite Earth Station, a southerly prospect only partially marred by an insect bite to my right knee, which had ballooned to the size of a cricket ball within minutes.

Deferring all treatment until I'd achieved the day's objective, I temporarily parted company with the LDP at Porthallow (which hereafter zigzagged its way across country), opting instead to skirt a trio of disused quarries before regaining the coast path at Godrevy Cove.

True to its name, the low-lying greensward beyond Lowland Point provided a fitting and leisurely climax to a largely enjoyable day – not least for the duel challenge of overcoming my infirmities and outpacing the weather. Since mid-afternoon, black clouds had been ominously rolling in from the east and now, on the very doorstep of Coverack, I was destined to be the first to our common destination.

Wednesday, 19th September. Choosing to ignore the old adage 'starve a cold, feed a fever,' I partook a huge 'blow-out' of a breakfast at the fair hands of my hosts, Mr and Mrs Jack Daw. Amazingly I'd retained a modicum of my sense of smell and taste – without which eating would be nought but a chore.

As I made ready for the off the weather abroad matched my fluctuating morale, veering from torrential rain to blazing sunshine and back again in the space of twenty minutes. Jack Daw concisely summed it up: "That's peninsular weather for 'ee!" And he should know. The walls of his dining-cum-sitting room were plastered with valedictory letters and illuminated addresses bearing witness to his deeds of derring-do aboard the now defunct Coverack lifeboat. And seldom an evening passed when he failed to tune his state-of-the-art radio receiver into the Coast Guard frequency. Old habits die hard.

Being largely open-plan in layout, Coverack lacked the intrinsic intimacy one associates with Kingsand or Polperro. It remains one of the Lizard Peninsula's more memorable villages nonetheless.

I departed in sombre mood, pessimistic as to my short-term weather prospects. In the wake of a series of post-dawn showers the rock-strewn coast path beyond Dolor Point was tantamount to walking on blocks of soap in bare feet – in short, positively treacherous. It was obvious also that my usually keen sense of smell had not entirely deserted me; even at Black Head I could still detect the unmistakable stench of Trewillis piggery, one kilometre to the north. At Beagles Point, with the sun at last assuming the ascendancy, I joined forces with two fellow ramblers, Francis and Robin, the latter being a Cornishman who had accompanied me briefly the previous day from Lowland Point to Coverack.

Despite the obvious disparity in our ages, backgrounds and walking experience, by hook or by crook we three remained together, joined by a common objective, for the rest of the day – a veritable walking triumvirate! And with the added benefit of three pairs of eyes and ears at our disposal, we missed not a single sight or sound of our magnificent coastal heritage.

Remaining ever alert to our surroundings, we took turns at the head of our little column – relay-fashion, while exchanging anecdotes and imparting our pet philosophies. And little by little the characters and idiosyncrasies of my neo-colleagues emerged. currently based in Holland, fifty year old Francis (shock-haired, goatee-beard, and thumbstick-cum-cudgel) looked every inch the latter-day pilgrim. Openly cynical and always amusing – at least to those not put off by his unbending 'take me as you find me' attitude – his passion for walking, and genuine disregard for authority, convention and responsibility, has taken him all over the world. Meanwhile Robin, so it would appear, was a far less complex character, yet no less interesting. A gardener by trade – married; no children – Robin walked purely for the love of it, for the love of discovering 'his' Cornwall. Francis, one suspects, had more convoluted motives.

As recommended by John Mole, I enjoyed a hot jam doughnut at Lizard Point Tea Room, the extreme southerly tip of mainland Britain. Pricey – but tasty! Indicative of the virtual water purity, every stream and brook was abundant with wild watercress – equally tasty (and all the more so for being free and gratis!). Francis, the voice of experience, suggested I lay my hands on a stout stick or staff; guaranteed to extricate one from all manner of tight spots. I took the suggestion to heart, resolving to obtain one at the first opportunity.

After a fine and eventful day on all counts, we three went our chosen ways at Mullion Cove, Robin and I to seek out B&B accommodation, Francis to discover a shop. Yet the story was far from over.

Having been turned away from Trenance Farm, I tried my luck at the Marconi Hotel – only to bump into Robin in the foyer. The Marconi had only two vacancies; a garden shed with a bed (!) at £8; or a single room at £16. Robin, by virtue of precedence, opted for the shed. Thus all was amicably settled. That is until I visited the local Spar store, where who should I meet but Francis. Our shopping complete, I invited him back to cast an eye over Robin's novelty accommodation. Which he duly did – and promptly gained permission to pitch his one man tent in the self same garden. Thus we three, thrown together by chance, are further linked by way of habitation

Thursday, 20th September. By the following morning Robin and Francis had departed, *sans* breakfast – and, more pointedly, *sans* payment! Gone but not forgotten.

Breakfast took somewhat longer than usual as I had to explain in triplicate all the ins-and-outs of the walk to each and every diner in turn – having inadvertently run out of explanatory appeal cards. One notable compensation was a particularly vivacious Black Country lass who foisted me with the extravagant sobriquet 'Blonde Giant'. Though to be fair, I suspect her opinion was partially coloured by the fact that her husband was all of five foot tall in his stockinged feet, and as bald as a coot!. But, more fortuitously, I shared a table with publisher Peter Groves and his wife Jean, a chance encounter that led directly to the very volume you are now reading.

Once abroad I fell back into my regular rhythm of walking; a comfortable pace I knew I could maintain around the clock. Villages and beauty spots came and went in quick succession – and I derived much reassurance from the old saying 'while the gorse is in bloom, Britain will never be conquered'. Particularly so for the fact that – like gorse the world over – the vast saffron thickets that fringe much of the Cornwall South Coast Path between Mullion Cove and Marazion are in bloom almost all the year round. I was intrigued, however, by the scarlet filament-like threads that adorned a few isolated shrubs. Definitely vegetable in origin, it transpired to be an example of the parasitic common dodder, among its more colourful folk-names, hellweed and devil's guts being most apt.

Midway between Gunwalloe fishing cove and Portleven, Loe Bar proved the ideal habitat for the once common sea holly. This massive shingle bank forms an ample buffer-zone between the sea and The Loe, a mile long freshwater lake, and its offshoot Carminowe Creek.

If talking to one's self is genuinely the litmus test of insanity, then my in-depth conversations well and truly marked me down as Bedlam-fodder. Though quite what the men in the white coats would have read into my alfresco singing remains open to debate. Certainly I favoured songs with a martial flavour that lent themselves to the rhythm of my moderato marching stride – current favourites being *Pick a Bale of Cotton* and *Onward Christian Soldiers.*

North-west of Porthleven the gaunt outlines of Wheal Prosper and Wheal Trewavas are stark reminders of Cornwall's mining heritage – in this case copper. The engine-house and chimney of the former, standing atop the granite promontory of Rinsey Head, was partially restored by the National Trust in 1970. The ruins of the latter are located half a mile to the east at Trewavas Head.

From Cudden Point the castle-capped island of St Michael's Mount hove into view.

At the village of Marazion I wolfed a freshly baked 'Tiggie-oggie', the best pastie I've ever had. On a broader front, not only did my grandfather sail on HMS *Marazion*, but John Mole's grandmother (née Hocking) was born there.

I entered Penzance via the huge crescent of sand that stretches westward from St. Michael's Mount. As arranged I met Barbara Dodgson and her husband in Penzance Station carpark, and was promptly whisked away to their comfortable Newlyn Coombe home, where Barbara put on a wonderful spread. As evening fell, I was conveyed to my accommodation in Penzance. Strewth! What with the proprietors' androgynous attire and the overtly feminine décor (which comprised: The Cerise Room, The Chartreuse Room, The Hyacinth Room, etc.) I could have sworn they'd booked me into a gay Guest House!

Before turning in I received a flying visit from my mentor, John Mole, and his exceptionally gifted daughter, Tamzin, *en route* to set up tomorrow's reception at Land's End. It was great to be reunited; it was even greater to be temporarily relieved of my burdensome non-essential equipment. As I drifted off to sleep I pondered upon the wisdom of wearing my ultra-shorts to breakfast...

Friday, 21st September. I stepped into a dull and overcast morning, a light breeze plucked at my wind-shirt. Gwavas Lake was the colour of lead and seemingly as solid. South of Penzance, Newlyn Harbour was tightly packed with trawlers and smaller fishing vessels. Newlyn benefited greatly from a new fishing quay in 1981, to the detriment of its once illustrious fishing-port neighbours.

Having chased away the last vestige of cloud, the sun broke through as I perused the narrow streets and stone-built cottages of Mousehole (pronounced 'Mowzel') for the first time since childhood. Circling the snug little harbour, I sought out the Kegwyn Arms. This former tavern is reputedly the oldest house in the village, being one of the few properties to survive a sacking by Spanish troops in 1595.

The Mousehole – Land's End leg of the Cornwall North Coast Path could well be described in terms once reserved for the pneumatic movie star Jane Russell – mean, moody and magnificent! Now on the very eve of completing the entire south coast, I was understandably in high spirits. My euphoria reduced hills to mere mounds, rocky terrain to a leisurely promenade; psychologically, Land's End was just a hop, step and jump away.

Porthcurno Beach was under military occupation. Revelling in the sunshine, squaddies old and young were abseiling from the high granite cliffs to the pliant sand below. Sadly, having been instructed to rendezvous at Land's End at precisely 3.10 p.m., I lacked sufficient time to pay an extended visit to the nearby Minack open-air theatre, other than a cursory glance at the romantic cliff-top setting. Approaching Land's End with some twenty minutes to spare, I bided my time at Pordenack Point where I offered up a prayer of thanks before gazing seaward in search of the 'mythical' drowned land of Lyonesse. Arthurian legend or reality? Certainly the Scilly Isles, twenty-eight miles to the south-west, contain clear archaeological evidence to suggest the latter. I for my part, retain an open mind.

John Mole and daughter Tamzin had done an excellent organisational job. As I strode the final few hundred yards across the tourist ravaged turf, a welcoming banner and balloon-waving throng of well-wishers were clearly visible on the forecourt of the State House Hotel complex.

I was formally greeted among others by Penzance Head Postmaster John White and Delivery Office Manager Malcolm Brown. High above the wave-lashed rocks which mark the south-western tip of mainland Britain, we posed for the media beneath the famous Land's

End signpost, now suitably modified for the occasion: 'John Westley 9,000 (miles) to go'. While shutters clicked and motor-drives whirred, and lensmen angled for the Best Shot, I reflected with satisfaction and pride upon the trials, tribulations and legion high points that so enriched the last forty-eight days and seventeen hundred kilometres...

Saturday, 22nd September. The State House was certainly a luxurious billet, and only within my price range due to a generous reduction by the management. My room, one of thirty-four deluxe *en suite* accommodations, was called Pedn-Mén-du; deriving its name from a local geographical feature. Only the brain-jarring din from a disco that extended into the early hours tarnished an otherwise perfect stay.

The swirling pea-souper that enveloped the hotel and much of west Cornwall the previous evening had dispersed by morning, giving way to a sullen, brooding sky. Rogue squalls swept in from the Atlantic, like the great grey hulks of airborne men-o'-war firing their turbulent broadsides of wind and rain. At present I was out of range, but definitely in the firing-line.

Despite the strong tidal crosscurrents and the roughest seas to date, Whitesand Bay to the north of Sennen Cove threw up the walk's first wet-suited surfer. Brave man, indeed!

Undeterred by the inclement weather, this section of coast path was particularly blessed with bird life. Stonechats and wheat-ears, for example, being as commonplace here as sparrows and starlings are in the city. At Cot Valley, due west of St. Just, I was amazed to find the area awash with hastily parked cars and telescope-toting birdwatchers (all Barbour jackets and green wellies!). This usually deserted country lane resembled Oxford Street in the rush hour. In questioning one serious-looking 'twitcher', I was curtly informed that a yellow throated verico from the USA had been spotted in the vicinity.

At Cape Cornwall, which misses by only 1,000 yards the distinction of being mainland England's westernmost point, I kept a weather-eye upon a particularly menacing squall converging from the west. I'd need fleetness of foot and good fortune in equal measures to avoid a soaking at the hands of that Black Beauty!

Covering some thirteen miles of highly demanding terrain, the coast path between Cape Cornwall and St. Ives is called The Tinners Way, along which tin was once transported for export to the Mediterranean and Celtic countries.

The last few kilometres were marred by a plague of devil's coach horses upon the badly eroded coast path, a foolhardy mountain biker who pointedly ignored my pleas for caution, and a series of brief but heavy showers.

From his Clodgy Point look-out, my young cousin Tim loudly proclaimed my approach. It had been a long and gruelling day. And after a cliff-top reunion (with the Mole family), under the watchful eye of a grey seal from the surf below, we repaired mob-handed to St. Ives for a well deserved cream tea – with lashings of real Cornish clotted cream.

Sunday, 23rd September. After a wonderful evening in the convivial atmosphere of Wilbur's Café I am somewhat reluctant to leave St. Ives. It would be so easy to join the town's 'café' society on a permanent basis.

Coincidences continue to occur. While in the midst of our breakfast, who should drop-in but Francis. Of all the guest houses in all the world how did he manage to pick on ours?

Post breakfast, Kathleen (John Mole's wife), Tamzin and I walked to Lelant via the LDP. It had rained torrentially from early evening until moments before our departure – when it fortuitously ceased. The going underfoot was sodden, making a mockery of the otherwise undemanding terrain. Particularly so for Tamzin, who was feeling decidedly under the weather; and Kathleen, who only days before had been felled by a large 'silverish' dog (a Weimaraner?). Not only did we each toss a coin into St. Uny's well and make a wish, but we also sampled fresh cob nuts from the ancient wind-gnarled nut groves above Carrack Gladden. Vacating the Cornwall Coast Path, we beachcombed the entire length of the dune-backed Porth Kidney Sands, before rejoining the LDP to the north of the fifteenth century church of St. Uny where the ashes of my grandparents were scattered some thirteen years earlier. Joined now by the remaining members of the family, we ambled to Lelant's 'Badger Inn', and the parting of the ways. I bade a reluctant farewell.

Having walked over one thousand miles into the wind, and having as if it were turned the corner, I now had what breeze there was squarely behind me. At the head of Hayle estuary, I skirted the bird-rich tidal mudflats known as the Saltings. In the once busy port of Hayle the all consuming issue of the day was vividly proclaimed from fly-poster and bumper-sticker alike: 'No Gwithian sewage outfall' In simplistic terms, it was proposed to pump sewage from Cornwall's southern coast to the north, before discharging it into St. Ives Bay off Gwithian Village. And to hell with the generations of holidaymakers who have swum off the Gwithian Towans! (Towan being Cornish for sand-dune.)

At Hell's Mouth – a cliff-girt white water maelstrom and notorious ship's graveyard – I paused in solemn mood to regard the surviving foam-washed aft-section of a beleaguered timber transporter ship, one of the only three wrecks I witnessed on the entire walk: three wrecks too many. In the tragic foreknowledge that one crew member had perished when falling from a breeches-buoy at the very moment of deliverance, I balked at the macabre sight of holiday-coaches disgorging their giggling camera-toting payloads. Nothing short of the unfortunate mariner's floating cadaver would satisfy these ghouls!

Monday, 24th September. My birthday – thirty-eight today!

The day was blustery, though warming nicely in accordance with my increasingly sunny mood. Back aboard the coast path, it continued to set me the most intriguing little conundrums. None more so than the conical-shaped metal baskets which littered the clifftops, like colossal fairy-rings. The size of an average garden pond, I correctly deduced these rubble-filled protuberances to be 'capped' mine and ventilation shafts; the whole area being honeycombed with former copper and tin mine workings.

Much of the day my route was restricted to a coastal corridor between precipitous cliffs and MOD fencing. These physical limitations apart, I vowed to derive the maximum benefit possible from each day – for these assuredly are the good times. With the onset of winter only a matter of weeks away, Halcyon days like these are to be relished and savoured to the full. This is as good as it gets! North of Chapel Porth, I paused to compose a photo of the ruined Great Wheal Charlotte mine, from where copper workings once extended far out under the sea, with the explanatory National Trust 'acorn sign' to the foreground. At the quintessential moment a huge raven (Kronk! Kronk!) alighted centre stage as if on cue – thus transforming a so-so snapshot into (one hoped) a photographic masterpiece.

My objective for the day was the former mining village of Perranporth; where I picked up my birthday cards and made inroads into my backlog of sweat-stiffened Thor-lo hiking socks at the local launderette.

Tuesday, 25th September. So much for the knowledge of locals! Within a couple of hundred yards of adopting the LDP to the north of Perranporth, the said 'good footpath' promptly gave way to calf-deep sand – the one surface I was assured I would not encounter. Having travelled too far to retrieve my steps, I was left with no viable option but to descend from the energy-sapping hummocky wilderness of Gear Sands to the wave-compacted foreshore below. Thereafter I trekked the entire length of Perran Beach, before rejoining the coast path to the east of Ligger Point.

With a surfeit of sunshine and the merest hint of breeze, I was soon forced to remove my windshirt in view of a soaring body temperature. Thankfully my cold symptoms had now completely abated; a happy situation I put down to plenty of exercise and an abundance of good, clean fresh air. Thus far spared the squalls of yesterday, the weather would actually do justice to a mid-summer's day.

Though always a joy to behold, I now saw grey seals with such regularity that individual recording would be too time-consuming and laborious. Cliff erosion at Penhale Camp prompted a slight detour, though it did afford the opportunity to witness the drilling of an eminently maladroit batch of raw recruits.

At Penhale Point I looked back beyond the myriad headlands to the ivory tower of Godrevy lighthouse, now just a speck of white in the violet middle-distance. In the afterglow of St. Uny's well, I pledged to make a donation and a wish at each and every well whose path I crossed, whether 'wishing' or otherwise.

Upon the threshold of my day's terminus, Mawgan Porth, I was stopped by three hikers who appeared to know my business better than I knew myself. Had they read about me in the press? Seen me on TV? Heard me on the radio? None of these. My notoriety, they confessed, was due entirely to one they unanimously described as a 'wild man' – Francis! If I caught up with him during tomorrow's Mawgan Porth – Padstow leg, I vowed to thank him for an excellent Public Relations job.

Wednesday, 26th September. The weather continued in the same benevolent vein – to such a degree, that I'm tempted to believe that 'somebody up there likes me!' A comforting thought.

I struck out for Padstow along the grassy cliff-top path, harried every step of the way by hordes of crane-flies – a day-long nuisance. At Porthcothan Bay – a narrow inlet of silver sand and aquamarine shallows bisected by a freshwater stream – a picnicking gentleman-farmer confided to having seen many a basking shark and a pod of white whales (beluga?) in these very waters.

Following the inland course of the River Camel beyond Stepper Point, I entered Padstow via North Quay and was immediately entranced by the drowsy tranquillity of this tiny fishing port and its sleepy Sunday afternoon feel – the absolute antithesis of contemporary life.

Thursday, 27th September. The sun stuck valiantly to its task, though it was fighting a losing battle. Despite the squint-inducing brightness, there was a distinct chill in the air I hadn't noticed before; the ice-spiked air one associates with the freezer section of a supermarket.

I embarked from Padstow via South Quay, pausing briefly to photograph Court House, the sixteenth century residence of Sir Walter Raleigh while he was warden of the stannaries of Cornwall.

From Padstow to Wadebridge I followed the Camel Trail – the picturesque estuarine route of a now dismantled railway. With both towns doing a brisk trade in bicycle rentals, to be on foot was to be out of sync with the world.

The tranquil ambience of Padstow, however, remained with me throughout the morning like a devoted dog, both comforter and companion – until Wadebridge, where my serenity took flight in the face of throbbing midmorning traffic and milling shoppers.

Masochist that I am, I actually chose to climb Brea Hill in the full heat of day, with rucksack, and by the steepest (north) face – purely to survey and photograph from on high the hedge-hemmed church of St. Enodoc, Trebetherick, so beloved of the late John Betjeman. But what a view! My effort was repaid threefold!

On the run in to Polzeath I noticed a young couple who appeared to be arguing as to which one should approach me. Eventually, after much heated deliberation, the girl was ushered forth, and in an American accent enquired: "Is – is it you?" I replied drolly to the affirmative. With the ice well and truly broken, the duo eagerly described the fateful day at Tintagel when my 'coming' was foretold – and went on, with uncanny accuracy, to paint a precise word-picture of the 'prophet' Francis.

Friday, 28th September. Peafowl were abroad in numbers as I took my leave of Polzeath. Apparently some years ago several birds were released, escaped or were abandoned. Whatever the case, the village now has a resident feral flock who – by virtue of their size and single-mindedness – feed where and when they choose. And this morning they chose to graze and defecate upon any lawn that took their fancy.

A wispy sea-mist hung over the village, decapitating the uplands and casting an opaque veil over the latent presence of a watery sun.

As I climbed the well-worn trail towards Pentire Point, still draped in the merest gossamer cloak, spectacular views across the wide mouth of the Camel Estuary were revealed piecemeal by the melting mist. None more so than the distant 'Daymark' crowned promontory of Stepper Point.

Beyond Com Head, the sun having vaporised the residual haze, I negotiated a glistening savannah of dew bejewelled broom tussocks. Yet even this visual feast was superseded by the wondrous expectation I experienced in surmounting each successive headland, comparable only to the thrill and promise of opening a Christmas parcel. Each newly won seascape was a blessing; each eyeful a bonus. And all the while the blue-black ocean below, though calm as a millpond at present, silently brooded… patiently awaiting its hour.

To the west of Port Isaac lies possibly the most ill-conceived stretch of Cornwall Coast Path on the entire LDP. Instead of adhering to the contours and natural undulations of the terrain, the powers that be have chosen to adopt a series of severe ascents and descents, some of which include steps obviously built with eight-foot giants in mind, which when lubricated with dew are nothing short of diabolical!

From feeling decidedly drained from the morning's slog, the immense kindness and concern shown by Mr and Mrs Cleave of Port Isaac Post Office rejuvenated me no end. I climbed out of the low-lying village laden with all manner of souvenirs, having promised to send them a postcard from Scotland (they even provided the stamp!). Even before this charitable act I felt a certain empathy with Port Isaac for it exuded a sort of grubby charm, like a threadbare jacket with which one is loath to part. Ashamed though I am, as the day wore on I found myself becoming increasingly blasé in regards the awesome scenery. Very much a case of bread and bread. Must strive to retain my sense of wonderment. No wet blankets, please – we're British!

At the tourist magnet of Tintagel Castle – legendary birthplace of King Arthur – I was brazenly swept along with the fervour of my fellow grockles; taking photographs of anything and everything – in duplicate – in the scatter-gun principal that at least one or two photos would hit the target and turn out half decent. At the height of my snapshot frenzy, two couples sheepishly edged into shot ("Hello, you're John Westley") to inform me that they were well aware of my exploits and that I was writing a book on the subject – which was even news to me at the time!

And so to Boscastle, where I found my digs without difficulty. Located to the west of the village, it overlooked Forrabury Common where the ancient Celtic land tenure system known as 'stitchmeal' survives to this day. Though the lady of the household undoubtedly did her best, bless her, my surroundings were hardly salubrious – in fact, I now know where flies go in winter!

Saturday, 29th September. Such was the rain, or continual threat of it, that I wore my dreaded weatherproofs throughout the day. With head bowed into a potent cocktail of wind and rain for much of the time, very little caught my eye. Certainly the popular surfing beach of Widemouth Sand looked cheerlessly bleak. Not even the mildly interesting titbit that the Downing Street – White House 'hot line' passed directly underfoot could dispel the utter gloom of the place. Though in all honestly, in such monsoon conditions most beauty spots would befall a similar 'damp squib' fate.

My introduction to Bude, Cornwall's most northerly holiday resort, was likewise 'moist', and initially unfavourable. Though on returning to town for a warming evening meal, my reappraisal was less jaundiced.

Sunday, 30th September. I shared my breakfast table with a fellow walker, a modest young lady who needlessly belittled her own effort on behalf of the cancer ward of a local hospital. Her departure preceded my own by some twenty minutes, I being a methodical packer. Catching her up became my prime target and motivation.

For the second day in succession I walked slap-bang into a virtual wall of rain. Despite wearing only shorts and T-shirt beneath my weatherproofs, this wildly concertinaed landscape of soaring promontories and deep river-gouged gorges ensured that I raised a good head of steam.

It was a grey day: the sky was grey; the sea was grey – the colour of soiled bath water; the few hardy souls who ventured abroad were grey (except the young lady, who was pink and vital). The low-lying nimbostratus, heavy with rain, did not so much obscure the uplands as drape them with a sombre grey blanket, which hung hammock-like from peak to peak. The result was a 'now you see me, now you don't' situation between the comparative visibility of the valley and the total obscurity of the summit.

Try as I might, I didn't catch up with my fellow guest until the rock-strewn foreshore of Sandy Mouth, where she understandably encountered some difficulty in scaling Stowe Cliffs. Her tenacious persistence impressed me no end. Laden with her own prodigious rucksack and soaked to the skin, she refused to entertain the idea of taking a breather, let alone calling it a day. We parted company at Duckpool – a shingle backed beach, flanked by steep and unstable cliffs – she to await the arrival of her husband, I to make an ascent of the treacherous Steeple Point.

As the deluge continued unabating, walking became nigh-on impossible. Every track became a runnel; every trail a brook; every path a river; every hollow a ford; every slope a rapid. To all intents and purposes the LDP was a single watercourse. The accumulated debris added a further perilous dimension. In addition to the general uncertainty of one's footing, I laid the blame for two minor tumbles squarely at the feet of my now slick-soled boots.

During one particular spell of white-out cliff-top walking – the first time I've actually walked with my head in the clouds! – I literally teetered on the brink of the abyss. No minor tumble this. Not for the first time I was forced to lean precariously into the prevailing head wind in order to gain the slightest leeway. One minute I was charging rain-blinded along the coast path – next minute, the nor'wester having suddenly shut down in mid-blast, I was airborne. One forward somersault later, I came to an abrupt halt some 200ft above the raging foam. My rucksack, so often the cause of many a downfall, had on this occasion come to my rescue, anchoring me firmly in the sodden cliff edge scrub.

At the secluded rack-and-pebble beach of Marsland Mouth, the usually sedate like-named stream of Marsland Water – which marks the Cornwall-Devon Boundary – was in full spate, a veritable white-water gusher.

From the awe-inspiring 'Promontory of Hercules', as Hartland Point was known to the Romans, Lundy Island was clearly defined and far larger and closer to the mainland than I had envisaged. East of Hartland Point, the rugged North Devon Coast Path commanded fine views across the broad, tide-ripped mouth of the Bristol Channel: the largest inlet in the British Isles.

I entered the time-capsule village of Clovelly by its steeply cobbled High Street – alternatively known as 'up-a-long' and 'down-a-long' – which plunges zigzag fashion to a faithfully restored eighteenth century quay. Lined with quaint whitewashed cottages, my tread-worn boots made this the most hazardous descent of the day.

As I made for the Red Lion Hotel, which overlooked the shingle-bedded harbour, I resolved to explore Clovelly more fully on the morrow – hopefully in blazing sunshine.

3   Wet, wet, wet

And did those feet in ancient time
Walk upon England's mountains green?
William Blake.

Monday, 1st October.

I WAS abroad at 8.30 a.m. and remained within the atmospheric environs of Clovelly, Devon's showpiece village, for the next hour. The rain of the previous two days had washed all traces of colour from the sky, yet the village remained as vibrant as ever.

Apparently if one can climb from the harbour to the first bend in the High Street and still hold a conversation one is considered fit. A test I passed with flying colours.

I headed east along the gently meandering Hobby Drive; a rough-shod three mile trackway flanked by wooded cliffs and lush vegetation. At one point I was caught in a cascade of beech mast, like rain, yet infinitely dryer.

Beyond Hobby Lodge a holidaying Malaysian nurse assured me: "We don't have Multiple Scleroses in Malaysia." Allied with the revelation of the previous evening – an American doctor informed me that MS. is widespread in Northern States and virtually unknown in the broiling south – the links between MS. and temperate climates would appear overwhelming.

As the walk unfolds I find myself identifying more and more with Christian, the central character of *The Pilgrim's Progress*; though unlike Christian I have yet to shed my burden.

Named after Charles Kingsley's adventure story, Westward Ho! came as a major disappointment. All chalets, caravans and hotels – and little authentic character. Appledore, however, was a different kettle of fish – boasting everything its neighbour to the south-west lacked; colour washed houses, shipyards and character to burn.

I met only two genuine walkers during the course of the day; an Englishman who was breaking-in a new pair of boots – or vice versa; and a Dutchman who didn't realise we had shops in this part of the world – and consequently was buckling beneath a mammoth rucksack and eight days provisions!

Tuesday, 2nd October. I set about my journey with renewed vigour – and counting my blessings with every stride. I crossed the River Torridge by Bideford's most famous landmark; with its twenty-four arches, the stone-built bridge has carried grateful passengers since the Middle Ages. Instow, to the north, was a significant improvement upon Westward Ho!. Just how that nondescript village could have inspired Rudyard Kipling to write *Stalky & Co.* is a mystery.

Between Instow and Barnstaple I followed the route of a dismantled railway, incongruously known as the Tarka Trail. An area less likely to harbour even a single otter I have yet to see.

Wednesday, 3rd October. I awoke to a foul morning of heavy rain and blustery wind. Having received my 'new' boots the previous day, I parcelled-up my original pair for immediate dispatch and re-soling.

Beyond the dune-sheltered village of Croyde, my 'new' boots didn't retain their pristine condition for long. My first excursion onto the Somerset and North Devon Coast Path was even wetter and muddier that the Bude-Clovelly section, thanks to a combination of inadequate drainage and constant tractor/cow traffic. The highlight of the morning was the tiny village of Lee, with its imposing hotel and spectacular cliff-scape backdrop.

I entered Ilfracombe, North Devon's largest resort, by the Torrs Walk on the town's western outskirts. I was soon regretting my vow to patronise each and every wishing well, which in Ilfracombe have reached plague proportions. Now decidedly short on the small change front, I took the A399 to Combe Martin with all haste.

Thursday, 4th October. Beyond the straggling valley-long village of Combe Martin, the western flank of Exmoor rose steeply away; a majestic cloud-haloed range of emerald green, with a cape of rust coloured bracken to seaward.

I was soon brusquely confronted by the first ascent of the day – Little Hangman (218m). This 'stiffish' climb was followed in rapid succession by Great Hangman (318m) and Holdstone Down (349m). The gradient of the intervening kestrel-hung valleys became ever more steep; these yawning ravines were additionally occupied by hardy sheep and the occasional low-level sortie of Hawk trainer jets. Considering the extreme terrain, intermittent squalls and constant westerly blow, it was not surprising that fellow walkers were noticeably absent.

Having suffered two dog attacks between Trantishoe and Highveer point, I followed Francis' advice and adopted a hefty stick in the hope of forestalling further bloodletting on my part. My *Pilgrim's Progress* persona was thus outwardly complete.

For the remainder of the walking day to my evening berth of Lynton I remained steadfastly road-borne, pausing only to marvel at the serrated limestone pinnacles of the Valley of the Rocks – featured in *Lorna Doone* – and known by such evocative names as The Devil's Cheesewring, Ragged Jack and The White Lady. I managed to capture the latter on film – between squalls – along with a herd of feral goats.

Friday, 5th October. Two months into the walk – yet it felt more like two weeks!

It was another awful start to the day: wet 'n' windy, and with a humidity level comparable to Kew Garden's Palm House; the mere thought of physical exertion prompted a head to toe varnish of perspiration.

From the word go I plummeted 500 ft to Lynton's sister village of Lynmouth by way of the plunging westerway footpath which passes the eccentric – and even steeper – water-powered cliff railway. Site of the infamous flood of 1952 which claimed thirty-four lives, Lynmouth's riverside road was still lined in part with sandbags. Memories, it would appear, are understandably long in these parts.

Travelling in an easterly direction, I vacated Lynmouth by the vertiginous 1-in-4 Countisbury Hill (A39). In days of yore stage coach drivers had to take a new team of horses merely to contemplate the continuous mile long climb. Much pleased with myself, I completed it without a single pause – even finding the resolve to decline a couple of prospective lifts on the way. From the summit of Countisbury Hill I took the footpath to Foreland Point, and thereafter followed the Hogs-back Cliffs which stretch without break clean through to Porlock.

I was seeing Exmoor in the raw: lush coombs, rambling moorland – and with the added atmospheric dimension of rain and mist. In such adverse conditions one could easily be convinced that *Lorna Doone* was a factual account. For before the advent of metalled roads Exmoor must have been a virtual no-go area for the forces of law and order.

Culbone Church is reputed to be the smallest completed church in regular use anywhere in England. Once the centre-piece of a thriving charcoal burning community, only one cottage now survives. As an avid churchyard browser, I noted with interest the high incidence of the surname Ridd. Further shades of *Lorna Doone*! The Boy Jesus is reputed to have visited Culbone Church in the company of his uncle, Joseph of Arimathea. And in kneeling in prayer before the tiny alter, I was achieving another of my long-time goals. Spiritually renewed, I repaired to the thirteenth century porch where disaster struck in the guise of an upturned can of Coke. As I scrambled on hands and knees to mop up the offending liquid, my simple maladroit act felt like a heinous crime, a blasphemy

As the weather deteriorated yet further (the wind was actually howling like a banshee), I took a path through the deer-rich Yearnor Wood to Porlock Weir. Etched into the steep slopes high above the sea, this partially gravelled trackway was carpeted with windfall chestnuts – both white of flesh and sweet to the taste.

At the chocolate-box village of Bossington I called it a day. Nestling in the lee of the partially aforested Bossington Hill, it exemplified the English village at its consummate best. In regards the utilisation of local materials, sympathetic maintenance, human scale and picturesque setting, Bossington was in a class of its own.

Saturday, 6th October. Following three consecutive days of rain, the sunshine that greeted me wasn't unwelcome – just unfamiliar. While I squinted into the morning glare, plumes of vapour rose from the sodden hedgerows like so many dormant geysers.

My first port of call was Allerford, which matched Bosington charm for charm – yet edged the contest with its cobbled double-arched packhorse bridge. The ancient packhorse trail led me to Selworthy – the final component of a stunning Somerset triumvirate. Purpose built for retired estate workers, this thatched, white-walled village, with its woodland setting and southerly aspect, was picture-postcard perfect.

From Selworthy I climbed through a memorable mature woodland before emerging at the gorse-gold summit of Selworthy Beacon (308m). Having attained this all-seeing vantage point, the sun promptly did a vanishing act, giving way to rain and wind in equal proportions.

Taking to the Somerset and North Devon Coast Path, my bleak wind-buffeted passage was brightened only by the sighting of a spotted woodpecker in flight and a weasel carrying its prey.

I entered 'old' Minehead by the steep slopes of North Hill, dominated by a fifteenth century church whose tower once served as a mariners' beacon. While the inclement weather remained non-conducive to sightseeing, I couldn't help noticing the prevailing cloying combination of brown stone and caramel coloured pointing. Though my enduring impression will be of sparsely peopled amusement arcades and a rain-swept mile-long sea-front. More pertinently, Minehead marked my completion of the South West Way.

Beyond The Strand the wind assumed the ascendancy, reaching a gale-force peak. Watchet – still recovering from the vagaries of the January storms – came as a blessed release from the elements.

Sunday, 7th October. I have been travelling in illustrious footsteps. Apparently Wordsworth and Coleridge were keen walkers of the cliff paths between Culbone and Watchet. Indeed it was while residing at a farmhouse in Culbone that Coleridge, after taking a draught of opium, was inspired to compose his brilliant dream-poem *Kubla Khan*. And more relevant still, it was from Watchet's small harbour that Coleridge's brain-child *The Ancient Mariner* set sail.

After the general high standard of upkeep and waymarking of the South West Way, the at times non-existent coastal footpath beyond the beautiful pond-thronged hamlet of East Quantoxhead came as a rude awakening.

Within a few hundred yards of rejoining the coast, I passed the red-brick oil Retort House – a remnant of the famed shale-oil strike of 1916. This is now all that remains of what was intended to be Somerset's answer to Texas!

Eastward views along the low, crumbling cliffs were dominated by the grey and navy blue bulk of Hinkley Point Nuclear power station, adjacent to which, I noticed with alarm, a number of sheep staggering and rolling on their backs, legs flailing. The whole inexplicable scene was reminiscent of a Monty Python sketch.

With its northerly aspect of Bridgwater Bay and flatland backdrop, the weather-beaten hamlet of Storford appeared most idyllic – though in all honesty a touch too close to Hinkley Point for my liking. And so to Bridgwater – 'District of Sedgemoor; site of the last battle on English soil'.

Monday, 8th October. I made tracks from the flourishing town of Bridgwater in ideal walking conditions: bright, dry and cool. A mercifully brief stint of road walking (A38) brought me to Dunball, where – after some trials and tribulation – I asserted my right of way through the dock area. Having gained admittance, I watched the Chilean ship *Hero* unload its pungent cargo of 100,000 tons of fish meal: protein supplement for animal feed. In view of the all pervading gut-churning odour, I tactfully curtailed my conversation with a female analyst who appeared quite immune to its effect.

As I drew level with Combwich, at the western limit of Pawlett Hams, the toll of the midday church bells ambled across the limpid water. Intermittent bank-side stockpiles of putchers, yard-long conical fish-traps of metal or wooden construction, bore witness to a seasonal abundance of salmon. Despite the high level of rainfall over the latter half of last week, the ground underfoot remained rock-hard. Estuarine walking, though comparatively undemanding, can be mind-numbingly dull, the lack of contours leading to an absence of scenic surprises.

Beyond the popular seaside resort of Burnham-on-Sea I hit the proverbial 'wall'. For what had been a far from fatiguing day, I was disconcertingly heavy-legged and footsore. More worryingly, I was beginning to feel quite disorientated. Mayhap my biorhythms were at their nadir? Or was dehydration the culprit? Whatever the cause, Uphill, in the county of Avon, couldn't have come too soon for my liking ... to sleep, perchance to rest!

Tuesday, 9th October. Not surprisingly Uphill's illustrious neighbour to the north, Weston-Super-Mare, was a virtual ghost town. After a long, and hopefully prosperous summer season, Weston projected a distinct 'morning after the night before' look. That is, somewhat dishevelled, yet putting on a brave face. Certainly the town appeared to have taken a terrible battering by the storms earlier in the year (Clevedon, as I discovered later in the day, suffered a similar fate). Only now were maintenance crews patching-up the sea-wall around the Marine Lake, which even now was unusually choppy for an ostensibly land-locked lagoon.

According to Ms Webb of the Tourist Information Board, St. Thomas's Head is an MOD property of a particularly 'sensitive' nature. Thus another route was sought. As a parting shot, Ms Webb alerted me to the plenitude and officious nature of the Somerset and Avon constabulary. To whit, don't risk walking the M5 (which would have saved me untold miles). As the only viable alternative left open to me was the long haul inland via Congresbury and Yatton ... then so be it.

The next thirty kilometres passed in a flash, my only recollection being the heart rending sight of two grounded pipistrelle bats, and the heady garlic-like aroma of wild hops that permeated many a hedgerow.

On the outskirts of Clevedon – the culmination of my day – having sought the witness-book signature of one WPC Nunn, Motorway Police, I casually enquired as to the consequences had I chanced my arm on the hard-shoulder of the M5?

"I'd have booked you!"

(Gulp!) You can't say fairer than that.

Wednesday, 10th October. I was not the only one bidding adieu to Clevedon. At the head of the newly restored Clevedon Pier *The Waverley*, the world's lone surviving seagoing paddle-steamer, was preparing for the off. Whereas I was heading for Avonmouth and a photo-call, *The Waverley* was destined for Bristol Dock and the starring role in a movie. Its piped trill remained audible long after the twin tri-coloured funnels were lost to sight.

A brace of enforced detours marred the early part of the day. First casualty was Lover's Walk, an atmospheric cliff-top footpath, ruled out through storm damage. I pressed on, only to be denied a second coastal access by the construction of a sewage works. I belatedly rejoined the coast south of Portishead, where a Royal Mail driver recognised me and put me on the right road for Pill. Here, once again, the poor beleaguered pedestrian gets the mucky end of the stick. What a roundabout way one is forced to take in order to cross the juddering Avonmouth Bridge. Quite literally, all around the houses!

My circuitous route brought me to the edge of Avonmouth's grim industrial heartland – and the incongruous luxury of the Miles Arms Hotel. Having received a handsome cheque on behalf of the fund from Tim Williams, Employee Relations, and the hirsute R. K. Thompson, Acting Bristol Head Postmaster, we repaired to the Hotel car park at the behest of the gentleman of the press where I posed upon a wall, daisy roots to the fore, while downing a pint of 6X (potent local brew).

Some hardship!

Thursday, 11th October. Not even the prospect of forty road-borne kilometres with the constant threat of rain could diminish my anticipation of the day ahead. Not only did I have the crossing of the Severn Bridge to enthuse me, but also by so doing I would be entering Wales for the first time. I fully intended to drink deep at the well of experience and savour every quaff.

Adhering to the A403 from the word go, I gained my first glimpse of the magnificent Severn Bridge from Crook's Marsh. From the distance it bore a striking resemblance to the Tamar Road Bridge. And from close quarters it was every bit as awe inspiring as Brunel's Prince Albert Bridge by virtue of its sheer enormity. With a single graceful span of some two miles, it took me a full half hour to cross, including photographs, notation and the odd chat.

From the Chepstow end of the bridge, my tight schedule determined I should adopt the A48 all the way to Newport (Casnewydd). Prior to this, experiencing some uncertainty as to whether I was actually in Wales or England, I popped into a village store.

"Am I in England or Wales?"

First shop keeper, dour, broad Welsh accent:

"Wales, man, Wales!"

Second shop keeper, Bristolian, mischievous, ditto Welsh accent: "Between you and me I don't know what I'm doing here. Right bunch of artists they are! Can't sing! Can't play rugby!"

A heated argument, initially light-hearted, ensued between the duo, whose opinions were diametrically opposed. As the exchange became increasingly vitriolic and fisticuffs were but a hairsbreadth away, I made a tactical withdrawal, sidling unnoticed from the premises – and still none the wiser.

On the outskirts of Newport my confusion was marginally clarified by a passing jogger, who took time out from his pavement-pounding to confide that even the Welsh rugby selectors invariably overlook players from Gwent, as they too misguidedly regard this low-lying fertile corner of Wales as part of England.

Friday, 12th October. Farewells aren't my strongest suit. Having posed for a couple of souvenir snaps, I hit the road post-haste. With sunshine all the way, I was clearly back in the weather's good books. Making my way through the Pillgwenlly district, the first genuine multi-racial neighbourhood since North Kent, I sensed a total and amicable integration.

Yet I couldn't leave without taking a look at the famed transporter bridge over the River Usk, Newport's engineering wonder. Built in 1906 to convey sheep and workers to the then adjacent pasture and steel works, it is one of only three in existence. Now lamentably out of commission, a sum of three million pounds is required to bring it back into full working order.

Beyond Maes-glas I followed the B4239 through a landscape of flat, fertile meadows and dykes to Cardiff (Caerdydd), the only worthwhile distraction being the sighting of a polecat at Pwll-Mawr, complete with mask and pale winter coat.

Approaching the impressive Civic Centre I was greeted by an array of civic dignitaries and Senior Royal Mail officials. Following a photo-call (presentation of cheque, foot in fountain, foot out of fountain, brandishing walking stick, et al), we repaired to City Hall for 'drinkies' and a welcoming speech which transmuted into a lecture. As had become a tradition, I sported my rucksack throughout the proceedings: I considered it a bad omen to off-load my 'burden' until the day's walking was over.

That evening, in the civilising company of John and Tamzin Mole, I voiced the desire to do something typically Welsh. Impish calls to sing, torch a holiday cottage or open a 'leek-u-like' fast food restaurant fell on deaf ears. For I was a new man, a convert, a Welsh-phile.

Saturday, 13th October. Armed with an ever expanding Welsh vocabulary I departed Cardiff in the knowledge that I was in for another fine day.

A familiar piped trill greeted my arrival in the former coal port of Penarth. From the century old pier I watched the departure of *The Waverley*. Its filming schedule complete, it was no doubt heading back to its River Clyde HQ.

From Penarth I took the gently rolling cliff walk to Sully by way of Lavernock. I was due at Font-y-gary holiday/leisure complex between 3 and 3.30 p.m. I made it within ten minutes of the latter deadline.

Sir Broke Boothby headed the reception committee, which included several familiar faces among the press corps. It was hoped that the ensuing publicity would give a welcome boost to both the appeal fund and the holiday/leisure complex, recently the subject of a £2m face-lift.

Chauffeured back to my accommodation in Rhoose, Lower House Farm proved an atmospheric billet. After a splendid repast, and way beyond the witching hour, my host Greg Rogers broached an outstanding mystery. Just why should the household moggy, in common with its alsatian predecessor, sit for hours on end staring at a seemingly innocuous handmade nail which protruded from the wall beside the original open hearth fireplace? What could they discern that our civilisation-dulled senses overlooked?

Your guess is as good as mine.

Sunday, 14th October. Having re-covered the dead ground between Rhoose and Font-y-gary I adopted the Glamorgan Heritage Coast Path at Leys Beach, overlooked by the twin-towers of Aberthaw Power Station.

West of the rocky headland of Summerhouse Point the path ran alongside a field of cultivated horseradish; one of my favourite herbs, whose piquant bouquet seasoned my cliff-top route for the next half-hour. To all intents and purposes it was a veritable midsummer's day; yet all around were signs of autumn. The seaward verges were a carpet of fairy rings. Field mushrooms galore!

I kept my 4 p.m. appointment at the straggling cliff-top village of Ogmore-by-Sea. A photoshoot and cheque presentation took place upon the sloping greensward above Black Rocks, with its stunning backdrop of Devon and Somerset across the Bristol Channel.

That evening Mike and Joan Walters, Ogwr MS Branch, treated me to a slap-up dinner. A lovelier, more sincere couple you couldn't wish to meet. Had he lived, their son – who died of MS. complications – would have been my age. I sensed a near parental concern for my welfare, and was touched by their open-hearted generosity.

Monday, 15th October.

As the prospect of winter loomed even larger – it was chucking it down outside – so my mornings fell under two distinct headings: camping and accommodation. When under canvas I rose and struck camp at first light – not wishing to prolong my discomfiture; when in accommodation – whether grotty or four star – I found myself procrastinating, putting off my departure until the last possible moment. Yet once abroad, and quite literally in harness, I invariably fell straight into the old routine with ease.

Such was the volume of rainfall overnight that the Ogmore River, fast flowing at the best of times, was haemorrhaging over the landscape, having burst its banks in several places. But more to the point, the ancient stepping stones at the foot of the strategically placed Ogmore Castle were totally annihilated by the white-water maelstrom. Fortunately a few-hundred yards upstream a foot-bridge came to my rescue.

Across a water meadow which resembled a paddy-field I made for the tiny grey stone and thatch hamlet of Merthyr Mawr; renowned as one of the prettiest in Wales. From the ruins of Candleston Castle, where the narrow lane from Merthyr Mawr came to an abrupt end, I picked my way through the shrubby, sand dune wilderness of Merthyr-Mawr Warren. Here the air was rich with the sweet savour of fermenting fruit. With willow-like leaves and clusters of orange berries, bouquet-wise negotiating the sea buckthorn thickets was evocative of walking through a vineyard. Quite intoxicating.

I suspected I had caught Porthcawl on a bad day. The town appeared to have its own private rain-cloud stationed overhead. The vast Coney Beach Amusement Park – closed and deserted – was anything but. And the serried ranks of vacant-eyed caravans depressed me no end.

My dark mood was partially lifted by a welcome cuppa at Porthcawl Police Station, courtesy of PC Burke. But from an wanted poster I noticed that the murderer(s) of walkers Gwenda and Peter Dixon on the Pembrokeshire Coastal Path – where I would soon be! – was still at large. Links with a similar double killing in 1985 were not discounted.

On the sound advice of PC Burke I abandoned the coast at Mawdlam, as the Afon (River) Cynffig would almost certainly be impassable.

The B4283 and A48 led me to 'Ty'n-y-Caean'; once the vicarage of the nearby ruined Margam Abbey. After a sumptuous evening meal – all home produce – Mrs Rhiannon Gaen tutored me on my Welsh pronunciation, before single-handedly drumming up a civic reception for me the following day at Swansea County Hall.

Tuesday, 16th October. Laden with Margam Abbey souvenirs – gifts from the generous Mrs Gaen – I made for Port Talbot along the A48. Located to the south-east of town and flanked by the secluded Margam Sands, the mammoth Port Talbot steel works obscured my view of Swansea Bay.

In the dead of night this grim industrial complex was a skeletal behemoth, black and foreboding, given flesh by pin-holes of cold-fire and belches of crimson flame. In the cool light of day the beast is debunked, slain, and the menace is no more.

Once over the River Neath I struck out for Swansea upon the A483. Sometimes trotting, always hurrying, the next twelve kilometres passed in a punctuality-obsessed blur of industrial dereliction and coastal beauty. And even then I failed to keep my appointment by a full quarter of an hour. My first late arrival; my embarrassment was complete.

Fortunately the reception committee – headed by Fred Kingdom, Chairman of the County Council, and the lovely ladies of Swansea MS branch – bore not the remotest ill feeling. Quite the contrary: "What's fifteen minutes after seventy-three days!"

Then it was all back to the Chairman's Chambers for drinks (no local brew! Tut-tut!), photos, chat, more souvenirs, signing of the visitors book, even more photos, and a round of farewell kisses (easily the best bit!) – from which the Chairman was pointedly excluded.

I followed the curving sweep of Swansea Bay to its southernmost limit, Mumbles Head, by way of a delightful promenade, the former route of one of Britain's earliest railways.

Beyond the coastguard look-out on the southern side of Mumbles Head begins a dramatic stretch of coastal footpath. Designated an 'Area of Outstanding Natural Beauty' in 1956, this was the Gower Peninsula at its challenging best. Reaching its zenith at Newton Cliff, with near-sheer rock-faces, scree slopes and seriously undermined trails, this was also cliff walking at its hairiest! And great fun for all that.

Despite the longest walking day in weeks, some nine solid hours, I was loath to jack it in. I was on a roll – and I wanted to ride my luck. Branched filaments of cirrus cloud pointed the way and bade me push on – the village of Southgate bade me rest over.

Southgate and common sense won the day.

Wednesday, 17th October. From the moment I left Southgate the elements conspired to negate the euphoria of the previous day. A uniform gunmetal blanket of cloud overhung the landscape, compressing the horizon to a luminous sliver of white. Downpours followed at random intervals to ensure my weatherproofs remained *in situ*.

Skirting Pennard Burrows, the cliff path descended to the broad sandy expanse of Threecliff Bay. Watched over by the ruined thirteenth century Pennard Castle from its rocky outcrop eyrie, I utilised the fortuitously placed stepping stones to cross the swollen stream of Penard Pill.

For the next hour or so I avidly beachcombed the sand dune backed crescent of Oxwich Bay. Amongst the tangle of beach-borne debris which marked the high-tide line, a marooned lion's mane jellyfish, fully a yard across its opalescent bell, and a Cinzano bottle, containing a sodden spliff and a mellow message ('Good luck in life – The Boys'), took the honours. Much of the household refuse was curiously of continental origin.

Mrs McNamara of the Oxwich Reserve Centre, hub of the Oxwich National Nature Reserve, pointed out the potentially treacherous nature of the coastal path between Oxwich Point and Worm's Head, concluding: "If you fall off no one will find you for a week – if then!"

Potentially treacherous, yes – but also wildly spectacular. None more so than the enigmatic Culver Hole, a 60 foot high stone construction built into a natural cleft in the cliff face, being of unknown purpose and origin.

I could quite legitimately have circumvented the barrow-like bulk of Rhossili Down by following the low-lying green shoulder to seaward – in the event I was glad I didn't. Climbing instead to the summit of The Beacon (193m) I was rewarded with a breathtaking southerly prospect of the appropriately named rock mass of Worm's Head. From Rhossili Down's northern heights the view was equally impressive, falling away towards the small island outcrop of Burry Holms and the hill-masked village of Llanmadoc – my scheduled stop-over.

Thursday, 18th October. I remained on roads for the full duration of the walking day: B4295, A484 and B4311 to name but three. The weather – merely overcast – was a vast improvement; though the scenery fell well short of yesterday's momentous heights.

Within half an hour I was in the august mist-collared presence of the fourteenth century Weobley Castle. Commanding an all-seeing panorama of the wildlife-abundant Llanrhidian Marsh and Loughor Estuary, I couldn't envisage a less warlike locale. Yet its seemingly impregnable defensive position didn't save it from attack and partial destruction in 1400.

Once across the River Loughor I was in the county of Dyfed. The once busy port of Llanelli proved to be a far larger town than I anticipated, with a comprehensive and atmospheric covered market, and boasting the most ornate branch of the Halifax Building Society imaginable. Its red tile-hung facade and black and white Tudoresque window frames and gables were an unexpected delight.

And so to Burry Port. Having survived the turbulent transition from small fishing village to booming coal port, it is now gaining status as a yachting centre. Though more laudable in my view was the aesthetically pleasing experimental wind farm which stands beside Burry Port's old coal fired power station. From the sublime to the environmentally unfriendly.

Friday, 19th October. A largely sleepless night – thanks to a succession of passing freight trains and a chill in the bladder – allowed me plenty of scope for reflection (when not urgently spending a penny, that is!). Such was my overall physical condition and mental toughness that I now had little doubt as to my ability to finish the walk ... barring any unforeseen disasters.

It was another dank unpromising morning as I set out for St. Clears.

"Pronounced St. Clares," corrected a Mrs Tibbitts – one of Burry Port's few citizens not sporting the otherwise *de riguer* cloth cap.

This was the second successive day that I was confined to the road – a full forty-five kilometres/twenty-eight miles – yet I took it literally in my stride.

With its tangible medieval air, Kidwelly provided some light relief. All the way up the gentle incline of Walter Street a battery of housewife-marionettes, wordless and totally engrossed, were frantically sweeping with a will. Rigidly restricting their compulsive activity to their own particular rectangle of pavement, I envisaged the whole perspective scene in photographic form, a still. This was living Wales, and it spoke volumes about the refreshing old-world conscientiousness and civic pride of its people.

By the time I'd aligned my camera only the silver haired Mrs Fisher remained – the rest having bolted rabbit-like into their two-up/two-down terraced burrows. Though not my original composition, I cut my losses by snapping the kindly Mrs F. – with her full and eager consent – at the height of her dust-swirling frenzy. Alerted by the commotion without, Mr Fisher emerged and offered to exchange my 'branch' for a genuine Government issue walking stick – an offer I politely declined. 'Old Faithful' and I had been through a lot together – it was now my talisman.

With increasing discomfort in my right knee, now drum-tight, I shared my northerly route (A484) with a column of spanking new white Porsches. So much for the recession!

Intent upon remaining as close to the Afon Tywi as metalled roads allowed, I exchanged the hurly-burly of the A484 for an ostensibly quiet country lane just south of Llwynhelig. Almost immediately a wild or outsize feral cat slunk across my path. By the time I reached a break in the hedgerow it had vanished.

Man's best friend, meanwhile, continued to dog my progress, the farmyard variety being the most consistent offenders. Fortunately most canines fled at the sight of a cocked stick, while others gave up when I left their 'territory'.

The hamlet of Croesyceilog proved the exception to the rule. As I drew level with a gap between a row of dilapidated out-buildings, a brace of snarling, slavering brutes flew at me. Pinned against a hawthorn hedge, I held the dangerous duo at bay with scything sweeps of 'Old Faithful'. Blessed with a high boredom threshold, I was prepared to hold my ground all day – in the interest of preserving life and limb. Eventually, frustrated by their inability to sink their teeth into me, the pair soon fell prey to squabbling, before falling upon each other in open white-fanged hostility – paving the way for my tactical withdrawal.

Below me to the west the Afon Tywi snaked its way across a verdant flood plain towards Carmarthen – our common destination. With just over half the day's schedule completed, I shot through the important market centre of Carmarthen double quick.

My evening accommodation, Gardde-y-Rebbecca (Garden of Rebecca), came not a moment too soon – monotony being, in my view, as fatiguing as physical exertion. The house was a shrine to Dylan Thomas with whom co-proprietor David Thomas shared a birthday. Though the real devotee was David's wife, Ann, who was at that very moment appearing in a local dramatic production.

By mid-evening, having been somewhat side-tracked earlier by an interview and photo-session for the local press, David let me into a little-known secret.

I had always assumed that Dylan Thomas' wooden hut – in which he wrote many of his most celebrated works, and to where I would be making a pilgrimage on the morrow – was entirely as the author had left it. Not so. For former English teacher Ann Thomas had in her possession the hut's original blue painted doors. As the story goes, she spotted two of her erstwhile pupils carrying the replacement doors – identical to their predecessors in all but the lack of wood worm – to the hut's cliff walk location.

"What are you doing with the old ones?"

"Chucking them away, Miss."

"Oh no, you're not!"

Thus they fell fortuitously into her hands – and have since graced the stage of, and lent unique authenticity to, many a Dylan Thomas revival.

Saturday, 20th October. The morning was murky, with an underlying air of hidden promise. With welling anticipation, the A4066 hastened me to Langhorne, pronounced 'Larne', where I did the full tourist round of Dylan Thomas haunts: his wooden hut workshop (from where he eloquently described the view of the 'mussel pooled and heron priested shore'); Brown's Hotel (his favourite watering hole); and his simple grave, in the local churchyard. Dylan said of Laugharne: "This timeless, mild, beguiling island of a town ". A pen-picture *par excellence*.

Pendine Village came as a welcome release from the tarmacadamed grip of the A4066. Even the earlier sighting of my first buzzard in weeks being waylaid by a clique of crows and jackdaws was no compensation for the off-road walking I so craved.

I scaled the stone rampart of Dolwen Point, pausing at the summit for a Mars Bar, a Coke and a much needed call of nature. Sandwiched between an extensive MOD missile testing range and Carmarthen Bay, Pendine Sands' six miles of wave-compacted, billiard table-flat foreshore stretched away to the east; all of which made it the logical site for numerous land speed record attempts in the 1920s.

East of the strikingly laminated Telpyn Point – which I gingerly rounded on a causeway of wave-lubricated boulders – I pumped one of two local prawn fishermen for the tricks of his trade: "You just probes the rock pools with you-er hazel switch to dislodge the little bligh-ters, then you nets them and pops them in you-er bucket. Sim-ple, isn't it." Though quite how one spots the 'little bligh-ters' in their near transparent pre-cooked form he omitted to divulge.

Beyond the former mining community of Amroth, a well maintained footpath heralds the start and eastern extremity of the 290km (180 mile) Pembrokeshire Coast Path, which for a while follows the general course of the long since wave-obliterated Old Coast Road. I meanwhile remained steadfastly beach-borne until I reached the tiny seaside hamlet of Wiseman's Bridge, where I joined the route of the old Saundersfoot-bound railway.

Fulfilling the day's early promise, the sun broke through as I emerged from the rail tunnel at Coppet Hall Point and the broad sandy expanse of Saundersfoot Bay fanned out before me. At other resorts I'd witnessed the odd erudite gull dropping shellfish onto rocks or road from a great height in order to extract the succulent flesh from within. Here in Saundersfoot it seemed that all avian life forms were skilled exponents of the art. Talk about raining tortoiseshell limpets and dog whelks! In the immortal words of the 1951 movie *The Thing*: "Watch the skies!" – or alternatively wear a hard hat!

Well meaning staff at the nearby harbour-side Tourist Information Centre estimated that the sometimes wooded, always rolling coast path to Tenby would take me a minimum two and a half hours. Nevertheless, one and a quarter hours later I was overlooking Tenby's impressive horseshoe of a harbour and admiring the surrounding pastel-coloured ranks of tall Regency and Georgian buildings.

Arriving at my Guest House accommodation the Italian born proprietress cautiously enquired "Youa for me?" before engagingly elucidating: "You getta lotta funny peoples!"

Sunday, 21st October. In his *Tour Through Britain* of 1724, Daniel Defoe described Tenby as 'the most agreeable town on the south coast of Wales, except Pembroke' – a comparison I too would soon be in a position to make.

Though bracing, the blustery conditions were positively exhilarating, as indeed was the challenging prospect of a complete day aboard the switchback Pembrokeshire Coast Path. Beachcombing the length of The Burrows was no hardship. I embraced it with a passion. A winding path then lured me across a mercifully quiescent firing range towards the headland of Giltar Point. Access to the point itself was by an ingenious device called a Dutch Ladder; a series of logs tethered by stout cords that enable one to cross sand dunes without causing erosion

Giltar Point was significant on two fronts: for its fine view of the monastic community of Caldney Island, barely a kilometre offshore; and my first encounter with a chough. Clearly unperturbed by my goggle-eyed presence, a pair of these red-legged crows continued blithely to comb the flower-studded turf.

On the geological front, having trekked in the oft towering company of Red Sandstone cliffs virtually all the way from Tenby, they finally gave way to grey carboniferous limestone east of Stackpole Quay. Beyond a flight of steps – once colonnaded with pillars and trees – led down to the dune-backed beach of Barafundle Bay. By virtue of its inaccessibility to cars and caravans, Barafundle Bay is regarded by many as the most idyllic coastal location in the county of Dyfed.

From Saddle Point, Broad Haven, I struck inland along the western bank of Bosherston's famous lily and fish ponds. Covering an area of some eighty acres, this wildfowl paradise was formed when the valley was dammed in the eighteenth century – thus exploding by some several centuries all claim to being, among others, the spot where the moribund King Arthur abandoned his sword Excalibur.

Monday, 22nd October. Located at the end of a winding lane some two kilometres south of Bosherston, St. Govan's Chapel was my intended initial port of call – followed by a brisk cliff-top yomp to the massive limestone pillars of Elegug Stacks.

So much for my intentions. Part way down the lane at Castle Tank Tower, which overlooks the 6,000 rolling acres of Castlemartin Artillery Ranges to the west, I was matter-of-factly informed by an army officer that the ranges – and thus Elegug Stacks – were off limits until 4.30 p.m. due to NATO tank exercises.

St. Govan's Chapel would therefore have to suffice. Huddling in a wave-battered cleft at the foot of a flight of rock-hewn steps – supposedly uncountable by mortal man (I made it seventy-four going down and seventy-three coming up!) – the 'Chapel in the Cliffs' is steeped in mythology. Being of a simple stone and slate construction, at the east end of the Nave (main body) is an altar, with steps leading to a sixth century hermit's cell. To the rear of the cell in a fissure in the rock wall, rib-like indentations are clearly defined. Here St. Govan is reputed to have hidden when pursued by a band of Lundy Island pirates. Legend has it that if a person makes a wish and enters the fissure, and is able to turn around, their wish will be granted. Despite my dwindling weight, this was a manoeuvre that was nonetheless beyond me.

Prior to leaving I dropped a coin into the now dried-up wishing and healing well outside – I hadn't forgotten my vow! – and made a further wish, the selfsame maternal orientated wish I always made.

Throughout the morning I'd witnessed increasing numbers of German military personnel – their civilian vehicles retaining their native license plates – but I was still amazed to see the German tricolour flying above Merrion Army Camp! Yet not half as amazed as when I reached the hamlet of Cold Comfort. For here I was overtaken by a diesel-belching column of tanks of the resident Panzer Division. According to one particularly irate Warren farmer, they've been here for the last thirty years – and their presence is much resented by most locals, many of whom lost relations in the tank battles of WWII's North Africa Campaign.

I finally departed the B4319 at the popular surfing beach of Freshwater West, pausing briefly on the southern headland to inspect the last remaining thatched seaweed collector's hut, used for the storing and drying of purple laver, central ingredient to the South Wales delicacy of laver bread.

Between Freshwater West and the gull and cormorant colonies of Sheep Island, the balmy weather was reminiscent of early summer. The terrain, meanwhile, was less accommodating. Though arduous at the best of times, this series of near vertical ascents and descents would no doubt prove an impenetrable barrier in wet or icy conditions. On such footpaths there is no room for error.

At the stroke of 2 p.m. a raucous siren rent the salty air (putting-up a quartet of browsing chough in the process, much to their vociferous 'Keeaar!' annoyance); though not unlike an air raid warning or an 'all clear' signal, it was in fact a routine emergency drill at the nearby (as the chough flies) Texaco refinery.

Beyond Angle Hall Quay, having neither seen nor spoken to a soul since Warren, I followed the private carriageway which fringes Angle Bay, before descending to a mud and shale beach for the final run in to Rhoscrowther, and my Crowther Inn billet. And what a billet! Situated right at the foot of the horizon-dominating Texaco Oil Refinery – boasting the largest refining capacity on The Haven (Milford Haven that is).

Tuesday, 23rd October. Chastened by a tangible drop in temperature and fortified by five days of dry weather, I was well prepared for the sheeting downpour that greeted my departure.

A montage of rain-blurred images were all I had to show for the next two and a half hours of sodden slog: Popton Castle, oil refineries, flame-plumed flare stacks…

Pembroke was a different kettle of fish, a vivid entity. Rain is always less intrusive in town – tending merely to damp-down the dust and clear the streets of less hardy souls. From the imposing castle-dominated upper end to the eclectic jumble of periods and styles of buildings that line Pembroke's main street I voraciously wolfed the sights

Swiftly crossing Haven Bridge – my awareness of its partial collapse in 1970 hardly encouraged me to dally – I trekked south to the peaceful, deep-water anchorage of Neyland and the secluded shingle and rock coves of Hazelbeach beyond.

During a lull in the rain, an unconvincing sun broke through in conjunction with my arrival in Milford Haven. The town's gridiron pattern street layout was conceived and begun by a colony of Quaker whalers from Nantucket who were invited to operate from the then new harbour by Charles Greville, nephew of Nelson's mistress Emma Hamilton. In spite of the fine facilities on offer, a desire to avoid fighting in the War of Independence was undoubtedly the whaler's prime motive.

Anticipating further rainfall at any moment, I made for my evening destination of Sandy Haven with all haste, only to be stymied by the tidal inlet of Sandy Haven Pill. According to misinformed locals the village would be accessible at this time of day via a broad expanse of red sand, or at worst a brief paddle away. Confronted instead by a stretch of creek at high water, I derived only marginal consolation from the knowledge that the picturesque anchorage before me was the favoured setting of many paintings by the late Graham Sutherland.

Seven unforeseen kilometres later, in reality but a few hundred yards actual progress, I arrived at Skerryback Farm, Sandy Haven – and was promptly welcomed by the Williams family as one of their own. And what a welcome! What hospitality!

I awoke at midnight with the rain hammering at my room's solitary window and what felt like a comatose St. Bernard across my chest. In my veritable rutted-hammock of a bed, the squeaky frame of which compelled my complete inertia, I lay supine beneath a winter weight duvet. The pitch-dark of my benighted room – that total all-enveloping blackout common to all truly rural areas – was intermittently raked by the probing beam of Great Castle Head's automatic lighthouse to the south, in whose short-lived, rhythmic wake the sable-gloom was all but re-doubled.

N.B. Given the choice of two beds, unbeknownst to Mrs Williams I'd plumped for the bed nearest the door – the unmade-up one!

Wednesday, 24th October. It was a dazzlingly bright morning, if discernibly cooler than its rain-lashed precursor. "The sun always shines on the righteous" intoned the kindly Mrs Williams as she bade me farewell. Humbled by her compliment and the gift of a comprehensive packed lunch, I headed south along a rough field-hemmed trackway towards Little Castle Head. The browning grass-stubble to the east was randomly dotted with black plastic-sheathed silage bales (worth £20 a piece on the open market), giving way to lush slopes of chartreuse pasture, and backed by flame-quenched flare stacks of the distant Esso Refinery, now in the process of demolition.

The gorse, blackthorn and bramble scrub which overran much of the Pembrokeshire Coast Path (now celebrating its twentieth year) between the transit towers west of Little Castle Head and Musselwick displayed not the slightest inclination to autumnal die back, much to the detriment of my exposed legs.

The first unbargained for deviation occurred at Musselwick, where the erstwhile cliff-borne pathway gave way to a stretch of rock-strewn beach walking – regular sprained ankle country! It did however, present the opportunity to photograph several fronds of purple laver.

Deviation number two was not so innocuous. Supposedly passable except for two hours either side of high tide, the creek which separated me from the village of Dale had been transformed into a virtual maelstrom by the precipitation of the last twenty-four hours. I certainly wasn't enjoying the best of luck with tidal crossings, preferring to play each day by ear rather than pre-plan my route in meticulous detail – though I consoled myself in the knowledge that each detour bumped-up the kilometres no end.

By the time I entered Dale via Mullock one hour later, with only eight kilometres and a niggling pain in my right heel to show for my trouble, I noted with wry irony that the self same inlet was now perfectly fordable. What a difference an hour makes!

No doubt a hotbed of water-sport activity in the high season, Dale is reputed to have more hours of sunshine than any other village in Wales. Suffice it to say, my arrival coincided with a monsoonish wet spell that blighted my entire crumbling-cliff-top route to Marloes Sands by way of St. Ann's Head.

By mid-afternoon the rain and scudding clouds had given way to sunny intervals. With low tide swiftly approaching, beyond the Iron Age settlement of Gateholm Island the sparse wreckage of the paddle-steamer *Albion* which foundered in 1837 was plainly visible in the ebbing surf.

As the anonymous saying goes 'When St. Bride's Chapel a salthouse was made, St. Bride's lost the herring trade'. My 5 p.m. touchdown at Upper Ripperston Farm was infinitely more fortuitous than the plight of the once flourishing local herring industry. 10 p.m. found me luxuriating, lead crystal in hand. The home produced beef had gone down a treat, complimented by an eminently drinkable Burgundy. Meanwhile, without, the rain once again made fluvial inroads from the west; so I'm reliably assured, a predominantly nocturnal phenomenon along this stretch of coastline.

Thursday, 25th October. After the evening's downpour the coast path, which I regained at Mill Haven, was a meandering morass of sodden sod. Every chance brush with undergrowth or foliage resulted in a delayed action cascade; a watery sword of Damocles. Judgement was everything. A moment's hesitation meant a thorough dowsing. Within half an hour I was striding through the mature plantation which extends eastward from Borough Head and where Gwenda and Peter Dixon were so ruthlessly murdered the summer before. It is widely believed that Mr Dixon, an avid radio ham, intercepted an IRA broadcast and went to investigate in the company of his wife. As if to confirm these suspicions, shortly after the discovery of their bodies an IRA arms cache was unearthed in the vicinity. Through a vista of wild pear and gnarled oak the glass-smooth Goultrop Roads was straddled by a varicoloured arc. In such a serene setting it was difficult to grasp the mentality behind such vile deeds. Yet was not original sin conceived in the ultimate serene setting – the garden of Eden?

Alternating between greystone promontory and deserted cove, the following twenty-four up-and-down kilometres were redolent of Cornwall at its idyllic best. With the added piquancy of yellow hammer-thronged hedgerows and battalions of squalls closing-in from the south-west.

Such was the ferocity of the wind on the cliff-top homeward stretch beyond the fiordesque Solva Creek, that I was shaken about like a rag doll, and this in spite of the anchoring weight of my rucksack. My Bude debacle still fresh in my mind, I henceforth resolved to steer clear of the cliff edge in such conditions.

And so to St. David's, founded by Wales' patron saint and whose name it bears. Among its many claims to fame it is Wales' most westerly village and, by virtue of its magnificent medieval cathedral, Britain's smallest city.

Friday, 26th October. Stepping into a morning of pallid sunshine, my initial priority was to photograph St. David's Cathedral before the weather closed in. As it turned out, no sooner had I captured its rich mauve stone proportions and tranquil valley setting than I was overtaken by a monumental cloudburst, which transpired to be the formula for the day.

Having rejoined the coastal path at Caefai Bay, the first instalment of an eventful day occurred at Porth-clais, formerly the harbour of the village city. Round the rim of this narrow banked inlet I was privileged to witness the incoming tide as it raced onward past the stiffly jutting jetty like a mini-bore. Presently, as I examined the carefully restored lime-kiln lined harbour, a seldom seen double rainbow materialised above St. David's. Perfectly formed and distinctly separate entities, one above the other, only the foul weather prevented me from photographing it for posterity.

Despite a summer-like brightness, the driving, freezing rain continued off and on throughout the morning, while the ominous blue-black tide-race between Ramsey Island and the mainland (Ramsey Sound) was sufficiently chilling in its own right. Heaven help the poor soul who falls into its Hellespontine clutches.

From my cliff-top vantage point of Maen Bachau I was horrified to see what I took to be a dog lolling in the surf below. Of course it turned out to be a seal – a massive bull grey seal. Both equally curious, we examined each other for several minutes, me through binoculars, he through painfully red rimmed eyes. Throughout the duration of our ephemeral eye-contact it appeared agitated and alarmed by 'something' in its watery presence – like the girl swimmer in the opening sequence of the movie *Jaws*, shortly before she was devoured piecemeal from below. From time to time its attention returned to me and I fancy I detected a plaintive expression. At that moment my heart went out to the forlorn creature – irrevocably manacled by natural selection to a grim existence in an inhospitable environment.

Just south of the rock-bound cove of Porthstinian, dominated by St. David's lifeboat station, I spotted the bobbing heads of some more seals, a family group at play: a dark coloured bull, barking voluminously; a speckled cow and her near pure white pup, which derived great pleasure in wallowing on its back. Even when I made my presence known with a sharp whistle the frolicking continued. No plaintive expressions here.

Overlooking the optimistically titled Whitesand Bay (Porth-Mawr), conceivably Wales' premier surfing beach, I spent an edifying few minutes with a most engaging couple, both devout Christians. Our all too brief intercourse stiffened my resolve no end. And a more pertinent venue for my spiritual elevation I couldn't imagine, for it was at Whitesand Bay that St. Patrick was inspired to convert Ireland to Christianity and from where he set sail.

It was on the red-soil foothills to seaward of the prominent, isolated granite mass at

Penberry (573ft) that I encountered Windy, a wind-tossed wild child from Melbourne: footloose and fancy free – as in free spirit; free love – as in love among the potato sacks. Verily love in a cold climate!

Now totally immune to the vagaries of the weather, and warmed by the afterglow of our alfresco liaison, it was rainbows all the way to Abercastle – single, plural, more than I saw in my entire childhood. From here I struck inland to Mathry, where I spent the evening reflecting upon my good fortune and my animated crock of Aussie gold.

Saturday, 27th October. I re-engaged the coastal path beyond Abercastle on a bitterly cold morning, made more so by a biting wind – yet mercifully no rain to greet my egress. But it was the calm before the storm. While coastal West Wales braced itself to bear the brunt of the tempest jetting in from the Atlantic – with wind speeds predicted to match, if not surpass those of the Great Storm of '87 – I was drawn to a bronze plaque on Goodwick Sands commemorating the surrender in 1797 of a 1,200 strong French invading force under the command of one Colonel Tate, an American citizen (surprise! surprise!). Interventionists even then. Some things never change.

I took time out in Fishguard to pop into a jewellers in order to get my digital wristwatch put back an hour (too complex for me!) in order to conform with the imminent end of British Summer Time. In 1971 Fishguard was temporarily re-dubbed 'Llaregub' for the filming of *Under Milk Wood*. In view of the town's legion public houses, one suspects that Dylan would have approved of the choice of location.

Having endured the stifling confinement throughout the day, I finally resolved to get out of my weatherproofs. And atop the ruins of the Old Fort (erected after American privateer John Paul Jones bombarded the town in 1779 – another damned Yankee!) seemed as good a spot as any, and with a prospect of Fishguard Harbour to boot. In stowing the offending garments I surveyed the departure of the Rosslare-bound ferry – and, more alarmingly, caught sight of an inrushing armada of darkling rain clouds. Even as I scurried eastward along the cliff path, ever mindful of the yawning drop to my left, the wind perceptibly freshened from seaward as though fleeing in the face of the impending turmoil. While offshore, white horses were the outriders of a growing swell.

The first marble-sized droplets were already darkening my shorts and windshirt as I scrambled, thwarted, back into my rainwear. As if taking its cue from my readiness the deluge descended *en masse*, filling the air with water whipped into a ferment by the violently veering storm-wind. I knew I had a battle royal on my hands. Roll on Newport – and sanctuary. I'd sleep well tonight.

Sunday, 28th October. This was my final day on the Pembrokeshire Coast Path and I intended to enjoy it to the full – though perhaps 'enjoy' is a little excessive. I ruminated upon my gentle introduction to the coastal path at Amroth. Since then the switchback terrain had grown ever more demanding by the day. Apparently, in the original charter, the powers that be decided to retain the natural craggy character of the coastscape. A decision unyieldingly adhered to! And the final leg to the outskirts of St. Dogmaels would prove a worthy and ultimately rewarding climax. In like a lamb – out like a lion!

Above Celbwr Bay, a narrow gap in the cliffs where coasters once landed their cargo, the wind, which up until that point had been stiffish, became positively rigid. Choughs revelled in the draughty conditions, diving and rolling like mini swing-wing jets. Surely the most accomplished flyers of the entire crow family – and don't they know it!

The recent wet spell (understatement!), allied with the ravages of countless free ranging cattle and sheep, had transformed the coast path into a glutinous quagmire. Yet not all ruminants lived to bite another day. In plumbing the depth of the stream slashed canyon of Pwllygranant I disturbed a pair of ravenous ravens in the midst of their grisly dissection of a long-dead sheep. So much for birds having a sense of smell!

My experiences in the holiday resort and market town of Cardigan were doubly novel.

Not only did I undergo the most vivid sensation of *deja vu* when crossing the Afon Teifa towards the metal-buttressed walls of Cardigan Castle, but on emerging from the local cop shop I was lecherously wolf whistled by a gaggle of teenage girls (no accounting for taste!). Now I know how it feels to be on the receiving end – bloody embarrassing!

Midway between Cardigan and my evening destination of Traeth-y-Mwnt, the erstwhile dry day had to go and blot its copy book in the form of an almighty cloud burst. Though decidedly unpromising on my OS map, the small sandy cove of Traeth-y-Mwnt was overshadowed by a spectacular variegated hill-headland of green slopes and red earth rising to a summit of grey stone, while at its base resided the 700 year old whitewashed Church of Holy Cross. A veritable mountain writ small!

Less than twenty minutes after gaining the welcome asylum of the farmhouse home of the Evans family, we came under siege from a hailstorm discharging hailstones the size and consistency of frozen peas. From my north facing bedroom window there was not a single light to be seen – just uninterrupted blackness. No interference from neighbours hereabouts – no neighbours!

Monday, 29th October. The wind that howled so mournfully throughout the night had ceased by first light – replaced by torrential rain, though this too had thankfully relented by the time of my 10 p.m. departure. The reason for the comparative lateness of the hour was due entirely to the wholehearted generosity of my bilingual hosts. Mrs Evans having selflessly risen at the crack of dawn to prepare a batch of my favourite Welsh Cakes for me to eat along the way, I could hardly rush off without so much as a by-your-leave. This preceded a grand tour of the pigsty – which had lost part of its galvanised roof overnight. Tour over, Mr Evans sent me on my way with the following prophetic proverb: "When you can see the Lleyn Peninsula, its going to rain; When you can't see it – it already is!"

This particular morning the Lleyn Peninsula was plainly visible to the north – and sure enough within twenty minutes it was chucking it down. As I passed the Government Missile Testing and Research Centre west of Aberporth, I witnessed the successful launching of a meteorological balloon – a huge off-white sphere towing an equally huge instrument pack. Both were soon swallowed-up by the low lying cloud.

I spent the whole walking day on roads, largely unclassified, which was quite a contrast to the cross-country rigours of the previous nine days. Yet beyond the cliff-sheltered tide-lapped sea-front of Llangranog I perceived a subtle change of atmosphere. Not only was the terrain increasingly mountainous, but Welsh speakers were also more thick on the ground. Could this be the start of 'Welsh Wales' as opposed to the 'Little England' of the south?

From the heights above New Quay I could make out the projecting arm of the Lleyn Peninsula in stark relief against the pale northern sky. But I was on the final downhill stretch now. I was home and dry.

Tuesday, 30th October. Within fifty rain-free yards of my billet it was once again bucketing down, babbling in the gutters and ricocheting a full foot off the tarmac. No wonder Wales is green – mould! (eighth consecutive day of rain, by the way – but who's counting!).

It was while residing in New Quay in the 1940s that Dylan Thomas penned *Quite Early One Morning* – in which the germ of *Under Milk Wood* can clearly be seen. I fancied I detected the prototypes of many of Dylan's extensive gallery of characters all about me: There was Captain Cat, there was Polly Garter and over there Organ Morgan – while the town's outlying environs were the undisputed province of rooks, squabbling in the leafless treetops like demented Daleks.

The outskirts of Aberaeron provided the first hit-and-run victim of the day – a mink (just enough for a small muff or a fur lined jock-strap!). In spite of the inclement weather the town itself was quite jolly. Ranks of pastel-hued Regency houses gave the harbour-side streets a distinct Mediterranean savour. Particularly fetching were the green and white bilingual street signs. But highly indicative of the recession in general, and the economic nadir of the principality in particular, when it came to real estate everything in Wales appeared to be *Ar Werth* (For Sale).

Even beneath a darkly malevolent sky Aberystwyth's irrepressible ebullience shone through, perhaps generated in part by the army of multinational students from the local college which forms part of the University of Wales. The festive mood was vibrantly enhanced by the many-coloured garlands which hung from selected lampposts.

By 10 p.m. the wind had picked up significantly and the same garland festooned lampposts beneath my third floor room were now swaying like bulrushes in a swell; my windows were rattling fit-to-bust in their ill-fitting frames; rain was in the offing. I pitied anybody abroad on such a night. While I, insulated from the elements, was as snug-as-a-bug-in-a-rug!

NB. At approximately 7.20 p.m. British and French engineers simultaneously broke through at the midway point in the Channel Tunnel, via a small bore hole. Momentous times, indeed.

Wednesday, 31st October. I couldn't bring myself to leave Aberystwyth without checking out the North Beach and promenade. Easier said than done. A conspiracy of wind and rain saw to that. Undeterred I fought my way to the front in the best walking-against-the-wind mime tradition. Marcel Marceau would have approved. Emerging from a side-street canyon, I walked slap-bang into an elemental brick wall.

Apart from the usual aches and pains I felt in remarkably fine fettle. Even so, I knew the stiff climb to the top of Constitution Hill was out of the question. The only alternative transport to the 430ft summit, the Victorian Funicular Railway (a 'conveyance for gentlefolk since 1896') wasn't running. I'd just have to forego the all-seeing eye of the camera obscura, claimed to be the largest in the world.

I repaired to a public shelter (*circa* 1925) in order to salvage a photographic record of the day from its west facing portal. Uniquely incorporated into the ground floor of a dignified four-storey sea-front building, as I angled for the best shot the rain probed ever deeper into my mushroom-enamelled wind tunnel. I was flogging a dead horse. But I wasn't alone in my dissatisfaction. "The piss-pot of Wales!" opined my fellow refugee, glaring at the rain-lashed promenade.

The 'big dipper' B4572 brought me to the holiday village of Borth. As I tramped the deserted, straggling main street it reminded me of a Wild West ghost town – all it needed to complete the illusion was some tumbling tumbleweed. Straddling a tenuous dry corridor between Cardigan Bay and the Cors Fochno Bog, Borth was a natural disaster just waiting to happen. Sure enough towards the northern limits of the village signs of flooding were in evidence: road-wide pools, overflowing drains, and sand-bogged doorways.

I strode into the town of Machynlleth – situated due south of the final road crossing of the Afon Dyfi before it broadens into the open sea – precisely on time (more by luck than by judgement) and was shaking the hand of big, bearded Midlander Barry Little as the rocket-shaped clock tower, under which we stood, struck 4 p.m. There's punctuality!

Barry drove me to his Aber-Tafol home where, joined by his wife Jean, an MS. sufferer for the past twenty years, we enjoyed a wonderful repast and discussed tactics for the future promotion of our common cause.

I had my marching orders for the day – and a chock-a-block schedule that read: 9 a.m.: pick up and be driven back to Machynlleth; 9.30 a.m.: begin walking; Midday: Aberdovey: reception/photo-call; 2 p.m.: Tywyn: reception/photo-call; 4 p.m.: arrive Llwyngwril. It left little room for error – and made no allowance for sightseeing, pressing-the-flesh, or any other equally pleasurable distraction.

I retired at 1 a.m. – my head reeling.

4   **On top of the world**

He who would travel happy must travel light.
   Antoine de Saint-Exupery

Thursday, 1st November.

RETURNING to Aberdovey from Machynlleth I entered the county of Gwynedd by crossing the Afon Dyfi (River Dovey) at Pen-y-Bont. The Dyfi itself was precariously close to bursting its banks as it slid gelatinously seaward through a lush water meadow, bracketed by densely forested hills of mixed woodland.

The sun broke through as I strode into Aberdovey (Aberdyfi) for photos and interviews with the local press. As I moved off to meet the growing throng in Tywyn I ploughed through yet another cloudburst, the umpteenth of the day.

Tywyn is a small seaside resort better known for a stone pillar thought to bear the earliest example of written Welsh. At the war memorial I was engulfed by members and officials of the Meirionnydd branch of the MS Society. Autographing press cuttings – one of which reported the exploits of a 'John Wheetley' – and photographs that even I wasn't aware had been taken was an odd sensation. Chatting to such a spirited and optimistic bunch was a humbling experience.

Leaving Tywyn, with good wishes and applause trailing after me, all went well until I reached the southern bank of the Afon Dysynni where the Bailey Bridge on which I'd intended to cross had inexplicably been dismantled. I was not only facing a profligate waste of precious time, but a long, long detour inland to the bridge at Bryncrug.

But deliverance was at hand. Enter MS live-wire and regular Welsh word-spinner Douglas Williams, who negotiated on my behalf a novel if precarious river crossing, seated – rucksack and all – upon a 'raft' of untethered canoes, ably manned by a party of Rolls

A piece of kayak. Rafting across the Afon Dysynni.

Royce apprentices attending an outward-bound course. Douglas caught the entire stunt on film and later circulated the results throughout the media.

Finding my lodgings in Llwyngwril was no problem. Pentre Bach, a large comfortable former manor house, visually beckoned from the end of a 260 yard private, tree lined drive. My satisfaction was enhanced by the stunning prospect of Barmouth Bay and the mountains of Snowdonia from my bedroom window.

Friday, 2nd November. I stopped off at Llwyngwril PO to dispatch a parcel of X-rated laundry under plain brown wrapper; health warning attached. The Postmistress, who knew all about the walk, sorely tempted providence by cheerfully guaranteeing me a rain-free passage (now where have I heard that before?). Within minutes of leaving Llwyngwril I was ushered back into my Gore-Tex cocoon – washout number eleven. "More liquid sunshine" I consoled myself, without conviction.

Looking north from the wooden pedestrian toll bridge that spans the beautiful Mawddach Estuary, Barmouth had a squat rainbow-column projecting from its midst, the arc being lost in a veil of leaden cloud.

My coast road route (A496) now snaked its way through a series of trim, stone-built villages: each blessed with its own stretch of beach; all nestling between hill and dune.

As I passed through Dyffryn Ardudwy ('Valley of Ardudwy'), a name which applies equally to the village and area in general, I jumped out of my skin at the sound and sight of jets from the nearby Royal Aircraft establishment performing victory rolls at rooftop level. A portent of things to come?

Saturday, 3rd November. A vestige of watery sunshine strove vainly to banish an autumnal chill from the air; a penetrating chill visually enhanced by the white-capped Snowdonia Mountains to the north. Winter draws on!

Lording it over the surrounding landscape from its bluff-top elevation, Harlech Castle – Edward I's massive fortress/bastion – cried out to be photographed, as did the scattered settlement that has mushroomed in its shadow. As one who hails from a smokeless zone, the marble tracery of a thousand coal fires was equally irresistible. This was living social archaeology. The only thing missing was a hansom cab!

As I dithered between map and skyline a sprightly, soft spoken old dear throttled down and voluntarily pointed out Mt. Snowdon: "The one with its night-cap on." She followed up with a cautionary tale: "Harlech is a quiet little backwater. Unlike Porthmadog or Ffestiniog – hotbeds of vice, they are." And as she beetled off: " It's nice to meet a God-fearing person. I shall pray for you!" Of that I had no doubt.

The sheer rock-face of Y Garth was definitely not the realm of the faint-hearted. And I had nothing but admiration for a team of intrepid mountain rescuers who were practising abseiling with a stretcher. At least I took it to be practice and not the real thing. Below the fissured eminence of Y Garth the Briwet toll bridge (Pont Briwet) provided a tantalising glimpse of Clough Williams-Ellis' Italianate masterpiece-cum-folly Portmeirion – closed to the public for the off-season. A bitter blow.

I entered the holiday centre of Porthmadog by way of the Cob, a mile long toll road/rail embankment that neatly bisects the picturesque Glaslyn Estuary. The town was a hive of activity: train spotters (lured by the painstakingly restored Ffestiniog Railway), backpackers/hikers, water-sport fanatics, etc. I was particularly taken by the numerous delicatessen and book shops. And not a hint of vice, hotbed or otherwise!

As the distant lights of Pwllheli hove into view through a curtain of drizzle I realised full well that I was breaking one of my most solemn vows – never to road-walk after dark. Even at close quarters Pwllheli was in a state of semi-darkness due to inadequate street lighting. A state of affairs that confounded the discovery of my digs for the best part of a rain-soaked hour.

Sunday, 4th November. First complete day on the Lleyn Peninsula, one of the least-changed parts of Wales. And what a start to the day; dazzling sunshine and a bracing salty tang. I was invigorated.

Usually the busiest town on the Lleyn, Pwllheli was all but deserted apart from the odd paper-boy and occasional chapel-goer. Two of the faithful stopped to bestow a now familiar blessing: "We'll pray for you."

Beyond Abersoch the twisting up-hill-and-down dale lanes had me freely perspiring, while random raindrops drummed out their ominous Morse upon my waxed-cotton cap. First dousing of the day.

With the curving crescent of Porth Neigwl (Hell's Mouth) behind me, the tree-lined climb to Rhiw by way of Treheli was the sternest test for some days. Having overcome one major obstacle, the pitter-patter promptly gave way to a full blooded downpour.

Gaps in the hedgerows and high banked verges continued to present a periodic visual treat of wild waters or distant cloud-capped mountains. But my accommodation called. Without further ado I ploughed on to 'Meillionydd Bach', my berth for the night, where the farmer and farmer's wife team of Hugh and Lowri Thomas gave me the red carpet treatment. Both were among the vast majority who voted to keep public houses closed on the Sabbath – the only place in Britain without Sunday licensing. Apparently the referendum takes place every seven years and is invariably a foregone conclusion – the Lleyn and its inhabitants remain an anachronism and a breath of fresh air in a jaded world.

Monday, 5th November. Lowri sent me on my way with a blow-out of a breakfast inside me and a fresh batch of Welsh Cakes in hand. I was loath to leave such a warm and welcoming household. – even more so when confronted by the brass-monkey temperature without. On the credit side it was another blindingly bright start to the day – the morning sun gilded the filigree hedgerows, all gossamer-draped with myriad spiders-web streamers.

By the time I reached the tiny fishing village of Aberdaron both the day and I were warming up nicely. Nestling snugly in a hollow in the rugged coastline, all was quiet on the Aberdaron front. From the knot of whitewashed cottages to the wave-lapped church all was vacant, un-peopled. I departed, as I came, accompanied only by the sound of my own footfalls.

West of Aberdaron I eagerly bartered unclassified road for cliff-top footpath: breathtaking scenery, muddy going, impeccable waymarking... for the first kilometre. By late afternoon Llangwnnadl was mine. "Make yourself at home, Mr Westley", invited the note pinned to the front door of my digs. The key in the lock confirmed it. This open house generosity was typical of my hosts Carys and Gareth Owen; characteristic of Lleyn folk in general.

Tuesday, 6th November. Today marked a watershed in weather and attire. Such was the bitter chill that I forsook my ever-present T-shirt for a warm-as-toast Helly-Hanson thermal vest in iceberg blue – to match my frigid extremities.

At Porth Colmon I rejoined the coast and headed north-east atop the grassy cliffs that tumbled haphazardly to beaches of golden sand. A cloudless sky and glassy sea were in perfect symmetry, presenting a boundless prospect of cornflower blue. The deafening silence was broken only by the dull murmur of surf-on-sand and the tic-tic alarm call of the ubiquitous robin. And while the bedewed sheep-shorn sward gave generously underfoot, the sun's lambent rays warmed me by degrees. I was in my element.

I was spending the night at Clynnog-fawr PO, the honoured guest of Mr and Mrs Damerell. The interior of the post office was an absolute revelation, like stepping back in time. And quite unchanged from the day Mr Damerell took it over some forty years ago – complete with original enamel 'Sunlight Soap' advertisement.

Wednesday, 7th November. It was another brilliant, if crisp morning (ah, how quickly we forget!). From the A499, Anglesey appeared within easy reach – though in reality still three days' hike away. In the middle-distance, the ultramarine millpond of Caernarfon Bay was carved deep with the iridescent furrow of a low-level pass from a pre-war biplane: pleasure flights had replaced the aerial-heroics of 'the few' at the old RAF station just north of Morfa Dinlle.

Bordering the wide, desolate inlet of Foryd Bay, the overgrown strand-line abounded with skylarks rising vertically heavenward like animated jump-jets from where they delivered their angelic warbling song so beloved of poet and composer alike. Where Foryd Bay abutted the Western Reaches of the Menai Strait, a large bull seal surfaced close to shore juggling with a butterfish; tasty eating by all accounts – though preferably cooked.

A brisk three kilometre walk along the foreshore brought me to the Afon Seiont where a foot-bridge disgorged its awe-struck charges at the very foot of Caernarfon Castle, surely the finest example of medieval fortification in Britain. Although a magnet for tourists, the town itself has retained a parochial 'Welshness'. East of Caernarfon I followed the meandering A4086 inland to the slate-working community and 'base-camp' village of Llanberis in preparation for tomorrow's big push. My assault on Snowdon!

Thursday, 8th November. From a prominent tourists' information booklet I learned that the distance between Llanberis station and the top of Snowdon (Yr Wyddfa) is but $4\frac{5}{8}$ miles; one hour by rack-and-pinion steam locomotive – somewhat longer by Shank's pony. Furthermore, the summit station has an integral café where, for the price of a special railway stamp, one can post letters and postcards at the highest post-box in Britain and obtain a unique cancellation for their effort.

Dry, cold and blustery though the weather was at ground level, the bulletin board outside a Llanberis camping shop predicted poor visibility and strong wind above 3,000 ft. I was undeterred. Mentally geared-up, boots Nikwaxed, legs embrocated, nothing would stop me now.

Still sporting my rucksack, though partially lightened for the ascent, I passed Llanberis station at 9.50 a.m. Beyond the last vestige of habitation I adopted the onward-and-upward Llanberis path, which vaguely follows the route of the Snowdon Mountain Railway.

Immediately above the tree line-windbreak I fell foul of a freezing down draught, unremitting boulder-strewn gradient and glaring sunshine. With back aflame from stooping into the prevailing blast, I was soon wishing I'd worn something more substantial than shorts and windshirt. This was a lesson hard learnt.

Log: 10.56: Snowline in sight; such is my elation it's all I can do to stop myself running all the way to the peak – if such were possible against this icy-blow. 11.00: close shave: nearly blown over the precipice by rogue gust! Now well into the snow field, 8 to 10 inches deep, compacted; boots all but useless, insufficient tread. 11.10: approaching cloud cover – eerie! 11.13: Vision obliterated – total whiteout! Zero chance of viewing Wicklow Mountains or Isle of Man. 11.25: Reached summit (3,560 ft.). "On top of the world, Ma!" Summit station/café shuttered and barred: snowbound, icicle-hung…

Thus denied the opportunity of dispatching my pre-written postcards – now null and void – I consoled myself by scrambling to the culmination proper, the conical concrete pinnacle – a risky business.

I met only one fellow mountaineer all morning, a local who had ascended by the Snowdon Ranger Path, and who emerged from the swirling pea-souper like a B-picture villain.

Having left my signature in the virgin snow in the time honoured manner (never eat the yellow snow!), I began my descent. What with the all-apparent wind-chill factor and the virtual blizzard conditions, I felt like a latter-day Scott of the Antarctic – and very nearly joined him in the hereafter. For what had been a head-wind on the way up, conversely became a tailwind on the way down. As I broke into a gentle trot I found myself hurtling uncontrollably towards the crag-edge. Had I been in possession of a hang-glider at that point

Brass monkey weather on Snowdon.

I'd have been back in Llanberis in seconds. As it was, I heard a disembodied voice cackling maniacally in my slipstream – my own! At the last conceivable moment I had the presence of mind to thrust my legs forward long jump-fashion, jamming my heels into the loose scree, and grinding to a bone-jarring halt, hurting my left knee in the process...

Back at Llanberis station, shaken and decidedly stirred, I stopped the watch: a round trip of 2 hours 43 minutes; a descent of 68 minutes – and almost a darned sight quicker!

Friday, 9th November. Pedestrian access to Anglesey across the turbulent waters of the Menai Strait is officially restricted to Thomas Telford's superb Menai Suspension Bridge – like it or lump it. I did neither, opting instead to plead ignorance of the law and cross by the more expedient Britannia Bridge (Pont Britannia); a notable erection in its own right.

Not being a physical extension of mainland Britain, I decided to swiftly bisect the Isle of Anglesey by way of the A5 – a tedious twenty-eight kilometre trudge across the low-lying hinterland, harried every step of the way by a constant stream of Holyhead-bound traffic. My only deviation was to purchase a souvenir platform ticket at the most famous small station in the world: Llanfairpwllgwyngyllgogerychwyrndrobwllllantysiliogogogoch or 'The-church-of-St-Mary-by-the-white-hazel-over-the-whirlpool-the-church-of-St-Tysilio-close-to-the-red-cave'! Try getting your tongue round that little lot after a couple of sherbets!

Saturday, 10th November. What an evening! Gone midnight and the temperature in my room was still a sweltering 80 degrees. Being situated above the kitchens was no laughing matter. Which also explained the infernal extractor fan going all night.

Lacking the usual energy – my get-up-and-go had got-up-and-gone – I completed the last short hop along the confounded A5 in little over an hour. Why rush? I wasn't meeting walk co-ordinator John Mole and his wife Kathleen until one.

Anglesey's largest town, Holyhead had much to commend it. None more so than the ladies of the Holyhead Tourist Information Centre who not only showered me with gifts galore – including a lifesaving Dublin Street plan – but also wangled me a free passage on the Holyhead-Dublin B&I ferry.

Having misjudged the distance from their Berkshire home, it was well after one when John and Kathleen arrived. No sooner had we snatched a bite of lunch than it was time to pick up my freebie ticket and board ship. It was an extraordinary long way to come for such a brief but vital encounter (new maps for old; punt for sterling), and I had no wish to detain them unduly on such a raw day. Yet such generosity of time and commitment would be their hallmark for the entire walk.

Drawn-out dockside farewells were not my forte, and besides I was emotionally drained from a hundred similar good-byes. A sincere embrace, a wave, and I embarked upon the blue-and-white liveried *Leinster*. Named after the ancient province, which includes Dublin, the *Leinster* was due to sail at 3.45, round about which time the ship's announcer casually ambled on-air in a characteristic laid-back manner that was to endear itself to me over the proceeding sixteen weeks!

"Well, good mornin' Ladies and Gentlemen... or rather afternoon... (ripple of laughter from passengers) well, we're just about all aboard, so we'll be off in about foive minutes or so... give or tec' a minute." Twenty minutes later we put to sea. No urgency please, we're Irish!

By seven the three-hour plus voyage was all but over, and the low lights of Dublin slid into view on the starboard side like a string of pearls against a black velvet curtain. As for disembarkation? Just like stepping off a bus: no searches, no declarations, nothing. Which, considering I still faced a six kilometres route march into Central Dublin, suited me down to the ground.

A further insight into the amiable Eireann psyche came at the Dock Gates. Here a brace of smartly attired customs officers was conscientiously stopping all traffic, inspecting driving licences and giving each vehicle the once over. Until I asked for directions, that is. At which point conscientiousness went out the window. Falling over each other to put me on the right track, they completely overlooked the stream of relieved motorists that were sneaking through unchecked on the blind-side...

Abroad the twilit back streets, however, it all felt remarkably like the Old Country: cars driving on the left; street signs virtually indistinguishable from our own. I was clearly a stranger in a not so strange land. Only when I encountered the wide trident-lamped boulevard of O'Connell Street did the flavour of what is after all a foreign country begin to emerge: green post-boxes, unfamiliar telephone ('Telefon') boxes, Gaelic lettering (even the graffiti!). And there was something unusual, something enigmatic about the hordes of night clubbers, theatre-goers, Saturday-night revellers. I couldn't put my finger on it at first – then I nailed it: the polite, easygoing, non-confrontational attitude of the young people. A welcome contrast to their inner-city UK counterparts.

"A hundred thousand welcomes," gushed my guest house landlady Mary Heely. I quickly discovered that as a foreign traveller I was not an anonymous tourist but a 'visitor and guest'.

"The Bretish are always welcome."

"Do you take sterling?" I impishly probed, fully aware of the advantageous exchange rate.

"Rather!"

Hospitable *and* shrewd; this was one on-the-ball Colleen.

Sunday, 11th November. As usual I'd overestimated my ability. In lumbering myself with additional maps, winter-wear and sundry items to cover my entire Hibernian sojourn I'd bitten off more than I could masticate. Packing was tantamount to squeezing a quart into a pint-pot: be it a 75 litre rucksack 'pint-pot'. One of the these days I'd wise up to my own shortcomings. In the meantime I'd ditch all non essentials. More parcels home!

O'Connell Street was just as impressive in the daylight as it had been after nightfall: central tree-lined pavement, statues galore, scaffold-clad General Post Office (headquarters of the 1916 Rising), dark theatre, shuttered cinemas, scurrying belated faithful. The lull after the storm; the morning after the gregarious night before.

At the southern end of O'Connell Street, beyond the statue of 'The Liberator' himself (Daniel O'Connell), I paused upon the triple-arched O'Connell bridge, one of Dublin's loveliest views and the city's main north-south artery. Below me the gull-dappled waters of the beloved River Liffey dawdled murkily; the selfsame sombre waters that gave Dublin its name – Duiblinn, or Dark Pool.

Beyond the Liffey, which neatly bisects the city into north and south, I made a beeline for the coast at Sandymount Strand. My clockwise circuit of Ireland was underway. And Dublin's Georgian heritage – fine squares, artisan villas, gleaming brass knockers, filigree fanlights – kept me riveted every step of the way. Noticeable too was the native penchant for green livery of various public services, including An poist (Post Office) and Coras Iompair Eireann (Buses and Rail). Truly the Emerald Isle.

South of the city it became immediately apparent that my Ordnance Survey (Suirbheireacht Ordonais) maps at half inch to one mile were totally inadequate. One could barely make out third class roads let alone footpaths. I decided to play it by ear.

Trials and tribulations apart, my witness book still required endorsing. Enquiries as to the location of the nearest police station drew many a blank look, while requests for the 'cop shop' met with absolute bewilderment.

"Sure you'll be wantin' the Gorda barracks." From that point forth the Garda Síochána Station became a prime daily destination and font of much local knowledge.

Throughout the day, potentially attractive coastal views were impaired by forests of towering, spindly TV aerials – invariably oriented to pick up the favoured British television broadcasts from 'across the water'. Equally unsightly were the ubiquitous grey-painted metal telegraph poles.

Churches of all denominations and flower sellers, the latter usually situated at the church gates, did a day-long roaring trade – as did the shops who cashed in on the head-scarfed hordes emerging from mass or those who had simply dropped-in to 'say a Rosary'. No anti-Sunday shopping lobby here!

A short trek down the coast from the brightly painted terraces of Dun Laoghaire (pronounced Dunleary), Ireland's premier yachting centre and ferry port, I came to Sandycove (Cuas an Gaincarrh). I particularly wanted to pay a call on the one-time Martello Tower-lodgings of Dublin's prodigal son, James Joyce. Prominently featured in the opening pages of *Ulysses*, it now houses the Joyce Museum.

Just across the border into County Wicklow – 'The Garden of Ireland' – I had my work cut out for me. Former work-mate Pat Doyle had suggested I look up his family ("ask anyone") in the once fashionable resort of Bray (Bré). Easier said than done. Not only was the town far larger than I'd been led to believe, but every other commercial premises appeared to have 'Doyle' emblazoned above its portal: Doyle's Bar, Doyle's Newsagent – and all had relatives in England. It was a needle in a haystack job. I contented myself with a sight so rudely denied me from the summit of Snowdon – that of the wild and forbidding Wicklow Mountains.

A little over five kilometres to the south, Greystones (Na Clocha Liatha) shared Bray's aura of faded elegance: old money, tree-lined streets, off-road parking, obligatory privet hedges. Greystones' railway station was the rallying point for a group of youthful, banner-toting protesters – though patently not of the town. Likewise, the serge-overcoated Gardai, impassively watching from street corners in twos and threes, had clearly been drafted in. Why such a genteel backwater had been singled out in this manner was incomprehensible.

Away from the sea front my incomprehension rose in direct correlation with the growing number of Garda officers materialising from the topiary. Cordoned by the temporary steel barriers, the house next to my 'Glendore' accommodation was evidently the epicentre of the impending storm of protest.

Once installed in the congenial, bohemian atmosphere of 'Glendore', my host Penny Hall clued me in hushed tones: "The gentleman next door is the Solicitor General responsible for the imminent extradition to Britain of IRA hunger striker Dessie Ellis."

Penny dissuaded me from popping out to photograph the proceedings: "In these situations the Gardai take no prisoners!"

Monday, 12th November. Unseasonably humid and sunny though the weather was, it more than complemented the abundant palm trees that lined my southerly route, which in turn bore witness to the warming influence of the Gulf Stream.

Beyond Wicklow (Cill Mhantáin), the county town at the foot of the Ballyguille Hill, the wandering coast road led me a merry if solitary dance. Flanked left and right respectively by a string of sandy beaches and the lower slopes of the Wicklow Mountains, I met not a soul all afternoon.

I should have known the weather was too good to last. Come 3 p.m. and a massive fog bank rolled in off the sea, obscuring the landscape and soaking me before I had time to don my weatherproofs. To add insult to injury, the very next bi-lingual/dual calibrated road sign callously announced ten miles/sixteen kilometres to Arklow (An Tinbhear Mór)! And there was me thinking I'd be there before nightfall. Fat chance.

From here on in it was rain, pain and inexorably failing light. In fact I'd picked up an hour of daylight in crossing the Irish Sea. During my last few days in Wales lighting-up time had been about 4 p.m. – here it was nearer 5.

Even so the final six kilometres into Arklow were a leap into the darkness: no street lamps here, and my previously reliable mini-maglite torch decided to pack-up on me. Sod's Law! But Old Faithful, my Pilgrim's Staff, came into its own. I was a regular Blind Pugh (tap-tap!). In the country of the blind, the audacious man is king!

Such was my single-mindedness that even the latent chime of spade-on-gravel vaulting through the blackness didn't faze me. Here we were, me and the phantom gravedigger (for all I knew!), assailed by driving rain in the darkest depths of rural Ireland – and exchanging pleasantries as if it was a commonplace, workday encounter. Oh well, when in Ireland…

With 52 kilometres/32½ miles under my soggy belt, Arklow came in the nick of time. In the blackout I'd overlooked the picturesque Vale of Avoca, which inspired Thomas Moore's poem *The Meeting of the Waters*. But in its place I'd struck alehouse-gold in the relaxed and friendly refuge of the Bridge Hotel, so named after its proximity to the Avoca River. And at that particular moment a wedge of Irish Brie washed down with a pint or three of pukka Guinness, lovingly drawn and 'scraped and topped', and an accompaniment of traditional live music was infinitely more inviting than a rain-swept, benighted valley.

Tuesday, 13th November. Another day, another county: Co. Wexford – and the sunny south-east. Statistically confirmed to enjoy up to an hour more sunshine per day than any other part of Ireland, this phenomenon is accredited in some quarters to a hole in the ozone layer above the Celtic Sea. So much for the good news.

Most Irish folk seem to have the gift of the gab. This particular morning the twin topics given a verbal airing were the outcome of tomorrow's Republic v. England European Championship football match, and the phasing-out of the punt note in favour of a coin – which, detractors claim, is difficult to differentiate from the 10p piece. Now where have I heard that one before?

On the weather-front the morning lived up to Wexford's four star billing: dry and sunny. After a brief spell aboard the N11 National Primary Road, I stuck with the mothballed Coast

Road. Its pot-holed charm served me well. I doubt if the Republic will ever have a long distance coastal path worthy of the name, as vast tracts of coastline are, alas!, in private ownership.

West of Courtown (Baile na Cúirte), which claims the lowest recorded rainfall in Ireland and thereby assures its resort status, I was taken by the volume and pluck of the native grey-and-black hooded crows, the piebald equivalent of our own carrion crow. Equally widespread were donkeys ('Moke') and their doe-eyed offspring ('Mini-moke?') – endearingly known as 'Irish bog-engines'.

Like junior school 'Hometime' the world over, Riverchapel was a joy to behold: fresh faced kiddies, squeals of delight, a convoy of bicycles (no stabilisers), excited chatter – no expletives either. An altruistic childhood this: substitute short trousers for Levis; stink bombs for glue-sniffing; scrumping for joy riding. These are salad-days Wexford style: callow, evergreen, ageless. No imitation adults here, no affectations: Not old before their time. Too soon will come the burden of riper years, the responsibility of adulthood. Until then...

As darkness descended I found myself defiantly whistling *Colonel Bogey* as I shambled towards Blackwater, and hoping-upon-hope for something more than the Spartan digs of late. For the second day on the trot walking lost its appeal. On the whole the last forty-eight hours comprised 10% pleasure, 90% endeavour.

Thus ensued another evening of dark-room obscurity (still no torch – must be the bulb!), star-less to boot. And now it's raining again: black gobbet sized projectiles at first, then a full-blown deluge. All hands to the heavenly pumps! My whistle gutters and dies – water-logged pea! A new sound reaches me, over the cascade-gush of downpour-on-tarmac. Hobnailed boots? Tap shoes? No matter. For a lane-wide troupe of ghostly apparitions hove into view; animated bed-sheets all. Sound, vision and vivid imagination combine to fashion an incongruous mirage, a phantasmagoric illusion: Ku Klux Klan in stilettos!! One bovine ululation later and the hallucination is debunked. Cattle-prod extended, I brought up the rear until the parting of the ways: I to bed and board, they to byre and fodder.

The last couple of miles dragged on interminably. Whether fallacy or reality, Irish miles appear significantly longer than the Imperial variety. I was dead on my feet.

At Blackwater (An Abhainn Dubh) post office-cum-stores I beseeched staff to notify my prospective host, Bridget Whelan, of my arrival in the village. Within minutes I was haring my way car-borne to Bridget's outlying homestead – 'Haven Farm'.

Wednesday, 14th November. No sooner had I recovered from last night's hair-raising wing-and-a-prayer drive to Haven Farm, than it was heart-in-mouth time once again for the return trip to Blackwater. And it came as absolutely no surprise to learn that many thousands of the Republic's motorists – at worst reckless, at best unconventional – received their licence without even taking a test!

Bridget's non-stop machine-gun chatter was both informative and a welcome distraction from the speed-blurred hedgerows. Subjects hastily glossed over included her fear of "t'under" and her pet gripe "Oytinerants" (gypsies). Such was the momentum of her pell-mell delivery that she actually gulped for air, guppy fashion, at the end of each sentence. A not uncommon mannerism in these parts.

By 9.30 a.m. I was pounding the tarmac south of Blackwater – frequently bestowed with the title 'Wexford's tidiest village'. So physically and mentally demanding is road walking that after two consecutive nine-hour days I was all in, more so for the fact that such protracted stints allow insufficient time for bodily recuperation. Though no doubt being over thirty-seven hundred kilometres (2,000 miles plus) into the walk had something to do with it.

Believed to be the home-town of my maternal great-grandfather William White, Wexford (Loch Garman) derives its English name from the Viking Weissfjord or 'White Fjord'. A quick flick through the phone book confirmed White to be the predominant surname hereabouts.

As I headed out of town along the wood-lapped crescent quay, past the bronze statue of local-man-made-good John Barry (1745-1803), 'Father of the American Navy', I was sheepishly accosted by two lads who took me for an Australian 'visitor' ("Got ten-pence, muster?"). This was a frequent misconception throughout my stay in Ireland – though in my book 'North London' and 'Strine' are poles apart. One look at their glum expressions told me that England had taken the lead at Lansdowne Road, Dublin (Eng-land! Eng-land!). Within half-hour the 'boot' was on the other foot and homeward-bound schoolboys, ears glued to transistor radios, were whooping with delight – London-born Tony Cascarino had equalised for the Republic. Honours shared.

Wonders will never cease. I actually reached my destination – Rosslare Harbour – before nightfall. Not fancying the isolation of the local Youth Hostel – so often tenantless at this time of year – I sought alternative accommodation.

"Come home with me," said the seventy year old man-mountain, "the wife and I'll do you B&B for IR£6". Jeremiah Foley by name; a grand name for a grand old gent. Standing at well over six feet, and as broad as he was tall, he must have cut a dash in his younger days in the Garda Síochána.

I was morbidly intrigued. Even as we trooped in silence to Jeremiah's converted coast guard station home, I wondered just what I'd let myself in for. At IR£6 it even undercut the flyblown, rock-bottom seven pounds B&B advertised in Margate. If nothing else, man should live to satisfy his curiosity.

Not for the first time since arriving in Ireland I retired to a bedroom that bore a greater resemblance to a Catholic shrine than to a bedchamber: a tableau of saintly figurines, Papal certificates, the odd crucifix, and a wall-mounted Holy Water dispenser (dried up) for crossing oneself. Though infinitely more spiritual than these desiccated, dusty relics was the view from my room – an endless vista of sea, sky and ferryport.

Thursday, 15th November. I didn't have to wait long to discover the secret of my bargain-basement B&B. Not only were all the basic facilities classified as 'extras' and charged at a punt a go, but the single major economy came at breakfast. As the very foundation on which I built my walking day, I required a substantial nosh to get me off on the right foot. What I got however was a cereal, bread and a mug of tea – and Jeremiah Foley seated beside me eyeing my every move like a malignant Finlay Currie. Every conversational overture on my part met with a monosyllabic reply. It was hard to swallow in more senses than one. Intimidation wasn't the word for it. I felt like Oliver Twist to Jeremiah's Mr Bumble. "Please, sir, I want some more." But came there none. Where was the fry-up, the cholesterol à la carte: dog rolls, bacon butties, egg banjos? On the basis of ever-diminishing returns, customer-wise, this was the ultimate false economy. Whatever happened to the 'send 'em away happy' ethos?

I decided to cut my losses and pick Jeremiah's brains – I certainly didn't need to pick my teeth. But to no avail. My host appeared less familiar with the surrounding area than I was. "What's dis say? What's dis say?" echoed Jeremiah dribbling over my map. I'd had considerable experience pressing-the-flesh over the last four months, but Jeremiah's was the firmest handshake to date. Evidently this gentle-giant had the brute force to back-up his considerable bulk should the need arise. And from his no-nonsense bearing I doubted whether he had occasion to take any lip in his Garda days, let alone prisoners. We parted on amicable terms: he well in pocket; I well out of sorts.

Throughout the day only a wealth of churches and castles alleviated the monotony of this otherwise flat and featureless terrain. Suffice to say, I gave Bastardstown a wide berth!

Bemused, bedraggled and bewildered, I off loaded my rucksack at my Grange lodgings, before heading on down to Kilmore Quay (Ce na cille Móire), tucked just below Forlorn

Point (Crossfarnoge). Increasingly uncommon in a county noted for its thatch, Kilmore Quay had a host of mop-topped cottages with whitewashed walls. But still the dearth of humanity continued. Not only were the Garda Barracks and the solitary pub both closed, but so too was the village's pride and joy – the retired lightship *Guillemot*, which houses a floating maritime museum.

I completed the round trip back to Coral House by way of Ballyteige Castle, having tarried awhile to watch and photograph a family group of Whooper swans (silent 'W'), the vociferous cousins of our native mute swans, foraging in a sugar-beet field. Another ornithological first on my part, and the undisputed highlight of a nondescript day.

Friday, 16th November. Not once since arriving in the Republic have I slept beneath a duvet. The trend hereabouts appears to favour a hundredweight of assorted blankets fit to crush the life from one's immobilised body, while facilities at large ranged from dire to non-existent. Though fundamental to my general air of disillusion were my fruitless attempts to discover just what makes the Irish tick. Admittedly I now knew that support for the IRA and its political wing Sinn Féin ('ourselves alone'), far from being widespread and deeply entrenched, was largely restricted to a young(ish) urbanite minority. Also that President Elect Mary ("You have a voice. I will make it heard.") Robinson is roundly denounced by her detractors as 'the smoked salmon socialist'. Yet these enlightening examples apart, I was no closer to plumbing the depths of the Irish psyche.

With my weatherproofs now a virtual fixture, it was in a mood of fatalistic anticipation that I set out for Fethard, some 46 kilometres (28¾ miles) distant. Not for nothing is Ireland called the Emerald Isle. With rainfall recorded three out of every four days on the west coast, and every second day here in the east, it could hardly be anything else but verdant.

From what was on the whole another nonentity of a day, sans breathtaking scenery and interesting characters, I suspect I might have salvaged one or two half decent snaps – notably a colossal multi-wagoned snake of a sugar-beet train at Wellingtonbridge; Tintern Abbey, in long shot; an IRA memorial overlooking Bennow Bay; Saltmill's village smithy; and a vibrantly painted horse-drawn 'Oytinerants' wagon (gypsies or diddikais never call them caravans!) in the grounds of Tintern Abbey.

But it fell to Fethard (Fiodh Ard) to provide the day's modest high point. Technicolor plates of Jimmy O'Leary's garage have graced nigh-on every Tourist Guide and travelogue since the year dot. And rightly so. Of crude breeze-block construction, the garish red and black facade is strikingly redeemed by a series of motifs, nautical and Eireann, lovingly picked-out in scallop shells, and further embellished with an array of redundant agricultural implements. At last I felt one step nearer the essential idiosyncratic Ireland I so religiously sought.

Saturday, 17th November. Fethard to Whitechurch by way of Hook Head was today's schedule; third class roads no wider than farm tracks the route. Frustratingly, rain – from monsoon to nebulous – continued, as normal, to follow hard on the heels of lack-lustre sunshine.

The inclement weather apart, the day peaked really early. Just north of Templetown two yuppie fillies – cut-glass accents, obligatory pearls, Fair Isle sweaters, matching Cabriolet – were all over me like a rash: autographs, photos, questions, platonic kisses... It would seem our chance meeting made their day. It most certainly made mine!

Set on the crescent-shaped King's Bay, the nineteenth century village of Arthurstown is dedicated to the memory of Irish born Arthur Wellesley, First Duke of Wellington. And there was me thinking he was the greatest 'Englishman' of all time. Ignorance isn't bliss – it's oblivion! Neither the exact date nor birthplace of the 'Iron Duke' is known for certain – though what with 'Wellingtonbridge' of yesterday and now 'Arthurstown', Co. Wexford must be front runner in the home-county stakes.

It was after dark when I arrived at my digs – back to the old routine! – though still half-an hour earlier than arranged. In the gloom of the unlit gravel driveway, I could make out an oversize shadowy form bounding about hither-and-thither at the outermost limit of my field of vision. Only when my scrunching footfalls broke the silence did the opposition give voice; a booming bark that stopped me dead in my tracks. Even as I gingerly backed away the 'phantom hound' was joined by two colleagues of equal dimension. What to do? Chance my arm (and other limbs!) with the pooches or mark time until my co-host's homecoming? Patience prevailed. And within ten minutes John Caulfield, ex-Royal Air Corps, ushered me into the passenger seat for the drive up to the house. A precaution well founded as the headlights promptly illuminated a trio of overgrown Irish Wolfhounds!

Sunday, 18th November. Rose at 8 o'clock for 8.30 Mass at Bally Kelly Roman Catholic Church, the parish church of Jack Kennedy, great-grandfather of assassinated US President John F. Kennedy, before his emigration to Boston. The Reading came from the Gospel according to St Matthew (25: 14-30), the parable concerning the master and his three servants. Now while I'm all for fulfilling one's potential and not hiding one's light under a bushel, I found the inordinate number of collections an imposition – particularly as I was almless at the time. Meanwhile, Mr and Mrs Caulfield (who slipped me a couple of bob) refrained from going up to receive the sacrament – they hadn't fasted for the prescribed one hour beforehand: it used to be twenty-four hours – but 'the times they are a-changin'!

We made a slight detour on the way 'home' to take in the isolated hamlet of Dunganstown, birthplace of Jack Kennedy and from where he fled to escape the ravages of famine in 1848. The modest Kennedy homestead is still occupied by descendants of the family and was visited by JFK before his tragic demise in 1963.

Back at Moorland House I proceeded to pack, while Mrs Caulfield prepared a four star breakfast. For the next two and a half hours, give or take an hour, we three dissected all matters Anglo-Irish. What an education on my part. For example not only was it news to me that two-thirds of Wellington's crack troops were Irish born but that, far from being neutral during WWII, Ireland selflessly exported all it could to sustain mainland Britain when alternative supply lines were all but severed. On top of which over one-hundred-thousand Irish men and women died fighting for the allied cause during two world wars – all volunteers. Some neutrality!

But on the subject of British intervention in Irish affairs Mr Caulfield remained stridently impassioned, yet clearly not so anti-British as to preclude his serving proudly in the Royal Engineers. According to my co-host, even Patricius (St. Patrick) was an interfering Brit who only succeeded in diluting the Celtic heritage. But special venom was reserved for 'Lord Protector' Oliver Cromwell – whose name is accursed to this day for his savage and barbaric treatment of the Irish for resisting his authority. The term 'by hook or by crook(e)' heralded one such grisly episode. Apparently, when lying off Hook Head in a storm that prevented both him and his 'Ironside' troops from landing, Cromwell reputedly vowed to take Waterford: "By Hook (Head) or by Crooke(town)." Yet through it all the Irish have retained an extraordinary capacity for forgiveness. Which, when you consider what a thorn in their side we've been down the years, is a veritable miracle. "Why *won't* they leave us alone to run our own lives?" beseeched Mr Caulfield penultimately.

Even as I bade my belated farewells he further implored me to do all in my limited power to offset the anti-Irish bias of the British media.

Consider it done.

Having valiantly withstood the morning's ear-bashing, it was gone mid-day by the time I legged-it from Whitechurch. And with a good 36 kilometres (22½ miles) between there and Waterford, I had little opportunity to survey the scenery – largely washed-out by a string of heavy showers. Though I could hardly overlook the John F Kennedy Arboretum. Nestling on the slopes of Slieve Coillte (Hill of the Forest) above the Kennedy ancestral home at

Dunganstown, the 580 lush acres contain some 5,000 exotic trees and shrubs; a fitting green memorial to the late president's enduring popularity.

On the agricultural front, sugar-beet harvesting was at its frenzied height, Ireland being self-sufficient in sugar, and both field and byway were indistinguishable beneath a uniform quagmire of red loam and sugar-beet debris. Meanwhile the pall of silence that cloaked this seeming pastoral scene had sinister undertones. Far from altruism on the part of the respective farmer, placards declaring 'Land Strictly Preserved Fur and Feather' referred to the jealous protection of shooting rights. Allied with the widespread practice of poisoning (toxic-spiked meat: 'Land poisoned'), it was little wonder that I had yet to see a single bird of prey. Though it was some minor consolation, while on the subject of airborne observation, that I had still to see or hear an aircraft since arriving here – let alone a wayward vapour trail.

Guided by the twinkling lights of Waterford's mile-long quayside, I strolled awhile in the beguiling society of a schoolmistress – O lucky children! – avidly scouring the grass verge in search of cans for the purpose of recycling. Thoroughly entranced by the Eireann smile and heavenly disposition of this pedagogue-angel, all too soon we parted company in the impersonal gloaming of the N25.

With Pilgrim's Staff and fourteen weeks salt 'n' pepper growth forward-most, as I prepared to cross the bridge over the River Suir into the ancient city of Waterford (Port Lairge) a group of high-spirited youths staggered in mock consternation and exclaimed as one:

"My God! St. Patrick!"

Monday, 19th November. Another county, another Province – Waterford and Munster respectively. With the ring of Kerry and Galway Bay to name but two jewels in Munster's scenic crown, the coming weeks held rich promise. In the meantime it was down to the workaday slog between the busy seaport of Waterford, home of the famous Waterford crystal ware, and the renowned holiday resort of Tramore.

On reflection the terrain over the last couple of days has grown evermore undulating, a trend that is certain to continue for the foreseeable future. As for the weather, those unlikely bedfellows sunshine and showers look to have set in for the duration.

According to my reckoning the first 1,600 kilometres (1,000 miles) took forty-five days and the second 1,600 kilometres took forty-three days, therefore I should be nudging 4,800 km (3,000 miles) – all going well – by mid-December. Roll on Christmas!

NB All Ireland appears to be awaiting the outcome of tomorrow's Tory party leadership showdown with bated breath.

Tuesday, 20th November. West of Tramore two jagged mountain ranges veered awesomely into view: Comeragh and Monavullagh. A nominal sweep of the head unleashed a contrasting panorama of mist-draped peaks, frost-dusted hills and a steel-blue millpond Atlantic. Blithe to the cold-fire rays of the dazzling sun, the rarefied wine-like air was chilled to piquant perfection. A thoroughly intoxicating ensemble.

At the head of a reed-fringed flood plain east of Annestown loomed the overgrown hilltop fortress of Dunhill Castle. With its rocky inlets, plunging cliffs and secluded bays this was south-east Ireland at its supreme best.

The rolling coast road between Annestown and Dungarvan was liberally punctuated with tranquil villages, all the more so for being bathed in a softly diffused afternoon light. The outskirts of Bunmahon (Bun Machan) threw up an honest to goodness beagle hunt, complete with Master of Hounds brandishing a furled bullwhip. Later, in the sleepy backwater of Stradbally (An tSráidbhaile) – for sleepy read comatose – I saw the amazing sight of a venerable old golden Labrador dozing in the autumnal sun with an equally aged Jack Russell terrier curled-up on its back.

Wednesday, 21st November. Second successive morning of flawless walking conditions: frosty, bright and invigoratingly chilly.

Throughout my Dungarvan-to-Grange walking-day the perception that I was somehow in the very midst of authentic Ireland was no groundless observation on my part. The peninsula of Ring (An Rinn) is a thriving outpost of the Irish language – be it laced with a broad Waterford accent – culture, traditional music and folklore. One of many small rural communities that have remained closer to their Gaelic roots by virtue of their remoteness, the Gaeltacht areas (Irish speaking) are now actively supported by the Government. As the Irish so rightly say: "A people without a language is a people without a heart."

I'll drink to that: "Sláinte! (Health!)"

Between Newton and my evening destination of Grange (a frequent place-name in these parts), I plucked a ready-made pilgrim's staff from an ash thicket. Strong, flexible and ramrod straight, the Gaelic game of hurling is played with an ash stick or 'hurley' for these very properties. Despite all the obvious advantages, I was loath to part company with dear weather-beaten 'Old Faithful' after all the scrapes we'd come through together.

Thursday, 22nd November. I took to the open road soon after sun up. Sporting weatherproofs, waxed cap and woolly mitts, I was well prepared for the seeming winterscape that greeted me. Draped in a velvet mantle of hoarfrost, the etiolated landscape was censored of all imperfection. I stoutly resisted the overriding urge to shatter the flawed pearlescence of a string of frozen puddles; to succumb would have been sacrilege.

Despite the finger-nipping chill my temperature rose according to the terrain, and I was soon able to dispense with hat and gloves – as indeed I'd earlier dispensed with the services of 'Old Faithful' (henceforth call me 'old faithless'!). Rather than abandon it completely, I left it in the safekeeping of my hostess. Mustn't let sentimentality cloud my judgement. Then, as now, I remain convinced that my actions were pre-ordained.

By midday I was afoot Ireland's largest County, Co. Cork. Strategically placed at the mouth of the River Blackwater, the ancient walled port of Youghal (Eochaill), pronounced 'Yawl', appeared in an advanced state of heavy-lidded languor beneath a cloudless sky of duck egg blue. An illusion. Dominated by an unusual four-storey clock tower which straddles the main street, Youghal was positively abuzz with news from across the water. Gossip, not religion, is the opium of the masses. And Youghal's teeming shoppers were rapaciously overdosing on the sensational disclosure of Premier Margaret Thatcher's resignation. It was clearly as Major (!) a talking point here as at home – perhaps more so, considering the 'Iron Lady's' popularity in the Republic (though more for her stateswomanship than for her domestic policies). My English accent brought out the newscaster in everybody – all of whom insisted on clueing me in on the big story. It seemed that the only ones not cognisant of the momentous happenings were the seals blissfully frolicking in the crystal waters offshore. And they were infinitely richer for wallowing in ignorance of the fact.

I, meanwhile, was preoccupied with 'momentous happenings' of a different nature. Apparently it was in the garden of Myrtle Grove, a fine but much altered Elizabethan erection, that Sir Walter Raleigh, versatile genius and one time Mayor of Youghal, grew the first potatoes and smoked the first tobacco in Ireland. In more recent times, Youghal achieved cinematic prominence as the location of John Ford's 1956 movie *Moby Dick* for which the town's stone-built facade was transformed with a temporary 'skin' of New England-style clapboard.

A sickle moon had already ousted the sun, and the deep-freeze of eventide had long since reclaimed its dusky domain, by the time I set foot in Garryvoe where, in the out-of-character cold snap of backwoods Co. Cork my fancy rigidly locked upon thoughts of food. And tonight I fancied Scotch Broth, Ballycotton plaice with mountains of piping vegetables, and sherry trifle sluiced down with a 'pint of plain'!

Friday, 23rd November. Come back Jack Frost all is forgiven! Roared on by a banshee of wind, it had been raining stair-rods since first light – if the meagre candlepower permeating the unbroken slate-grey cloud cover could be so described. To say that I was reluctant to leave my warm – well, lukewarm – lodgings was an understatement. Despite all the hype to the contrary, driving horizontal rain will eventually penetrate any and every shell-garment. And my modest weatherproofs – a misnomer if ever there was one – were no exception to this depressing rule.

At times like this I had to constantly remind myself of my good fortune. After all, as I'd been told so often: "Most people would give their right arm for the opportunity to walk around the British Isles". Opportunity, however, didn't lessen the enormity of my task – it merely paved the way for my attempt.

With my hood-blinkered visibility restricted to a bare minimum, for all I saw of Ballycotton (Baile Choitín), Whitegate (An Geata Bán), Cork Harbour and the like, I might as well have cut straight across country to my Cahermone objective. As it happened, the common courtesy of Irish motorist for the saturated pedestrian went some way to atoning for the foulness of the day. Meticulously slowing down at puddles to avoid drenching me further, they invariably acknowledged me on passing – when not offering me a lift (stoically declined on all counts). Throughout the rain-swept day the metalled roads shone like rivers, a network of third class tributaries besmirched by rafts of pulped sugar-beet and carrots, the product of many an encounter between overladen lorry and pot-hole.

I had long since given up lunch breaks; an hour's midday inertia needlessly extended the walking day by a similar period after dark. Instead I harnessed my hunger, turning it to my advantage. What greater incentive to put one's best foot forward than the prospect of a blow-out spread at the end of the line? And how better to get to know a people, a race, than to devour its distinctive cuisine?

Saturday, 24th November. Today inauspiciously took up where yesterday left off: cold and wet; or in the Gaelic *fuar* and *fluich*. Like its predecessor, this wasn't a day for blithely wandering off the beaten track and I restricted my passage to link, trunk and national primary roads accordingly. I was thankful also for the frequency and clarity of road signs – as my water-logged South Cork map was on the verge of disintegrating.

Adopting the N25 at Cahermone, I bypassed the thriving market town of Midleton (Mainistir na Corann) with a view to making Cork – the Republic's second city – by early afternoon. Alas, the wind was in the wrong direction to catch a freebie-whiff of the aromatic vapours wafting from Midleton's state-of-the-art distillery, which incorporates the world's largest pot still with a liquid capacity of 33,333 gallons!

From the off I felt an instant rapport with Cork – an anglicisation of Coraigh – 'The Venice of Ireland'. Sandwiched between the north and south channel of 'The Lovely (River) Lee', the main business and shopping centre of the Republic's second city is remarkably compact. In the aptly named Grand Parade the svelte-uniformed ladies of the Tourist Information Centre agreed to make a collection on my behalf and post the proceeds on. While waiting for the centre to re-open after lunch – not so much a lunch break, more a siesta – I dropped in on the English market, an eighteenth century covered forum, now a flea market of high repute and a faithful evocation of Cork life in microcosm.

Thoroughly captivated by the 'City of Spires', I stayed far longer than intended. Even then it was a major wrench to sling my hook. Procrastinating to the very last, it was inevitable that the run in to Weaver Point would be consigned to the realm of darkness. Fringed by woodland and lapped by Lough Mahon, Cork Harbour and the Owenboy River, my link road passage was a magical if precarious business. When not transfixed by the headlights of the occasional startled motorist I extinguished my mini-maglite torch – which had miraculously decided to work of its own accord. Once more at one with my nocturnal surroundings, the mud-flats, reed-beds and woodland floor of my shadow world came alive with the croaks, rustlings and fluted calls of a million latent life forms. My only visual contact was with a flight of large bats randomly silhouetted against the horn-ed moon. My imagination ran riot as I drew alongside Drake's Pool, a silver-furrowed reach of the Owenboy River, where Sir Francis Drake holed-up while on the run from Spanish Men-o'-War in 1587 – the year before he took on the might of the Armada.

Beyond Crosshaven (Bun an Tabhairne) I escorted a mother and son through the pitch-black lanes for a kilometre or so to the Helm Hotel, Weaver Point, where we went our separate ways. My good deed for the day. For their part they remained genuinely indifferent to my concern for their welfare. All credit to Ireland's law-abiding majority.

Pronounced locally 'Helum', the Helm Hotel was far from the swankiest hostelry I'd encountered on my travels. Its saving grace, however, was the composite telephone-radio in my otherwise Spartan room on which 'Six hours of non-stop hits of the 60s and 70s' transported me back to the golden days of pirate radio (showing my age!). My paperwork took a back seat as I wallowed in wet-eyed nostalgia.

Sunday, 25th November. The morning was radiant – as was my irrepressible state of mind. I was even inspired to chronicle my experience in song; something I hadn't done for the best part of a decade. And what better proving-ground for my new compositions than the rarefied alfresco acoustics of the undulating red-soiled farmland, delightful bays and richly wooded valleys of my Weaver Point to Kinsale flight path. And it was a far from audience-less recital. Apart from a number of locals walking strings of baying greyhounds, my Pied Piper delusions were fuelled by a landscape awash with a verminous tide of brown rats frantically seeking the sanctuary of verge and hedgerow, having gorged on their favourite food – sugar-beet. Such was the rodent aggregation that at times they resembled animated fur rugs fleeing the approaching tractor-drawn sugar-beet harvesters *en masse*. Once loosed, the greyhounds had a field day; but this wasn't sport, it was a turkey shoot, carnage. And still they came...

Kinsale (Cionn tSáile), where I was spending the night with an American couple, Art and Ruthann Moran-Salinger, has had a chequered history: John Wesley, preacher and founder of Methodism was lionised here – having been stoned in Cork, just eighteen miles due north; in 1915 the inquest into the sinking of the Lusitania by a German submarine was held at Kinsale Court House; in recent years an extravagantly picturesque harbour and frequent gourmet weeks have combined to make this ancient seaside town a tourist attraction for more peaceable reasons.

Monday, 26th November. Following a sublime night's kip in a 200 year old four-poster bed I was ready and willing to take on the world. Fortunately I had only the earnest repartee of Art and Ruthann to contend with, both of whom had their own particular pet subjects: Art was into genealogy in a big way, being utterly convinced that the Salinger aspect of his double-barrelled surname is an anglicisation of the Norman/Irish St. Leger – of Doncaster flat-racing classic fame. Ruthann's abiding interest was less obvious, and only came to light in the process of saying goodbye. Suddenly aghast with wide-eyed awe, a simple farewell handshake provoked Ruthann – a qualified faith healer – into the euphoric revelation that I too was likewise blessed. Apparently in the simple act of pressing-the-flesh, the heat and 'vibes' from my hand had been the give-away. Whether I chose to pursue a direct hands-on approach or 'absent healing', I was left in no doubt that I had 'the gift' and that, furthermore, I was obligated to follow it up: "It's a great source of hope to the otherwise hopeless."

Sandwiched between a cloudless azure sky and the cobalt blue of Kinsale Harbour, the town was even more attractive – if such were possible – than steeped in the rose-hues of last nights bloodshot sunset. Here was a place where I could settle down and write, paint, compose... vegetate; whatever mood took me.

My brown study didn't last very long. In passing a shop-front I caught sight of my image in the plate-glass window; and jolly disquieting it was too. Now shaggily hirsute and with a loping staff-assisted stride – as opposed to the staccato gallop of old – I had assumed all the physical characteristics of Francis (see Cornwall). In the same way that a common life-style and stimuli produce a common beast, perhaps it is the lot of all latter-day pilgrims to assimilate the outward appearance of their humble Middle Ages counterparts?

Sheltered by steep green hills on all sides, Kinsale marks the beginning of scenic West Cork. It also marked the departure point of one Alexander Selkirk aboard the 90 ton *Cinque Ports* in 1703, and whose consequent marooning on the Pacific Island of Juan Fernandez inspired the Daniel Defoe novel *Robinson Crusoe*. I was following in distinguished footsteps, indeed.

Throughout the brisk yomp to the Old Head of Kinsale, a bird-thronged promontory sixteen kilometres/ten miles to the south, I occupied my time adding the finishing touches to yet another lyric. With the melody almost complete, two further lyrics in the pipeline and one in the bag, I wasn't kidding when I said I could work here. The Muse was definitely with me! It was off the dramatic cliffs of the Old Head that the Cunard liner *Lusitania* was torpedoed on May 7, 1915, with the loss of 1,198 lives.

Overlooking mud-flats and dominated by the extensive mellow-stoned ruins of a fourteenth century Franciscan Friary – the destructive handiwork of English parliamentary forces in 1642 – the village of Timoleague (Tigh Molaige – 'House of Molaga') stands at the head of a silty creek. I wasted little time in telephoning Dr Ann Nicholson. It seemed an eternity since she and her husband Mike had extended an invitation to stop over; in reality but seventy-nine days ago in the sun-kissed surroundings of Portloe, Cornwall.

Tuesday, 27th November. Ann hastened me back to Timoleague at breakneck speed aboard her wing-ed chariot, Mike having departed at dawn for a job interview (fingers crossed!) in Bremen, Germany.

Once renowned for the Spanish wine that could be shipped up these waters with comparative ease, the diversity and concentration of bird life upon the now unnavigable mud-flats of Timoleague had to be seen to be believed. Though certain species, namely ducks, were noticeably apprehensive on account of the wholesale wild-fowling.

Heading west along the shore-embracing coast road I came to the popular family holiday resort of Courtmacsherry (Cúirt Mhic Shéafraidh); as I recall, a straggle of raggle-taggle dwellings hemmed by hill and strand-line. Gently collared by an effervescent spinster keen to show off her latest couturier creation – plaid slacks hot off the Singer – my approbation was amply rewarded with a detailed inventory of 'the Divil's own goings on' in the 'big houses' across the bay. Scandals apart, from an architectural viewpoint, the most interesting by far was Coolman Castle – now owned by the Disney Corporation.

Beyond Barry's Point I paused to plunder my rucksack for the sandwiches (ham and mustard – consumed on the move) and After Eight mints deposited there by Anne. Far below me the recumbent butter-wouldn't-melt Atlantic daintily nuzzled the southernmost promontory of Seven Heads peninsula. O capricious ocean! Even the halcyon weather contrived to lull me into a false sense of security; it bore a greater resemblance to spring than autumn – and a glorious spring at that. Such balmy interludes would undoubtedly stand me in good stead for the deluge to come. Photographs were a no-no. Not even the likes of David Bailey could do justice to the consummate Clonakilty Bay!

On the home stretch now, and as I skirted the winding inlet towards my evening destination, the lively market town of Clonakilty (Cloich na Coillte), I mentally catalogued the various forms of visual acknowledgement exchanged between motorist and pedestrian. After two weeks of conditioning I was well accustomed to the Irish foot-slogger's tradition of waving to each and every vehicle that passed one by – though these well intentioned gestures weren't always reciprocated. Worst culprits were usually tourists or visitors – most of whom merely registered a puzzled expression. It was left to the natives to exhibit the full spectrum of gesticulations: from the barely perceptible wink or inclination of the head;

through the mid-range broad grin or nod of recognition, to the ultimate full blooded wave and double honk. Though no less heedful of the etiquette of the road, the more laid-back motorists restricted their acknowledgement to a nonchalant raising of the index finger from the steering-wheel, while tractor-borne farmers and joy-riding teenagers were among the most demonstrative. Stern-faced hell-for-leather ton-up merchants were invariably of the single digit variety.

Wednesday, 28th November. A strong character with opinions to match, Dorothy Jennings ruled her 'Dessert House' protectorate – my free and gratis lodgings – with the unwavering conviction of one thrown in at life's deep end. Here was a graduate of the school of hard knocks. Husband or no, here too was a survivor. Over breakfast Dorothy introduced me to my fellow guest – a salesman who travels in socks (don't we all!). I was clearly the first Anglo he'd spoken to in a month of Sundays and he was positively bursting to chew-the-fat over John Major's Tory leadership victory:

"I wonder if he'll find a cabinet post for Maggie?" enthused the hosiery salesman.

Pigs might fly, thought I.

Despite the blenched and outwardly cheerless sun, the bitter chill of a landscape white with rime was right up my street. Physical toil in such conditions was a doddle. Lured by the prospect of fresh discoveries beyond each successive tongue of land, the autumnal beauty of whitewashed creek, cove, sheltered bay and estuary drew me remorselessly onward. Carried away by my hurly-burly pursuit, time was all but suspended. Seemingly immune to the brilliant sunshine now in evidence, the brackish backwaters to the west of Clonakilty Bay remained resolutely ice-bound, while rock-tussocks of bladder-wrack exposed by low-tide were fetchingly adorned with frost-starched tutus.

On arrival at my Kilfinnan Farm digs I was well-and-truly 'mothered' by Anne Mehigan, without doubt the most angelic and softest spoken person it has been my pleasure to meet. While Anne ably catered to the needs of the inner man I was entertained by the boisterous high jinks of the farmer's three children, just home from junior school. And what an engaging trio! Untarnished by crass commercialism and pop culture, TV played no part in their lives – the hill behind the farmhouse blocked the incoming signal. Instead their conversation revolved around books; books as friends – not an imposition. Roald Dahl's recent death was a personal tragedy to each of these kids; they could rattle off the titles of all his brain-child progeny without prompting. Their enthusiasm and humility – they aspired to become postman, priest and nun respectively – spoke volumes. As for the 'Teenage Mutant Ninja Turtles'?

"Who are they?"

All power to the hill!

With the kiddies safely tucked-up in bed Anne reappeared and ushered me to the dining room for a meal of banquet-proportions. Again all home produce. Ann Nicholson would have approved! She put my dramatic weight loss down to insufficient calorie intake.

Thursday, 29th November. Bereft of yesterday's fog, Glandore was a sight to behold. Overlooking a stunning natural harbour – a sapphire in a verdant setting – the pub-cum-grocers Hayes' Bar is the real community centre, as are Irish bars in general. Both Glandore and its twin across the harbour, Unionhall (Bréathtrá), were vaguely reminiscent of Cornish fishing villages; white and pink washes being very much in vogue. Indeed, fish was the abiding all-permeating odour. The colloquial greeting of "Grand Mornin'" came at me from all sides in a variety of accents (English, Dutch, German… even Irish), reflecting Glandore's cosmopolitan make-up.

The terrain and landscape now were undoubtedly changing, becoming ever more rugged by the hour. The erstwhile tranquil pasture-land was increasingly boulder-strewn and gorse-gold; undulations became more acute.

Skibbereen (An Sciobairín), the 'little boat harbour' and sleepy market town, is generally regarded as capital of the Carberies. To my traditionalist eye the chance pairing of Christmas decorations and brilliant sunshine were somewhat incongruous, though no-one, least of all me, was complaining. The streets were unaccountably full of individuals – apparently at a loose end: standing, watching, waiting.

Midway between the harbour-side village of Baltimore (Dún na Séad) with its fine island-dotted vista and my Rathmore billet, I passed considerably more than the time of day with an ex-patriot English woman out 'cycling' her dogs: she aboard a mountain bike tethered to two black Labradors by a taut length of lingerie (black tights?). With the sun rapidly descending in the west, the moon already present to the east, and the bitter cold seizing-up my joints, she barely paused for breath. An expansive lady to say the least, she promptly clammed-up when I commented upon her hacking cough, merely mumbling something about 'more serious than that'. I took it to infer either consumption or lung cancer. Whatever the case, I decided to pray for her. I was certainly giving the old 'absent healing' miracle-mongering a thorough workout.

Friday, 30th November. Past the midway point of Hollyhill, the remote and unspoilt terrain evolved further into a collage of moorland, peat-bog, crag and peak; a Hibernian Exmoor. To the south, beyond the patchwork of emerald fields, Roaringwater Bay stretched off into infinity, blue with the floats of legion mussel farms. From time to time I took to the lanes or 'boreens' which criss-crossed the landscape; little more than glorified farm tracks with a mane of grass sprouting from the crown, they go under the endearing nickname 'dual cabbageways'. As early as 1.30 p.m. we were losing the light.

Perched on a hill-side with gaily painted houses, shops and pubs, and boasting a wealth of resident literary talent, though the visual arts are no less well represented, the village of Ballydehob (Béal an da Chob) provided my first encounter with an Irish mink. Agitatedly patrolling the riverbank opposite the local landmark twelve-arched bridge, its pelt slick from a previous dive, it took a header on sensing my presence and vanished from sight.

Just outside the small town of Skull/Schull (An Scoil – 'School') – take your pick – on the Mizen peninsula, I reported to 'White Castle Cottage' for my overnight stay. Fabricated of Cornish granite and assembled on site, the raking sweeps of the now automated Fastnet Lighthouse, the western turning-point in the biannual Fastnet Yacht Race, penetrated my condensation-misted bathroom window with ease. The ultimate complimentary bath-night light show.

5   Climb every mountain

A sedentary life is the real sin against the Holy Spirit.
Only those thoughts that come by walking have any value.
   Nietzsche

Saturday, 1st December.

RENOWNED for its ultra-mild climate (exotic flowers and shrubs flourish all year round), Schull and its environs well deserve their appellation 'Irish Riviera'. Though little in the way of 'mildness' was evident this morning, as my departure was greeted by a stiff sou'wester. Sheltered from the northerly winds by Mt. Gabriel (1339 ft.), and comprising little more than a single main street of brightly-hued terraced houses, shops and the inevitable bars, Schull commands a beautiful view across the like-named natural harbour.

Beyond Goleen I jettisoned my rucksack and weatherproofs at my Collaros digs and struck-out for Mizen Head (Carn Uí Néid), with a view to completing the 16km/10ml round trip by nightfall. Emerging from the barren hinterland, the coast road followed the reed-fringed course of Barley Cove: an idyllic holiday haven ringed by mountains and flanked by lakes aimlessly plied by shoals of young pollack. With the nearby villages of Crookhaven (An Cruachán) and Goleen, Barley Cove forms part of a delightful triangle collectively called 'God's Pocket'. Here too, thatchers were busy cutting and bundling the medium of their specialised craft. Swaths of khaki reed-stubble bore witness to their urgent industry.

With its 700 ft cliffs affording a seascape spectacular of Atlantic rollers and wheeling gannets, Mizen Head is Ireland's Land's End and the Republic's most southerly point. Across Barley Cove, the neighbouring promontory of Brow Head was barely discernible in the rapidly failing light. It was from here that Marconi transmitted his historic telegraph message to Poldhu in Cornwall.

Back at Collaros I committed the ultimate *faux pas*: I ate the skins of my baked potatoes (the tastiest bit in my book!). According to the lady of the house this Irish taboo harks back to the bad old days of the famine of 1846-7, when only the utterly destitute or desperate consumed their potatoes – if they were fortunate enough to have any – skins-and-all.

Sunday, 2nd December. Departing Collaros – 'Land that juts out into the sea' – just before 9 a.m. I backtracked to Goleen through a mountainous panorama accompanied by a haunting combination of a crowing cock and church bells before heading across country to join the southern shore of Dunmanus Bay. My objective for the day, Kilcrohane, was now directly opposite on the lower slopes of the Sheep's Head peninsula.

Up until now I was fairly sceptical of Ann Nicholson's theory that middle-aged couples in the Republic actually preferred 'bland' new bungalows to traditional homes which 'reek' of Ireland's colonial past. Yet here before me was the irrefutable evidence: superior older properties left to rot while inferior contemporary erections thronged the coastline. Thank goodness that a growing body of discerning youngsters with an aesthetic eye and a healthy disregard for outmoded prejudice are at last waking-up to the DIY potential of these modestly priced desirable dwellings.

On to the Sheep's Head peninsula now, and the sight of herring gulls peppering the coast road with shellfish evoked an illusion of *déjà vu*. Though unlike the gulls of Carmarthen Bay, their Eireann equivalents have a distinctly upmarket palate. Not for them the common-or-garden mussel. Nothing short of tarmac-tenderised sea urchin was good enough for these birds.

East of Ahakista, halfway between Durrus and Kilcrohane, I paid my respects at the memorial 'to all those who died in the air (India) disaster, 1985'; Ahakista being the final landfall the fated aircraft passed over before exploding some 100 miles to seaward. The stone and granite monument, which bears the names of every victim, is sensitively located beside a gently shelving shingle beach; so permitting the grieving relatives the opportunity of total immersion in the limpid waters of Dunmanus Bay in accordance with Hindu custom.

After a day of head-scratching I was still thoroughly nonplussed by the strange hieroglyphic-like chalk markings that adorned the road at regular intervals. But in the dungeon-darkness of backwoods Kilcrohane all would be revealed.

Down wind of the action, a swell of voices came to me on the breeze – the partisan clamour of betting men. Injecting a bit of pace into my stride, I soon caught up with the shifty throng: comprising the players, 'handlers', bookies and spectators of a clandestine game of road bowls. A predominantly Irish pastime thought to have been brought here by the soldiers of William III, my initial visual impression was the shower of sparks thrown-up by the impact of a 28 oz. iron ball as it ricocheted off the metalled road. Launched underarm, windmill-fashion, after a thirty-pace run-up, woe betide the spectator who wanders into its juggernaut flight-path. Where the ball, or 'bullet', leaves the road an impartial adjudicator chalks an interwoven monogram of the respective players initials – the strange 'hieroglyphics' – from where he is obliged to take his next throw. The object of the game is to cover the three mile course in the fewest number of shots. In this fortuitous instance, both the game and myself shared a common objective – Kilcrohane, where the winner was happy to pose for a souvenir snap. And he had every right to be happy – sure wasn't he IR£3,000 the richer!

Monday, 3rd December. Resembling an enormous natural rockery, the landscape of the Sheep's Head peninsula must be a sight to behold when the heather is in full magnificent bloom. It can be no coincidence that the world honey-making champion hails from this nectar-gatherers' paradise.

After a rewarding trek to and from Sheep's Head, I scaled the mountainous spine which ran the length of the peninsula and provided a magnificent aerial view of Dunmanus Bay. At once I found myself descending into an idyllic valley of babbling brooks – the overriding sound – white cottages and burgeoning holly trees, the proliferation of waxen berries far out numbering leaves. It brought to mind the verdant crater of an extinct alpine volcano, and all it lacked was the melodic tinkling of cowbells to convince me that I'd been transported to Switzerland, for cows there were aplenty.

From the rim of my bowl-contoured paradise I gained my first glimpse of the much vaunted Bantry Bay – one of the world's largest and most stunning natural harbours. A diaphanous veil of mist only added to the allure. Likewise enchanting was the entire 28 km/17½ ml run-in to Bantry along the appropriately named Goats' Path: a rambling switchback of amber-pooled bog-lands, mountains far and wide, and the ever-present deep water and sheltering arms of Bantry Bay.

Constricted by steep green hills and bay, Bantry nonetheless manages to carry off its varied roles – market town, tourist centre, fishing port and gateway to Ireland's mountainous south-west – with considerable panache. Having given the town a brisk once-over and impatient for my digs, I buttonholed a laid-back Jack-the-lad.

"I'm looking for 'Shangri-La', mate."

"Aren't we all", he replied sagely, breaking neither stride nor sweat.

Tuesday, 4th December. It was a frosty morning and biting cold, though significantly brighter than of late, as I headed off around Bantry Bay in an anti-clockwise direction. My N71 route wove through an ever increasingly wild and glorious terrain before swooping down upon Glengarriff (An Gleann Garbh). Located at the head of the islet-dotted Glengarriff Bay, the town is a veritable subtropical oasis. Thanks to the Gulf Stream, a protected southern exposure and consequent near-Mediterranean climate, rhododendron and fuchsia flourish year-round beneath the umbrage of giant eucalyptus, palm and oak trees. A town to consign to one's memory.

Wednesday, 5th December. Burden marginally lightened after parcelling-up and dispatching a stockpile of souvenirs, exposed films and used maps, I set out rejuvenated for Allihies by way of Garnish. Soon the jagged vertebrae of the towering Caha Mountains gave way to the equally impressive Slieve Miskish Range.

It was perhaps naive of me to imagine that I could remain impassive to the inspirational, kaleidoscopic input of sights, sounds and acquaintances forever. And now the feedback was flowing thick and fast. Naturally enough there were casualties of my abstraction. Castletown Bearhaven (Baile Chaisleáin Bhéarra), principal town of the peninsula and second largest fishing port in Ireland, was one such example, coming as it did in the midst of a particularly prolific spell of lyric writing. Sheltered by mountains to the north and Bear Island to the south, even I couldn't help but notice the town's multicoloured ranks of laid-up fishing boats, but it was only later that it emerged that this was due to the fact that the vessels in question had already caught their allocated annual EC fish quota and were now impatiently awaiting the coming of the new year. Notable laws unto themselves, however, were the plethora of Russian, Polish and Japanese factory ships who ply these waters regardless of season or EC directive.

The sky above the scattered hamlet of Allihies (Na hAilichi) was shot with red and gold, like the glow of a distant conflagration. Likewise burnished, the surrounding patchwork of fields shelved down to a sea of cadmium yellow, while the three remaining sides of this idyllic enclave were bounded by a stark skeletal silhouette of Slieve Miskish Mountains.

Before turning in for the night, I followed a boreen up to the Old Mine workings. Allihies was once a major copper mining centre, last worked in 1962. Myriad mine-shafts remain, now the unsightly repositories of Allihies' household refuse.

Thursday, 6th December. Fellow guest Rosita Boland was up and showered – cold shower! Spartan lady! – long before I stirred my stumps. Over breakfast Rosita confided that she was hitching around Ireland, still a comparatively safe undertaking here, and fully intended to write a book recounting her exploits. Entitled *Sea Legs* (New Island Books), she promised to give me a good plug therein – a reciprocal arrangement. So impressed was she by the interlude in question, that I gave her my unequivocal blessing to utilise the 'Road Bowling' anecdote. A parting gesture. Nothing rekindles a memory like an odour – or words to that effect. Henceforth the sweetly aromatic fragrance of *Aloe Vera* and Rosita are forever inseparable; the one will always evoke the other.

Leaving Allihies the brooding and rugged scenery was unparalleled. No sign of Rosita – clearly she'd experienced no trouble thumbing a lift. Before long I came to the 'Mass Rock'; a well fashioned stone altar and cross perched high on a heathery rock-strewn mountainside. Having completed the testing climb, I offered up my own solemn prayer – as many a persecuted Catholic had done before me. From the prodigious vantage point of this eucharistic eyrie, one couldn't help but observe that by prohibiting the celebration of Mass the occupying British forces of those bad old colonial days had done the faithful a considerable favour. For what parish church could match the spiritual oneness of receiving the sacrament at this outlawed alfresco altar?

At 3 p.m. I entered the spectacular kingdom of County Kerry. Less than one kilometre brought me to Coolounig on the shore of Ardgroom Harbour. My hostess Mary Lynch hadn't anticipated my arriving quite so early and had only just returned from a clam collecting expedition on the adjacent beach. The shell-colouring of this local delicacy varies according to habitat (gravel, sand, mud, etc.), though local restaurateurs snap them up irrespective of hue as fast as Mary can harvest them.

That evening I received a telephone call and an unexpected change of plan. With a severe weather front anticipated later in the month, my assault on Carrauntoohil (Corran Tuathail), Ireland's highest peak, was brought forward to this coming Sunday. This automatically ruled out my long intended Hags Glen (Coomb Callee) route to the summit, a comparatively easy 'tourist trail' accessible only from the Killarney side of Macgillycuddy's Reeks (Mountains). Instead I was pitted against the daunting, near vertical South face!

Friday, 7th December. Thrusting deep into the Kerry coastline the broad, beautiful and misnamed Kenmare River – beside which I now journeyed – was patently an inlet of the sea. To the north the glassy surface reflected the awesome symmetry of white-capped mountain and coastal scenery of the Inveragh Peninsula: the massif hub of the 'Ring of Kerry'.

Either side of Lauragh (An Laithreach) the road was enveloped by lush vegetation; the luxuriant presence of bamboo and yucca making a nonsense of the dwindling temperature. At noon, beyond the trout-rich Cloonee Loughs, my path was traversed by a primarily nocturnal hunter – a young dog fox in full magnificent winter coat. Whether driven abroad by hunger or the desire for its own territory, its amber eyes paid me scant attention as it maintained its stately passage.

Saturday, 8th December. In spite of the comparative shelter in and around the colourful market town of Kenmare (Neidín), I don't think I've ever felt so cold. Not the superficial 'my tiny hands are frozen' type cold, but a thorough-going intestinal chill. If such was the case at sea level, what sort of temperatures would I encounter during Sunday's big climb when high altitude and wind-chill factor came into play?

North-east of Kenmare the N71 led me to the massive stone portal of Moll's Gap, across a mean and moody bog-land of snow and ice growing deeper and crisper with every stride, the penetrating cold ever more keen. At over 1,000 ft., the road through Moll's Gap – gateway to the Black Valley, Killarney – was a sheet of ice. Here my staff or 'third leg' came into its own, while the icy-blast that howled through the break in the ridge reduced me to a ponderous shuffle.

Gingerly I proceeded onward and downward into the very bowels of the Black Valley, cautiously seeking out the soft powder-snow of the pristine verges for maximum traction. As forewarned, I ran the gauntlet of harebrained competitors of the 'Rally of the Lakes' every step of the way. What with black-ice, drifting snow and loonies tearing up the tarmac, I now knew what it meant to 'walk through the valley of the shadow of death.'

And what a valley! Ringed by the towering snow-capped peaks of the poetically named Macgillycuddy's Reeks and the rugged cliffs near Moll's Gap, home to chough and hooded crow, the valley was unmistakably redolent of a Zen garden, a stylised landscape in miniature: burgeoning holly trees – naturally dwarfed by harsh conditions – with not a branch misplaced; lichen-clad boulders; scaled-down snow-fed rapids and waterfalls provided the audio accompaniment; while the reflective qualities of Upper Lake were indispensable. A truly serene setting. I was immersed in meditation, and totally at one with the world.

As the temperature dropped yet further, I plumped for the soft option of farmhouse B&B. Camping was definitely out; I had no desire to finish-up like Captain Scott and Co. – which in these Antarctic conditions was a distinct possibility. Hillcrest Farm was to be my base camp for the next two nights.

Having gorged a mammoth repast of soup, lamb and veg., apple pie and custard, and an entire pot of tea, 9 p.m. found me swaddled in thermal undies and dorma blankets, my breath vaporising in plumes before me as I addressed a batch of postcards. My teeth were as yet uncleaned – both water tank and mains supply were frozen solid. The wind meanwhile, having steadily picked-up since nightfall, now whined like a soul in torment. My heart went out to the hardy mountain sheep. I knew from bitter experience that such privation focuses the mind like nothing else upon the basic necessities of survival – a warm body and a full belly.

Sunday, 9th December. After waiting in vain for the clouds to recede – which was a bit of a choker after two comparatively cloud-free days – I set out at 10am, liberated of all but essential items of equipment: camera, Pilgrim's Staff, packed-lunch, whistle, compass, torch, etc.

The summit of Carrauntoohil (1039m/3414ft) was only 8 km/5 ml distant but such were the extreme wintry conditions abroad that host Mary Tangney refused point blank to let me go until I produced a written breakdown of my intended route and estimated time of my return – following the expiry of which she was honour bound to call out the rescue services.

Beyond Black Valley's An Óige Youth Hostel, I walked the length of the glaciated Cummeenduff Glen beside Gearhameen River and islet-studded ribbon lakes. Bearing north-west at the foot of Brassel Mountain the 'green road' corkscrewed onward and upward before petering out just past the final outpost of habitation – a semi-derelict hill farm. I was now well into the snow-line with not even a sheep for company; most having long since been driven down from these inhospitable upland pastures. And while the snow grew ever deeper, nudging four feet to the leeward of boulders the size of double-decker buses, the wind steadily rose – as did my temperature. With sleeves already pulled up and weatherproof jacket agape, glacier glasses were the first to go – they kept steaming up – followed by cap and gloves. By the time I drew level with a leaden Curraghmore Lake every inch of exposed flesh was glowing crimson. Allied with the air of Himalayan rarity, I was euphoric.

Before me loomed a wall of black rock and compacted ice, the near perpendicular base of Carrauntoohil, its mountain spire lost to low-lying cloud. Here began the climb proper. Hand over hand, foot over foot; my slip-and-slide progress cried out for a pair of crampons. After two hundred feet or so, and a drop of several degrees, I made the most of my camera before disappearing into the cloud cover. From here on in I was climbing blind. Two hours of intermittent snow flurries, frequent compass readings, and the odd dousing in snow-concealed mountain streams brought me to the summit – clearly marked by a large steel cross. Prior to retracing my steps I prised a few souvenir pebbles from the permafrost underfoot.

If anything the descent was more dangerous than the ascent, and I was lucky to get away with only a barked shin. The sight which greeted my emergence from the cloud-base was as startling as it was unexpected. Gone was the snow-field – no doubt washed away by a sudden cloudburst. In its place a bog of sphagnum moss bejewelled with melt-water pools – some of which were deceptively deep – shelved away to Cummeenduff Glen.

Task accomplished, goal achieved, I returned to Hillcrest Farm beating the 5 p.m. deadline by minutes – much to my own satisfaction and the relief of Mary Tangney.

Monday, 10th December. The anniversary of my arrival in Ireland one month and 1,179 km/737 ml ago. Awoke shivering at 6.30 a.m. to the news that upwards of eight people had frozen to death in England over the weekend, with numerous other individuals still missing across Italy and Spain. Only now am I fully aware of the severity of this Europe-wide cold snap. No wonder Mary Tangney did her utmost to dissuade me from venturing out on Sunday.

With two mountains down and four to go, and as yet not a single summit-view worthy of the name, I was now banking on Ben Nevis next spring to provide a cloud-free unhindered photo-opportunity. Certainly one couldn't question the visual clarity this morning: every jagged-edged pinnacle was there for all to see. Yet why, oh why, couldn't it have been so yesterday? What a difference a day makes!

Tuesday, 11th December. My first full day on the legendary Ring of Kerry – a scenically contrasting byway of lakeland, mountainscape, and coastline. Before heading out for Caherdaniel at the head of the Inveragh peninsula, I interrupted my journey at the lace making centre of Kenmare to dispatch thirty postcards and to purchase a rubber ferrule for my Pilgrim's Staff.

Within the hour the rain returned in torrents, sweeping down from the adjacent red sandstone peaks like a Hibernian Niagara Falls and penetrating my already sodden boots with consummate ease. Water ingress was a perennial catch-22 never resolved: my evening stop-overs afforded insufficient time and opportunity to dry out my boots; but until they were thoroughly dry applying waterproofing wax was an utterly futile exercise.

Beyond the gaily painted cottages of Sneem (An tSnaidhm) I found myself alternately battered by head winds and swamped by rain. Throughout the final few benighted kilometres to Caherdaniel I was spiritually transported to the 'dark flat wilderness' of Dickens' Kent. And while ghostly clouds scudded the night sky and the wizened digits of wind-harried trees reached down... down... I expected at any moment to come face to face with Magwitch!

Within striking distance of my destination, and during a brief lull in the nigh-on continuous downpour, I felt obliged to lift my eyes to the heavens – and was immediately stopped dead in my tracks by a starscape-canopy of indescribable beauty: stars as thick as daisies on a neglected lawn – each effulgent speck individually defined.

Wednesday, 12th December. Suitably fortified with a blow-out breakfast I skirted the foothills of Cahernageeha Mountain, climbing all the way into a stationary bank of sea mist which effectively obscured the wide sweep of Ballinskelligs Bay and the twin promontories of Hog's Head and Bolus Head. If ever I'm asked for my opinion of the spectacular views afforded by the coastal section of the Ring of Kerry, my only conceivable reply can be: "What views?" For what with rain, darkness and now sea-mist, my visual frustration would appear to be pre-ordained.

Lying on a strip of land between Lough Currane and Ballinskelligs Bay, the seaside resort of Waterville (An Coireán), once the favourite holiday haunt of Charlie Chaplin, was my first stop. Other celebrities to frequent the town were George Bernard Shaw and Walt Disney.

As the winter set in and tourists and pedestrians in general were ever more thin on the ground, I was obliged to seek solace in my own company. Yet never once did I feel isolated in any shape or form. On the contrary, in the wise words of the old adage: 'he is never alone that is accompanied by noble thoughts'.

I struck up an instant rapport with my hostess for the night Mary Sigerson: we shared a common passion for London. While she'd lived there for several happy years before returning to Ireland to marry and have children, the fact that her husband was a London Underground worker wasn't the only reason she pined to return to 'the smoke'. Dungeagan, she felt, was too quiet, too limiting, and with insufficient scope for her first love – charity work. In London she ran the Kerry Man's Hostel by day and fed the inhabitants of 'Cardboard City' by night, and she longed to get back into harness. Her absentee husband managed to get home every couple of months, but she would dearly love to up-sticks and join him.

According to Bunyan's *The Pilgrim's Progress* – my current reading matter – the backpack burden so stoically toted by Christian, is said to signify 'the gilt of sin which effort cannot remove'. And there was me thinking I was just carrying a rucksack!

Thursday, 13th December. What a morning! Sea-mist and showers all the way to my destination of Cahersiveen. Though bodily cold at the outset, I soon warmed to the task of scaling the numerous hills that overlook the sea hereabouts. At least I assume that to be the case – for I was singularly unable to see a damned thing for the third successive day. And as for sighting a puffin, my avowed objective, I couldn't even make out the Puffin Island bird sanctuary on which they apparently congregate.

The zigzag ascent to the top of Coomanaspig pass was as steep as the view was unrewarding. And, at 1,000 ft., it is one of the highest places in Ireland accessible by car.

Leaving the obscurity of the summit, I descended blindly to the village of Portmagee, reputedly named after the eighteenth century smuggler, Theobald Magee. Just visible through the murk and obtainable by bridge was the barren sea-girt holiday resort of Valencia Island, the European terminus of the first transatlantic telegraph cable (1866).

Maintaining an eastward tack, I rejoined the Ring of Kerry beyond Aghnagar Bridge. Then, following a lengthy detour to and from Reenard point, took the sweeping N70 to the capital of the Inveragh peninsula, Cahersiveen (Cathair Saidbhín). Not to be missed is the towering ruin of a police barracks, burned to a shell in 1922. Originally designed for the North-West Frontier of India, due to a bureaucratic cock-up it was inexplicably built in Cahersiveen instead!

Friday, 14th December. Sallying forth into a cold, bright and virtually cloudless morning I resumed my journey along the easterly course of the main coast road. Just outside Cahersiveen, on the northern bank of the Carhan River, I visited the humble birthplace of Ireland's liberator, Daniel O'Connell (1775). Now little more than a derelict ruin, for a shrine of national importance it was woefully neglected.

Throughout the day, my route paralleled that of an overgrown cinder track, the origin of which was unmistakably announced by the lofty presence of a redundant railway viaduct north of Kells. According to Ann Nicholson, after gaining full independence in 1923 the powers that be were gripped by a 'get rid of everything British' fever. A prime casualty was the rail system –dismantled on a scale which exceeded even the devastation wrought upon our own rail network by the Beeching Report. Yet now the Irish populace to a person wished that the Republic's founding fathers had retained it.

Descending coast-ward through the thinly wooded Valley of Kells I gained my first awesome vision of a turquoise Dingle Bay and the soaring hills of the distant Dingle Peninsula beyond. Nightfall found me at the small holiday and fishing resort of Glenbeigh (Gleann Beithe) sharing the open-house hospitality and down to earth company of the McCarthy family. As 8 o'clock approached, the streets emptied into our sitting/dining room for this week's instalment of the cult National Lottery TV spectacular *Winning Streak* – prizes upward of IR£250,000. In common with the entire Republic I was hooked and decided there and then to risk a punt or two every week until I departed the Emerald Isle in March.

Saturday, 15th December. Such was the breathtaking view from Glenbeigh – four miles of golden sand, and the mountains of Dingle rising above a startlingly wide Dingle Bay – that it was well worth enduring a teeth-chattering evening beneath a summer-weight duvet for the privilege.

Through a coastal plain of bog-land and enormous sandbars to seaward, I proceeded to the market town of Killorglin (Cill Orglan) situated above the salmon-rich River Laune. My arrival in this former fishing village signified my imminent departure from the Ring of Kerry and the completion of my clockwise circuit of the sometime scenic – weather permitting – Inveragh peninsula. I was swept along on a flood tide of Christmas spirit: street decorations were audibly embellished by a backdrop of pre-recorded carols; hordes of quietly desperate shoppers hustled-and-bustled with seasonal courtesy; Christmas tree sellers barked-out their bargain-basement prices; while pimply hyper-polite youths collected on behalf of 'Concern' (for the third World).

Beyond Castlemaine (Caisleán na Mainge), the departure point for my tour of the Dingle Peninsula, the straight-as-a-die R561 arrowed its way to Boolteens and my evening accommodation. On arrival my company was monopolised by five year old Carleen. While my post-walk cuppa grew steadily colder, my diminutive inquisitor kept-up a non-stop stream of questions. Thoroughly parched, I hit upon a table-turning ploy:

Ask Carleen a question and wet my whistle while she answered.

Author: "Are you in a big class at school, Carleen?"

Carleen: "Oh yes, eight or nine of us."

(Now eyeing my short-shorts – which had 'ridden up' with wear)

"Are you in a big class at school?"

Before turning-in for the night I took a bath in what resembled hot Lucozade. A perfectly natural phenomenon in these parts on account of the water's ultra-high iron content, the soft-drink illusion was soundly kicked into touch by an unsavoury union of rusty-nail flavour and metallic bouquet.

Sunday, 16th December. My introduction to the Dingle Peninsula – a fuchsia-lush sliver of land jutting some 48 km/30 ml into the Atlantic – was everything the Inveragh peninsula was not: dry, if cold, and thus far with crystal clear visibility. At the eighteenth century shipwrecker's haunt of Inch (Inse), that fair-weather friend the sun put in a most welcome if overdue appearance. Location for scenes from *Ryan's Daughter*, the four mile arc gently receded into a gilded sea. From this point forth sand bars gave way to severe fulmar-patrolled cliffs and rocky coves; a duality that re-awakened my passion for cliff-top walking.

The attractive single-street village of Anascaul (Abhaim an Scáil) marked the conclusion of a thoroughly enjoyable day. Secreted between Dingle Bay and mountain peaks, the 'South Pole Tavern' commemorates the exploits of one Tom Crean. Born here in 1877, he was a member of Scott's ill-fated Antarctic Expedition of 1911/12 and discovered the bodies of Scott, Wilson and Bowers who died of exposure on their return journey.

Monday, 17th December. Preoccupied by the reoccurring thought 'will I ever feel warm again?', I set out from Anascaul into the post-dawn gloaming of a mist-thwarted morning. Adopting the meandering course of a third class coast road, south-west of Anascaul I passed the blackened shell of Minard Castle. Once the largest fortress on the peninsula, Cromwell's troops destroyed it in 1650 after a protracted siege.

West of Lispole (Lios póil) I joined the Dingle-bound R559. Skirting Dingle Harbour I kept my eyes peeled – in vain – for 'Fungie' the Dingle Dolphin. Regarded by some as the town's financial saviour, this friendly bottled-nosed dolphin was first spotted in 1984. But if Fungie-mania (merchandising, memorabilia, boat trips, etc.) is the icing on Dingle's cake, fishing remains the bread and butter industry.

Eager to learn the tricks of the trade I picked the brains of a retired fisherman who willingly let me on one or two wrinkles of the lobster/crawfish trade. For example, did you know that hens of the aforesaid species carry their eggs beneath their abdomen like outsize prawns? Or that an EC ruling forbids the landing of such specimens? NO? Well then you certainly wouldn't be aware of how the fisher-folk outmanoeuvre the regulation by removing the incriminating eggs while at sea – only to retain the orange eggmass for their own private delectation. Not a lotta people know that. I, for my sensibilities, wish I wasn't one of them.

Beyond Dingle, reputedly the most westerly town in Europe, I penetrated the 'Shamrock Curtain': an invisible border between the predominantly English speaking east and the Gaeltacht region of Corca Dhuibhneknown. From here to Dunmore Head, mainland Ireland's westernmost point, the coastal plain was dotted with hamlets where Gaelic culture and language still thrive.

But the superb crescent-shaped beach of Ventry Strand was a flawed paradise. Protected to seaward by a range of marram grass-topped sand dunes was the greensward winter quarters of a band of travellers that resembled the rubbish dump of a medium sized town. According to Rosita the Irish are terrible litterbugs. Even in the midst of such visual splendour, household garbage continues to besmirch virtually every beauty spot.

Comprising some 400 'clochans', dry-stone beehive-shaped huts or cells, the Ventry (Ceann Trá) to Slea Head Road boasts perhaps the richest concentration of antiquities in all Ireland. In rounding the wild and beautiful tip of the Dingle peninsula, I briefly encountered Slea Head and Dunquin Village (Dun Chaoin) – both integral locations for *Ryan's Daughter*.

Two kilometres offshore, the Blasket Islands, uninhabited since 1953, breached the Atlantic swell like a pod of monstrous hump-backed leviathans.

With darkness and cold descending in equal measure, I came upon Ballyferriter (Baile An Fheirtéar). Curling seductively at the foot of the 1331 ft. Croaghmarhin Mountain, this pretty half-moon of a village is the spiritual hub of this Irish-speaking enclave.

Tuesday, 18th December. Through a contrasting landscape of Golden Strand and harsh farming country, where ancient dry-stone walls overgrown with turf and briar divide skimpy long-abandoned parcels of land, I gave the elements a run for their money. It is also the traditional home of the 'Currach' – primitive canoe-like boats made of tar-impregnated canvas stretched over a wooden frame. During the course of the day I was fortunate enough to witness both the high-prowed fishing currach (Glashabeg) and the low-browed hybrid racing variety (Dingle Harbour).

After lunch (a Mars Bar!) the weather closed in with a vengeance – saving its cloudburst worst for the outskirts of Dingle. In completing my bat-out-of-Hell round-trip to Dingle – via Smerwick Harbour and Brandon Creek – I was now some 281 km/175 ml short of the magic 3,000 mile mark!

Wednesday, 19th December. Deterred from so doing by yesterday's culminating downpour, I took full advantage of this morning's cool but sunny entrée by avidly devouring the sights and sounds of this Olde Worlde fishing port and tourist centre. Bounded on three sides by majestic hills of green and purple, Dingle's steep streets, handsome buildings and colourful harbour had won me over after just two fleeting visits. Such was the universal sense of well-being engendered by a combination of balmy weather and stunning scenery, that everybody it seemed was in the market for a chinwag.

Ahead of me to the north lay a further five kilometres of steadily ascending gradient; the narrow winding road followed the rim of a vast green bowl before soaring to the 1500 ft. apex of the Connar Pass – the highest mountain pass in Ireland. At the midway point who should step from a passing car but Rosita! Following an emotional reunion, we sailed to the dizzying heights of the Connar Pass bringing each other up to date anecdote-wise as we went.

At the summit we sat upon a stone-hewn parapet and tucked into a snack of tea (black) and sandwiches (Irish blue cheese), courtesy of Rosita. My sole contribution to the proceedings was to record the moment for posterity; a photograph which later adorned the back cover of *Sea Legs*. The northerly prospect was stupendous to say the least; Rosita was visibly staggered. Flanked left and right by breathtaking lake-bejewelled mountains, including Ireland's second highest peak – Brandon Mountain (3127 ft.), a desolate boulder-strewn landscape of subdued autumnal tones cambered gently to a verdant shoreline. And all the better for being a shared experience.

Vacating our Connar pass eyrie the road corkscrewed down past towering cliffs and rock-cluttered hills towards Brandon Bay, where we parted company: Rosita to resume her hitching; I to walk to Stradbally via the waterside village of Cloghane.

Thursday, 20th December. Apart from the occasional dryish interlude, I was rain-lashed and wind-buffeted for the entire day which saw my completion of the Dingle peninsula. If there was little in the way of visual distraction, I had much to occupy my mind having been good-humouredly ticked-off in a Castlegregory (Caisléan Ghriaire) bar: Never refer to the six counties in the north as 'Ulster' – for the present day province comprises only two-thirds of the original nine counties. 'The North' will suffice.

Now a fertile coastal plain opened up before me – the Vale of Tralee. During an all too brief window in the weather I managed to photograph Ireland's only remaining commercially operated windmill at Blennerville, just south of Tralee (Trá Lí). Standing stark-white against a brooding ebony backdrop (easy to see why Don Quixote mistook such structures for giants!), it marked the highlight of a rain-impaired day. Celebrated in *The*

Rose of Tralee, my initial impression of the market town in question was somewhat tarnished by the unwholesome alliance of driving-rain and gull-thronged municipal rubbish tip which preceded Tralee to the south. Though falling well short of Dingle in terms of character buildings (the result of two conflagrations in the seventeenth century), Tralee's dearth of architectural heritage is amply compensated by the International Festival held annually in late August/early September. The high point of this week long binge is the 'Rose of Tralee' beauty contest, which attracts female contestants of Irish origin – no matter how tenuous – from all over the world.

Friday, 21st December. Within minutes of leaving Tralee I was engulfed by a rainstorm – the template for the day ahead; a day which saw me pay a flying visit to the now major port of Fenit (An Fhianait) – birthplace of St. Brendan the Navigator and from where he is said to have set sail for America some 1400 years ago – before trekking northward, taking in Ardfert (Ard Fhearta), once the ecclesiastical capital of Kerry, and Banna, a stone's throw from the Ring-fort where Sir Roger Casement, British diplomat, Irish patriot and revolutionary leader was arrested on Good Friday 1916 for 'aiding the King's enemies'. All of which I saw precious little.

At Ballyheige the rain momentarily left off, permitting me to take my first and last photograph of the day: the bronze statue of a handcuffed Roger Casement (1864-1916) against a suitably sombre sky – a sky which promptly split asunder once again. So much for the resort's claim to enjoy the driest and brightest weather in Kerry!

Blessed with long sandy beaches lapped by the Gulf Stream, Ballyheige is dominated by the shell of a neo-Gothic Castle built for the Crosbie family in 1812. My guest house abode for the evening was somewhat humbler, but infinitely more welcoming.

Later that night the National Lottery was won by a schoolgirl to the tune of IR£266,000. I contented myself with a hot-water bottle and a roof over my head.

Saturday, 22nd December. A sulphurous morning of gales, torrential rain and bitter c-cold, not even this further deterioration in the weather could deflect me from buying a lotto ticket – you've gotta be innit to winnit! – and phoning home to a sickeningly dry and bright Cheshunt!

From Ballyheige I legged it westward beside Ballyheige Bay for the wave-lashed promontory of Kerry Head across a bleak terrain of windswept bog-land. In the auspicious setting of a golden summer's day the mere sight of the two 2,000 year old crumbling, semicircular forts which denote the westernmost point of the headland might inspire noble thoughts; in the present adverse climate it seemed scant reward for such a foot-slog.

Doubling back from Kerry Head, the rugged north Kerry coastline and mouth of the Shannon remained tantalisingly out of view – whether obscured by rain or inaccessibility – for the remainder of the walking day.

Sunday, 23rd December. I didn't think it possible, but if anything the weather was even worse than yesterday. And if gale force winds and freezing rain are deemed moderate by the hardy farming community, just what climatic treats await me in January when the 'bad weather' begins?

I managed to dry-out the vast bulk of my kit apart from boots and rucksack which remained stubbornly saturated despite a night-long grilling on a radiator. Thus began without doubt the wettest single day since the Bude-Clovelly deluge in September. And as I consequently discovered in no uncertain terms: Irish rain reaches the parts that other rain doesn't reach!

With little desire for sightseeing – and even less opportunity – the many unexplored charms of this northern corner of County Kerry remained just that. After six consecutive days of rainfall the River Shannon – at 230 miles, the longest river in the British Isles – had burst its banks in several places. The resulting network of canals and pseudo-paddy fields that fringed the shore was simply flood plain reverting to type; a type which effectively damped my spirit of exploration.

Throughout today's easterly looping route-march every other settlement was Bally-this and Bally-that ('Bally' being the Gaelic prefix for town): Ballyduff (An Baile Dubh), a farming village with a handsome new heritage museum and interpretative centre – albeit closed for the season; Ballybunnion, a popular little seaside resort whose myriad attractions include the only hot seaweed baths in Ireland (June to September); and Ballylongford (Béal Átha Longfoirt), a tiny farmland village within sight of Lislaughtin Friary, an ivy-clad ruin to the north. The weather, meanwhile, was Bally awful throughout.

At Sallowglen Mr and Mrs Walsh welcomed me with open arms – literally. But I had significantly more than the acquisition of a well appointed, centrally heated and hyper-friendly billet to celebrate – in the course of the day I'd completed the first third of the walk!

Monday, 24th December. After an evening ravaged by thunder, lightning and God knows what other apocalyptic delight, I hoped upon hope that the tempest which raged until dawn had seen off the last vestige of rain-cloud for the foreseeable future. Came the morn and my wishes were only partially answered. A sparkling calm-after-the-storm start to the day gave ample reason for optimism – the weather forecast begged to differ.

Once abroad, the aftermath of last night's meteorological blitzkrieg was much in evidence: hail and snow congregated in hedgerow and hollow, while a heavy frost clung on defiantly till noon. Thoroughly rejuvenated by the winter-sun and frost-bite chill I struck out for the Shannonside village of Tarbert (Tairbeart), where I made a bee-line for the post office. Disaster – it was closed! In all the methodical ritual of my pre-walk preparation I'd overlooked the consequence of day and date – Christmas Eve! Having lugged three weighty parcels all the way from Sallowglen for immediate dispatch, I had no option but to retain them until after the holiday.

From Tarbert to Foynes I hugged the southern shore of the reposeful Shannon Estuary. Suspended above my right shoulder, a crescent moon remained visible around the clock. Equally illuminating, several mentions on Kerry Radio had heightened public awareness of the walk and I found myself much in demand by passing motorists: "Good man yourself!"

Shortly after mid-day I crossed the county boundary into Limerick – a landmark which coincided with the inevitable cloudburst.

The village of Foynes (Faing) was once as synonymous with trans-Atlantic air travel as Heathrow is today. In those far off heady days of the late 1930s, lumbering four-engined flying-boats regularly utilised the placid Shannon between Foynes Island and the village as a watery runway. Half a century later several rust-bucket cargo ships rested at anchor where luxurious seaplanes once soared skyward or splashed down.

I was not the only first time visitor to Fynes. In clothes more suited to southern climes, a black ship-hand paced a deserted quay, shoulders hunched against the cold, hands thrust deep in pockets and unresponsive to my seasonal greeting. Christmas can be a most joyous occasion in the company of loved ones, but when you're far from home, the loneliest.

Having anticipated my arrival before nightfall, my hostess Maura Galvin had all but given up on me. And it was with genuine relief that Maura and her dairyman husband Tom – celebrating the imminent dawning of his one day off a year – pushed the boat out and lavished me with every conceivable Christmas fare. Five convivial hours and as many triple brandies later I hit the hay. Anaesthetised to the cold, I sat up in bed updating my journal and plotting tomorrow's route till 2.30am, when the second power-cut of the evening/morning prompted me to call it a day – Christmas Day!

Tuesday, 25th December. My first Christmas away from England, but I couldn't have been better looked after. Homesickness didn't get a look in. Would that the black seaman of yesterday fared as well. As I prepared to take my leave of Killeen House the world outside was a ferment of hail and thrashing branches, as it had been throughout the night – a night in which 80mph gusts had cut a swath of destruction down the length of Ireland's western seaboard, severing overhead power-lines in the process. More of the same filthy conditions were forecast over the next few days.

Ireland's fourth largest conurbation, Limerick City (Luimneach – 'Bare Spot') wasn't at all what I'd expected. Rosita had candidly described it as the 'pits of the earth'. I couldn't agree. Any city where taproom regulars are actively encouraged to sing is okay by me. Certainly our own juke-box orientated alehouses could take a lead from Limerick landlords.

Hastened by the heaviest hailstorm to date, I arrived at my lodgings just after 3 p.m. – slap-bang in the middle of the Queen's speech. Big mistake! For my hostess and her numerous house guests were devout Royalists. As, I'm reliably informed, are many Republicans. For the second night on the trot I ran the full intoxicating gamut of Irish hospitality.

Wednesday, 26th December. Boxing Day or, as it's known in Ireland, St. Stephen's day. God alone knows how I got up this morning – never mix the grape and the grain.

Pre-departure gale warnings to 'remain indoors' went unheeded. The conditions abroad were exhausting and frustrating in equal measure, veering head winds rendering forward momentum a constant uphill struggle. Storm damage was rife: shattered chimney pots, dislodged roof tiles, fallen trees. At least the Great Storm of '87 eased off after a few hours – this beaut had now been on the rampage for two days with no sign of abating. Throughout my northerly sweeping N18 route to Ennis (Inis) I was alternately dive-bombed by jets bound for Shannon airport and pebble-dashed by hail. Some hail showers gathered such momentum on the icy down-draught that drivers were forced to sit it out, while I cowered, extremities stinging, letting my rucksack bear the brunt of the impact.

Crossing into County Clare I witnessed two impressive castles; Cratloe Castle (more a tower house really), once the power base of Clan MacNamara; and Bunratty Castle, Ireland's most complete and authentic fortress.

On entering the village of Clarecastle (Droichead an Chlair), I was singled-out by a motley crew of blacked-up, cross-dressed individuals who said they were 'Wrenboys' and demanded a donation in return for posing for a 'team' photo (a bit like 'trick or treat' with menaces). I mistakenly assumed it to be an obscure charity stunt – and shelled-out accordingly. Only later was I informed by Mr Cahill that the sole object of the exercise, apart from the 'crack' (fun of it), is to finance one almighty booze-up. While I snapped away, the 'Wrenboys' – who in bygone days carried a live wren in a cage – tunelessly warbled the following ditty:

> The wren, the wren, the king of all birds,
> St. Stephen's Day 'twas caught in the furze.
> Up with the kettle, down with the pan,
> Give us a penny to bury the wren!

Worth 70p of anyone's money!

Thursday, 27th December. My route now followed the northern shoreline of the ever-broadening Shannon Estuary, the foul weather showing not the remotest inclination to subside. But while the wind remained a constant hindering factor, each successive cloudburst, hailstorm or snow-flurry was now interspersed with the most beautiful pastel blue sky imaginable. But just where was this inclement weather coming from? According to local consensus, it was well out of character.

On a hill above Killimer village, the northerly terminal of the Co. Clare – Co. Kerry (Tarbert) ferry, stands a bronze monument to nineteenth century 'murder of convenience' victim Ellen Hanley, whose drowning while crossing the Shannon was dramatised as the *Colleen Bawn* (*Shining Girl*) by Irish playwright Dion Boucicault.

Towards the outskirts of the bustling market town of Kilrush (Cill Rois) I popped into a shop for directions and, feeling lucky, purchased a *Winning Streak* scratch card. What do you know – a IR£5 win! Which left me a 'massive' IR£3 ahead in my lottery dealings to date.

Friday, 28th December. Despite the sledge-hammer blow of an IR£82,000 tax bill, guest house proprietors Joe and Bridie Kiely not only waved all payment but also presented me with a substantial donation and enough fruit to open a greengrocers.

I departed the Grove Guest House at 9.30 a.m. – and it promptly bucketed down for my benefit. A word to the wise. It pays to memorise the following Gaelic gender distinctions in order to spare your blushes at the public convenience: *Fir* = Gentlemen; *Mna* = Ladies. I didn't and I wasn't!

At Garraun I plumped for the network of narrow pot-hole pocked lanes which fringe the Loop Head peninsula's southern coastline. Now well off the tourist trail, the general feeling of desolation was further enhanced by a flat and barren hinterland and surf-lashed shore. While tenuously strung between outlying settlements, overhead power/telegraph poles lolled drunkenly at precarious angles. I gave the former a wide berth.

Just east of Kilbaha (Cill Bheathach), a loosely scattered hamlet around a small rock-aproned bay, and my journey's end, all hell broke loose. A rapidly darkening sky preceded a nerve-jarring fusillade of thunder and fork lightning directly overhead. Both stirred and decidedly shaken I journeyed on, only to be assailed by a barrage of hailstones the size and consistency of marbles and the velocity of air-gun pellets, which left me yelping in pain and defiance of the elements.

No sooner had I gained the sanctuary of widower Nora Haugh's tiny sea-front cottage, than Clare FM News were on the phone hoping for an interview: "You sound out of breath?" After seven solid hours battling into gale force head winds and assorted filthy weather I had every right to!

Following my fourth turkey roast in as many days, a good natter and draught or three of Nora's home-made *vin extraordinaire*, I turned in. Fatigue was finally setting in. Even so, it was 1.30 a.m. before I extinguished the bedside lamp – journalistic duties called. But what a bed! Distinctly cambered on all sides, it rose to a central sierra of eiderdown quilt; while the ancient feather mattress, as high as it was broad, had all the inviting qualities of an outsize soufflé. This time-warp illusion was aided and abetted by the welcome addition of a stone hot-water bottle – Philpott's original foot warmer!

Saturday, 29th December. In walking gear still cold and damp from yesterday's exploits, I set out for Kilkee via the treeless promontory of Loop Head, the most westerly point on the peninsula. There was a certain nobility in the headland's grim defiance in the face of a systematic pounding by the combined forces of Atlantic roller and winter-gale. But I was in no humour for photographic mementoes. The icy blast was cutting through my already sodden shell garments with impunity and leaching away my precious body-heat in the process.

All too aware of the potential seriousness of my predicament, I veered north for Kilkee and respite. Wending my way along tide-wracked thoroughfares frequently made impassable by encroaching seas, the oceanward prospect fluctuated between spume-washed strand and dramatic blowhole-riddled cliffs; each towering white-water ejaculation heralded by the distinctive boomed report of wave on rock.

Long before I reached my evening accommodation of 'West Winds' (how appropriate!) I was shivering uncontrollably and walking in a state of trance. On the outskirts of Kilkee (Cill Chaol) the unreality of my situation was made more so when the telephone box from which I was phoning home was totally enveloped by a snow-storm. And though I managed to disguise the anxiety in my voice, there was no doubt that I was in trouble with a capital T.

An evening of cosseting in the accomplished hands of Emily Troy and her teenage daughter failed to snap me out of my lassitude; I almost fell asleep over my meat and three veg. The more I yawned the more I shivered; the more I shivered the more drowsy I became. Emily put it down to a bout of the 'flu'; I put it down to hypothermia.

Sunday, 30th December. Awoke for the umpteenth time at 7.30 a.m. after a fitful night's sleep. And while the storm still raged without, I continued to shiver beneath my winter-weight duvet despite the valiant efforts of the central heating and a combined bed-attire of thermal combinations, woollen mitts, loop-pile walking socks and a fleecy jacket. I rallied a little over breakfast, only to revert to a state of light-headed lethargy on returning to my icebox of a room.

Benefiting greatly from the resistance of a moderate head wind and stiffish climb out of Kilkee – the most 'British' of Irish holiday resorts; complete with marine parade and bandstand – I began to warm-up almost immediately; a welcome rise in body temperature I was able to sustain by keeping-up a daylong hell-for-leather pace and by vigorously attacking every climb. I was well on the road to Spanish Point – and recovery; an enervating and eye-opening byway which marked the renaissance of my appetite for wild seas, salt spray and marram grass-knitted sand dunes beneath darkling skies. All of which I savoured to the full.

Beyond the resort village of Quilty – where cliff-top gardens had already been swallowed-up by the ever hungry sea and adjacent cottages looked set to follow suit – I witnessed a most bizarre game of soccer. Though patently the superior footballing side, the green team (what else?) were continually thwarted in their offensive efforts by the prevailing north-west gale which refused point blank to let them get the ball out of their own half of the field. I've heard of wind-assistance but this was ridiculous!

Monday, 31st December. Though the wind was as keen as ever (typical understatement), at least I had the unexpected advantage of a dry morning. From my digs I proceeded to Spanish Point, the barren headland as opposed to the village of the same name. As the name infers, Spanish Point recalls the events of 1588 when two Armada ships – *San Sebastian* and *San Marcos* – ran aground there. Several hundred crew and soldiers promptly drowned, but they were the lucky ones. The 'survivors' who made it ashore were summarily butchered by locals loyal to the crown. Elizabeth I may have had the body of a weak and feeble woman, but she clearly had no qualms about issuing a 'no survivors' directive. Further up the coast a limestone plaque commemorates the visit of King Juan Carlos and Queen Sophia of Spain in July 1986.

Ten kilometres north-west of Lehinch (An Leacht) – where craft shops and bars with impromptu traditional music abound – the cliffs of Moher rose above the foaming Atlantic to a height of nearly 700 ft. Erected in 1835 as an observation point for 'strangers visiting the magnificent scenery of this neighbourhood', O'Brien's Tower was the focus of a knot of English visitors. In stark contrast to the familiar brogue of the local populace, their precise clipped diction sounded discordantly harsh to my now 'Eireann' attuned ear. Dialects apart, we shared a common awe of the brooding rough-hewn cliffscape which ribboned north and south for a spectacular six miles.

Looming large to seaward, the Aran Islands appeared to have been under daylong siege from a resident rain storm; a leaden-hued weather-front that had now abandoned its offshore abode and was ominously heading this way. In imminent danger of a thorough drenching – the worst I'd endured thus far today was hail – I descended without delay to the Spa town of Lisdoonvarna (Lios Duin Bhearna – 'Fort of the Gap'), arriving well after dark but having successfully outrun the elements. Consisting of one street and nineteen bars, what better location to be billeted on New Year's Eve!

6   A walk on the Wilde side

He knows not his own strength
That hath not met adversity.
   Ben Jonson

Tuesday, 1st January, 1991.

GUSTING wind and pelting rain were already in full swing by the time I vacated my Lisdoonvarna digs. Ahead of me lay a clockwise coastal sweep around the north-west corner of the Burren (Boireann – 'Rocky place'): a 500 square mile lunar landscape of pavement-like limestone slabs crazed with deep fissures ('Grikes') and scattered with boulders. An outwardly inhospitable terrain at the best of times, this morning it was positively forbidding. Ludlow, Cromwell's general, described the Burren as a land 'yielding neither water enough to drown a man, nor a tree to hang him, nor soil enough to bury him'. But for all its grim austerity, it harbours a seasonal treasure-trove of plant life. With some 1,100 species recorded to date, it rates as one of Europe's richest botanic areas.

After six teeth-chattering, wind-tossed hours – it felt more like a life sentence – I came upon the nineteenth century fishing village of Ballyvaghan (Baile Uí Bheacháin). My hostess for the evening, Anne Martin, came to pick me up in her car, an exercise which took considerably longer than anticipated for many of the outlying roads were submerged beneath several feet of water. On the drive back to Leagh South, Co. Galway, I saw for myself the full far-reaching extent of the flooding. And with further precipitation forecast every day for the coming week, folk living in the low-lying coastal districts had better pray for a miracle or invest in a pair of water-wings.

Wednesday, 2nd January. Tom, Annie's builder husband, drove me back along the coast to Ballyvaghan from where, sandwiched between the northern edge of the Burren and Galway Bay, I trekked eastward through a water-logged landscape. Just over the County boundary into Galway – Ireland's second largest county – I paused at the foot of the incline which led to Villa Maria and waved optimistically in the hope that either Anne or Tom might be looking out. Ireland as a whole is one of the most sparsely-populated countries in Europe, and Connaught – of which Galway constitutes but one fifth – is the most sparsely populated province.

Inconvenienced only by the odd heavy shower, usually when a likely photo-opportunity presented itself, I arrived at the Winkles Hotel in the colourful fishing village of Kinvarra (Cinn Mhara) in the late afternoon. Even at this early hour, the bar was unexpectedly chock-a-block with well oiled revellers. Drawing me into the thick of it, proprietors Phil and Tony Moylan plied me with piping soup and draught Murphy's until my room was made ready.

Thursday, 3rd January. East of Kinvarra I stopped to check out Dunguaire Castle – in actuality a majestic sixteenth century Tower House that holds sway over the adjacent Kinvarra Bay – then headed north deviating between the scalloped eastern shoreline of Galway Bay and a rolling landscape of lush pasture criss-crossed with lichen encrusted dry-stone walls.

Either side of a bright interlude at midmorning the weather continued in the same foul vein as the previous four days. Thus I arrived in Galway City, former Norman settlement and mediaeval trading post, in the midst of a thunderous downpour. Yet nothing could dampen the contagious enthusiasm and youthful exuberance of this thriving cathedral and university city, still resplendent in its Christmas decorations.

Friday, 4th January. Just over the Corrib River, beyond Galway's ancient city walls, the tidy suburb of Claddagh is famed far and wide as the origin of the Claddagh Ring: the traditional method by which a girl could alternately announce her availability for marriage or that she was 'spoken for' according to which way up and on which hand it was worn. Made of either silver or gold and readily distinguishable by the unique design of two hands proffering a crowned heart, they are to this day manufactured in the locality and successfully exported throughout the world.

Due west of Claddagh the scenic R336 links a loose chain of Irish-speaking villages that straggle along the northern shore of Galway Bay. The most comely and compact by far, and coincidentally my billet for the night, was Spiddal (An Spidéal). What a picture it must be in the halcyon summer months when boats regularly embark from Spiddal's large working quay for the Aran Islands, and Currach Races take place offshore.

But it was an evening of high anxiety. Hurricane force winds, touching twelve on the Beaufort Scale, were anticipated overnight, a night in which my hosts' two sons had planned to return by ferry to England where they worked. Mrs Barbara Curran would have none of it; sea travel was out of the question. Mr Curran remained philosophical; the 'boys' remained intransigent. In the event a radio announcement just after midnight resolved the issue: all scheduled ferry departures were cancelled until further notice. Barbara could sleep easy.

Saturday, 5th January. For once the Met. Office were as good as their word. By 12.40 a.m. much of Ireland's western seaboard was under the meteorological cosh. And while rippling roof tiles played a jarring arpeggio, the roaring vortex without excluded all hope of slumber. Needless to say when sleep came it was deep and hard earned, and the entire household overslept.

Came the morning and far from having blown over, it now sounded as though a test-bed mounted jet-engine was gunning outside my window. Two power cuts and one breakfast later, Barbara tried to dissuade me from venturing abroad – even volunteering to transport my rucksack to my next port of call if need be. Emboldened by the Met. Office update that it would be all over by 3 p.m., I wouldn't hear of it.

Such was the duration of the walk that it was inevitable that at some time I would encounter the winter. And Ireland, as opposed to Scotland, looked the safest bet for a temperate and trouble free passage. How wrong can one be! While Scotland enjoyed the mildest winter for years, Ireland was experiencing the type of once in a lifetime natural disaster that had all the hallmarks of a national emergency. But the Irish are made of stern stuff. And their general 'mustn't grumble', 'show must go on' outlook was as admirable as it was infectious.

With all the manual dexterity of a down-at-hoof dray-horse pulling a fully laden cart, I plied the R336 through a featureless terrain of untameable bog-land. Suffice it to say, my progress was ponderously slow. Those few trees that had previously defied the elements now lay prostrate, having invariably brought down power-lines in their descent. At the pretty Gaeltacht settlement of Inveran (Indreabhán) dry-stone walls and hastily abandoned lorries rocked like so many cardboard cut-outs, and a whimpering border collie rolled across my path, an animated ball of tumbleweed.

In full view of Ballynahown's lone general store I was blown three times into a rain-filled ditch; three times I battled to regain the tarmac. Extricating myself on the third occasion, sanctuary beckoned. Between ditch and general store I performed an involuntary strip-tease: press-studs popped, zips-fasteners unfastened, jacket billowed, over-trousers inflated and descended. Soaked through and thoroughly frustrated, I burst into the candlelit emporium almost colliding with the shopkeeper who referred to my antics in the ditch with deadpan detachment: "I thought you were picking flowers".

As the weather deteriorated still further the stroke of four o'clock found me on the outskirts of Kinvarra (familiar name, different location) hanging-on for grim death to a metal post at the roadside. For what seemed like an eternity I was slammed first one way then the other with all the self-determination of a windsock in a cyclone. Never before or since have I felt so powerless, so out of control and at the mercy of the compassionless elements. And all the while my eyes clamped shut against the ever marauding hail.

But deliverance was at hand in the fortuitous guise of a motor-car carrying two lads from a local fish-farm and the youngest daughter of Mrs Mary Joyce – my hostess for the evening! What luck! Within half-an-hour I was safely installed in my Turlough digs on the Rosmuck peninsula, be it in the middle of a round-the-clock blackout.

Having weathered the storm, Mary Joyce relieved me of my saturated garb and draped them over the turf-fired range. Following the novelty of a candlelit bath, I spent the evening trading 'hurricane' anecdotes and knocking back hot brandy toddies.

Sunday, 6th January. The lights were still out this morning, but the dazzling brightness which illuminated the day made electricity and candle power redundant. Not so the need for warming winter clothes, and mine were as crisp and dry as toast, if fetchingly salt-caked from the flying spume. While I breakfasted and prepared for the off, the Joyces' embarked for Mass *en bloc* – perhaps to give thanks that they weren't among the fourteen hapless souls who came to grief in yesterday's turmoil.

I cadged a lift back to Kinvarra with a belated churchgoer. What a contrast to Saturday! Today all was peaceful and serene, as if the erstwhile turbulence had denuded the air of all vitality, leaving in its wake a vacuum of inertia. And now that I could actually open my eyes without imminent risk of blinding by a rogue hailstone, I could see the full splendour of my surroundings: the rugged coastline now caressed by a millpond calm sea; the boggy heartland replete with autumnal mantle of russet-brown and beige of bracken and moor grass respectively; and tiny pine-clad islets mirrored in land-locked loughs of vibrant blue. Thus unfolded a day of consolidation, a day of westerly snaking Cois Fharraige and an equally scenic home stretch of minor coast road, punctuated throughout with periodic squally showers. But after yesterday's elemental excesses, even this was a welcome relief. Such is the accommodating, passive nature of the terrain that the only tell-tale indication of the hurricane's passing was a truck which had turned turtle at Flannery Bridge.

With close-on 40 km/25 ml under my belt, I rounded the tip of the Cnoc Mordain peninsula at 4.30 p.m. A host of offshore islands were visible in all directions and to the north the snow-capped Connemara peaks rose dramatically beyond the deep-water Bertraghboy Bay. Within half-hour I made the bay-side village of Glinsk (Glinsce), the still air imbued with the sweet heady scent of turf-fires.

Monday, 7th January. Thought my luck had changed this morning. Awoke to find a winsome wench in my room... In fact she was bringing me breakfast in bed – full English (she Anglo-Irish). A welcome touch of luxury nonetheless. While I tucked-in, the wind moaned in the eaves and waves of hail beat a tattoo on my skylight window.

Fortunately by the time I made my adieus the sky had cleared, leaving behind a bitterly cold head-wind which continued to strengthen throughout the day. In such conditions each photograph and hastily snatched notation was a major achievement. The scenery, meantime, remained much the same as of late – breathtaking – prompting me to elevate coastal Connemara alongside the Black Valley and Schull as my favourite parts of Ireland thus far.

Ahead of me lay a north-westerly loop around the edge of Bertraghboy and Cashel Bays, and to finish a clockwise lap of Roundstone Bog: 10,000 lake-spattered acres of uninhabited blanket bog. And one of the few European outposts where otter still thrive.

Apart from the occasional flurry of sleet I thought I'd got away with a comparatively mild day. No such luck. As darkness and temperature fell with every stride, a mile or so short of my Ballyconnelly quarters the heavens opened – freezing rain! As fortune would have it my hosts were as generous as they were accommodating. And while the electric lights – which contrived to flicker like guttering candles – left a lot to be desired, I wanted for nothing.

Tuesday, 8th January. Over breakfast we discussed the ever deepening crisis in the Middle East. Only seven days now remained for Iraq to withdraw from Kuwait in compliance with the UN ultimatum. The overriding mood was increasingly pessimistic.

I now moved inexorably northward through a progressively etiolated landscape of snow, blenched beaches and thatched whitewashed cottages while, always in view, the Twelve Pins or Bens (Ben being Gaelic for 'Peak'), the mountainous hub of Connemara's 5,000 acre National Park, provided a grand backdrop for the coastal steppe.

However, the distinction 'scenic highlight' of the day fell to the Clifden peninsula. Rising westward out of Clifden town, 'Capital of Connemara', the fittingly named Sky Road soared above the peninsula's southern shore to astonishing heights, providing exhilarating coastal views in the process. But it wasn't all plain sailing. From beginning to end – be it the handiwork of vandals or the wind – I encountered not one road sign pointing in the right direction. Though with the aid of my map and trusty compass I did my damnedest to correctly orientate each and every one. My good deed for the day.

Wednesday, 9th January. The weather forecast was snow and gales, with temperatures falling to minus five. As for Saturday's 'war of the elements', the Irish Met office now confirm that in terms of sheer destructive power it exceeded even Hurricane Charlie of '86, in which eight died in storm related incidents.

Cleggan and its gently rolling environs were still partially masked by drifts of powder snow, though nothing could disguise the fact that it had taken a hell of a pasting. And it wasn't only the stone-built pier that had incurred structural damage. The Letterfrack coast road was closed for emergency repairs – though propitiously not to pedestrians. The reason for its closure was soon evident. Along the narrow causeway between Lough Anillaun and the sea, huge blocks of mangled-masonry, which once constituted the sea wall, now littered the highway; a highway now indistinguishable beneath a crazy-paving of mud and rubble. On the southern approaches the tarmac was pocked with gaping craters, the infill of which now peppered the adjacent field like a bounteous crop of bitumen.

With a growing regard for the all-powerful elements I journeyed eastward to the Quaker-founded village of Letterfrack (Leiter Fraic), from where I veered NE in the lee of the white-capped Tully Mountain (1172 ft.) to the end of the promontory. Here the crumbling remains of the fourteenth century Rinvyle Castle dominate the scene. Once the tower-house stronghold of the O'Flaherty's, it now stands silent sentinel over an extensive sandy beach with views extending to a handful of tiny islands.

Rejoining the N59 at Tullywee Bridge, I resumed an easterly tack, my meandering Lough-side route fringing a trio of well stocked salmon and sea-trout lakes; the property of Kylemore Abbey Fishery. Kylemore Abbey itself, a neo-Gothic castellated pile, rises from the shore of Fannon pool, backed by the densely wooded lower slopes of Doughruagh Mountain (1736 ft.) – a favourite photographic composition with coach parties and ultra-distance walkers alike.

By 4 p.m. I was comfortably installed in the Kylemore Pass Inn Hotel – Irish hospitality at its magnanimous best. All in all it had been a fairly unremarkable walking day by recent standards, marked by sleet and snow showers, perishing cold and little in the way of mental stimulation. News that the polar temperatures were expected to continue for the best part of a week didn't exactly have me jumping for joy. Hearts of oak, that's the spirit!

Thursday, 10th January. As forecast it was another radiant if wickedly cold morning – even the ubiquitous mountain sheep were running about to keep warm! After a sumptuous breakfast I retraced my steps to the white-rendered village of Tully Cross where, five-days after the event, tilers were still busy patching-up the storm-damaged roof of the parish church. From Tully Cross I trekked eastward completing my bi-part circuit of the peninsula by way of the mountain-hemmed Lough Fee. What appeared destined to be another dank and uneventful day suddenly burgeoned with promise. My host had suggested I look-out for the one-time holiday home of Oscar Wilde and his distinguished parents, located on a tongue of land projecting from the Loughs northern shore. Lo and behold! There it was, snuggled amidst the pinery of its demi-island setting – Illaunroe Lodge! Ignoring the crude 'Keep Out' sign I persevered up the overgrown, rhododendron-choked drive, picking my way between puddles and a quagmire of leaf-mould. Long before I achieved my goal, a pair of vociferous guard-dogs betrayed my approach, though the comforting rattle of chains declared the duo to be stoutly tethered. Reassured by this knowledge, I proceeded to the front door of the scarlet-liveried lodge via three stone-hewn steps. Gaining no response from the verdigris-encrusted dolphin knocker, I slipped round to the tradesmen's entrance. Following a couple of raps on the window live-in caretaker Delia McDonell peered round the door. For the next hour I was taken on a grand tour of Illaunroe Lodge's part-refurbished/part-dilapidated interior. Pride of place went to a fresco in the entrance hall reputedly the work of Oscar himself. Though not a covetous man by nature, here was one property I would dearly love to renovate and occupy – unlike its absentee Irish landlady.

But the day was far from over. Bombarded every stride of the way by either rain, hail or snow I trudged northward to Killary Harbour, Ireland's only true fiord. My spirits instantly soared! From the raised southern bank I espied my first wild otter. Totally oblivious to my presence, it blithely alternated between duck-diving and consuming its prey while floating on its back in a manner reminiscent of the sea otters of California. Despite being wet through and chilled to the marrow, I watched transfixed for many a rain-spattered minute, unable to tear myself away. But sanity prevailed, and with the west wind at my back I flew along the harbourside N59 to Leenaun (An Lionán), where I mounted the slope to the guest house/home of the Hoult family. Immediately divested of all sopping garments I was shepherded before a roaring turf-fire for coffee, biscuits and a cosy chat. And with the promise of a hot soak in the tub and a slap-up meal yet to come, this was the icing on the proverbial cake. Truly the perfect end to a well-nigh perfect day.

Friday, 11th January. Apart from one mercifully brief deluge I was privileged to see Killary Harbour at its mussel-rafted, salmon-caged best. Steeply banked on the northern Co. Mayo side by the Mweelrea Mountains and Ben Gorm, and by the russet-sloped Maumturk Mountains on the southern Co. Galway side, the winding deep-water anchorage was now bathed in the most glorious winter sunshine.

Retaining the shore-hugging coast road, within the hour I rounded the head of the capacious inlet, where Killary Harbour meets the inflowing Erriff River, crossing into Co. Mayo in the process. From this extreme landward point the Atlantic Ocean was some nine miles due west.

In the ample shadow of Ben Gorm (2303 ft.) I traced the northern shoreline of Killary Harbour as far as Bundorragha, where I turned inland for Cregganbaun via the Dhulough Pass: a glaciated U-shaped valley bounded by the snow-dusted Mweelrea Mountains and the great phalanx of the Sheefry Hills.

Just short of the pass proper, the secluded settlement of Delphi is well worthy of mention. It was built in the 1830s as a fishing lodge for the second Marquess of Sligo, Lord Byron's travelling companion in Greece, and remains to this day a visual delight of wooded dell, lough and mountain stream.

From Cregganbaun I wheeled south-westerly around the copper-glow foothills of the ever-present Mweelrea Mountains, regaining a panoramic sea-view shortly thereafter. Having caught the flack of a spate of late afternoon showers, I claimed a grisly souvenir from the roadside herbage: a sheep vertebra. Between Killadoon and my evening objective of Thallabaun, four kilometres to the south, I must have passed ten decomposing carcasses. Apparently in extreme weather conditions sheep invariably seek the shelter of ditch or culvert, where they are frequently snowed under. Come the thaw and all is pungently and gruesomely revealed.

My co-host Mr Morrison met me at the top of the lane which led to the family homestead, 'Bayside': Hemmed by serrated uplands and dune-lined shore, its muted pastoral setting appeared utterly tranquil. But appearances were deceiving. Only last week the Morrison's had lost IR£3,000 worth of fencing to the 'hurricane', and two prize bullocks to storm-severed overhead power-lines.

Thus concluded the twenty-fifth consecutive day of precipitation of one form or another. And to think I griped about a mere thirteen wet days on the trot in Welsh Wales. Didn't know I was born!

Saturday, 12th January. In the knowledge that my walking day was comparatively short by my own standards, after a leisurely breakfast I strolled round Silver Strand Bay with a view to paying a call on singer, TV celebrity and MS sufferer, Maisie Tilsley. The morning was glaringly bright and the light dusting of frost lent a deliciously astringent nip to the air.

"Wipe the shit off your boots!" invited the waggish ex-private secretary of Woodrow 'Woody' Wyatt. A sense of humour was an essential defence-mechanism of this erudite and indisputably ladylike lady; a racy wit that had seen her through many a trial and tribulation.

"Ah, John, my lucky name. Good things always happen to me when I meet a John." And if anybody deserves a stroke of good fortune, it's Maisie Tilsley.

Inspired by Maisie's selfless and courageous example, my spirits soared along with my body temperature. In my rapture the fast receding snow-flecked Mweelrea Mountains were colossal inverted cream horns, complete with icing sugar dusting. Thanks to the sea-level flatness of the archaeologically-rich coastal pasture stretching from Killadoon to my evening stop-over of Louisburgh (Cluain Cearbán), the stark, soaring pinnacle of Croagh Patrick (2510 ft.) dominated the skyline to the east throughout the latter part of the day. Surmounted by the alabaster Temple Patrick, it put me in mind of the blanched nipple of a mammoth ivory mammary.

Having pinpointed the whereabouts of my Louisburgh accommodation I made an off the record excursion to the ruins of the medieval Kilgeever church, two kilometres to the east. Renowned for its association with St. Patrick and as a devotional station for pilgrims *en route* to Croagh Patrick, my motives were of a more corporeal nature. From the adjacent well of Tobar Ri an Domhnaigh (The well of the King of Sunday) I filled three small bottles. A proven curative for all manner of ailments, they would soon be winging their way homeward, along with a figurine of Knock Water, courtesy of Martha Morrison of 'Bay Side'.

Back at my hotel I was all set to follow the example of the Welsh-born saint by fasting until after tomorrow's planned barefoot assault upon Croagh Patrick – only to succumb to a fireside feast, all home produce, compliments of the establishment. I didn't want to appear ungrateful after all.

Sunday, 13th January. After what was officially designated the coldest night of the winter so far, it was a blustery, frozen-puddle, hard frost morning that greeted me – unlike the windless, climbing-conducive day I'd hoped for.

From the car park of the Croagh Patrick pub – a short distance from the greystone ruin of Murrisk Abbey, which is once said to have housed Fiacail Padhraic (St. Patrick's tooth) and Clog Dubh (The Black Bell of St. Patrick) – the massive conical peak of Ireland's holy mountain loomed majestically before me, and upon which St. Patrick reputedly spent forty days and forty nights of Lent in AD441. Indelibly etched by the feet of some 60,000 pilgrims annually, the broad path was visually discernible virtually all the way to the summit despite a blanket of snow beyond the halfway mark.

Sans boots and socks, judiciously secreted 'neath a bush near the car park, I began my abortive ascent. Even before I reached the snow-belt I realised the error of my ways. In a bid to insulate my feet against the bitter chill, I took the pre-climb precaution of spraying them with Deep Heat. This served only to accentuate the grinding agony of it all by ensuring they retained an acute sensitivity long after the numbing cold would have rendered them devoid of sensation. Under the millstone weight of my rucksack every excruciating step was tantamount to walking on broken glass, burning coals... the ultimate penance.

But it wasn't my feet that beat me in the end. That dubious distinction goes to the north wind. The sheltered lower slopes gave no indication of the icy-blast aloft. But after ninety minutes gruelling progress, and with Temple Patrick so tantalisingly near, I found myself hopelessly pinioned upon the mountain's exposed eastern shoulder, stomach-uppermost in a good foot of snow. An ungainly posture but a necessary one. Any other stance and the wind probed beneath me, manhandling me bodily towards the edge of the mighty south-facing precipice. It was from this lofty vantage-ground that St. Patrick rang Clog Dubh, inducing a lemming-like suicidal tendency in Ireland's reptilian species, all of whom – apart from the Natterjack Toad – leapt to their deaths. The low-lying peat-land vista of this isolated corner of Co. Mayo was all very impressive, but I had no desire to go the way of the snake. In order to further gauge the strength of the wind I tossed a couple of fist-sized rocks into the air – and watched with abject disbelief as they sailed out over the yawning drop like crumpled crisp packets. That confirmed it. Withdrawing to the north face I trained my camera upon the spacious Clew Bay, an agrarian archipelago of a hundred or more soft-hued islets, a fleet of 'drowned drumlins', stretching northward to the cloud-draped Nephin Beg Range. Thus a mountain scaled by the elderly and infirm in fine weather had defeated me in foul. But I was far from downhearted. The ecstasy of the view alone was ample compensation for the discomfort of the climb.

Having added a cow's horn to my macabre souvenir collection, I literally blew into a deserted Westport (Cathair na Mart) – a consummate example of late eighteenth century town-planning. From the front doorway of my 'Anglers Rest' lodgings a distant white-capped Croagh Patrick appeared serenely becalmed – a cruelly deceptive image.

Monday, 14th January. The ruddy-cheeked proprietor of 'Anglers Rest', whose general well-being prospered no end from a bottle of 'Tobar Ri an Domhnaigh' water, sped the parting guest with a traditional Irish *bon voyage*:

> May the road rise up to meet you,
> May the wind be always at your back,
> May the sun shine warm upon your face,
> The rains fall soft upon your fields,
> And until we meet again,
> May God hold you in the palm of his hand.

Beyond Newport (Baile Uí Fhiacháin), the seventeenth century town, angling centre, and former home of Princess Grace of Monaco, I swung westward along the northern shore of Newport/Clew Bay, overlooked by the imposing Nephin Beg Range. In its sheltered corner of Clew Bay the straggling seaside village of Mulrany commanded a splendid view of an extensive sandy beach, Mulrany Strand. Looking southward from my digs, the distinctive cone-shaped prominence of Croagh Patrick played a taunting game of peek-a-boo from behind a candy floss cloud-bank. Landlady and farmer's wife Sheila Moran was endowed with considerable culinary skills and was not adverse to lavishing her *piéce de résistance* with all manner of exotic herbs and spices – unusual in Ireland, a land where unsophisticated but filling meals are generally preferred to 'fancy' foreign fare. And in such epicurean circumstances, where better to spend two nights?

After supper Sheila presented me with a parcel. At last my replacement boots had caught-up with me. Which was just as well – for I'd been walking on my uppers for two days!

Tuesday, 15th January. Having left behind all nonessential baggage, before setting out on my round trip of the Corraun peninsula I back-peddled a few yards to Mulrany PO where I sent off a parcel: down-at-heel boots, rancid souvenirs, etc. (woe betide the inquisitive customs officer!).

Jerked from my initial torpor by the saline rush of negative ions and the invigorating 'edge' of a crisp nor'wester, today's anticyclone gave no cause for complaint. So why, on such a God given morning as this, was everyone bar none so fatalistically obsessed with the prospect of war? Even the young girls of Mulrany Junior School on the outskirts of the village – and who thought I was French (makes a change!) – were morbidly anticipating an all-out conflict. Though they, by virtue of their tender years, knew no better. Not so Mr Moran, who favoured annihilating Saddam Hussein's Iraq now before he had time to develop 'The Bomb'. So much for exhausting diplomatic avenues!

For the first time in weeks I required neither map nor compass. Not even I could get lost on what was virtually the peninsula's only road. At some 32 km/20 ml in circumference – excluding excursions – the appropriately named Atlantic Drive lapped the elliptical headland providing a wealth of spectacular coastal scenery, while the tri-eminent mountainscape to landward, in soaring above heather-swathed foothills and patchwork fields, added a welcome sense of the dramatic.

Long after the diesel-chug of workmen repairing the storm-devastated pier of Mulrany Strand had been lost to the mew of wheeling gulls, I came upon the Co. Mayo Armada Memorial. Though not much to look at, it bore mute testament to the loss of the *San Nicholas Prodaneli*, one of twenty-two Spanish ships which foundered primarily upon Ireland's treacherous west coast.

Between Belfarsad and Tonregee I diverged from my intended route. Achill Island, Ireland's largest offshore island and also its most inspiring, was only a comparatively short bridge crossing away. Although islands weren't strictly within my walking parameter (with some 942 off mainland Britain alone, they were far too numerous), the mere act of setting foot upon Achill, even for the precious few minutes I permitted myself, was a tremendous morale booster.

For the final half-mile, which brought me full circle to Mulrany, I was escorted by two young lads toting toy Armalite rifles (how symbolic!). The chatter was all war! War! And though both were certainly better informed of world events than I was at a similar age, their knowledge apparently didn't extend to the ability to tie their own shoelaces. There must be a moral in there somewhere! "Hello Father", chorused the boys to the approaching black-garbed churchman, who enquired of me: "Are you walking for peace?"

All but in name, father, all but in name.

Wednesday, 16th January. Apart from the odd watery episode – such as the storm-shattered salmon cages which lined the shore of Bellacragher Bay, reduced to matchwood by the triple impact of wind, wave and rock – today's northerly trek to Bangor saw the erstwhile rugged terrain give way to a bleak treeless-tundra, with temperatures to match its Siberian Steppe appearance; an endless bog-land vista which stretched out on either side of the windswept byway.

Irrationally motivated to secure an outward sign that peace would prevail in the Middle East, I carried out a daylong hunt for a symbolic white feather – which until this point in time were plentiful. Instead, with due irony, I found only a model balsa-wood Spitfire perched atop a solitary, wind-stunted bush in the middle of nowhere. A definite ill omen. From that moment forth I had no doubt that conflict was imminent. The storm clouds were gathering in more ways than one...

Just south of Bangor (Baingear) the already desolate landscape was further laid waste by mechanised turf (peat) extraction; a horizon-wide wilderness of dark, velvety plain watched over by a solitary canary-yellow behemoth, a caterpillar-tracked turf cutter.

Unable to have my usual midweek flutter on the lottery – the Bangor-Dublin computer link had been down since the hurricane – I plotted a course for my evening billet where, after doing ample justice to a succulent sirloin steak, I joined the Cosgrove family for the recorded highlights of Spurs latest match, only to find it axed from the TV schedules at the eleventh hour – US Airforce high-level bombers and RAF Tornadoes had begun bombarding Baghdad! Operation Desert Storm was underway, the liberation of Kuwait was at hand! And there we remained, morbidly mesmerised until the wee hours. The portent of the Spitfire all too luridly realised!

Thursday, 17th January. Gulf War Update: no reports thus far of any casualties incurred by the Allied Forces, but rumours abound that several air force personnel have been taken prisoner.

Teeming rain and fresh winds were the order of the day as I legged it south-westerly from Bangor beside the serpentine estuary of Tullagham Bay. The barren and grimly threatening terrain was much the same as of yesterday – unusually flat, though the moorland monotony was alleviated in part by the odd striped plantation, rhododendron windbreak and isolated farmstead. This area is known collectively as Erris, and is one of the largest tracts of blanket bog in Ireland.

Beyond the small seaside village of Gweesalia, where the rectangular peninsula juts out into Blacksod Bay, the moisture-laden Atlantic atmosphere blotted out the potentially awe inspiring seascape, a visual impediment which dogged me all the way to the scattered settlement of Tullaghanbaun, at the peninsula's southern flank. Despite arrangements to the contrary 'Achill View' was locked and barred, my prospective hosts being nowhere to be seen. With only a boisterous canine to keep me company, I hung about for a full half-hour before making tracks for the neighbouring community of Doohooma (Dumha Thuama) where I discovered that the 'Achill View' household had inexplicably decamped for a midwinter break, leaving yours truly up the well-known creek without a paddle.

Gweesalia postmaster Michael Henry, who was in the process of date-stamping my witness book, suggested I try my luck at the village's only hotel, Óstán Synge (after the author), rather than backtrack to Bangor. A providential suggestion. Thus, instead of re-crossing the desolate Erris bogscape, by 7 p.m. I was getting to grips with an exquisite three-course meal served by the porcelain-complexioned Margaret – whose Gaelic forename defied both spelling and pronunciation. Over coffee she brought me up to date with the latest happenings in the Gulf: the US had suffered the first Allied casualty – a pilot – while the crew of an RAF Tornado on a low-level bombing mission were now officially designated as missing.

Friday, 18th January. The foul weather bore all the muscle-flexing hallmarks of a full-blown Atlantic gale: Tullagham Bay was whipped into a crosscurrent-cappuccino of frothy coffee, diluted to taste by a periodic deluge and fanned cool by the hotel's wildly flailing topiary. It was during a brief lull in the downpour, if not the wind, that I made a bolt for Belmullet.

Not for the first time the occupant of a Garda patrol car took pity on the hapless wanderer and offered me a lift – but by this time Belmullet (Beal an Mhuirthead) was within sight. The largest conurbation in Erris and the gateway to the Mullet peninsula, Belmullet is situated at the narrowest part of the isthmus between Blacksod Bay and Broad Haven. The biggish Christmas tree which sprawled across the town square where it had lain since the climatic shenanigans of a fortnight ago, seemed to epitomise the apathy of a town that had patently seen better days. An apathy which certainly wasn't shared by my hostess Eileen Gaughan, who is regarded as a positive saint in local circles for her unflagging charity work.

Towards evening Maureen, a reflexologist friend of Eileen, dropped in and immediately remarked upon my 'radiant aura', apparently indicative of a latent ability to heal. She proceeded to predict – quite rightly – that I'm prone to headaches of the frontal lobe region. Which begs the question, why can't I heal myself?

Saturday, 19th January. What began as a most promising day of blue skies and placid waters soon reverted to the now familiar pattern of wind and rain. Though significantly less bleak than the Erris bog-land of late, today's southerly trek down the ragged farmstead-dotted tongue of land that is the Mullet Peninsula remained a total nonentity until I happened upon Aghleam and the time-warp general store of Mary Maughan. All I required was a Mars Bar 'fix', but what I got was a good half-hour's verbal travelogue of all that's best on 'The Mullet'. Having illuminated my day, Mary set me on the road to Fallmore, my evening's abode, and St. Dervila's Well ('Tobar Dairbhile'), whose water is said to be most efficacious in the curing of eye disorders. As an endearing parting shot she recounted the symptoms which prompted her own recourse to the Holy Waters of 'Tobar Dairbhile':

"Oi saw everyt'ing two. Everyt'ing two."

From Aghleam I proceeded to the southern tip of the peninsula around the scenic Fallmore Drive, which laps the headland between Termon Hill and the wind-blown shore. After filling a small lemonade bottle at the blue and white shrine which marks the foreshore site of St. Dervila's Well, I made for the neighbouring farmstead of Bridie and Harry Keane; a delightful, easygoing couple who bent over backwards to settle me in and to make my stay a memorable one.

Sunday, 20th January. During breakfast we three listened to a local radio request programme; a quaintly comforting broadcasting of fond familiar melodies and songs, followed by a brief bulletin of 'Death Notices' – which in this far-flung, sparsely-populated corner of Ireland, is often the only way of hearing about the demise of a friend or acquaintance along with when and where to pay one's last respects. For my part I was still intrigued by the constant wind which whipped across this exposed headland. Even now the shrill fluctuations from without were tantamount to residing beside Brands Hatch on race day.

While the Keanes readied themselves for eleven o'clock Mass, I struck out due east for Blacksod Point which, with its rows of mangled lobster-pots and abandoned hulks, was certainly the worse for wear after the recent bout of storms. Some things never change. It was on this very spot in 1588 that one of the larger Armada ships, *La Rata Encoronada*, ran aground and was torched by her crew.

For once I circled a promontory in a counter-clockwise 'widdershins' direction, returning to a deserted Aghleam by early afternoon. For all its rugged grandeur, the wave-gnarled coastline of The Mullet boasted some remarkably fine sandy beaches. And on my return leg north, none grabbed my attention more so than the dune-rimmed inlet of Elly Bay.

Gulf War Update: A third RAF Tornado has gone missing. Israel has agreed not to retaliate, despite the provocation of a second night of attacks from Iraqi SCUD missiles. Allied aircraft, meanwhile, are destroying Saddam's missile sites and mobile launchers as fast as is humanly possible.

Monday, 21st January. Vacating the R313 at Barnatra, I swung up-country around the bulging headland beside the outer reaches of Broad Haven and Sruwaddacon Bay. In between offering up a prayer at each and every shrine and grotto, a vow I was determined to keep at all costs, I grabbed the opportunity to chin-wag with a string of likewise conversation-hungry old characters who appeared to have all the time in the world at their disposal. One in particular, a bicycle-riding shepherd who collared me west of Dooncarton megalithic tomb (un-signposted), wasted no time in lambasting Saddam Hussein ("The Bast'ad") for threatening to use POWs as a 'human shield'.

After a bracing and overcast day afoot, I crossed the welcoming threshold of the Seaview bar-cum-guest-house, Pollatomish village, by late afternoon. While I downed a 'Hot Irish' (whiskey – with an 'E', lemon, cloves, brown sugar and boiling water) a regular joined me at the bar. Why didn't I send my nearest and dearest some poteen? Not only could he introduce me to a 'reputable retailer', but he could let me in on the best way to bamboozle the "pe'ple of the Customs and Excoise" – disguise it as a bottle of Holy Water!

Gulf War Update: It has now come to light that one unfortunate US pilot who ejected over Baghdad was murdered by a mob before Iraqi troops could intervene. Meantime, a group of British pilots were paraded live on Iraqi television; all of whom had been beaten black and blue while in custody. So much for the sanctity of the Geneva Convention.

Tuesday, 22nd January. While doing the rounds of Sruwaddacon Bay and the beautiful pine-fringed estuary of River Glenamoy I reflected upon my crusty 'attitude problem' at the beginning of the walk. At that unenlightened time I recall becoming insufferably indignant at the slightest setback or spell of adverse weather, taking it as a personal affront. Now, six months into the enterprise, I've begun to 'mellow out', take the rough with the smooth, and above all to accept all meteorological excesses for what they truly are: natural phenomena.

But this was one day that my 'laid back' frame of mind would not be put to the test. Cold, dry and with barely sufficient sea breeze to ruffle my sun-bleached thatch, I was in my element.

Only since growing a beard have I attained facial symmetry. This conclusion I arrived at while catching a fleeting glimpse of my hirsute visage in the window of Mary Monaghan's post office, Ross Port. Here was a lady with whom I shared a deep affinity. In common with my own current fund-raising efforts, all but a single square foot of Mary's counter space was likewise devoted: collection boxes abounded in all manner of shape, size and colour, each vying for the well-intentioned copper or conscience-salving bank note, and with such diverse recipients as a donkey sanctuary and a local hospice.

Following an amusing twenty-minute natter, I beat a retreat from this cul-de-sac village at the northern confluence of Sruwaddacon Bay and Broad Haven, veering north-westerly to the Irish speaking hamlet of Stonefield. Along with Carrowteige and Kilgalligan, the neighbouring settlements to the east and west respectively, Stonefield looked to be in a thoroughly depressed state – an observation freely corroborated by Mrs C. who met me at the gate of my vacant bungalow lodgings and who confirmed that official unemployment figures for the region topped 80% while, unofficially of course, the black economy was booming. One direct outcome was the abundance of unregistered and unauthorised B&B accommodation.

With two days paperwork to catch-up on, I retired soon after dark – I'd done my share of carousing the previous night. And, besides which, I was quite looking forward to the herbal fragrance and flickering shadow-play of the turf fire in my bedroom – all well and good when the down draught wasn't blowing the smoke back into my room!

Wednesday, 23rd January. The novelty had worn somewhat thin by morning. As if the all pervading damp-chill and uniform dusting of turf ash weren't bad enough, it's a sad state of affairs when one is loth to lay down one's tooth brush for fear of catching something. And as for the towel pointed out to me on arrival, and which I'd used in good faith, in the cold light of day it looked like a cross between an engineer's oily rag and a black and white minstrel's face-cloth. Needless to say I made do with a lick-and-a-promise, and put the whole grimy episode down to experience.

A 'wonderful wilderness' would best describe the rugged tract of brownish-green bog and upland moor stretching from Stonefield to my secluded evening stop-over of Carrowmore (one of two settlements so named in the Ballycastle area), some 48 km/30 ml to the east. With the initial drizzle growing conspicuously heavier all the while, beyond the lobster fishing centre of Porturlin the coast road petered out, giving way in turn to *boreen* (green road) and mountain pass track; the steeper the gradient the closer each resembled a mini-cataract in spate. Among the many pre-Christian archaeological discoveries unearthed (or to be more precise 'un-turfed') in the area in recent times, the New Stone Age community of 'Céide Fields' (pronounced 'Kay-Jeh'), midway between Belderg and Ballycastle, is one of the oldest and most exciting in Western Europe, dating back to 3,000BC.

In spite of the thoroughly miserable conditions, the kittiwake-graced cliffs of Benaderreen were a photographic must. Once the subject of wholesale slaughter in order to supply feathers for the hats of fashion-conscious Victorian ladies, since it was given legal protection the kittiwake has flourished and can rightly be called one of the few ornithological success stories of this century.

Remaining virtually daylight until 5.30 p.m., darkness fell with power-cut abruptness shortly thereafter without so much as a semblance of twilight or gloaming. In the ensuing Hibernian nocturne the street lights of Ballycastle swam in haloes of carbon monoxide from a row of driverless vehicles ticking-over outside the grocers-cum-papershop. It was lottery night and no punter worth his salt would risk missing the 8 p.m. deadline.

Flitting from fluorescent pool to fluorescent pool I headed out of town past the funereal-gloom of Ballycastle cemetery for my hilltop eyrie of Carrowmore. Not for the first time nor the last I was staying on a farm: the proprietor – for reasons you will promptly discover – shall remain nameless, though not unappreciated. Having gorged myself on the umpteenth steak of the last fortnight, Mr O. broke out a flask of that illegal fire-water – poteen. Generous measures all round. According to Mrs O. this was the 'genuine article', the 'Real McCoy'. But for all its authenticity it did absolutely nothing for me – apart from reducing the roof of my mouth to a tatter of shredded flesh!

Thursday, 24th January. Having ascended to my temporary domicile of Carrowmore in the depths of darkness, I was ill prepared for the peerless panorama that radiated before me this morning: a range of thrusting hills lorded it over a gently cambering coastal pampas of variegated greenery and Atlantic washed shores. I couldn't wait to get at it.

Descending towards Bunatrahir Bay, I turned northward for the blowhole-pitted promontory of Downpatrick Head – according to legend, the site of a no-holds-barred showdown between St. Patrick and Old Nick himself – before pounding ever eastward through the maze of dog-leg lanes which skirt Lackan and Rathfran Bays. Amidst the mystical ambience of an ancient stone circle to the north of the burnt-out shell of Summerhill House I took a well earned breather. Such was the sublime duality of bird song and gambling lambs, their catkin tails all aquiver, that one could actually believe that spring was upon us.

Beyond Palmerstown Bridge I exchanged the R314 for a dead-end coast road which meandered its way to the head of a sandy inlet and the waterside hamlet of Ross. As I approached my digs for the night, I was inexplicably overcome with melancholy. But my spirits were soon restored by my hosts Peter and Mary O'Hara. As has been the norm of late, with only the odd exception, my arrival prompted scenes reminiscent of the return of the prodigal son – with roast chicken substituting for the fatted calf.

Lullabied by a chorus of barking foxes, it was 2.30 a.m. before I finally hit the sack. A satisfying end to a satisfying day.

Friday, 25th January. It was a crisp morning with sunshine galore and despite a modicum of sleep-deprivation, I felt on top of the world. For the initial north-south leg of today's straightforward circuit of Killala Bay and the Moy Estuary I followed in the footsteps of General Humbert, whose 1,100 French troops began their ill-fated attempt to overthrow English rule just north of Ross, at Kilcummin Strand, in 1798. Having disembarked from three French men-o'-war, first to fall to the Gallic invaders was the unassuming coastal town of Killala (Cill Ala), possessor of a fine limestone round tower dating from the twelfth century. Next in line for 'liberation', some fourteen kilometres to the south, was Ballina

(Béal an Átha), the second largest town in Connaught. To this day the road to the north of Ballina is known as Bothnar na sop (the 'Road of Straw'), for it was along this thoroughfare that sympathetic locals lit straw to guide the advancing Franco-Irish forces.

Dominating the verdant shoreline between Killala and Ballina the comparatively complete ruins of Moyne Abbey and Rosserk Friary bear witness to the wanton destruction of Elizabeth I's over-zealous Governor of Connaught, Sir Richard Bingham.

Beyond Ballina the paths of General Humbert and I diverged: I to hug the coast northward to the dapper little holiday resort of Inishcrone (Inis Crabhann) on the eastern shore of Killala Bay; General Humbert and his troops to march southward towards an ignominious surrender.

Gulf War Update: Allied troops have retaken a small island off the Kuwaiti mainland. In summary retaliation Saddam Hussein has released millions of gallons of crude oil into the Persian Gulf and has threatened to set it alight. Even in its un-ignited state, it represents an ecological disaster of catastrophic proportion.

Saturday, 26th January. The weather throughout today's north-easterly tramp around the massif nub of the Slieve Gamph or Ox Mountains continued in the same idyllic spring-like vein as its predecessor. And with its stunning Atlantic horizon and three unblemished miles of golden sand Inishcrone shamelessly contributed to this dog day illusion. But the town's major draw and principal claim to fame is Kilcullen's Bath House where, for a modest fee, one can luxuriate in a piping hot bath of seaweed-enriched sea water. Highly recommended for the treatment of the symptoms of rheumatic and arthritic disorders.

Twelve kilometres down the road I gained my first view of Sligo Bay glinting invitingly in the winter sun. I noticed also a subtle, almost indefinable change in the light. Changing too was the prevailing local dialect which now bore a striking resemblance to a diluted Ulster brogue. An accent, I'm assured, that would grow ever broader the farther north I travelled.

And so to Ardnaglass, my evening quarters between Skreen and the coast, a settlement of such minuscule dimension that it wasn't even shown on my map, save the copperplate abbreviation which denoted the presence of a derelict castle. That night I had my biggest lottery win to date. Only two numbers short of the jackpot, I should clear IR£30 minimum. (hope the money doesn't go to my head!).

Sunday, 27th January. Today's walk revolved entirely around the sun-dappled reaches of Ballysadare Bay. The increased afforestation along this predominantly low-lying stretch of coastline was a welcome development from the treeless tundra of late, lending the landscape an intimacy not experienced since the Gulf Stream days of West Cork.

At Balladrihid, midway point on the day, I veered north-westerly towards the monopolising presence of Knocknarea, the 'Hill of Kings' (described by Yeats as a 'cairn-heaped grassy hill'). The summit is indeed surmounted by a huge passage grave and cairn, that is thought to be the tomb of Queen Maeve of Connaught ('Queen Mab' of English folk tales). On closer examination, from the worm's-eye-view of the tidy bay-side settlement of Culleenduff, the near sheer scree slopes were precariously grazed by steely-nerved sheep. Sooner they than I.

Rounding the headland by late afternoon, I called it a day at the seaside village of Strandhill, a popular holiday resort with an eighteen hole golf course and a vast sloping beach of compacted sand.

Gulf War Update: From my *Sunday World* newspaper I gather that at least 45,000 US troops and 500 British troops (including several SAS personnel) in the Gulf are either Irish or of Irish descent. Food for thought.

Monday, 28th January. Eight short kilometres due east of Strandhill was the county town of Sligo, and the first opportunity to redeem my lottery winnings. Forever linked with the hyper-talented Yeats family (Sligo Art Gallery contains works by John and Jack Butler, father and brother respectively of the more illustrious William Butler), the association is further cemented by the numerous retailers which bear the family surname, including pubs, a sandwich bar and a coffee shop (whose motto is 'Poetry is food'). As for Sligo's positive wealth of eighteenth and nineteenth century buildings, W. B. Yeats described them as having 'a kind of dignity in their utilitarianism'.

Beyond Sligo I adopted the windswept R291, swinging north-westerly to the headland resort of Rosses Point. Crossing over to the peninsula's northern shore I hoofed it eastward, before terminating the day's exertions at Rathcormack and my digs for the night. That evening I taped my most recent batch of songs and carried out timely repairs on my worse-for-wear shorts – which I'd worn continuously since day one.

Tuesday, 29th January. Could this current Arctic reverse simply be the death throws of winter? I do hope so. For I've been terribly stiff and rickety of late. And not only is my sprained ankle getting no better but my metabolism, like the slumbering landscape, appears to be in a state of recess during these dormant winter months.

Pulling out of Rathcormack for Drumcliff the traveller cannot fail to be impressed by the sheer limestone plateau of Benbulbin. Rising from the greensward terrain like the verdigris encrusted hull of a capsized ocean liner, it holds sway over this entire coastal strip. Ten minutes up the road, 'under bare Ben Bulbin's head', I paused to pay homage at the final resting place of W. B. Yeats, whose grandfather had been rector here at St. Columba Church of Ireland (Protestant), Drumcliff, from 1811 to 1846. Coincidentally, I missed the anniversary of the writer's death (28-1-39) by just twenty-four hours – which perhaps explained why the grave was so spick-and-span (an island of marble chippings in an ocean of weeds!). Yet for all the tomb's solid dependency, there exists a school of thought that casts doubt as to the identity of the remains therein. Could it conceivably be that after his death near Roquebrune in the south of France the wrong body was later (1948) re-interred here in Sligo? Certain French scholars believe so. Perhaps the powers that be should hedge their bets and take a tip from a recent acquaintance of mine who advocated letting the grave run to weed in order to give it that 'lived-in look'.

Two kilometres west of Drumcliff, overlooking the wide expanse of Drumcliff Bay, Carney Post Office was quaint even by Irish standards. Doubling as a living room, its fittings comprised a tiny desk-cum-counter and a three-piece suite arranged around a glowing turf fire. The elderly proprietors were highly supportive of my cause, having lost a much-cherished daughter to MS some five years ago. I made a tactful withdrawal, mindful only of having reopened old wounds...

Doused by the first rain in five days, I plodded out to the foreland village of Ballyconnell before swerving up-country, flanked by Benbulbin and Sligo's untamed northern coast, towards my evening abode. In such atrocious, wintry conditions – the air temperature had taken a nose-dive – I was glad to get a roof over my head.

Wednesday, 30th January. Like most folk in the region, my hostess buys her petrol in 'The North'. Indeed, the frontier crossing at Belleek is less than forty minutes drive away. Many locals purchase their Christmas drinks there too, such are the bargain-basement prices, but officially non-residents must remain in the 'province' forty-eight hours thereafter.

Beyond Grange (An Ghrainseach) the unmistakable signs of spring abounded, belying the ongoing cold-snap. Drifts of primroses littered the hedge-banks – a full month ahead of schedule. While, heralded by a short triple bark, a glint of red-brown drew my eye to a pair of foxes embroiled in a heated game of follow-my-leader – vixen beating a retreat, dog-fox in hot, lusty pursuit. Mating season is upon us!

Ten kilometres north of Grange, on the southern approaches to the fishing village and holiday resort of Mullaghmore, the century-old Classie Bawn Castle holds centre stage. This was the summer home of Earl Mountbatten of Burma until his assassination in 1979 when his fishing boat was blown up just offshore in Donegal Bay. I didn't need to look far in order to gauge the strength of Republican feeling hereabouts. The approach road (R297) to the village was daubed with a pro-IRA slogan ('BLESSED ARE THOSE THAT HUNGER TO DEATH'), which served only to remind me how close I was to 'Bandit Country'.

Things were happening thick and fast now; county gave way to county. 2.30 p.m.: Goodbye Co. Sligo, hello Co. Leitrim. 3.00 p.m.: Goodbye Co. Leitrim, hello Co. Donegal. It was hard to keep track of my whereabouts. It was also sad to leave Sligo. Sligonians are a happy breed on the whole and prone to welcome one with open arms. At Tullaghan (An Tulachán), the only village on the two mile stretch of Leitrim which borders the sea, I phoned home from a sweat-box of a telephone kiosk, dazzled by the sun's deceptive arc light intensity.

Retaining a north-easterly tack, next in line was Bundoran (Bun Dobhrain), Donegal. Resembling a down-market Hastings, it nonetheless featured one or two choice examples of late Victorian and Edwardian elegance – none more so than 'The Great Northern Hotel' – while the adjacent sandy beach of Tullan Strand is claimed to be the cleanest in Europe. Game, set and match Bundoran.

Thursday, 31st January. Like many a housemaid or 'tweeny' of old, I woke up to a frost-bound Ballyshannon in an equally frost-bound attic. The sun was still glaringly in evidence, but it was the friendliness of the town's citizens that I warmed to – that and scaling the succession of gently rounded hills which hampered my northerly passage. The first of which led me past the town's imposing clock tower and the grave of Ballyshannon's most famous son, poet William Allingham, whose best known poem *The Fairies* reflects the local belief in 'the wee folk'.

This was my first full day in Donegal, the most northerly county in the Republic of Ireland, and one of the nine counties of the ancient province of Ulster – with dialects to match. A couple of kilometres out of town on the Rossnowlagh Road, beyond the partially renovated remains of Assaroe Abbey, my path was crossed by the gliding flight of a peregrine falcon. An unremarkable event in itself perhaps. But elevated in significance by the fact that this was the first bird of prey I'd seen – as far as I could recall – since arriving in Ireland!

Beyond the tiny resort town of Rossnowlogh, the 'Forked Headland', the twenty kilometre tramp to Donegal Town encompassed all that is best in the wild and rugged Donegal landscape: rocky hills, wooded glens, secluded strands of golden sand, and reed-fringed lakes (part frozen).

Despite being laid-low with a bout of the blues earlier on (Seasonal Affective Disorder? Homesickness?), I finished the day in the best frame of mind for some weeks. And Donegal Town, whose Gaelic-Irish name – Dún na nGall – means 'fort of the foreigners', played a prominent part in my dramatically improved humour. Sited at the confluence of the River Eske and Donegal Bay, it boasts perhaps the finest centre-piece of any town in Ireland – the Old Market 'diamond' (actually a triangle, but let's not be pernickety). Surrounded by three and four storey shops, hotels and ultra-dignified houses all built of the local mellow sandstone, the Old Market and the town as a whole reminded me of St. David's in Wales.

Noticed my stomach in the mirror of my 'Castle View House' lodgings. Never been flatter, nay concave. Can't still be losing weight, surely! At 9.30 p.m. my reverie and Donegal's fragile silence was shattered by a fair impression of an air-raid siren – shades of Baghdad – followed by a cacophony of flirtatious feminine shrieks which continued into the wee small hours. A lively town, Donegal.

Gulf War Update: Allied troops have retaken a small Saudi town that was overrun by Iraqi ground forces the previous evening.

7   Londonderry air

One travels more usefully when alone, because he reflects more.
Thomas Jefferson

Friday, 1st February.

NOSOONER had I embarked upon the westward leg of Donegal Bay's ragged northern shore than the snow set in; a maelstrom of cottonball flakes that blemished the tarmac like gull droppings. But for all the Siberian chill, sticky-buds burgeoned from every hedgerow. Four kilometres into the walk I quit the N56, adopting instead a web of minor roads and trackways for a rudimentary loop around the Doorin Point headland before rejoining the N56 at Inver (Inbhear). A further 8km brought me to the village of Dunkineely, a popular fishing centre north-east of St. John's Point.

Off-loading rucksack and other non-essentials at my billet, I set off on a kilometreage-boosting round-trip of the promontory's landward end: outward, along Inver Bay to Ballyederlan; across country to Riggy Keugh; and homeward to Dunkineely, beside a mussel-floated McSwyne's Bay and Castle Murray (recently sold).

Saturday, 2nd February. Proceeding westward at a fair lick, I fled the N56 and the buffeting attentions of a fleet of inconsiderate Killybegs-bound fish lorries at Milltown.

The big-league fishing port of Killybegs is a town with a personal hygiene problem. Even from two miles upwind (no doubt even when impaired by a stinking cold!) the town's distinctive fishy niff is all but tangible; an all pervading pong which emanates from upwards of ten fish processing factories which congregate around a colourful and noisy gull-thronged quayside. Amidst scenes reminiscent of Hitchcock's *The Birds*, I watched the trawler *Western Endeavour* disgorge ton after bloody ton of mackerel. My thoughts returned to that momentous day in Fowey, Cornwall. Could these fish be part of that self-same mammoth shoal?

Beyond the tight-knit community of Killybegs the scenery changed dramatically: harbour frontage gave way to the rust-coloured hues of bracken-clad cliffs and indigo sea; Victorian terrace gave way to pockets of stone-built thatched cottages (many with keys in the front doors!).

Between Fintragh Bay and my evening abode of Kilcar the big-dipper of a coast road, with its mountainous backdrops, provided me with my stiffest physical challenge for some time. A challenge to which I rose with relish. These exertions sent my body temperature soaring. Another couple of degrees and I'd have shed my shell-garments – a couple of degrees which lamentably didn't materialise.

Despite the recent closure of Kilcar's largest tweed factory-shop – with a resulting loss of fifty jobs – smiles far outnumber frowns. But none of the village's beaming souls had a broader more winning smile that the angelic Caroline, the infant daughter of mine host Teresa Molloy. Shirley Temple, eat your heart out!

Sunday, 3rd February. What a breakfast! Spent in the enthralling company of Caroline. Never again will I be able to watch 'Tom & Jerry' without subconsciously hearing her exultant cries of: "Tigger Wabbit! Tigger Wabbit!"

Less cheery was the weather; blustery wind, bitter cold and relentless driving rain – the deadly triumvirate! (to walkers and sheep alike). Beyond the craggy coastline and mountainous views of the initial Kilcar to Carrick section, I bisected the lough-dotted headland. Continuing westward through a spectacular if inundated terrain of mountains and blanket bog I made for the small beach resort of Malin More, outflanking the mighty Slieve League cliffs in the process. I kept my spirits up by singing (though *Singing in the Rain* was strictly taboo), stopping occasionally to urinate (in these temperatures, tantamount to finding a needle in a haystack) and generally acknowledging the acknowledgements of sporadic startled motorists (either going to or coming from Mass).

From Malin More I followed the rain-swept coast road north-easterly beside a spume-furrowed Glen Bay to Glencolumbkille – location of the BBC TV serial *Murder In Eden* – whereupon I paid the penalty for ignoring my intuition. Two kilometres previous at Doonalt I had had a vivid premonition that the nameless white-rendered dwelling perched high above the ferment of Glen Bay was my evening accommodation – a suspicion confirmed by the only pedestrian I saw all day. I vowed henceforth to abide by my instincts.

Monday, 4th February. Talk about a room with a view! Bereft of the cloud cover and sheeting rain of yesterday, my first floor picture window presents a panoramic outlook of big-screen, Technicolor proportions. Even in recline Glen Bay hogged the lime-light, its world-weary white-horses effortlessly clearing the shoal at the mouth of the bay before collapsing listlessly upon a gilded tract of sand.

In retracing my steps to Glencolumbkille I had a good look around the picturesque if deserted Gleann Cholm Folk Park. This faithfully reproduced huddle of cottages, a school and a lime-kiln gives a vivid insight into eighteenth century rural life.

Beyond Glencolumbkille I held my course, proceeding to the head of a funnel-shaped valley – the 'Glen of St. Colmcille' (like the village, deriving its name from the sixth century Saint Columba of Iona). From the crest of the valley the serpentine byway undulated in a general north-easterly direction through a near empty landscape of bog, lough and occasional rocky outcrop; the entire terrain richly draped in a mantle of browns, greens and ochres.

Mirroring the meandering course of the Owenteskiny river, from the snow-bound upper slopes of Glengesh the breathtaking glacial valley plummeted through the tree line to the very doorstep of my evening destination of Ardara.

Ardara is the handmade knitwear and hand-woven tweed capital of Ireland, a distinction confirmed by just one look at the twin main streets of this pretty village, which comprise no less than nine knitwear and tweed shops.

Tuesday, 5th February. Today signals the anniversary of the walk's beginning six eventful months and well in excess of 6,700 kilometres ago. A milestone marked by another perishing day in which the bulk of the scenic splendour was obscured by mist.

Beyond Ardara the further north I travelled the dialects became broader, the landscape more wild and wonderful; a painted landscape which reflected the subdued tones of traditional Donegal tweed – from where the natural dyes were originally obtained (local herbs, lichen, etc.).

Skirting the southern shore of Kiltooris Lough, my eye was taken by a wavering skein of brent-geese flying in to roost. Later, in cutting across the lakeland rockery of Dunmore Head to Portnoo, I walked part of the way with a laconic shotgun-toting wildfowler.

Q: "What do you shoot?" A: "Anything."

Brent-geese beware!

Gulf War Update (Day 21): 110 Iraqi planes have fled the battle zone for the sanctuary of Iran. Ground War still to begin in earnest.

Wednesday, 6th February. On the evidence of today's showing West Donegal has to be the most rugged and thinly populated area I've visited to date. And a veritable paradise for walkers and anglers for all that.

East of the wave-sculpted rock formations of Crohy Head, the blue sky and white sand of Maghery belied the sub-zero temperature. Lining the upper shore of this compact fishing hamlet, ranks of purpose built trestles were piled high with the freeze-dried stalks of sea kelp, all destined for the Meenmore iodine extraction plant.

Accompanied by the florid hues of a rosy-fingered sunset, I completed the remaining seven kilometres to Dunglow by early evening. Not only is Dunglow (silent 'g') the capital of the region known as 'The Rosses', but it is also the heartland of the largest Gaelic speaking population of any Irish county.

Thursday, 7th February. From Dunglow I set out on a scenic tour of the 'The Rosses' (or 'Na Rosa' in Irish, which means 'The Headlands') along a coastal corridor which snaked its way northward between a barren and rocky shoreline and lough-studded hinterland of reddish coloured peat bog. To seaward, Aran Island was just half-an-hour's 'chug' away by ferry from Burtonport. This being a staunch Irish-speaking enclave, the English translations were noticeably omitted from the erstwhile bilingual road direction signs. Towards the latter half of the day crude pro-IRA graffiti became increasingly commonplace, their daubed slogans defacing roads and prominent roadside boulders alike – though many were partially erased by diplomatic-minded authorities. Such was the dwindling temperature throughout that Lough Meela and the salt-water inlet of Inishfree Bay were frozen solid – much to the befuddlement of countless immature, first-winter, herring gulls.

Newsflash: For the first time on mainland Britain mortar bombs were today remotely fired by members of a London-based IRA active service unit. The target: Downing Street. Fortunately, nobody was hurt.

Friday, 8th February. It was snowing steadily, great fluttering flakes the size, colour, and aerodynamic quality of swarming cabbage white butterflies; each delicate arrangement of ice-crystals destined to augment the ever deepening pristine carpet. Over breakfast cautious radio pundits advised wary citizens to remain within. On the assumption that fortune favours the bold, I hit the open road…

From Bunbeg, possessor of possibly the smallest working harbour in Europe, I shaped a northerly course for Bloody Foreland. Here the snow had all but vanished, revealing a wind-parched tundra boisterously gleaned by mixed-flocks of buntings and finches, with yellow-hammers in the ascendancy. What a muted contrast to the fiery evening skies which lend this rocky cape a vivid blood red hue, from which it derives its forename.

Eight miles due north of Bloody Foreland lies the bleak and treeless Tory Island – from the Irish 'Toraigh', meaning 'outlaw'. The name 'Tory' was originally adopted by those who opposed the accession of James II (1679-80), and later by the forerunner of the present day Conservative Party.

Following a stimulating loop around the multi-branched inlet of Ballyness Bay, I arrived at the welcoming Gortahork home of Padraig and Úna Nic Giolla Chearr ("Please call me Agnes"). An enthusiastic hiker in her own right, Agnes was keen to accompany me for at least part of tomorrow's walk to Carrickart – but was obliged to attend the 'one-month-Mass' of her late mother-in-law beforehand. While I earned my keep by drying-up and Nikwaxing the walking boots of mother and daughter, Agnes rang round her hiking colleagues in order to drum-up some company for me during the morning stint. But the weather had other ideas.

Saturday, 9th February. From first light – as the less hardy conscripts developed cold feet at the sight of the still deepening blanket of snow – the telephoned cancellations came in thick and fast, eventually leaving just Agnes, who would catch me up at Falcarragh, and her good friend Barbara McLaughlin, whose home I would pass *en route*.

The 'cry offs' didn't know what they were missing. Stepping into a winter-wonderland of consummate walking conditions – the air! the glare! the brittle crunch of boot on snow! – it was all I could do to hold myself in check. For hold myself I would need to do if I wasn't to overshoot the rendezvous, which, in the event was timed to perfection by all parties. For the next thirteen kilometres we three tramped eastward in delicious isolation, at one with our snowbound surroundings. Apart from one or two notable ornithological observations and general 'good-to-be-alive' comments, our conversation touched upon many and varied topics – none more ill-founded than the incredulity of media-manipulated German tourists who simply cannot believe that English 'visitors' are still welcomed in the Irish Republic with open arms: "But zure-ly zey are your en-em-y peo-ples!"

The small resort village of Dunfanaghy, sublimely situated on a picturesque inlet of Sheephaven Bay, marked the parting of the ways. The companionship of Agnes and Barbara had been much appreciated and a welcome change to the usual solitary slog.

Ahead of me lay a twenty-two kilometre yomp around the broad tranquil reaches of Sheephaven Bay, its unpolluted waters apronned by dunes of gold and green. And at every turn, the prodigious backdrop of Muckish or 'Pig' Mountain, so called for its resemblance to a reclining porker. Fourteen kilometres later the sun was setting fast, gilding the saltwater inlet which separated me from the massive keep of Doe Castle.

It was long after dark when I attained my goal for the day, 'Hill House', Carrickart. A gem of a billet – if only the entire Doherty family weren't smitten with filthy colds. Respiratory diseases apart, the Doherty's children Brenda and Sean were role models for young people the world over: courteous, inquisitive, outgoing – and with that heart-melting habit of referring to their mother as 'Mammy'.

Sunday, 10th February. Further overnight snow-fall having enhanced the winterscape, I departed 'Hill House' in a buoyant mood. West of Carrickart I crossed the sheep-grazed isthmus which lies between Mulroy and Sheephaven Bay; a flatland of golf links and pasture that was this morning the domain of exuberantly cavorting young rabbits, for whom the novelty of snow had yet to wear off. It was also the gateway to the spellbinding Rosguill Peninsula.

Bounded by the seven mile switchback of Atlantic Drive, the views from the Rosguill Peninsula are reputedly the best in Donegal – to which I wholeheartedly attest. Ocean vistas, secluded beaches, lofty promontories, it has the lot!

On completing a memorable circuit I returned to the Victorian 'estate' village of Carrickart, before trekking south-westerly along the partially afforested shore of Mulroy Bay to the mountain-hemmed village of Milford. In the wake of a bout of early evening showers, the forest plantation which flanked the home stretch gave off a musty odour redolent of second-hand book shops. Forty kilometres (twenty-five miles) had passed in a trice.

Monday, 11th February. With an anticipated two million IR£ riding on Wednesday's draw, I made a point of purchasing my penultimate lottery ticket before heading out of Milford for the austere beauty of the Fanad Peninsula.

For the umpteenth consecutive day the now infamous left ankle was playing-up merry hell. Rather than jeopardise the outcome of the entire venture I decided early on to curtail my immediate schedule. Thus emerged my revised itinerary: north to Ballyhiernan Bay beside the crenellated sea loughs of Mulroy Bay and Broadwater; across country to Doagh Beg, bypassing Fanad Head in the process; then south along the shore of Lough Swilly to the seaside resort of Portsalon and the sandy phalanx of Ballymastocker Bay; from there my destination lay inland at Ballynashannagh, where my accommodation had been arranged at Swilly View Farmhouse. And, at a distance of thirty-five kilometres on the day, no mean feat in the circumstances.

Tuesday, 12th February. My hostess, Margaret Borland, despatched me with a complimentary packed lunch and a word of comfort for Mary (*author's mother*): "A crown awaits you!"

South of Bunnaton I passed through the final Gaeltacht area of my journey. The importance of these state subsidised regions cannot be undervalued. For as their loquacious inhabitants will readily tell you: "A people without a language is a people without a heart." And the Gaeltachtai have heart aplenty.

At the small fortified town of Rathmullen, mid-point on the day, I nipped into the sea-front post office on a whim to buy a 'winning streak' scratch card (my 'Mystic Meg' stars for the week advised me to look out for a lady in green who would bring me luck). Sure enough Postmistress Angela Crerand was sporting an emerald green blouse – and I came away IR£10 the richer!

Well pleased with my nouveau affluence, my get-up-and-go – absent of late – returned with a jolt. Nothing stimulates like financial gain! A further ten kilometres through a waterlogged coastal strip, 'Road liable to flooding' warned the sign, fetched me up at the plantation town of Rathmelton, which spans the gorge-like estuary of the River Leannan. 'Plantation', in this instance, refers to the seventeenth century colonisation by English and Scottish Protestants. On the directions of the jovial manager of a quayside butchers shop, I left Rathmelton via The Tank, a near vertical hill due south of the river

True to its Gaelic place-name origin, my digs for the night, 'Ards' (meaning: high or height), was on the crest of a hill. Half-way up it the rain clouds parted dramatically and I was compelled to witness the dying rays of the setting sun. It was an emotional experience – I genuinely mourned the sun's temporary passing. After what felt like months of rain and funereal darkness, I saw the life-giving orb, the 'Eye of Heaven' in a new appreciative light. I was at one with those Inca sun worshippers of yore…

Wednesday, 13th February. With visibility at a premium, descending The Tank presented its own unique problems, not least the precarious blend of black ice and stationary vehicles. Turning right at the quayside my route paralleled the winding course of the Leannan Estuary before linking-up with the still waters of Lough Swilly at Shellbrook. Thanks to the fog-induced myopia my view was largely restricted to the odd rime-hung hedgerow and darkly skeletal tree. And apart from the ivy-covered ruins of Killydonnell Friary (Franciscan suppressed in 1603), my southerly shore-side ramble was as featureless as the terrain.

Only on the very threshold of my scheduled stopover, Letterkenny, Donegal's liveliest town, did things begin to look up. Media coverage of the walk had been fairly extensive of late and thanks to my new found celebrity status I was developing a pronounced swollen-head. Enter one tow-headed whippersnapper who gave me a scathing once over: "Are you in a circus?"

Result: One inflated ego well and truly deflated!

'Swilly View' (*deja vu?*) was at the top of Kilmacrennan Road, an arterial thoroughfare double-parked with gypsy wagons, wrecked cars and associated piles of scrap metal. At the nudged instruction of their Faganesque father, two didicoy youths approached me separately for money, their sob stories honed by frequent telling. Pleading poverty, I drew their attention to my collection box – which cooled their ardour in a flash. Local residents have been campaigning to get the travellers moved-on for five years; five years of verbal intimidation and creeping eyesore against which the Garda appear powerless to act.

'Swilly View' MKII post-dated its Fanad peninsula namesake by the best part of a century, but in terms of welcoming atmosphere the two were on a level par. Soft spoken hosts Salina and John O'Hagan informed me soon after my arrival that Letterkenny's premier eatery was standing me a meal. 'Skippers Restaurant' had everything going for it: great ambience, great food – and with the additional ingredient of canned 60s music (Capital Gold with nosh!).

Thursday, 14th February. The pelting rain which marked my egress from 'Swilly View' continued throughout the day, eight and a half hours and 50 km/31¼ ml without discernible respite. Declining the gracious offer of a second breakfast at 'Skippers', I slipped out of Letterkenny before the roadside scrap-metal dealers were up and about.

Due east of Letterkenny I picked-up the 'Inishowen 100': a scenic 100 mile coastal tour of the wild and often formidable Inishowen (Owen's Head) peninsula; the vast bulk of which I would be covering over the next few days. Though visibility was again impaired by the vagaries of the weather, one couldn't overlook the sudden simultaneous emergence of innumerable clumps of snowdrops, their drooping, green-flecked alabaster blooms fair igniting the darkling hedge-banks like embers of cold fire.

For the final half-hour I ran the gauntlet of the busy R238 in Stygian gloom, by which time the complete ineptitude of my 'weatherproofs' and the increasing weight of my rain sodden backpack had between them resurrected the excruciating ache in my left shoulder. I finished the day with my Gore-Tex gloves tucked beneath the offending shoulder strap – effectively reducing the pain but exposing my hands to the freezing elements.

And so to Buncrana on the eastern edge of Lough Swilly, principal town of Inishowen and one of the biggest tourist draws on the peninsula. Though on a rain-lashed February evening its appeal totally eluded me, a disenchantment soon remedied by the homespun hospitality of Mary McEleny of 'Kincora', my ministering angel.

Friday, 15th February. Even before I left the northern outskirts of Buncrana, having stopped on the way to buy my final lottery ticket before crossing the border on Monday, the drizzle-laden fog had saturated my outer garments. While visibility was down to a scenery-obliterating twenty-yards. Thanks to this 'atmospheric moisture', part weather, part mood, a day which should have provided spectacular views aplenty failed miserably to deliver the scenic-goods.

For example, ten kilometres north-west of Buncrana I should have seen Dunree Fort, the crowning glory of Dunree Head. This – so I'm reliably informed – impressive fortification once controlled the entrance to the then strategically important Lough Swilly. Now open as a military museum from April to October, in the early days of World War I it witnessed the assemblage of the British Grand Fleet. What I witnessed, however, was neither grand, impressive nor glorious, but a formless blur.

Six kilometres to the north the Gap of Mamore, which passes between the mountainesque hills of Urris and Mamore at a dizzying height of 800ft above sea level, promised a majestic panorama of heather covered hills, low fertile plains, long golden beaches and the sweeping Atlantic Ocean beyond. A visual treat promised but rudely denied. Though far from downhearted – for the man sound of body and mind there is no such thing as bad weather – I made do with pottering about the well and two grottos at the summit before beginning the serpentine descent.

Gulf war latest: Saddam Hussein has agreed in principle to withdraw his forces from Kuwait – with certain provisos. With the war as good as lost, his twin motives now appear to be saving face and safeguarding his position at home.

Saturday, 16th February. A raw morning; blustery and dry – a welcome improvement upon the excessive 'moisture' of the last couple of days. West of Ballyliffin I skirted the dune-fringed wildlife sanctuary of Trawbreaga Bay via Carndonagh, the hub of Inishowen. The bell in Carndonagh's Presbyterian church is believed to have originated from *La Trinidad Valencera*, the largest ship of the Spanish Armada which was wrecked in Kinagoe Bay in 1588.

Due north of Carndonagh, the chocolate-box seventeenth century plantation village of Malin radiates from a neat triangular village green, randomly planted with cherries, limes and sycamore. Worthy winner of the National Tidy Town competition in 1970, Malin is approached by a ten-arch bridge which spans the inlet – the second largest stone-built bridge in Ireland.

As one of Donegal's premier attractions Inishowen is frequently referred to as 'Ireland In Miniature' because it embodies all the scenic characteristics of Ireland as a whole. Equally alluring for those wishing to 'get away from it all' is the pastoral tranquillity of the place, where – as a rule – feral goats outnumber cars, and cows outnumber people. However in the wake of the recent media blitz Inishowen was anything but tranquil. Spotting 'Wonder

Walker' (my new tabloid sobriquet) was the 'in' pastime for weekend motorists. One family even drove over from Ballymena in Northern Ireland to lend their moral support.

In between pressing-the-flesh and politely declining invitations – time was pressing also – I noticed that with the sheep population too I was suddenly the flavour of the month. Whereas in the past they fled at my approach, now they literally flocked towards me in a welter of guttural-bleats and lanolin-whiff. Now it was my turn to be mystified.

With only two hours of daylight remaining, I still had the full circuit of Malin Head to complete before I turned in. A lone herdsman eased my concern with a timely adage: "Frost in the air – slow to darken."

With such evocatively titled geological features as Devil's Bridge and Hell's Hole, even in repose Malin Head could never be anything less than dramatic. Further round the coast Banba's Crown, topped by a derelict Martello Tower, is officially Ireland's most northerly point.

Sunday, 17th February. No sooner had I set out than the sheep mystery resolved itself. In the neighbouring field a shepherd proceeded pied-piper fashion from feeding trough to feeding trough. Over his shoulder he carried a green polythene sack of high-protein pre-lambing pellets – the self same green as my rucksack. And, according to the shepherd, the favourite food of expectant ewes. Hence my sudden popularity! Proof positive that sheep can't be colour-blind. I asked him why his sheep had 'nicks' out of their ears: "It's all to do with this 'ere EC sheep subsidy," said he smiling mischievously, "so's we don't claim twice on the same beast."

Today's route took me across the northern seaboard of the Inishowen peninsula, the rolling terrain ensuring no lack of bodily heat – despite the glacial efforts of the torrential rain which set in by the late morning.

At the hillside settlement of Portaleen my ego received a further setback. Apparently impervious to the downpour, a band of angel-faced urchins pumped me remorselessly. My reply falling upon deaf ears, their sing-song Ulster brogues trailed away behind me: "Whort awe yow, mus-ter? ... Hey, Mus-ter!... Whort awe yow?" What indeed?

A further 20 km brought me to the popular resort of Greencastle – so named after the extensive ivy-clad ruins which are the prime feature of this quaint fishing village – and my first sight of Lough Foyle and the cloud-topped peaks of County Londonderry, Northern Ireland, beyond. From Greencastle I veered south-westerly along the shore of Lough Foyle to Moville where a room awaited me at the Foyle Hotel.

That evening I was wined (well, Guinessed) by Garvin Kerr and his charming wife Marie. As the appointed Royal Mail representative, and a tireless charity worker, Garvin was here to finalise arrangements for tomorrow's triumphal entry into Derry City (or Londonderry, according to one's religious/political proclivity). He had already worked wonders on my behalf, not least in organising a checkpoint waiver for the entire party (I was to be accompanied for the final eight kilometres by an honour guard of placard-carrying postpersons from Great James Street sorting office). And if the cordial companionship of Garvin and wife Marie was anything to go by, I was in for a high old time in The North.

Monday, 18th February. I set out from Moville somewhat the worse for wear after last nights bevy. My delicate state wasn't aided by the dazzling sun which had me squinting from the word go. With the appalling news that IRA bombs had gone off in two London main-line stations still fresh in my mind, I plotted a southerly course for Derry City beside a shimmering Lough Foyle. County Londonderry, across the water, was lost in the haze. With every border-ward stride the road surface and fertility of the land visibly improved: a rich dark humus soon replaced Donegal's recalcitrant top soil.

Within minutes of approaching the outskirts of the small border village of Muff – now dominated by the triple towers of the giant Du Pont works, Derry's biggest employer –, the sudden appearance of an Ulster TV crew had a beneficial effect upon my hangover – it took my mind off it completely.

The exact chronology of events thereafter escapes me, for I was swept along on a rip-tide of euphoria and public acclaim. But the mood, the overriding feeling of goodwill and solidarity emanating from all those present will abide with me forever. Certainly I remember the enthusiastic reception at the frontier post from Royal Mail colleagues, customs officers and the media. I remember too the endless retakes for both TV and the gentlemen of the Press; and how foolish I felt marching on the spot for a 'wild-track' recording to be used as background noise on an interview with Radio Foyle.

*A rousing welcome in Londonderry (or Derry, according
to one's political/ religious beliefs).*

I recall also the steel fences, the tank traps, the battery of surveillance cameras and the helicopters circling above the checkpoint just south of Muff. And who could forget the gaunt features of British squaddies on sentry duty. Dwarfed by their weapons and heavily but necessarily encumbered by flak-jacket and body-armour, they resembled children playing deadly games, games with which they had long since become disenchanted.

Of the walk from the checkpoint to the city centre I recall only the blistering pace set by Frances Thompson, Derry's only post lady; the odd fragment of Garvin's non-stop running commentary; and the exhilarating sense of 'home coming'. Thirteen weeks of assimilation into the southern way of life, green pillar boxes, bilingual road signs and 'funny' money were unceremoniously ousted by pillar boxes of a familiar red hue, monolingual road signs and even 'funnier' money (banks in the North issue their own banknotes – none of which are legal tender in England). Moreover, Northern Ireland 'felt' more British than mainland Britain.

As for the reception at Great James Street sorting office – for sorting office read 'Fortress Royal Mail' – my recollections are only marginally less sketchy. Again the media turned out in force, as did members of staff and representatives of the local branch of the MS

Society. I was dazed by it all – a fact eminently conveyed by my glazed expression which continued to adorn Northern Ireland's newspapers throughout the following week.

With the reception winding-down, before escorting me to my digs Garvin took me on a whistle-stop tour of the city, 'his' city, the second largest in Northern Ireland after Belfast. Under Garvin's street-wise tutelage I gained a privileged insight into Derry and its inhabitants not accessible in any tourist guide. And despite twenty years of 'troubles', I had nothing but admiration for a people whose motto – indeed that of Ulster as a whole – is 'business as usual'. If Derry is a city under siege, as the British media is apt to imply, then somebody forgot to inform the inhabitants.

Tuesday, 19th February. Before leaving Derry, also called the Maiden City because its massive surrounding walls have never been breached, Garvin accompanied me to the neo-Gothic red-sandstone Guildhall where I was presented with a civic plaque from Lord Mayor Cllr. David Davies, whose chain of office was presented to the city by William III. All too soon it was time to bid farewell to Garvin, my mentor, whose pet salutation is forever consigned to my memory: "How's yer form!"

I took my leave of Derry via Craigoven Bridge, one of the few examples of double-decker bridge in existence. As a result of the continued blanket coverage of the walk, my progress throughout the day was reduced to a snail's pace. But I wasn't complaining. I positively thrived on the goodwill. If it wasn't motorists offering me a lift or merely slowing down to wave, it was fellow pedestrians earnestly seeking my first impression of the 'province'. My genuine approval invariably met with a favourable response: "Yer a good mahn!"

To the north-east of Derry the flatlands reclaimed from the River Foyle many centuries ago were dotted with small townships and villages. Ballykelly, a garrison town, fair bristled with fortifications, observation towers and armed sentries – for whom all movement above walking pace was restricted by their cumbersome body-armour. Street names appeared deliberately provocative to those of a Republican persuasion: Churchill Road, Queen's Street, King's Road ... And for those left in any doubt as to the religious/political proclivities of those residing hereabouts, the red, white and blue kerbstones and lamp-posts hammered home the Loyalist message. A state of affairs endorsed also by the marked decline in the number of shrines and grottos.

On the western outskirts of the largely restored eighteenth century town on Limavady, its Irish name means 'leap of the dog', I asked a couple of immaculate green-clad, heavily armed RUC officers for directions. While one attended politely and efficiently to my request, his oppo vigilantly covered him from behind. No matter what their detractors might say to the contrary, there can be no doubting that in terms of dedication and bravery the RUC are head, shoulders and flack-jacket above your average 'bobby'.

Wednesday, 20th February. No sooner had I sat down to a mouth-watering breakfast than things began to happen thick and fast. In between chewing the fat with a steady stream of notable visitors – including the Mayor of Limavady Cllr. Jack Dolan, snatching the occasional bite to eat, and withdrawing to the front garden for the presentation of a cheque, I was called to the telephone for a 'live' interview on Highland Radio. I felt exhausted before the day had begun.

Already well behind schedule for my 4 p.m. reception in the sedate market town of Coleraine, my departure from Limavady was further delayed by hordes of well-wishers who insisted upon slapping me on the rucksack, thrusting money into my hands (later transferred to collection box), and dragging friends and relations into the street to see "thart mahn orn TV".

In the interests of clawing-back some lost time, I decided immediately to restrict my efforts to the A2, wending my way north-easterly through a coastal plain overshadowed throughout by the craggy nub of Binevenagh, which means 'terrifying promontory', and a towering range of fulmar-squatted cliffs, liberally punctuated with waterfalls, which extend to Castlerock. The fertility of the soil remained consistently high, and it came as no surprise to learn that the world ploughing championships were to be held here later in the year.

Precariously perched on its cliff edge eyrie due east of Downhill, the splendid Mussenden Temple – an exact copy of the Roman Temple of Vesta – marked my departure from the coast. Climbing steadily inland, within eight kilometres of my destination I was joined by fellow 'posties' Steve, Jim and Billy who – taking up the entire near-side lane with an enormous welcoming banner – preceded me through the town to Coleraine's New Row sorting office. Here the media shenanigans began in earnest, all consummately orchestrated by Mrs Phil Kelly, Post Office Public Relations manager, Northern Ireland. This was my first meeting with the delightful Phil, who was to mastermind my entire campaign in the 'six counties'.

That evening Joe and Lesley Wishart, my hosts for the next two nights, threw an intimate dinner party in my honour: Lesley's mother, May, and family friends Dorothy and Dougie Chandler completed the guest list. The occasion went swimmingly, not least for the friendliness of those present and my belated introduction to the local tipple, Bushmills Irish Whiskey – the Water of Life!

Thursday, 21st February. In order to accommodate tomorrow's tour of Bushmills distillery, today's walking stint – Coleraine to Portstewart, then along the coast to Portballintrae – was a little on the short side (26 km). And in order to rendezvous with Joe Wishart at 4.15 p.m. in Portballintrae, it was necessary to limit my pace to a dignified saunter – even though the weather conditions, cold and misty, were hardly conducive to such a leisurely promenade.

The intriguing near-Scottish Coleraine accent – affirmations of "Och aye" are not uncommon – was not the only indication that Scotland was but a 'short leap across water'. The proliferation of Orange Lodges, the meeting place of this once secret order, confirmed that cultural traffic has not been all one way.

Flanked by a superb two mile stretch of Golden Strand, the west tip of Portstewart was a hyper-swanky enclave of large detached residences. Like Hove – with sand-dunes! Seven kilometres to the east, Portrush – just over the boundary into County Antrim – was a horse of a different colour. Though well endowed with an attractive harbour and a superabundance of sand, the rash of amusement arcades which mar the main street were not to my taste. Like it or not, this diversity of appeal has established Portrush as Northern Ireland's leading holiday resort.

Throughout the day a pair of RUC officers in an unmarked patrol car kept careful tabs on me. My wish was their command. At one point I was joined by a couple of well-meaning, if down at heel, youths. Sure enough my guardian angels stepped up their surveillance, appearing at every turn – just in case.

Back in the urbane surroundings of Lodge Road I barely had time to change and grab a light snack before I was whisked away for an enthralling evening with members and supporters of the Coleraine MS 'Self Help' group, 'Self Help' being the operative words. No defeatists these. A more irrepressible, courageous bunch one couldn't wish to meet. I drew strength from their strength; resolve from their resolution. With the presentation of several cheques duly recorded by the local press, I came away with batteries recharged, my sense of purpose redoubled.

Friday, 22nd February. A day which began with an 8.30 call from Joe Wishart and a generous donation from him and his wife. Scarcely had I time to pack and gulp a rudimentary breakfast than Trevor McBride of the *Daily Mirror* arrived for a pre-arranged photo-shoot. Having tried a variety of set-ups, he settled upon an unlikely pose of me seated beside my rucksack on the Wishart's driveway examining my bare feet. Caption: Upon my sole! My beaming smile belied the polar chill.

With the photo-shoot out of the way, Dorothy Chandler, MS fund-raiser and fellow dinner party guest of two nights ago, drove me to the Old Bushmills Distillery – in operation since 1608, making it the oldest licensed distillery in the world. After an initial false start, in which an alarm bell had us all scurrying for the exit, Bushmills' PR Rep. and tour guide Sheila Croskeny proceeded to paint an intoxicating word picture of the entire whiskey making process in all its fragrant intricacy. Away we trailed from one heady bouquet to another (my sort of aromatherapy!): From 'mash tun' to fermenting vessel, from fermenting vessel to copper pot still, from pot still to blending vat (give or take a stage). At the end of the line all those present received either a complimentary nip or a hot toddy. Along with the vast majority, I plumped for the latter.

Once again at the mercy of the elements – it was now raining pitchforks – I set out for the Giant's Causeway, five kilometres to the north. World Heritage Site, eighth Wonder of the Natural World, and perhaps the best known tourist attraction in the whole of Northern Ireland, the Causeway consists of some 37-40,000 basalt columns rising from a sea-level crazy-paving of hexagonal stepping stones. Each slab, slightly higher or lower than its predecessor, has been polished by millennia of tidal action and two centuries of tourists feet. It was to these cliffs that I now made my way.

For the next seven kilometres I followed the perilous (in winter) course of the Causeway Headland Walk. Cut into the rock-face, roughly mid-way between the rain-swept cliff top and the boiling surf, the path, as narrow as a yard in places, takes in all manner of weird and wonderful rock formations with names to match: the Honeycomb, the Organ, the Wishing Chair, the Giant's Granny, the Chimney Pots and the King and His Nobles. And while the seascapes are nothing short of stupendous, the Headland Walk is not for those of a timorous disposition. Particularly so during inclement weather when rock-falls and mud-slides are commonplace.

From the scant remains of Dunseverick Castle, the traditional crossing point to and from Scotland in prehistoric times, I struck out along the Antrim Coast Road for Ballycastle, seventeen kilometres to the east. This is the largest town in the Antrim glens and home of the famous Ould Lammas Fair, where traditional confections include 'Dulse', edible dried seaweed, and 'Yellow Man', a bright yellow jaw-breaker of a toffee. Though on such an inhospitable winter's evening as this my appetite lay in a more savoury direction.

Saturday, 23rd February. It was a different Ballycastle this morning. Gone was the rain, sent packing by a fresh nor-wester. In its place alternating spells of sunshine and cloud lent the town a whole new mellow complexion – a total contrast to my own state of mind. I was becoming increasingly cowed by my celebrity status. Not that I didn't appreciate the public interest and acclaim, but when it became intrusive I felt guilty for craving a little anonymity. But that would come soon enough. According to Andy Warhol's prophecy, I was already well overdrawn on my fifteen minute allocation of fame. "Saw you on TV last night. Good luck on the walk", boomed the tooled-up RUC officer, inclining from a shop doorway. Apparently I'm good for an overdraft...

Taking to the pliant sand I skirted Ballycastle Bay to Pans Rock, from where I ascended to the world famous Corrymeela ('Hill of Harmony') Peace and Reconciliation Centre. Founded in 1965 as a neutral venue where Protestants and Catholics could meet in order to bridge sectarian rifts, Corrymeela also has support groups throughout England, Scotland, Wales and Germany. No sooner had I expressed my solidarity with the community and its aims than Daphne O'Connor, a Catholic from Donegal, took me on a guided tour of the centre's comprehensive facilities and features. A spiritually uplifting experience.

From the winding Antrim Coast Road, more roller-coaster than thoroughfare, one wild vista succeeded another, each more dramatic than the one before. Situated at the foot of Glendun, the attractive village of Cushendun is under the protectorship of the National Trust. Designed by Clough Williams-Ellis – the architect and founder of Portmerion in Wales – at the behest of Lord Cushendun's Cornish-born wife, Maud Bolitho, the rows of slate-roofed whitewashed cottages embody the distinctive folk architecture of her ladyship's West Country origin.

Sunday, 24th February. Before embarking from Cushendun, I wandered out to the headland to explore the Cushendun Caves. Gouged from the sandstone cliffs by the action of the waves, this network of vaulted galleries brought out the troglodyte in me.

Managing at long last to tear myself away, I departed Glendun, the 'brown glen', wildest of the 'nine glens of Antrim', by way of Knocknacarry. Continuing in a southerly direction I scaled the 675ft peak of Cross Slieve before dropping down into Cushendall, 'The Capital of the Glens'. Dominating the steeply sloping streets is the red-sandstone Garrison Tower, built in 1809 as a prison 'for riotous persons'. Prior to Cushendall the weather had been a copy of that of the day before. But by mid-day it clouded over – before bucketing it down for the best part of an hour.

Undeterred by the dreadful conditions, the Antrim Coast Road remained a positive joy. When not marvelling at the coastline of high plateaus and plunging cliffs, a succession of idyllic glens lure the eye inland to a magic realm of forests, tumbling waterfalls and ancient sites, where the 'little pe'ple' are said to lurk.

The Caledonian influence was never far from the surface. Every shop was owned by a Mac-this or Mac-that. Scottish newspapers too were available everywhere. One aesthetically pleasing development was that fully fledged houses now outnumbered bungalows, while a glut of litter bins – virtually non-existent in the South – reflected the 'Keep Ulster Tidy' drive.

At the conservation village of Glenarm a machine-gun toting policeman waved me over to the checkpoint which he was manning outside a fortress-like RUC station: "We knew you were coming", said he handing over the proceeds of a generous whip-round among his fellow officers. And when these boys say "We knew", one is inclined to believe them.

Thereafter things began to go awry. Far from being located in the village, as I'd been led to believe, my evening's abode 'Rockview', was still nine kilometres away at the head of the glen, way up in the hills. My elevated route did however provide me with a breathtaking twilight panorama of the deer-rich Glenarm ('Glen of the Army') forest, which runs the length of the valley floor.

Gulf war update: Operation Desert Storm has entered its final phase. Coalition ground forces are now advancing on all fronts.

Monday, 25th February. By way of a change, I returned to Glenarm down the opposite side of the glen. Same views; different perspective – made doubly so by the generous blanket of frost which now draped the hillscape; all was a glistening white.

Back at the coast I was greeted by a keen southerly head wind, whose day-long attentions failed to diminish my profound appreciation of those 'boys from the Glynnes' (glens), who built the Antrim coast road between 1832 and 1842. By degrees the road beyond Glenarm assumed a higher elevation, hugging the uplands to yield tantalising glimpses of white shores below.

Temporarily dropping back to sea-level, the sea-front of the spick-and-span resort of Ballygalley is overshadowed by the Scottish Baronial style Ballygalley Castle – now converted into an upmarket hotel. Here I enjoyed a complimentary cup of coffee, before pushing on to the nearby gift shop where I purchased and despatched another addition to George's (*author's father*) walking stick collection: in this instance, a blackthorn knobkerrie.

Lying eight kilometres south-east of Ballygalley, Larne is the second largest port in Ulster as well as its premier ferry terminal. It was also the home of one or two half-decent folk artists, whose works, in the form of massive Loyalist street murals, adorned the gable ends of every terrace – with the emphasis upon: 'God save *our* Queen'! The village of Glynn,

Larne's neighbour to the south, resembled the aftermath of an explosion in a paint factory – whose entire colour range comprises only red, white and blue.

For the second night running I concluded my walking stint well after dark. In the normal order of things this would be of little consequence, but here on Island Magee (in fact a seven mile long peninsula which projects into the sea like a giant crooked arm), with its reputation for witchcraft and diabolical happenings, it lent an added piquancy to the final couple of hundred yards to Ballystrudder.

Tuesday, 26th February. With my arrival in Belfast deferred until tomorrow, today's consequentially abbreviated trek entailed a complete circuit of Island Magee, once the sole province of the Bissett family who held the tenancy in Elizabeth I's reign, but now the inhospitable domain of downpour and uncompromising head wind.

On the outward leg, beside the low-lying backwaters of the virtually land-locked Larne Lough, the only distraction from the elements came at the village of Ballylumford. There, in the front garden of an otherwise unremarkable house, was a dolmen – a single-chambered grave, comprising a horizontal capstone and four vertical support stones – dating from around 2,500-2,000BC. At the head of the peninsula I crossed over the headland to begin the long haul south to Ballystrudder and refuge – a homeward leg marked only by the tragic sight of a spread-eagled waxwing; all that way (Arctic Circle) just to get creamed on the Queen's highway! In the event the weather continued in the same malevolent vein until I reached the home straight – at which point the clouds parted and the sun peeped through.

Just yards from my digs I was confronted by a pair of leather-clad crash-helmeted bikers who barred my way. Far from spoiling for a dust-up, the more talkative of the two grabbed me by the hand and continued to shake it vigorously throughout our short if moving conversation. It transpired that he and his sidekick had been scouring the coastline to thank me on behalf of the former's father who, like many an MS sufferer, was no stranger to heart-ache and despair. But, difficult though it is to believe, following my exploits had given him a whole new lease of life.

Wednesday, 27th February. On the weather-front, the Met. Office predicted a repeat of yesterday's formula: wet morning; dry afternoon. As it happened the outcome was quite the reverse.

The seaside town of Whitehead was my first port of call of the day. More widely known as the headquarters of the Railway Preservation Society of Ireland, steam events are held here throughout July.

Now veering south-westerly beside Belfast Lough, no sooner had I entered the precincts of Carrickfergus than a flurry of gobbet-sized raindrops darkened the pavement, the outriders of an imminent deluge. As castles go, Carrickfergus Castle takes some beating. Jutting from the basalt promontory on which it is built, the castle's 90ft keep holds sway over skyline and harbour to dramatic effect. One could envisage the day in 1690 when William of Orange, 'King Billy', stepped ashore (marked by a plaque at the landward end of King William pier) *en route* to the Battle of the Boyne.

Beyond Newtownabbey, within sight of Ulster's trouble-torn capital city, the traveller is funnelled into the northern, primarily Loyalist, districts of Belfast by Cave Hill – known locally as Napoleon's Nose – to the west and Belfast Lough to the east. With the rain now in full spate, in the vicinity of Fortwilliam Recreation Centre I was joined, in the now time honoured fashion, by an escort of hardy Royal Mail personnel. Whether volunteers or conscripts, I certainly appreciated their company – not least for taking my mind off my aches and pains.

But this wasn't the Belfast of TV newsreels or jaundiced hack writers. Where was the bomb damage, the broken windows, the blasted buildings? It was more like pristine Carrickfergus – no litter in sight. Maybe the rain had washed it all away? Maybe my 'postal pals' were taking me the scenic, Government-approved route? Or maybe, just maybe, there was no mileage to be had by the media in depicting Belfast, Ireland's 'Athens of the North', in a good light?

I was given a rousing welcome at my 3 p.m. reception at the Queen Street Head Office of Royal Mail Belfast, where – following, a lively if saturated photo-call and the necessary issuing of security badges – we repaired to a hospitality suite for a post-walk get together, buffet, presentations, more piccies, an interview on BBC Radio Ulster and a campaign brief from Phil Kelly.

Thursday, 28th February. So much for the sanitising illusion of rain. If anything, in this morning's frost-nipped radiance, Belfast was even more presentable. It seemed a long way to come for such a cursory visit. But time was of the essence. Bangor and 'Downtown Radio' called! I made do with a quick recce – the Albert Memorial, Belfast's answer to Big Ben, noticeably skew-whiff; Custom House, surely the finest building in the city, now a V.A.T. centre – before crossing the steel-grey River Lagon. Heading north-westerly, the industrial landscape to my left was a veritable *Who's Who* of Belfast's key employers: Harland and Wolf Shipyard, the largest in the UK – it's twin mustard-yellow cranes, affectionately known as Samson and Goliath, monopolising the skyline like mammoth goalposts; Short Brothers Aircraft manufacturers; Belfast City Airport…

I arrived at Bangor for a 'live' telephone-interview with less than ten minutes to go before air-time. Interviewer Linda Jane settled my nerves with her easy going manner. Like falling off a log! By the time the interview was at an end, a reporter/photographer from the local rag had turned up. While I gave him a brief résumé of the walk to date, Linda dedicated the next record to me: *Show me the way* – by Styx.

With the media high jinks over, I was determined to salvage something from the remainder of the day. And what better location for an afternoon constitutional than the bays of Bangor, Ballyholme, Cove, Sandeel and Sandy. Travelling west to east around the immaculate Groomsport promontory, I could only hazard a guess as to what visual grandeur I'd overlooked in my headlong charge to keep my radio engagement. The North Down Coast Path, for one.

On the outskirts of Donaghadee I presented myself at my pre-arranged lodgings. Much to my astonishment the couple in residence – let us say Mr and Mrs 'X' – had no recollection of such an arrangement. More to the point, they were not and never had been in the guest house business. All of which appeared totally irrelevant, for without further ado they took me in, bag and baggage. Stay the night, stay two! Typical Ulster hospitality. After a blow-out supper I telephoned walk HQ: an out of date accommodation guide was the culprit – that and the fact that each thought the other had made the booking.

With the inner man duly replenished, Mr 'X' suggested I accompany him while he drove his mechanic – who had just returned his newly serviced car – back to his home in Newtownards. Only when we were negotiating the network of pitch-dark lanes which criss-cross the Ards peninsula did he let me in on his 'little' secret: he was, by profession, a senior firearms officer in the RUC. Now he tells me! Only then did it dawn on me why he vigilantly checked his rear-view mirror every few seconds – he was a prime IRA target! Whether ambush or landmine, neither one of us knew what awaited us around the next corner. I disguised my disquiet as best I could. Mr 'X' took it in his prodigious stride. If given their heads, he maintained, the RUC could 'solve' the entire paramilitary problem within three months. Be it the IRA, INLA, UDA, UVF, or UFF, the membership of each of these outlawed organisations was known to, and documented by, the authorities. Adding wistfully: "Uff only oor harnds weren't teyad bey der Juduciary."

And why was he prepared to give me the run of his house – even trusting me to lock-up before I left in the morning? With a glint in his eye: "Uff ye geyat upty arny mischuff ye'll nort geyat four." With the entire resources and manpower of the RUC at his disposal, he had a valid point.

8   A blistering feat

No matter how many miles a man may travel,
He will never get ahead of himself.
    George Ade

Friday, 1st March.

MAKING urgent tracks for Donaghadee proper, I swept past the golf links to the large lighthouse-lorded harbour in whose sheltered waters I watched a lone seal blithely frolicking. For such a comparatively small town, Donaghadee has played host to many distinguished celebrities down the years – albeit *en route* to or from the Giant's Causeway: James Boswell, John Keats, Franz Liszt and William Wordsworth, to name but four.

Weather-wise I couldn't have wished for a more salubrious introduction to the Ards Peninsula. An absolutely sparkling morning caressed by the merest spring-like zephyr, it was certainly living up to its reputation as having one of the sunniest and driest climates in the North. Deriving its name from the Irish *Ard* meaning rock, the vast bulk of the shoreline is hemmed to leeward by a particularly scenic coast road and to seaward by a treacherous chain of rocky shoals. Inland a range of drumlin hills runs the length of the peninsula; evocatively encapsulated by C. S. Lewis, a native of County Down, as 'a layer of earth-covered potatoes'.

From here on in it was due south all the way to Cloghy or Cloughey, my evening abode. In between charming fishing villages, sandy beaches and tiny settlements dotted with whitewashed thatched cottages, my eyes were inexorably drawn to the north-east where, barely twenty miles distant across the North Channel, the Mull of Galloway was just visible beneath a pall of cotton wool cloud. An enigmatic foretaste of my forthcoming Scottish sojourn.

At the sleepy village of Ballyhalbert I was press-ganged by the patrons of the Ship Inn to drop in and "Weyat yer whistle". Several pints of pukka Guinness later ("Kip yer marny in yer pocket") I emerged somewhat merry if marginally disorientated.

Five kilometres further on, the major fishing port of Portavogie is famous for the giant prawns which bear its name. More significantly, it boasts bevies of the most beautiful girls imaginable. Among these comely colleens turtle-neck cardigans were all the rage and worn to stunning figure-hugging effect, the near diaphanous cashmere accentuating every titillating jiggle … get a grip, man!

One such sweater girl paused – in every sense of the word – to make my day with a donation and a smile that could melt the ice-cap, before driving on to Cloghy to alert my host of my impending arrival. The local bush radio was clearly working overtime. Throughout the final kilometres to the Roadhouse Hotel several households came rushing out to wish me well and to relate their own harrowing tales of MS in the family.

I was warmly greeted in the hotel's foyer by the sweater girl – looking even more attractive in the soft-hued lighting – and the burly proprietor of The Roadhouse Sam Anderson, former Irish Heavyweight Champion, who informed me that everything was on the house (which set the tone for the Ards Peninsula as a whole).

Gulf war conclusion: Hostilities are now officially at an end, US forces having earned the dubious distinction of killing more British troops than the Iraqis, in a bizarre series of so called 'friendly fire' incidents.

Saturday, 2nd March. Over breakfast in the fire-lit hotel bar a retired fisherman dropped in for a 'hair of the dog'. His tongue duly oiled, he confided that his all-time favourite fishing ground was across the Irish Sea – just off Sellafield: "Wharkun greyut feyush theyur far the teyukum – arn no competition". No doubt the close proximity of the offshore outflow pipes from the controversial nuclear fuel reprocessing plant had some bearing on their unopposed monopoly.

The lone Catholic outpost on the otherwise staunchly Protestant Ards Peninsula, Portaferry, radiates from an elevated square of handsome Georgian buildings and quaint shops. With the sheeting rain showing no inclination to ease up, I waited to be met at 2 p.m. by a deputation from the local MS branch who sought my advice regarding their forthcoming sponsored wheelchair push around Northern Ireland. As the deadline approached I braved the elements; descending Castle Street past the Aquarium and the discoloured molar of Portaferry Castle to the rain-swept quayside-terminus of the Strangford Ferry where I watched the black-hulled craft make two crossings of the turbulent 'narrows' – with no sign of the deputation. On the verge of calling it a day I was intercepted by the wheelchair-bound Sean, and conducted back to the 'Fiddlers Green' public house – and a generous roar of approbation from the assembled throng. If the streets were deserted, the 'Fiddlers Green' was packed to the rafters. An explanation was swift in coming: A cock-up on the communications front had led them to believe that I was arriving on the two-something ferry from Strangford. Hence the lack of urgency. For the next hour and three-quarters I succumbed to the overwhelming ambience, drank in the atmosphere (along with alternating draughts of Guinness and Hot Irish) and basked in the fervent goodwill, promising to return that evening for a fund-raising pub-crawl.

Gone three-thirty now and it was still chucking it down. Ahead of me lay a twenty-one kilometre trudge along the green and fertile shore of Strangford Lough to Grey Abbey and beyond. It was well after dark (seven o'clock in fact) when I finally put in an appearance at my 'Abbey Farm' billet. No sooner had I wolfed my dinner than the lads from the 'Fiddlers Green' were at the door.

I thought the drive to Newtownards was hair-raising enough, but it wasn't a patch on tonight's little episode. Of my three compatriots Gabriel – like myself – was a non-driver; Billy – a hirsute Dubliner's look-alike – was banned; and Sean – an MS sufferer – had only minimal control of his limbs. Suffice it to say, Sean did the honours, the stop-go drive to Portaferry taking nigh-on as long as I took to walk it. Throughout which Sean – whose iron resolution inspire all who meet him – kept us on the edge of our seats with the cautionary tale of how he wrote-off a Vauxhall on this same strip of road in his twenties. After three push starts, two breakdowns, a series of unexpected dragster-like accelerations and a near fatal head-on collision ("Ohh, booger it!" quoth Gabriel) – we eventually ran out of petrol outside the home of Ulster TV Newscaster Jeanie Johnson. While Jeanie went for petrol we pushed the car off the unlit country lane, before finally pulling into Portaferry at ten. For the next two and a half hours we 'hit' most of the town's 'twelve' pubs; each one throbbing to its own particular brand of music: live or canned; traditional or contemporary. At the last call but one the landlady invited me to "Rise on up there" and join her resident musician (guitar and drum machine) for a sponsored sing. As my Mystic Meg horoscope had already foreseen such an eventuality, allied with the fact that I'd also put away enough complimentary sherbets to shed any inhibitions, I bowed to the inevitable and regaled the long-suffering regulars with a half-cut rendition of *Needles and Pins*. At our final port of call we teamed up with Sean's twin brother for a night-cap and a final reckoning: a healthy £120 and a wealth of treasured memories to the good!

Sunday, 3rd March. Still distinctly woozy from last night's excesses, I returned to Grey Abbey and the coast. Deriving its name from the ruined Cistercian Monastery (founded 1193) to the east of the village, Grey Abbey exudes a monastic calm discernible through even my morning-after-the-night-before haze. The weather was mercifully cool and overcast. Brilliant sunshine would have totally wiped me out.

Home to Ireland's largest colony of common seals (upwards of 800 in early summer), basking shark, giant skate (pushing 200 lb.) and a host of other marine and bird life, Strangford Lough was the focus of today's shore-side ramble to Newtownards – which, contrary to its name, dates from the thirteenth century – before swinging south via Comber beside the islet-freckled western shore.

Due north of Killyleagh a car pulled-up beside me. Well-wishers I presumed. The gamine young lady in the passenger seat flashed a smile which spoke volumes. She wanted to thank me, fully intended to thank me, had rehearsed thanking me – but instead broke down in a flood of tears. As the driver departed with his sobbing charge, I suspected her to be newly diagnosed as suffering from Multiple Sclerosis.

As late as six o'clock the sky was an horizon-wide vault of robin's egg blue. The twin-towered fairy-tale castle perched high above Killyleagh cried out to be photographed. I duly obliged. It was in the library of Killyleagh Castle that the young Hans Sloane began his self-education. Sloane (1660-1753) went on to become court physician to George II and founder of the British Museum and Kew Gardens; his own library of 500,000 volumes and a herbarium of 800 species forming the nucleus of each collection respectively. The current Baron Killyleagh – and occasional visitor – is Prince Andrew, Duke of York.

Beyond the small harbour of this town the seaside road trailed north amid hill and surf to Holm Bay and my accommodation, the Fool's Penny Country House. Presently occupied by Adam and Joan Capper, he a martyr to MS, the 'Fool's Penny' of the title alludes to the amount of profit per pint of ale which financed the building of the house by its original owner, a publican.

Monday, 4th March. Overnight applications of liquid Savlon to my gammy heel had failed to improve matters. Quite the reverse in fact. With a mountain to climb in two days, it was the worst possible scenario.

Matters were hardly improved by the near gale force wind and torrential downpour which greeted my emergence onto the stone-flagged terrace. Where the wide reaches of Strangford Lough should have fanned majestically into infinity, an impenetrable curtain of rain now obscured the view. Among the photo-opportunities thus denied me were Downpatrick – reputedly the final resting place of St. Patrick, the Apostle of Ireland; and Kilclief Castle – built around 1413 by John Sely, Bishop of Down, who was later discharged for 'adulterous liaison' with the deliciously named Lettice Savage. In short, a total washout.

The one spot of light relief from the otherwise grinding monotony of rain and pain occurred east of Tully Hill, where a thunderous sea raked the narrow shore road at irregular intervals. Throwing caution to the wind I made a bolt as best my ponderous backpack would allow – only to catch the full maelstrom impact in mid dash. As the white-water cascaded about me I was in two minds whether to laugh or cry. I settled for the former.

My farmstead quarters were located just over two kilometres inland from the sprucely painted houses and five tower-house castles of Ardglass, in the midst of a fertile flood plain. I was to be the first paying guest, but no heating, a dearth of hot water, curtains too small to draw, nothing *en suite*, unmade bed (for bed read hammock), a smoke alarm that 'chirruped' every minute on the minute and a homicidal Jack Russell terrier made this a less than memorable night. Cold Comfort Farm indeed!

Tuesday, 5th March. Seven months into the walk – amazing how time flies when one's having fun! Weather conditions were perfect: dry and sunny, with a gentle waft of sea breeze. Incredible how a fine spell brings out the best in folk – it also brings out their wallets and purses. Forty pounds on the day; for such a thinly populated stretch of coastline a tremendous figure. One Scottish contributor advised me that his native land is divided into two distinct regions: midge (west coast) and midge-free (east-coast). As if prompted by all this talk of creepy-crawlies, clouds of basking sand flies periodically rose from the sun-baked tarmac at my approach.

I dined that night with Phil Kelly and Danny Carty, chairman NI Post Office Board, who would be accompanying me on tomorrow's assault upon Slieve Donard (2,796ft), Northern Ireland's highest peak.

Wednesday, 6th March. Weather-wise, how can two consecutive days be so dissimilar? After yesterday's balmy interlude, I was banking on more of the same. What I got, however, was a dull-as-dishwater, overcast morning with teeming rain of monsoon proportions.

At eight-thirty Danny Carty called at my sea-front accommodation with a view to transporting my non-essential items of equipment to Bloody Bridge (remembering a group of prisoners who were massacred here after the rebellion of 1641) where it would be restored to me after the climb. Undeterred by the foul conditions, a surprising number of people had turned up to show their solidarity. Several of the MS supporters who braved the elements had travelled from as far afield as twenty miles.

By 9.45 we were on our way. If anything, the conditions deteriorated still further as we broke through the tree-line. Danny was well wrapped up, a light pack securely anchoring his cagoule, while my patently inferior rainwear shipped water like a sieve. If coldness was my initial problem, as the incline became increasingly steep, the terrain ever more demanding, I began to overheat. Between rocky outcrops, the going was an ankle-deep morass of mud, moss, cotton grass and heather. Springs and rivulets bubbled-up all over the show, the product of precipitation nearer the peak. For much of the ascent we walked blind, a dense hill fog beheading the entire range. And as fatigue set in, minor spills were unavoidable.

Heading east in the ample lee of the Mourne Wall – a twenty-two mile long livestock exclusion barrier built 1904-22 to a height of eight feet – we entered the par-melted snow-field for the final back-breaking push to the summit, the culmination of an eighty minute scramble. In this weather, an amazing feat.

So inhospitable was the top of Slieve Donard that no sooner had we devoured a caramel bar than we began our descent. A descent which – on account of chatting to the occasional masochistic rambler, from one of whom Danny managed to extract a £10 donation, and two foolish young ladies sporting casual shoes whom we tried in vain to dissuade from climbing further – took as long as the ascent.

The final few kilometres to my evening berth in the harbour village of Annalong were among the most excruciating in many a long day, my torso being a mass of abrasions from the friction of sopping-wet undergarments. Moved by my pitiful plight, landlady Dorothy Stevenson steered me towards an interim snack of tea and cakes, with the promise of a hot soak and a roast to follow. Hospitality *par excellence*.

Thursday, 7th March. No sooner had I stepped into the dismal greyness of the Annalong morning, than the weather promptly resumed where it knocked off yesterday: pelting rain and penetrating chill all the way to the doorstep of the Diplomat Inn, Warrenpoint.

Throughout the day I plied a strip of chequered farmland between the cloud-shrouded Mourne Mountains and the sea-cum-Carlingford Lough, known as the 'Kingdom of Mourne'; an idealised image of Mother Ireland which focuses the homesickness of many an ex-patriot. The re-emergence of dry-stone wall field divisions was an aesthetic bonus. And yes, the Mountains of Morne really do 'sweep down to the sea'!

Approaching the quiet resort town of Rostrevor from the east, the low slopes of the densely-wooded Slievemartin (1597 ft), a National Nature Reserve, were teeming with browsing fallow, red and Sika deer.

Friday, 8th March. It never rains but it pours! My final day in Northern Ireland and still the same dreadful weather persists. A non-stop three day drenching which has left me with an agonising twinge in my lower back and a gut-dread of approaching cumulo-nimbus. A thoroughly inauspicious end to an otherwise memorable idyll of scintillating personalities and sumptuous scenery. But having shared the convivial company of a broad spectrum of Ulster folk, the euphemistically dubbed 'troubles' appeared as irresolvable as ever. A depressing admission.

Pursuing a north-westerly heading the confluence of Carlingford Lough and Newry River is commanded by Narrow Water Castle. It was in the vicinity of this substantial stone tower that upwards of eighteen British soldiers were killed when a troop carrier and helicopter were blown to smithereens by two remotely controlled bombs. In the ensuing mêlée a member of the Queen's household domestic staff who emerged from woodland on the opposing Republican side of the river was fatally shot by a British squaddie who mistakenly assumed him to be responsible for detonating the devices. The scene of the carnage was marked by a scattering of weather-beaten wreaths – a sad reminder of man's inhumanity to man.

At the first convenient crossing point I exchanged river banks, returning in the direction from whence I came beside the Newry Canal. Completed in 1741, the canal runs cheek by jowl with the Newry River and predates England's first artificial navigation waterway by twenty years.

Eight kilometres south-east of Newry, Ferryhill customs post-cum-National/County boundary consisted of little more than a Portacabin and a 'Welcome to Co. Louth (the smallest county in Ireland) & Eastern Ireland' sign. What a contrast to the hi-tech security conscious frontier post at Muff. But what it lacked in sophistication was amply compensated by the compassion and common humanity of its three man crew who dismissed my request for an official endorsement to my witness book until after I'd helped them put away an exquisite beef stroganoff. While we tucked in, a 'Stop Customs' barrier was erected in the middle of the road and any motorist foolish enough to comply – and by no means all did – was gently persuaded to contribute to the campaign fund. Scarcely had we ingested our meal than I was whisked off on a whistle-stop motor tour of 'Bandit Country', a sinister mountainscape of mist, rain, crag, gorse, legend and unapproved border crossings high above Ferryhill ("You're safe wi' us"). A reassurance that was severely tested when we paid an impromptu visit to the riverside location where the member of the Royal Household met his death, now commemorated by a stone. In the time it took us to reverse out of the secluded cul-de-sac we were surrounded by armed security forces (army and Garda) – who promptly melted away at the sight of my white-capped companions. Clearly they were as good as their word.

Two hours having elapsed since my arrival, I bid a reluctant farewell to begin the homeward haul to Carlingford. For the initial three kilometres I was accompanied by a friend of the 'Ferryhill trio', whom I escorted to her home in the former Gaeltacht village of Omeath. The youngest of fourteen, she didn't so much as bat an eyelid while recounting the not so distant episode when Ireland's largest ever terrorist bomb (1500 lb.) was discovered within sight of her bedroom window! A cool customer, and no mistake.

On the other side of Omeath I trekked the kelp-strewn shoreline of Carlingford Lough, my unwavering course mirrored by a grey-hulled patrol boat of the Royal Navy. Like a red rag to a Provo-bull, it frequently comes under land-borne small arms fire.

I arrived at the medieval town of Carlingford by the last pallid light of day. Famed as much for its oyster fishery as its abundance of castellated buildings (the latter once numbered thirty-two!), Carlingford remains a charming charactersome town with citizens to match.

Saturday, 9th March. Certainly milder and brighter than of late, today was the first dry day in four. With the obscuring cloud-cover rapidly lifting, I surveyed my surroundings with new eyes. At the very limit of small arms range, the Royal Navy patrol boat lay at anchor in mid-reflection of the Mourne Mountains. Carlingford too had risen in stature, now backed by the scenic grandeur of the heather-covered Cooley Mountains, the wild and rugged backbone of the Cooley peninsula. Indeed, today's journey comprised a clockwise orbit of the beautiful Cooley peninsula concluding, beyond a salt-marsh-bordered bay, at the busy port and county town of Dundalk. Not long into the walk I was angelically regaled by the 'sweet silver song' of a skylark, the first of the year.

Sunday, 10th March. Extricating myself from the maze of back-doubles that is Dundalk was but the first inconvenience of the day. But while a dearth of street signs can be easily overcome with a simple vocal request, the profusion of large dogs running amok – alsatians, dobermans and huskie-types – took considerably more getting used to. Likewise the exorbitant prices of even the most basic of shop bought items. Welcome back to the Republic!

On an infinitely more jolly note the air, scenery and folk at large remained in a rarefied class of their own. From Dundalk to Ganderstown, County Louth's eastern seaboard is one immense flatland of coastal plain and sandy shoreline broken only by the rocky projections of Dunany Point and the magnificent vantage ground of Clogher Head.

The nearby fishing village of the same name was playing host to what was possibly the biggest game of bingo in Ireland. From the modest recreation hall venue stretched acre upon solid acre of bumper to bumper gridlock. Not a blade of grass in sight. From the air the scene must have resembled a multi-coloured automotive mosaic.

Within ten minutes I had my first gander at Ganderstown. Not so much a town, more a low-density hamlet overlooking the Irish Sea. With a superbly appointed home and a ribbon of golden sand virtually on her doorstep, my hostess, Mary McEvoy, recently returned from Australia, had the best of both worlds.

Monday, 11th March. Any hope of a repeat of yesterday's unimpaired visibility was dashed by a swirling cauldron of sopping sea fog. It wasn't until I reached the periphery of Drogheda, eight kilometres to the south-west, that it began to disperse. In so doing, it revealed a suburban calm quite out of keeping with the region's turbulent past. Schoolchildren on either side of the Irish Sea are well versed in Cromwell's barbaric excesses following the storming of the walled city of Drogheda in 1649. But what isn't generally known is that many of Drogheda's most heroic defenders were the English officers who perished alongside their Irish brethren.

This formerly strategic medieval city straddles the River Boyne where a ford once gave access to a Viking trading settlement. Now spanned by, among others, St. Mary's Bridge, it was here that I took time out to photograph Drogheda's extensive river frontage. Eight kilometres up-stream 'on the grassy slopes of the Boyne' is the site of the fateful battle in which Catholic James II was defeated by his Dutch Protestant son-in-law William of Orange, a débâcle which quashed once and for all the claim of James to the English throne.

Tuesday, 12th March. After seven months practice on a daily basis, farewells came no easier. Withdrawing from the happy home environment that hosts Bob (an old friend) and Claire Pease had conjured between them was harder than most. Even the children's hacking coughs were curiously reassuring. Particularly so that of the elfin Amy who sounded like a Chihuahua with a fur-ball stuck in its gullet! I'd miss them all. Unlike the weather – and nothing could dispel the misery wrought by the unholy trinity of mist, drizzle and sheer physical discomfort.

Assuming a southerly course from the outset, the low and rolling coastline of long sandy beaches and picture postcard fishing villages went largely unheeded, such was my preoccupation with my deterioration in the foot department. As I recall there was a slight descent into the centre of Rush, followed by a general levelling off as I pulled into the tiny village of Lusk. Apart from infrequent off-road interludes, these last couple of days aboard the main Belfast-Dublin drag-strip were tantamount to taking one's life in one's hands. Definitely not for the lily-livered.

Now in a critical state, I concluded the day with a cursory hobble round the Donabate peninsula, south to the dormitory town of Swords, then due east to the exclusive seaside resort of Malahide. God alone knows how I made it. Sheer bloody-mindedness I suspect. Whatever the case, I was in no fit state for sightseeing, though genteel Malahide had already secured a niche in my affection as the place where a cornucopia of hitherto unpublished James Boswell manuscripts and journals had come to light at the stately, greystone Malahide Castle.

At four I bowled into my temporary Biscayne abode. Though perhaps 'bowled' paints too energetic a picture, for by this time I was reduced to a leaden footed limp. Almost immediately my presence was required elsewhere, and I was driven off to a beach-side photo-session for the *Irish Independent*. On returning I received a telephone call to finalise arrangements for tomorrow's reception in Dublin. Media commitments concluded, I sank into a hot tub. The accumulated aches and stiffness needed soothing away. What I didn't need was the curious numbing sensation which preceded the disquieting rusting of the water at the foot end of the bath as my coagulated composite heel-dressing detached itself, taking with it a sizeable swatch of anaemic flesh and revealing a red-raw pulp of weeping dermis. Back in my room I removed a further several grams of surplus tattered skin, before taking a few souvenir snapshots for posterity. Strictly X-certificate plain brown wrapper jobs!

Wednesday, 13th March. The recuperative powers of the human anatomy continue to amaze me. Overnight applications of liquid disinfectant had left the abrasion dry but supple. An intermediate buffer of non-stick gauze completed the treatment. I was ready if not raring to go.

My 3 p.m. appointment in Dublin left precious little time for rubbernecking – just as well, for the resumption of mist and rain were hardly conducive to a casual constitutional. Consequently, I put my best foot forward (no prizes for guessing which one that was) and shaped a southerly path for Dublin Bay. Undoubted high spot of an otherwise weather-censored walking day – excluding the Dublin reception – was a round trip of the Howth peninsula, a one-time island gently enfolded by a scenic coast road. And while Howth Castle, a trawler-serried harbour and Baily lighthouse each slipped from sight in turn, the central heights of the Ben of Howth (560 ft) remained ever present beneath the gull-speckled sky. According to H.G. Wells, the cairn-topped summit commands: "The most beautiful view in the world." Sadly this much vaunted pinnacle was beyond the scope of my tight schedule.

Entering Dublin some moments before the arrival of the delegate from the UCW afforded me ample time for reflection. Was it really sixteen weeks and 4,548 kilometres ago that I departed 'dear, dirty Dublin'? So much had happened in the meantime, not least that Dublin had succeeded Glasgow as 'European City of Culture'. An accolade long overdue. But the significance of becoming the first person to walk the entire coastline of Ireland didn't fully register until many moons later when I received a telephone call from a soon-to-retire Ulster civil servant who, while congratulating me on my achievement, confided that I'd stolen his thunder in beating him to his lifetime's ambition.

Conducted to the nearby UCW headquarters I was introduced to larger-than-life character Ned O'Dowd over a reviving cuppa. A retired London postie of forty years service, Ned was now living in his native Sligo, from where this six-foot tall septuagenarian had travelled at his own expense for this one off engagement. Rigged out in the full Pipe Major's dress uniform of the Royal Irish Rifles, his old regiment, he cut a striking dash. While my hosts Chris Hudson and Brian Shanney concentrated on last minute arrangements, I spent a good half-hour being put through the hoop by a fastidious lensman of the 'art for art's sake' school of photography. At a given signal, Chris sped Ned off by car to the junction of Amiens and Sheriff Street to await the arrival of Brian and myself on foot. In perfect synchronisation, as I turned the corner Ned resurrected his lifeless bagpipes with a hefty thump amidships. The initial strangulated strain giving way to a stirring march, we set off down the length of

Sheriff Street, beneath an acoustically-superb railway bridge, towards Dublin's Central Sorting Office. The cheer that greeted our emergence from the shadowy underpass would have done justice to the winning goal in the cup final.

Thursday, 14th March. After four solid months of walking in the hallowed footsteps of Saint Patrick and the swathe of destruction wrought by 'that man' Cromwell, it was my last day in the Emerald Isle. My one regret was to be leaving just three days before the St. Patrick's day celebrations. But my departure would prove slightly more convoluted than that of my arrival. Catching sight of the *Irish Independent* stop press, I choked on my porridge:

B&I SAILINGS HIT BY STRIKE

Of all possible scenarios this was the worst. While I had no objection to remaining here a few more days, to do so would undoubtedly render the entire record attempt null and void. Under *Guiness Book of Records* regulations, I was obliged to maintain a steady forward progress on a daily basis. Marking time till the strike ran its course definitely would not suffice. Suddenly devoid of appetite, I hit the road in search of deliverance. As the fates would have it, I hit the jackpot immediately. After exchanging my remaining punt for sterling, my first resort was to the office of the *Irish Times*, who had been most generous in their coverage of the walk. For twenty-minutes the telephone lines buzzed non-stop. By which time a rescue package was hatched: the *Irish Times* would pick up the tab for a taxi to Dublin Airport, whereupon Aer Lingus flight 606 – courtesy of the airline – would shuttle me across the Irish Sea to Manchester, from where walk co-ordinator John Mole would transport me to my original destination of Holyhead. In the event I opted to leg it to the airport under my own steam. With four hours till takeoff, I had ample time to boost my figures.

The thirty-five minute flight went swimmingly. Just after three I linked up with John Mole. He looked exactly how I felt – all in! Having risen early to drive from Berkshire to Angelsey, organised – and cancelled – a quayside reception, before hurtling back across country to Manchester at short notice, his fatigue was hard earned. Following a belated lunch, John ferried me west to Holyhead where I resumed walking.

After a sluggish start, I completed the eight kilometre twilight dash along the dreaded A5 to Valley by 6.45 p.m. John too decided to spend the night at The Bull Inn. A wise decision – which looked even more prudent after a succulent steak and several pints apiece. But sleep – when the product of honest toil – needs little coaxing. As I sank remorselessly into oblivion I pondered upon the overall benefit of my Eireann escapade. In the words of one of George Bernard Shaw's characters: "Ireland is like no other place under heaven, and no one can touch its sod or breath its air without becoming better or worse" ... consciousness faded.

Friday, 15th March. Anglesey's climate contrasted dramatically with that of Eastern Ireland. Where mist and drizzle were the worst the elements could throw at me of late, a fusion of sheeting rain and prevailing westerly wind redressed the imbalance. The temperature too had dipped alarmingly.

But the weather was not the only disparity between these two Celtic lands. The scenery also was strikingly dissimilar. Unlike County Dublin's plage-fringed coastal plain, Anglesey's thinly-inhabited northern seaboard is a varied and picturesque heritage coastline of sheer towering cliffs and pebbly coves.

Shaking off an initial bout of lethargy, it was by way of this remote and tranquil seascape that I began the return leg to continental Cymru (Wales). I'd had my fill of the expedient but grim A5. One immediate reward for opting for the more circuitous route was the gladdening sight of host upon host of wild golden-trumpeted daffodils, the national emblem of Wales. It must have been on such an outwardly loathsome day as this that Shakespeare wrote of daffodils:

That come before the swallow dares, and take
The winds of March with beauty.

Due east of the vast bulk of the Wylfa nuclear power station I hove-to amidst the clutter of cottages that is Cemaes Bay in search of respite and an endorsement to my witness book. Repairing to the Pioneer Stores for a Mars Bar (a full ten pence cheaper than in Ireland) the sprightly proprietress suggested that I make a point of calling into shops and pubs along the way on the pretext of making some small purchase or seeking directions, in the hope of picking up a few donations from staff and customers in the process. There's artful!

The Welsh are not as demonstrative or outgoing as their Irish counterparts, but those that did approach me were invariably generous with their praise and well acquainted with the walk and its aims. Less complimentary were the stifled sniggers from a gaggle of gangly schoolgirls on the approach to the once busy little shipbuilding port of Bull Bay. Do I really cut that comic a figure?

Saturday, 16th March. It was certainly good to be back in the land of flint cottage, chapel and catkin – if only the atrocious weather would dry up. No wonder the moisture-loving willows were thriving. And while the adverse conditions had a detrimental effect donation-wise on the 'passing trade' the 'shopping pretext' ploy continued to pay handsome dividends. Though as a non smoker I was rapidly reaching saturation point in the match department. Pubs, on the other hand, remained few and far between.

Worked-out quarries, crumbling out-buildings and under utilised harbours punctuated my easterly passage, bearing witness to a considerable industrial past. With its rundown quayside, smelting shops and dilapidated warehouses, the old port of Amlwch once shipped-out 80,000 tons of top-grade ore a year from the nearby Parys Mountain copper mine. But by 1815 the boom years were over. Similarly, twenty-four kilometres down the coast, the shipbuilding days of Red Wharf Bay, like Bull Bay before it, were long gone. In the wake of this industrial decline, tourism now ruled the roost, a calling to which the Isle of Anglesey is eminently qualified and fortuitously endowed.

As if to confirm my observation, the further east I travelled the incidence of sandy beaches began to outnumber the shingle variety. The terrain too became increasingly undulating as the day wore on, achieving a switchback climax at Anglesey's easternmost corner. With forty-eight kilometres (thirty miles) completed, at six o'clock I free-wheeled into the hill-hemmed village of Llangoed where quarters had been engaged on my behalf.

Five Nations update: In beating France this afternoon, England's Rugby Union team completed the Grand Slam. More power to the elbows of Captain Will Carling and his boys.

Sunday, 17th March. Separated by the turbulent waters of the Menai Strait, the serrated peaks of Snowdonia remained veiled in rain cloud the day long, a day which witnessed my return to mainland Gwynedd. In the interim, I walked south to the immaculately maintained little town of Beaumaris (from the Norman-French *beau marais*, meaning 'beautiful marsh'). Pride of place goes to Edward I's magnificent and virtually impregnable fortress, Beaumaris Castle. Of the few stalwart sightseers who roamed the rain-swept streets, almost all fell prey to my new forthright appeal technique: march right up; state my case; proffer collection box; express gratitude; depart. Worked a charm.

The verdant Beaumaris – Menai Bridge shore road (A545) is bounded by many exquisite and exclusive residencies. None more so than the elevated, landscaped *pied-a-terre* of an affluent Mancunian couple with whom I partook elevenses. How the other half live!

The stunning Menai suspension bridge, which conveyed me to the cathedral and university city of Bangor at a height of 100ft above the treacherously swirling waters, must rank as one of Thomas Telford's greatest works. Works which include – surprise! surprise! – St. Katherine's Docks (1826-28), my original point of departure.

Like many a campus city before it, Bangor – a hotbed of Welsh Nationalism – exuded a relaxed bohemian atmosphere. Amid the delightfully undistinguished maze of Old Bangor a seductive sophomore from Idaho – all ear-to-ear enamel and sit-up-and-beg bicycle (obligatory mode of transport for the politically correct student) – pulled into the kerb to give me a donation and an off-the-cuff lesson in the Welsh language. There are no silent letters; the spelling is phonetic; and the letter 'y' can be pronounced 'u' or double 'e'.

My *Cymraeg* tutorial duly digested, I swung north-easterly along an ever narrowing coastal corridor between Conwy Bay and the impenetrable massif bulk of the Carneddau Range. Contrary to expectation, legging it up the hard shoulder of the A55 towards the slow-moving oncoming traffic proved a real money spinner. From Penmaenmawr – the favourite summer resort of Prime Minister William Gladstone – to my evening retreat of Conwy I picked up a steady stream of contributions from the reluctant participants in a ten kilometre long tail-back. My eye-catching MS sash and bedraggled demeanour potently combined to prick the mass conscience of my captive audience.

Having tramped in excess of eighty-eight kilometres (fifty-five miles) over the last two rain-marred days, a good nosh was uppermost in my mind. Sadly many landladies, bless their tasty titbits, have little concept of the appetite and nutritional requirements of the ultra distance walker. I had some calorific catching up to do. Seduced by the tantalising tang wafting from Conwy's premier fish 'n' chip shop, I joined the expectant queue, my taste buds tingling in anticipation, my gastric juices percolating in time with the deep fat fryer. I scanned the wall-mounted menu. What was it to be: saveloy, onion rings and chips? Fish cakes, mushy peas and chips? Or pasty, beans and chips? Finding myself before the vinegar-irrigated counter, I promptly flipped and ordered the lot in a fit of EBTB (Eyes Bigger Than Belly). When in doubt, pig out!

Monday, 18th March. It was another sombre day of pelting rain. A chill March wind keened out of the north-east across Conwy Bay. Undeterred, the Kodak and pack-a-mack brigade were out in force. For their pains, these stolid English day-trippers set eyes on probably the most perfectly preserved of Edward I's walled towns and one of the great fortresses of Europe, Conwy Castle.

Of the three bridges that span the wide estuary of the Conwy, on which the town stands, I chose to cross by the clean-lined modern road bridge that runs parallel to Telford's aesthetically superior suspension bridge. The latter was purpose designed to blend with the medieval walls and turrets of the dramatic castle back-cloth, an effect that it consummately achieves.

As one of Wales' major holiday centres, Llandudno boasts not one but two fine beaches: West Shore, where Lewis Carroll stayed and wrote part of *Alice In Wonderland* (Carroll's association with Llandudno is commemorated by a statue of the White Rabbit on the sea-front); and North Shore, with its scimitar sweep of sand, broad promenade and elegant echelons of balconied, bow windowed hotels. In between, the awesome limestone eminence of Great Ormes Head looms above the town like a facsimile rock of Gibraltar. My plans to walk the entire circumference of the headland aboard the oft precipitous Marine Drive toll road came to an abrupt halt just north of St. Tudno's Well, where an obstructing rock-fall necessitated a zigzag diversion inland to the towering crags of Great Ormes' 679 ft summit. Even in the grip of a demi-monsoon the place was a hive of Spartan activity. I could only hazard a guess as to the crowds and commercialisation which must beset this designated country park in the summer when the funicular railway and Britain's largest cable lift bring it within reach of even the most passive of holiday makers.

Leaving behind the genteel elegance of North Shore, I held my easterly course along one of Britain's most popular holiday coasts – a tapering coastal strip compressed by encroaching hills and Abergele Roads (the nautical variety), dotted throughout with a chain of resorts ranging from sleepy hamlets to sprawling holiday camps and caravan parks.

In the gathering dusk I trudged wearily through the bungalow-land of Kinmel Bay and crossed over the River Clwyd into the outlying western districts of Rhyl; the amusement park end of town, where giant funfairs and a sun-centre, mothballed for the winter, reclined in the rain-swept murk. The banshee-like wail of the wind in the canvas shrouds and the doleful knell of chain on girder served only to heighten the sepulchral gloom. I laboured on until the blazing lights of my guest house beamed a welcome in the wet darkness. Apart from myself, the only other guest in residence was Jim, a dour Lancashire coal-miner from Burnley. He was presently employed at Talacre Colliery, due east of Prestatyn, one of only two working mines in the whole of North Wales.

Tuesday, 19th March. After a fitful night's sleep I returned to the land of the living with a right royal sore throat. Swallowing was absolute agony. Crisps and cornflakes were definitely off limits. If I hadn't had them removed yonks ago, I'd have sworn I had tonsillitis. Pinning my hopes on medication and blind faith, I sucked a lozenge. Grin and bear it, that's the way. I even managed a beaming smile for a photographer from the *Rhyl and Prestatyn Visitor.*

Rhyl's brash and bracing promenade stretched clean through to Prestatyn, with scarcely a break in the motley ranks of bungalows, Victorian hotels and yet more amusement parks. Six kilometres beyond Prestatyn's coastal defences, Talacre marks the eastern terminus of North Wales' busy holiday coast. A broad foreland of wild sand-dunes, caravan site and pithead, my thoughts turned to Jim toiling away far below in the bowels of the earth in mine workings that run out up to a mile beneath the treacherous currents of the Dee estuary. I thanked my lucky stars.

As I approached the tiny harbour of Mostyn, Alister Walker of Royal Mail Employee Relations roared-up on his high-powered motorcycle to seek confirmation of my appearance at our scheduled afternoon engagement. In confirming the arrangement I committed myself to a frenzied dash along the A548 beside the swirling silt, shifting sand and muddy foreshore of the River Dee.

Even then, I reached The Packet Inn, Greenfield, some twenty minutes beyond my 1.30 p.m. dead-line. Red faced as much from embarrassment as from my exertions, on arrival I was presented with an outsize cheque on behalf of Royal Mail colleagues in Chester and North Wales. Much relieved by the eventual outcome, Alister ushered me to the lounge bar where a pub lunch had been laid on and where I remained for the next hour in the congenial company of a delegation from the Delyn Multiple Sclerosis group.

Having developed a distinct penchant for Greenalls cask conditioned bitter, I found the remaining twelve kilometres somewhat arduous. Particularly tough on my feet was the rutted bone-hard verge between Greenfield and my desired objective of Connah's Quay. But the day had an elemental sting in its tail. After threatening all afternoon, the heavens finally opened as I homed-in on the massive power station cooling towers which flanked the home straight.

Checking in to the Albion Hotel at six, I had precisely two hours to freshen-up, change, eat and make and receive a number of telephone calls before being transported back to Flint where I was the honoured guest at the Delyn MS social evening. Full credit to the Buckley Theatre Club who kept us entertained with a memorable selection of songs and sketches with a smattering of topical feet/walking gags thrown in for my benefit. The buffet, meanwhile, gave me ample opportunity to stoke-up on carbohydrates. All in all a wonderful night made doubly so by the selflessness of the volunteer helpers and the indomitable spirit of their charges. The perfect antidote to self-pity.

Wednesday, 20th March. A stone's throw down the straight-as-a-die A548 I turned sharp left at Queensferry. Not only providing the first landward road bridge over the Dee, Queensferry also marks the spot where the wide Dee Estuary contracts into a manageable canalised waterway. At this point the weather was being bounteously kind to me. But it wasn't to last. Sure enough the bright and breezy conditions gave way to an afternoon of wintry cloudbursts, the first of which overtook me as I crossed the national/county boundary between Wales/Clwyd and England/Cheshire. What a homecoming!

Turning my back on the steel and chemical plants of north-east Wales, I struck the western shore of the Wirral peninsula at the dormitory suburb of Neston, the birthplace of Lord Nelson's mistress Lady Hamilton. My chosen route, The Wirral Way, England's first linear park, follows the course of the now defunct Hooton to West Kirby branch railway line overlooking, on occasion, a seemingly endless horizon of sinking sand and never-present sea. North of Neston I entered my third county of the day: Merseyside. Sandwiched foursquare by the estuaries of the Mersey and the Dee, and Liverpool Bay, the Wirral's green heartland of commuter villages forms a rural buffer zone between the docks and urbanisation of Wallasey and Birkenhead and the industrial landscape of Deeside.

Considering the grotty conditions, I received a staggering number of unsolicited donations along the way. Particularly profitable were the coastal conurbations of Heswall, West Kirby and Hoylake. No less forthcoming was my target for the night – New Brighton, a seaside resort on The Wirral's north-eastern tip. Whitewashed terraces of generously proportioned Victorian dwellings harkened back to the town's prosperous heyday – a heyday which included the English conducting debut of Finnish composer Jean Sibelius. And a prosperity which effectively came to an end when the town lost its ferry-link with nearby Liverpool.

For the second evening on the trot I was billeted at the Albion Hotel: same name, poles apart. This was my introduction to the instant familiarity and open-handed generosity of Merseyside legend. I was swamped by the kindness of the Albion's regulars; overwhelmed by the largesse of the management. Not wishing to let the side down I propped up the bar long after discretion decreed otherwise. Deeply appreciative though I was, all I really yearned for was my bed. I was dead on my feet.

Thursday, 21st March. So that was the River Mersey: an indigo sheet of breeze-ruffled water backed by the mighty metropolis of Liddypool (so dubbed by John Lennon). So near and yet so far. Though only ten-minutes distant by road tunnel or one of two passenger ferry terminals located further to the south, the 'rough cyclopean masses' of the city's massive dock buildings were still two days and over seventy kilometres away by Shank's pony.

Moments earlier I set out from Nude Brighter (another Lennonism) in a euphoric mood. Such was the infectious good humour of the Albion's landlord, Liam, and his fellow wise-cracking Merseysiders, that any other frame of mind on my part would have branded me a kill-joy of the lowest order. Mind you, the weather played its part. Like dormant flowers induced into radiant bloom by the sun's warming rays, a bevy of bare-armed, bare-backed, bare-legged New Brighton belles flaunted their femininity in gossamer-like summer frocks, drawing admiring glances from, and raising temperatures in, all quarters. It was grand to be alive. But while the spring sunshine was a positive boon, it was the public spirited generosity of the people – many of whom were unemployed – that put the proverbial icing on the cake. Robert Browning captured my disposition to perfection: God's in his heaven – and all's right with the world!

I continued to have unsolicited donations pressed upon me all the way to Seacombe, which abutted the desolation and empty berths of the once busy Birkenhead Docks. Wandering off the main A554 north-south thoroughfare, I found myself in the midst of what I took to be either a red light area or a window-cleaner's convention. Some of the ladies in question were taking the air between clients on the doorsteps of their redbrick terraced houses: arms crossed, micro-skirts up to their armpits ("Mornin', chuck!", "Nice legs, shame about the beard!"). Where the lady of the house was 'otherwise engaged', an army of window cleaners teetered on the topmost rungs of their ladders, ostensibly chamoising the upstairs windows, eyes shiftily focused on the goings-on within. Was such a scene the inspiration for the famous George Formby song?

After a further five kilometres down the western bank of the River Mersey I came to the garden village of Port Sunlight. Built in the nineteenth century by William Hesketh Lever, who later became the first Viscount Leverhulme, to provide 'a new Arcadia, ventilated and drained on the most scientific principles' for the workers in his soap factory, this picturesque example of enlightened town planning takes its name from the chief product which financed it: Sunlight Soap. The roofscape of mock-Tudor chimney-pots was a particular delight.

Rigidly avoiding the M53 for fear of prosecution, I arrived at Ellesmere Port, Cheshire, via a roundabout route of minor and B roads. The shoreline, at this point, being out of bounds. For the next hour or so I hot-footed it through an industrial landscape of hellish proportions – namely, the giant Shell Oil refinery, the largest petrochemical complex in Britain. Redolent of the nightmare realm of Hieronymus Bosch, plumes of steam haemorrhaged from an intricate ligature of chromium and aluminium pipework, while flare-stacks on all sides belched smoke and fumes into the atmosphere. My nostrils were assailed by the resulting cocktail of noxious odours. The one saving grace of this otherwise disagreeable interlude came at the outset, where an imaginative system of docks, locks and warehouses recalled Ellesmere Port's finest hour as England's elite canal port, yet another Thomas Telford masterwork, now metamorphosed as the Ellesmere Port Boat Museum.

By late afternoon it began to cloud over. But it was too late to mar a near enough perfect day. The sunshine had done my ailments the world of good, not to mention my morale. For the final few kilometres to Runcorn New Town I kept faith with the meandering A56 above a patchwork flatland bordering the Mersey, bestrode by pylons and bisected by the grey ribbon of the M56 motorway.

Friday, 22nd March. Spruced-up in readiness for a 3 p.m. reception at Liverpool's Copperas Hill Sorting Office, I was somewhat long-winded in extricating myself from the spaghetti-junction of underpasses, flyovers and cycle paths which ring the town. By the time I plied Runcorn's Meccano-like bowstring girder bridge – once the third largest of its kind in the world – over the collateral waterways of the Manchester ship canal and the 300 yard wide River Mersey, I had significantly less than five hours to reach central Liverpool. My lofty vantage point commanded a magnificent aerial view of mile upon mile of chemical plants which line the Widnes side of the Mersey, to the north. Though doubtless beneficial to the local economy, such a heavy concentration of industry did little for one's olfactory organ. The air around Widnes was permeated with a rancid smell redolent of dried urine.

Despite the beguilingly bright conditions, there was a distinct nip in the air which dovetailed nicely with my need to set a brisk pace. Sightseeing would have to take a back seat, punctuality was of the essence. Veering left at Woodend, I slogged it out upon the rock-hard margin of the Speke-Widnes Link Road. The mammoth Halewood motor works drifted past in a welter of industrial blight and stockpiled vehicles. And still the signs read Central Liverpool 8 miles, 7 miles, 6 miles. A sense of dread set in – the dread of letting people down, keeping them waiting. Hillfoot Road, Menlove Avenue, Penny Lane (no sign of the fireman with an hourglass, let alone his clean machine). Pressing on 'beneath the blue suburban sky', my effort was presently given sharp focus. Looming large to the north-west Liverpool's two cathedrals vied for prominence. To the left, the red sandstone Anglican cathedral, possessor of the largest organ and heaviest peal of bells in Christendom, and, to the right, the circular Roman Catholic cathedral, affectionately known as 'Paddy's Wigwam'. I might make it yet. There was still time.

Now on the very threshold of the city, my objective within reach, I was intercepted by Mr and Mrs Ron Graham and Phil Henney of the Liverpool MS Branch, who had been frantically searching for me in order to relay a last minute change of plan. Due to industrial action at Copperas Hill Sorting Office – word was that I wouldn't be allowed to cross the picket line – the reception was redirected to the Town Hall. How fortuitous! The picket's loss was my gain. With no time to browse in the myriad bookshops in Renshaw Street, I made a beeline for my new destination, gaining my first sight of the imposing municipal edifice via the pink metalled canyon of Castle Street on the stroke of 3.05 p.m. Considering the eleventh hour diversion, five minutes leeway was quite admissible.

Utilising the granite-faced Town Hall as a backdrop, I was joined by a spirited bunch from the local MS branch and several Royal Mail notables for a protracted photo-session under the auspices of, among others, a stunning supple-limbed lenswoman. But this Liver bird wasn't just a pretty face. Over the ensuing twenty-four hours the fruits of her labour were featured in each and every one of Liverpool's evening and daily newspapers. With cameras temporarily stowed away, we adjourned as one to the Town Hall's inner sanctum for a spot of light refreshment, cheque presentations, more photos, and a round of introductions. Lady Mayoress Dorothy May Gavin set the tone for my entire Liverpool stopover: "Call me Dot", invited the cordial councillor. I was certainly moving in rarefied circles. Only this morning none other than Her Majesty the Queen had been taken on this self same grand tour – with the accent on grand.

The Town Hall's cavernous interior was reminiscent of Dr Who's Tardis: far larger on the inside than the outside would suggest. Among the wealth of treasures on show, I was particularly taken by the magnificent domed roof, the hangar sized ballroom, the panelled Council Chamber and the second biggest chandelier in the world. It was easy to see why the place was in such demand as a film location: Its credits included *Chariots of Fire* and *Mountains of the Moon*. News that the much reviled former city council supremo Derek Hatton had this very day been arrested on the charges of illegal property dealings sent the Town Hall staff into fits of quiet ecstasy.

As the reception drew to a harmonious conclusion, Phil Henney escorted me on foot to my digs. *En route* he took on a brief recce of the exuberantly revitalised city centre, a revitalisation which cocks two fingers at the city's numerous detractors in the media. Our tour included 'Cavern Walks', an exciting multi-storey arcade of shops and offices located above the rebuilt Cavern Club in Matthew Street. The nearby Beatle Street wasn't the only reminder of the 'Four lads who shook the world', their vital early platters chorused from every bar and boutique. Phil's civic pride was evident.

Did I have the temerity to call them digs? The Adelphi Hotel is to digs what Dom Perignon is to plonk and what beluga caviar is to lumpfish roe. From the classic lines of the stately pale stone facade to the unadulterated luxury within – rose-tinted marble pillars, burgeoning palms, spectacular chandeliers, oak panelled walls, lavishly appointed suites of massive proportion – this was patently one of the world's ritziest hotels. I was indebted to the local Royal Mail bigwigs who were footing the bill. Though it was a pity I had neither the energy nor the appropriate garb to take advantage of the comprehensive in-house facilities: two night clubs, gymnasium, saunas, solarium, squash courts and a splendid swimming pool. In my languor I contented myself with a slap-up room service meal and a couple of hours of satellite TV before turning in. My definition of satellite TV: umpteen channels and nothing worth watching on any of them.

Saturday, 23rd March. Crowned by effigies of the mythical Liver Birds, the clock on the awesome Royal Liver Building, Britain's largest timepiece, read ten-thirty. The remaining two erections of this famous Pier Head trinity – the domed Dock Board Offices and the Cunard Steamship Co. headquarters – were equally as impressive. The mere sight of the latter transported me back four months to the Old Head of Kinsale, Co. Cork, off which the Cunard liner *Lusitania*, sailing from Liverpool to New York, was sunk by German torpedoes during WWI. Scattered pieces of the universal jigsaw were increasingly coming together in this manner to flesh out major events from the past. I can think of no better education than to witness first hand the broad canvas on which history and the history makers have left their indelible mark. Such is the virtue of travel.

Returning to the present, even the gigantic art deco Mersey Tunnel ventilation funnel is a work of art, and is in no way out of place beside its more illustrious neighbours. One could in fact explore Liverpool's labyrinthine waterfront for a month or more and still not be familiar with every fascinating facet, odd corner and secret garden. Not for nothing is the exhilaratingly restored Albert Dock complex – the largest group of grade one listed buildings in the country – also the nation's most-visited heritage attraction.

Like millions of emigrants before me, I bade farewell to Liverpool ('Capital of North Wales', 'Suburb of Dublin', call it what you will) with nothing but fond memories of my all too brief stay. The road north provided a seemingly endless panorama of dock practices old and new. From the lines of vacant berths and idle cranes, glimpsed through gaps in the eighteen foot high dockyard wall, it was difficult to believe that Merseyside was actually handling more cargo than at any time in its long and colourful history. But one port's loss is another port's gain, in this instance the giant container terminal down river at Seaforth. The heartening spectacle of the sun-spangled salt-breezy River Mersey set me in good stead for the day ahead.

Three miles downstream the Mersey Estuary empties into the Irish Sea. Meanwhile, to landward, beyond the beach-side marina and Georgian charm of sea-front Crosby, Liverpool's northernmost coastal suburb, the urban sprawl came to an abrupt halt. Pastures new, indeed; Hightown, Formby and Ainsdale being the only sizeable conurbations between Crosby and Southport. On the approaches to Ainsdale a motorcade of black limousines and police motorcycles outriders swept south on the A565, an attendant helicopter tracking the speeding column from aloft. Having addressed the Tory faithful in Southport, Prime Minister John Major was heading home.

At the first opportunity I curved left through the Ainsdale Hills following the metalled course of an old railway line. On the further side of the holiday camp at Ainsdale-on-Sea, I bartered tarmac for the equally firm and flat Birkdale Sands which stretched before me like an infinite khaki steppe. The sea had evidently gone out and forgotten to come back. So compacted was the sand that cars were using it as a shortcut to neighbouring Southport.

Sunday, 24th March. My grimy walking gear vanished overnight. Hostess Marion washed it without my knowing and returned it, pressed and aired, along with a veritable cornucopia of a packed lunch. Husband Tony chipped in with a sizeable cheque. Even while I loaded my burdensome backpack into the car, Tony and Marian touted for donations among their obliging neighbours. Their confidence in my ability to finish the task at hand was most reassuring: "See you at Tower Bridge!"

Restored to the land-locked promenade, the genial morning sun was just what the doctor ordered. With barely two-hundred yards under my waist band, I checked my stride and strolled awhile with an elderly widow and her grown-up wheelchair-bound son. From her harassed features it was clear that the distress of her son's malady and the sheer physical demands upon the carer were all too much. I offered her a few well-chosen words of encouragement in an effort to give her flagging morale a much needed boost.

On the outskirts of Crossens my doubtful expertise as a counsellor was called into service once again, this time by a wan young housewife who beseeched me in a manner I felt utterly unable to decline. Patently at the end of her tether, she was recently diagnosed to be suffering from MS. In the confines of her own home she confided to being near suicidal. If nothing else, I consider myself a receptive listener. She proceeded to lift the veil on her private emotions, lay bare her innermost thoughts. I let her talk herself to a standstill. Then, over the ensuing hour and a half, I gently coaxed her from the depths of her depression. It was hard going – but ultimately rewarding. Not only did I leave her in an infinitely better state of mind than when I found her, but I derived as much from our intimate tête-à-tête as my ladyfriend. Pedestrian heal thyself!

Fiddler's Green marked my departure from Merseyside. Welcome to Lancashire, the Red Rose county. For much of the remaining daylight hours I skirted the marshes and mud-flats which flank the southern shore of the Ribble Estuary. Halting at Preston only to get my witness book date-stamped at the local cop shop, I took off along the Ribble's northern bank. Certainly less scenic than the southern side, I was spared further disillusion by the onset of evening which overtook me as I approached the straggling village of Freckleton. But darkness was a double-edged sword. With breath vaporising in the frosty air, I trudged on to the neighbouring aerodrome-dominated community of Warton. Starved of visual distraction, the final pain-wracked walking stint severely tested my powers of endurance.

Monday, 25th March. Thanks to Rodney's wife Sandra I was packing a sufficiently sizeable doggy-bag of tasty tit-bits to see me through the day. These I consumed piecemeal whenever ennui or physical discomfort required staving off – a form of edible security blanket. As it transpired, it was a day of extreme contrasts – ranging from rampant commercialism to sequestered rural charm – which constitute the broad, flat Fylde peninsula.

At the junction of the Ribble Estuary and the Irish Sea I set course for Blackpool aboard the arrow straight promenade, my eyes firmly focused upon Lancashire's rust-red landmark – Blackpool Tower. For seven of the promenade's ten mile length it is served by enchanting green and cream trams which ply one of Britain's few remaining tram networks. At the end of the season these relics from a bygone age will have transported many of Blackpool's six million annual visitors, the vast majority of whom return time and time again for the sheer unabashed vulgarity that is the 'Golden Mile': a multi-coloured ribbon of fortune tellers, amusement arcades, Gothic hotels ('Two minutes from the sea'), discos, bars, waxworks and fun fairs, with a trio of spindle-legged piers thrown in for good measure. Torremolinos-meets-Las Vegas!

My maternal grandmother always longed to visit Blackpool, Britain's largest holiday resort, but never quite made it. Now I was here in her stead. Along the front. the braces-and-knotted-handkerchief brigade were noticeably absent. Apart from stationary cliques of loud-voiced youths blocking the pavement (school had already broken-up) and knots of quiet-spoken pensioners, the place was a hive of earnest cosmetic activity: a lick of paint here, a touch up there and all in preparation for the anticipated Bank Holiday rush. Now if only the good weather would hold, all parties would have cause for celebration. Nan would have loved Blackpool. I know I do.

The promenade terminated at the former (thanks to the 'Cod Wars') deep-water trawler port of Fleetwood, on the Fylde's northern tip. With no alternative route open to me, other than the passenger ferry to Knott End-on-Sea, I doubled back beside the roll on-roll off container ship terminal which fringes the mouth of the River Wyre.

From this point forth the walking day was memorable for all the wrong reasons. My rucksack was playing merry Hell with my lower back and hips, and I nibbled the last of Sandra's 'tasty tit-bits' in a vain attempt to take my mind off my troubles. It was patently clear that I was carrying way beyond my personal weight threshold. As a rough guide to backpacking in comfort, the average male should limit his load to one quarter of his body weight – slightly less for females. According to this theory I was toting the load ascribed to a twelve stone man, whereas I was down to a lean eight stone!

Indicating the upstream limit for sailing boats on the Wyre, I crossed the privately owned toll bridge (pedestrians 1p) between Skippool and Hambleton a little after six. Half an hour later – though it felt immeasurably longer – I entered the sumptuous portals of White Lodge Farm. As they say in these parts: "Where there's mook there's brass" – my farmer host brought most of it into dinner on his boots! Reet piquant it were too! (to use the vernacular). But for all his quaint ways, he did relate a most thought provoking anecdote. Apparently his eldest son, presently on light duties after a cow fell on his neck (!), keeps peafowl as a hobby, one of whom managed to find its way onto the menu via the wheels of a tractor. All agreed that the flesh at best has an acquired taste. The odious by-product only emerged – quite literally – some time later when those who partook of the bird discovered that their urine was tainted with a most unpleasant odour. Which begs the question (spelling inconsistencies apart): was the peafowl – considered a great delicacy in Tudor times – so named in recognition of its pungent after effect?

Tuesday, 26th March. Over breakfast I received a phone call from Chris Greenwood, sub-postmaster of Silloth PO, Cumbria, who wishes to accompany me on my ascent of Scafell Pike (April 1). This was duly arranged.

The overnight gales had subsided to a chill nor'wester by the time I set foot outside. Vacating the scattered hamlet of Sower Carr I bisected the rich and fertile coastal plain of Wyre district, a black-soiled market-gardening country which supports many a prosperous farmer and stone and brick built village alike, regaining the coast at Knott End-on-Sea. From here I followed the wind-raked foreshore north-westerly between alternating expanses of mud and sand to seaward and a billiard table-flat heartland of sheep-shorn marsh.

South-west of Cockerham I abandoned the featureless prairie of Cockerham Marsh for the more expedient – if monotonous – A588. I had less than two hours to cover twelve kilometres; a race against time and the on-coming traffic – and all that that entails: the passive in-take of carbon monoxide fumes, a buffeting from pillar to post and serial near misses. Having developed a ticklish cough in the aftermath of last week's sore throat, I rendezvoused in the old town and city of Lancaster just prior to 4 p.m. to be warmly received by members of the Lancaster and Morecambe MS Society. After regaining my puff, I accompanied secretary Penelope and Co. on a bucket collection around the historic city centre – a chastening experience which brought home to me in no uncertain terms the plight of the disabled in general and the wheelchair-bound in particular. Narrow pavements and a dearth of ramps, to name but two insurmountable obstacles. City planners take note.

Thus the town that gave lodging to Bonnie Prince Charlie and his army on their ill-starred march south during the Jacobite Rebellion of 1745, now played host to yours truly – though hopefully my journey would have a more propitious outcome. Now all I need is the energy to make inroads into my current batch of two dozen postcards (Blackpool) before they get too far out of date. Oh, for an early night wi nowt to do!

Wednesday, 27th March. The morning was clear and cool with sunny intervals. Tiny wisps of cloud skated over a chill powder-blue sky as I made my way north for the River Lune and Greyhound Bridge.

Under the panopticon gaze of the massive square stone keep of Lancaster's Norman Castle, perched high above a bend in the fatally silted river – a navigational calamity which cost the town its prestige as one of the busiest ports in the whole of Great Britain – the Lune's western bank led me south to the marsh-hemmed village of Overton. From the triangulation point overlooking the village, I plotted a north-westerly course for the nuclear power station at Heysham. At the last moment I veered away from this latter-day blot on the seascape, preferring instead the narrow winding streets of Old Heysham to that of the freight harbour and ferry terminal of contemporary Heysham to the south.

Without so much as a signpost to indicate the transition from village to town, north of Heysham I entered the holiday resort of Morecambe. Morecambe's chief asset is its promenade, which faithfully traces the gently indented coastline of Morecambe Bay for fully four miles to stunning effect. The sweeping panoramic view must be seen to be believed. From the vast expanse of the bay itself to the soaring peaks of Southern Lakeland, the prospect is never short of exhilarating.

The Cumbrian village of Kents Bank, seven miles away across the wide reaches of Morecambe Bay, looked invitingly near. But would-be pedestrians beware: the tide-rips and quicksands which abound in this transitional zone are notoriously treacherous, as borne out by the parish records and tombstone inscriptions in Cartmel Cemetery. In the absence of a qualified guide (formerly appointed by the Duchy of Lancaster), I pursued the safer but no less atmospheric Hest Bank Coast Road.

Beyond the once busy industrial town of Carnforth – iron ore was processed here until 1931 – all was suddenly limestone: from the towering rocky eminence of Warton Crag – riddled with Bronze Age caves and abandoned quarries – to the dry-stone field divisions and sheltered stone-hewn homesteads that drowse in this wooded backwater. The whole pleasing ensemble was more indicative to my eye of Cumbria rather than Lancashire. One couldn't avoid the sneaking suspicion that someone, somewhere had drawn the county boundary too far to the north.

It was getting on for five when my laboured footfalls disturbed the hushed tranquillity of Silverdale, an enchanting outpost of winding lanes and wooded walks overhung with pollen-oozing catkins bounteously disseminating their liquid gold. The adolescent Charlotte Brontë, who stayed here in the village with friends, must have gleaned much in the way of scenic inspiration from the experience. For my part, Silverdale galvanised me to pull my finger out and knock off the long overdue postcards. Bed: one am. Acute writer's cramp.

Thursday, 28th March. On the way to despatch my picture-postcards at Silverdale's quaint sub-post office – better late than never – the shade-dappled avenue framed a tantalising vista of the distant haze-hung sea. Once possessing direct frontage onto the River Kent, the village is now high and dry, the capricious deep-water channel having shifted further westward in the 1920s.

Somewhere between Silverdale and Far Arnside I completed the final stretch of the North Lancashire coast. From here on it was Cumbria all the way to the Scottish border. And a more serene introduction one could hardly conceive. Gone was the prairie-like flatland of Wyre district. This was a rolling, verdant landscape lovingly enfolded by the green depths of motionless foliage. I was well and truly in my element – though occasional sorties of low-flying jets did their damnedest to disturb the quietude.

Beyond Arnside, the long haul around the mud flat margin of the Kent Estuary lacked the lush intimacy of Silverdale, an intimacy that only resumed on the afforested approaches to the gardeners' paradise – on account of its sheltered position and mild climate – of Grange-over-Sands, a genteel Victorian watering place backed by lovely wooded fell scenery that sweeps right down to the sea.

At Kents Bank I received a donation and a smacker of a kiss from a lady who saw me in *The Sun* (not on page three I'll wager!). Shortly thereafter a homeward bound cab driver contributed his entire day's tips to the fund. More generosity!

Heading inland towards my evening objective, the pleasant little village of Cark, a soothing carillon of bells drifted down on the tepid air from the hilltop church of Allithwaite. It had been a most satisfying day on all fronts: visually (a wealth of rustic architecture and my first Red Admiral butterfly of the year), physically (no new injuries) and financially (approaching three figures).

Friday, 29th March. I withdrew as soon as propriety would permit, having been woken at 6.30 by the sun's dazzling rays streaming into my room – a brilliance which masked a perishingly cold morning. If anything, the keen edge lent an added piquancy to the heady brew of ozone, leaf mould and coal fires that assailed my nostrils. Like a full-bodied, aromatic white wine chilled to perfection, the countryside is most fragrant at a low temperature.

Less than one kilometre out of Cark, I strolled for a time beside the extensive grounds of the fine Tudor mansion of Holker Hall. The grounds encompass a spectacular display of rhododendrons and azaleas and a 120-acre deer park, all accessible to the general public. From Holker Hall the B5278 meandered north through a thickly wooded terrain to Haverthwaite, the departure point of the steam-hauled Lakeside and Haverthwaite Railway which connects with regular steamer sailings on Lake Windermere, just five kilometres to the north-east.

After negotiating the water-meadowed confluence of the Rivers Crake and Leven, and the cobbled streets of Old Ulverston (the birthplace of Stan Laurel), I recovered the shoreline proper at Bardsea. The coast road ran south to Rampside, affording a scintillating, uninterrupted aspect of Morecambe Bay in its full panoramic glory: 150 square miles of flash tides and glistening sand. For this reason alone the grassy seaward verge of the A5087 is a magnet for picnickers and sightseers alike, many of whom recognised me, inundating me with donations and requests for souvenir photos and the occasional autograph. One couple in particular had been awaiting my passing since lunch-time (my schedule was featured in the local press). So appreciative were they of my undertaking, that both were near to tears as they recounted the tragic moment two years ago when it was discovered that their beloved daughter was stricken with MS.

This emotionally charged encounter fired me up for the final cross-country push to the industrial town of Barrow-in-Furness. From the window of my digs I watched the setting of the roseate sun over Vickerstown and the cream-coloured cathedralesque 'hangers' where Britain's nuclear submarines are fabricated. One such grey-hulled leviathan sat high and dry on the hanger apron, while on all sides cranes loomed large like petrified dinosaurs. The entire dockscape was grimly mindful of a prehistoric graveyard; the final resting place of the great outmoded.

Good Friday had lived admirably up to its name.

Saturday, 30th March. After breakfast, landlady Pat Lumb organised a photo-session with the *North-West Evening Mail.* Like Coronation Street, everyone in Barrow appeared to be on first name terms. For my part I now took the media and public attention in my stride, regarding it all – apart from the charitable aspect – as a marathon public relations exercise on behalf of Royal Mail. I like to think I gave value for money.

Before heading out of Barrow I succumbed to the lure of the submarine complex which I'd seen from my window, the dock bridge presenting an unhindered viewpoint of the scaffold-clad beached leviathan. With camera cocked I was suddenly surrounded by a posse of uniformed walky-talky linked security guards. With three 'photographers' arrested in as many days – still to be released – they thought I was the vanguard of tomorrow's CND march. A simple explanation and I was on my way, photos intact.

From Barrow I trekked north beside the marsh-fringed reaches of the broad Duddon Estuary. Between my destination, Millom, and me lay Duddon Sands, a dangerous expanse of sinking sands and rapidly encroaching tides. Fully two miles at its widest point, it is criss-crossed by a network of footpaths albeit largely forgotten. The mysteries being known only to a handful of locals, I was resigned to a forty-eight kilometre yomp round the byways.

At one o'clock the rain set in. I couldn't complain – it was the first wet day in ten. Thanks to the recent press coverage everybody appeared to know of the walk, several even sent their heartfelt regards to Mary – my inspiration.

Now well off the beaten track, the need for Witness Book authentication impelled me to climb the wooden steps to the signal-box eyrie of signal-man Roger Tyson. The hamlet of Foxfield itself was utterly deserted; Foxfield Station represented my last resort. Roger likened his job to that of a lighthouse keeper: he was his own boss. But this was no Spartan workplace: with the addition of an easy chair, a music centre and the obligatory accoutrements for brewing tea he had personalised his environment into a brown-linoleumed snuggery. On the work front, Roger was hardly run off his feet. Throughout a day of tracking the general course of the West Cumbria line I saw only two trains, leaving plenty of time to sit back with a mug of Lapsang Suchong and let the haunting melodies of Tchaikovsky wash over him…

At Broughton in Furness the cagoule and compass fraternity were out in force; usually slumped against a dry-stone wall, having bitten off more than they could chew, or propping up the bar of the nearest hostelry prior to braving the elements. Whatever the case, they remained a jolly personable bunch – which was handsomely reflected in the host of voluntary contributions and oodles of admiration that came my way. In retrospect, I strongly believe that most all-weather walkers have pronounced masochistic leanings. No gain without pain!

Having seen off the last of the 'Furnesses', at Duddon Bridge, which marked my actual turning point, the riverbank was ablaze with daffodils. An utterly breath-snatching sight. And who could hold it against the wild daffodil that it is without perfume? Further upstream from this Wordsworthian spectacle the scenic course of the River Duddon Valley is immortalised by the poet himself in no less than thirty-five individual sonnets.

Beyond Duddon Bridge I walked south beneath the bare summits of the Cumbrian Mountains; to my left the impatient ocean surged to reclaim its sandy realm after the best part of a day in abeyance. The terrain grew increasingly rugged – and interesting. The bonsai-like combination of weather-stunted trees and undulating boulder-strewn fells (not unlike Black Valley, Co. Kerry, in many respects) was certainly to my taste.

I was in the midst of running through my appeal spiel for the benefit of the camcorder of a quartet of enraptured well-wishers who had driven out expressly for the purpose, when Millom postmaster Mr Evans arrived on the scene. For the remainder of the day I consigned myself into his capable hands, foremost on the agenda being a cheque presentation at Millom Sorting Office, courtesy of Millom and Barrow postal staff, duly recorded by the local press.

Sunday, 31st March. Easter Sunday. Christ is risen. Summertime, as far as the clocks are concerned, is upon us, British Summertime having come into operation in the early hours of this morning. It's a pity the weather isn't aware of this joyous event. Muggy and murky, with frequent showers being the climatic recipe for the day ahead. In such conflicting conditions, selecting the appropriate attire is always a headache.

Sans one hour's sleep I hit the road soon after ten (as far as my body clock was concerned it was still nine). Today's inverted L-shaped route march covered an area of Britain largely bypassed by holiday makers bound for the Lake District, while the shoreline, to a great extent, is inaccessible. Not for nothing is this region known as 'the forgotten coast of north-west England!'

Eating, sleeping, talking, walking (always walking) – that was the pattern of my days. With no feasible hope of let-up for at least six months, would I last the pace? Only time would tell. Also, I had finally come to terms with the immutable fact that gnawing discomfort was to be my constant companion for the foreseeable future. Like a drowning man, I grasping at each and every straw of distraction in the vain hope of diverting my mind from my bruised and battered body: how like the cry of a human baby is that of a new-born lamb; the high incidence of place names hereabouts that end in 'garth' or 'thwaite'. By midday I was unable to reflect upon the undoubted merits of the Lake District without conjuring the dual image of rain and daffodils – in that order, an association that persists to this day.

North of Ravenglass, the seaward terminus of the Ravenglass and Eskdale Railway, the first narrow-gauge railway in England, I forsook the coast and cut inland along the roller-coaster length of the tranquil and unblemished valley of Eskdale.

The deeper I probed the more the twisting, humpbacked, stone-wall bordered byway resembled the Yellow Brick Road of *Wizard of Oz* fame, right down to the skeletal trees which appeared to reach down to grab one. Like Dorothy, I was entranced. In common with the Ravenglass and Eskdale Railway, known locally as "T'laal Ratty" (The Old Ratty), my destination lay at the wilder, rock-flanked, upper end of the valley. In the case of "T'laal Ratty" the end of the line was Dalegarth Station; in my case, the Brook House Hotel, in the beautifully situated village of Boot (a most appropriate name for this ramblers Mecca).

9   I'll take the low road

Climb every mountain,
Ford every stream,
Follow every rainbow
Till you find your dream.
     Oscar Hammerstein II

Monday, 1st April.

EASTER MONDAY. The torrential rain thrummed upon my window since the first ashen light of dawn filtered through a chink in the leaden cloud cover. Parting my curtains I chanced a peek without. The surrounding mountains were lost to an all enveloping white-out of hill fog. In a fit of cold feet – in all senses of the term – I dove back beneath the invitingly warm coverlets, allowing myself the unadulterated luxury of five minutes grace. The mind was willing but the flesh was weak. From the sanctuary of my candlewick cocoon, my heart went out to the guys and gals of the 'Fiddler's Green', Portaferry, who were scheduled to begin their 'round Northern Ireland sponsored wheelchair push' today. I hoped for their sakes that they were faring better in the weather stakes than I.

Chris Greenwood put in an appearance at 9.30 on the dot. As we braced ourselves for the off the irony that today was also April Fool's Day was far from lost to us. Chris marked our departure with the astute observation that one would have to be 100% certifiable to attempt to scale Scafell Pike on such a day. Certifiable or not, we set off up Esk Dale into the oncoming sheeting deluge. Even by the Lake District's notoriously high rainfall level, it was clear that this was no run of the mill day.

At the foot of the near perpendicular Hardknott pass we abandoned the comforting solidarity of unclassified road, swinging left to follow the stately course of the swollen River Esk. Once off the beaten track the going underfoot became a squelchy morass of humus and sphagnum moss. The higher we climbed into the heathery foothills so the River Esk changed in character from its erstwhile majestic incarnation into a gushing torrent.

In making our assault from the south – via Throstle Garth (not a thrush in sight), Great Moss and Broad Stand – we were adopting what is generally deemed the 'Iron Man's' route. Even the hardy Herdwick sheep, reputedly the toughest of the tough, were looking decidedly green about the gills. All around, the exposed upland slopes were awash with newly risen rills and vigorously percolating springs; cataracts were two a penny. And still it chucked it down.

Beyond the disquietly yielding blanket bog of Great Moss our otherwise faultless orientation went somewhat awry. With visibility now down to a matter of yards, accurate compass readings were impossible. In such a meteorological miasma it was inevitable that we would lose our bearings. And lose them we did in spectacular fashion. The culmination of five hour's remorseless onward and upward slog found us atop the 3,162 ft. bulk of Sca Fell – as opposed to our avowed objective, the cloud-obscured neighbouring summit of Scafell Pike. With insufficient daylight hours remaining to make this second ascent and get back to Boot before nightfall, we reluctantly bowed to the inevitable and called it a day. At once, free from the concerted effort of climbing, we were all too aware of our sorry state; wet through and chilled to the marrow. After a brief consultation we began our incident-packed descent with necessary urgency, hampered initially by the slippery scree slope of Lord's Rake. Be it an optical illusion or aberration of the failing light, but part way down I'm convinced I saw a ptarmigan in transitional white/mottled spring plumage. In Britain ptarmigan are thought to be exclusive to the bleak and inhospitable tops of Scottish mountains. Be that as it may, I know what I saw.

Highly improbable though it may seem, conditions actually worsened on the way down. Streams and runnels that we crossed with consummate ease on the way up – whether in a single bound or by stepping stones – were now a succession of raging rapids. In preference to the long-winded manoeuvre of outflanking each maelstrom watercourse at source, we opted to ford them as and when confronted, resulting in a series of waist-deep dousings.

Great Moss benefited no end from this meeting of the waters, doubling in area, not to mention depth, in little over an hour. Further downstream the two waterfalls either side of Throstle Garth gained much in the way of awesome grandeur from the fluvial influx, as the cataclysmic cascades thundered their way seaward in a white water extravaganza.

Back on the valley floor beyond Brotherilkeld, the Esk had burst its banks. To all intents and purposes the surrounding 'pastures' were paddy-fields. The common consensus was that we two had gotten off light. Apart from turning my suspect left ankle a couple of times – on the scree slope and the bed of a mountain stream – I emerged comparatively unscathed.

Returning to Brook House – if not triumphant, then certainly relieved – Chris joined me in a consolatory cup of char before driving back to Silloth. I sensed that he still held himself responsible – quite unfairly – for the 'wrong turning'. Only later, with hindsight, did he correctly apportion blame when he confided that today was the worst day weather-wise in all his twenty years climbing in the fells.

Tuesday, 2nd April. Though the conditions were only marginally better than those of yesterday – frequent showers as opposed to a constant downpour – I wended my way back to the coast with all the self-assurance of one who has endured the worst the elements can throw at one and come through with flying colours.

Resuming my seaside safari at Drigg, Cumbria's coastal corridor stretched north-westerly between the Lakeland fells and dune-bordered shore. A wildly undulating seaboard dominated initially by the four cooling towers of Calder Hall, the first full-scale atomic power station in the world, and thereafter by three industrial centres which mushroomed in the eighteenth century when miners exploited Cumbria's extensive coastal coalfields.

Set at the foot of a vertiginous valley, the village of St Bees signalled my transition from unclassified road to the footpaths which lead to and from the red sandstone promontory of St Bees Head; these sheer, fissured ramparts, set above a gem-strewn beach, are the only cliffs worthy of the name on the entire north-west coast of England and the most conspicuous natural feature by far.

Rounding the steeply shelving rim of Salton Bay, past North Head lighthouse, I caught my first glimpse of the working port of Whitehaven, the most southerly of the aforementioned industrial centres. Benefiting no end from the Wren-style gridiron layout initiated by Sir John Lowther in 1690, Whitehaven was the first purpose planned town in England since the Middle Ages. The impressive town centre includes a wealth of tastefully restored Regency and Victorian buildings.

Wednesday, 3rd April. The air was clear and crisp with all the sharpness of an autumn morning. A spate of showers post lunch (a Mars Bar) completed the autumnal illusion. Like St Bees before it, Whitehaven occupies the ample cleavage of a steep sided coastal valley. No gentle introductions this morning. So stiff was the climb out of town that the head of steam I built up in the process saw me in good stead for the day ahead.

Maryport, the last of the three aforementioned industrial areas, and by far the smallest, nevertheless ranks high as a traditional maritime centre. At its peak Maryport handled over a million tons of seaborne cargo a year, primarily Cumbrian coal and railway lines. Christian Street in the heart of town is named after the first officer and leader of the mutiny aboard the ill-fated HMS *Bounty*. Fletcher Christian was born just outside Maryport in 1764.

Beyond Maryport's Roman fort of Alauna, sections of the ramparts still being visible, my route embraced the Allerdale Ramble for the rest of the day. At twenty kilometres from end to end, this undemanding seaside saunter threads its way north upon a grassy margin beside an extensive low-tide acreage of muddy sand and shingle. The ramble can in fact be accomplished upon either surface, though I struck by the less energy-sapping greensward.

Between Allonby and Silloth I couldn't help but notice a number of danger signs which alerted the unwary beachcomber to the presence of 'Live Bombs – if seen contact Police.' It wasn't until I reached the straggling hamlet of Beckfoot that a laconic local put me squarely in the picture. During WWII the broad waters of the Solway Firth, whose southern shore I now trod, was nicknamed Hudson's Bay on account of the returning Hudson Bombers who used it an unofficial bomb dump. To this day an average of half a dozen bombs are washed ashore each year.

With 53 kilometres covered, I pulled into the dapper little holiday resort of Silloth just in time to catch the last vestige of the setting sun as it sank behind the lilac-hued hills of Dumfries and Galloway. Won't be long now.

On a more mundane note, the drinking water hereabouts is opaque. Like Pernod – minus the kick!

Thursday, 4th April. From the start the weather fluctuated between bright intervals and squally showers: the one constant factor was the bitterly cold head wind whipping in from the Solway Firth which anticipated my every turn and re-aligned itself accordingly. On the injury front, my left ankle is now in a state of permanent sprain, while the soles of both feet are severely bruised after Monday's punishing scree slope descent.

Completing the final stretch of the Allerdale Ramble at the tiny village of Skilburness, chosen by Edward I – the Hammer of the Scots – as the unlikely launching pad from which to attack his enemies north of the border, I battled my way south-westerly through a wild tract of goose-grazed salt marsh to the small farming community of Abbeytown. Dissolved by King Henry VIII in 1538, only the nave of Holme Cultram Abbey – which gave the village its name – survives as the parish church of St Mary.

Beyond Newton Arlosh, founded by Cistercian monks in 1303 after the greater part of Skiburness was swept away in a flood, I lurched from downpour to downpour. Even in the vice-like grip of a mini-monsoon it was hard to conceive that the rural idyll of coastal meadows and scattered slumbering settlements, through which my peregrinations now led me, was once regularly plundered and robbed by ruthless feuding raiders from across the Solway – and vice versa.

Within hailing distance of Anthorn, at the southern edge of the grassy plain that is Bowness Common ('Bow' as in Bow-shaped; 'Ness' as in peninsula) the village was dwarfed by a NATO radio booster station, the spindly arrangement of masts and cables being more suggestive of an oversize runner bean frame than a high-tech security establishment.

I now swung around the headland hugging the gorse-gold coastline all the way to the sleepy backwater of Bowness-on-Solway. Here the Solway Firth is at its narrowest – the Scottish Shore being just one mile away – placing Bowness squarely in the front line in those dim distant days of tit-for-tat raids. But the village's chief claim to prominence is as the western limit of Hadrian's Wall, which here was simply a rampart of clay, turf and wood.

A native of Newcastle, Jean Annise, landlady of the King's Arms, who was providing me with bed and board, has therefore lived at both ends of Hadrian's Wall. But surely never in such august surroundings at those at present. In the days before Cumbria was annexed to England, Robert the Bruce reputedly slept at the King's Arms while on a tax gathering mission. Certainly the hostelry is contemporary with the period in question – having not only been fabricated from the remains of, but built on the site of the Roman fort of Maia, the largest fort on the entire wall.

I pitied Robert the Bruce that Jennings bitter wasn't on tap in his day – he'd have slept the sounder for it.

Friday, 5th April. The sky was blue, the sun bright, the air ozone fresh. To all intents and purposes I was enjoying the perfect spring day. At least I was until late morning when the mother of all rainstorms took a firm hold. In the meantime I grasped the opportunity to scout out the last scant remnants of Hadrian's Wall – with negligible results. I made do instead with a snapshot keepsake of the Vallum, which crosses the patchwork fields to the south-west of Bowness. Running the entire length of the wall on the English side, in its heyday the Vallum was a gigantic earthwork some 120 feet across. Now little more than a soggy ditch at best, current thinking suggests that it fulfilled the function of a military demarcation line. Civilians keep out!

As fate would have it, my route and that of the non-existent wall were one and the same – be it as far as the historic border town of Laguvalium (Carlisle). At least I could take comfort from having walked some fourteen of its seventy-two mile course. For the best part of four and a half hours I zigzagged from hamlet to deserted hamlet. The thirty-four changes of direction incorporated into the wall's well documented easterly progress were unprecedented for the usually straightforward Roman engineers. No doubt when it was completed in about AD127 the great mural barrier ran parallel to the high water mark. Now, almost two-thousand years later, it was landlocked; separated from the natural moat of the Solway Firth by gorse-garlanded salt flats.

As confirmed by its name, the sad little single street 'village' of Port Carlisle was once the seagoing outlet of the prestigious Carlisle Canal, along which, in 1829, Stephenson's Rocket was carried by barge *en route* to Liverpool and locomotive immortality. At the time of its inception plans were afoot to lavish Port Carlisle with wide boulevards and Tuscan-porched houses – all of which came to naught. The few visible signs of the canal, and that of the railway which replaced it, are fast disappearing. All that remains of the original grandiose commercial venture are two terraces of cottages either side of a handsome Georgian house.

In common with Bowness and Drumburgh before it, Burgh by Sands stands on the site of a Roman fort (Aballava). The castellated St Michael's Church at the centre of which harkens back to a time when it served an additional role as a refuge from Scottish raiders. Its finest hour, however, came in 1307 when it was chosen for the lying in state of Edward I after his death at nearby Lanercost Priory while on his way to renew the war against the Áuld Enemy.

It was still bucketing down when I turned into Junction Street, the city centre locale of Carlisle's Royal Mail MLO (Mechanised Letter Office). Both press and a border TV camera crew were in attendance to chronicle the event where I was presented with substantial cheques for the National Campaign and local MS research. The TV cameraman in question contrived to miss my original arrival and asked us to run through it again (and again) for his benefit. Suffice it to say, each repetition lacked the spontaneity of the original 'muffed' take.

I checked into Howard Lodge Guest House on cue to catch myself on the goggle-box for the first time. A painful never to be repeated experience!

Saturday, 6th April. It was a dull and overcast morning – giving way to rain in the afternoon (eight wet days running now and plenty more in the offing). It came as no surprise to discover that Carlisle wasn't mentioned in the Domesday Book, for it was still very much part of Scotland when William I's great Record of the Lands of England was compiled in 1086.

My north-westerly course to the Scottish border bisected the mud-flats and marshland flanking the estuaries of the Esk and Sark rivers. These bleak borderlands were once the domain of lawless Reiver families – the land-borne equivalents of the coastal raiders further to the west – who systematically stole each other's herds, chattels and goods over a period of three-hundred barbarous years. Their unscrupulous activities gave us such words as 'bereave' and 'blackmail'.

Feeling perceptively colder with every northward step, I crossed the River Sark into Scotland at precisely 13.10 p.m. At Gretna, the first settlement over the border, I paused for a celebratory pot of tea and round of salad sandwiches at 'Ye Olde Toll Bar', right next door to the famous 'First House' marriage room.

Veering now to the west, a three hour trek along the rich black-soiled farmland and tidal mud-flats of the fast-flowing Solway Firth's northern shore brought me to the Victorian red-sandstone town of Annan, the 'capital' of Annan and Eskdale district, with its wealth of Scottish vernacular architecture.

A hot soak in the bath at my lodgings for the night, provided ample scope for reflection upon my introduction to Caledonia. Such is the power of television that I received recognition aplenty throughout the day. Donations too came flooding in – which effectively scotched the myth of the 'tight fisted' Jock (largely propagated south of the border). And how wise of Scotland to retain the pound note.

Sunday, 7th April. In readiness for an anticipated daylong buffeting I donned my weatherproofs – and was immediately thankful as showers too became a prominent feature. In crossing the River Annan I caught up with and overtook a column of inadequately garbed teenagers walking on behalf of Leukaemia Research. Assuming yours truly to be the leader of this merry little band, by virtue of my 'advanced' years and sensible attire, a reporter/photographer requested an ad lib interview and an accompanying photo. Before disclosing my independence, I exacted a promise from the hapless journo to run my story in full, including appeal details. A good, if devious, morning's work.

I both began and ended the day aboard what locals refer to as 'The Low Road' (B724), as opposed to 'The High Road' (A75). In between times I walked the deserted seashore from the lighthouse dominated Barnskirk point to the minute hamlet of Moss-side. With eyes streaming from the constant chill head wind I turned my back on the sand and shingle sea-front and headed up-country for the cloistered village of Ruthwell – the only viable route around the marsh-bound mouth of Lochar Water. For such a tiny community it has much to commend it. Not only is Ruthwell the home of the world's first Savings Bank, founded in 1810 by Dr Henry Duncan, and still going strong, but also the Ruthwell Cross – a magnificent example of seventh century stone carving, inscribed with verses from the earliest-known English poem, *The Dream of the Rood* – is housed in a specially designed apse in the parish church.

Re-engaging the low road west of Thwaite, I paused to sample the metallic-tasting waters of the famous, some say infamous, Brow Well. For it was here in July 1796 that Robert Burns came as a last resort, on the incompetent advice of his doctors, to bathe in and drink the frigid waters in the vague hope of curing his ongoing malady. Before I left, a Mr Williamson from a nearby cottage came racing over, camera in hand, to take my picture 'for posterity'. As far as he could recall, I was the first 'celebrity' to visit the well since he photographed John Merrill on the same spot during his 1978 mainland UK walk. Though unlike me, my predecessor refrained from partaking the waters. Wise man. Mr Williamson concluded by letting me in on a little known secret: "Within a month of drinking from the well 'Rabbie' Burns was dead!" Now he tells me!

Once again ploughing a solitary furrow, I bypassed Caerlaverock National Nature Reserve – a network of deep channels and occasional quicksands rendering the 13,000 acres of Merse, or Saltmarsh, extremely hazardous to walkers – before picking-up the coast proper to the south-west of the red sandstone ruins of Caerlaverock Castle. Robert Paterson, 'Old Mortality' of the Sir Walter Scott novel, was buried in the kirkyard within the moated castle. Commanding sumptuous views over the Merse and Solway Firth it positively demanded to be photographed. But my eye was taken by the inordinate number of dead lambs scattered about the intervening pasture. The deadly combination of wind and rain had levied a heavy toll.

Without seeing so much as a single pub or shop all day I reached Dumfries shortly before five. The final twelve kilometre leg along the eastern bank of the tidal channel of the River Nith was memorable primarily for the welcome volume of patently alive and hyper-active lambs, periodically gambling and demanding to suckle with a swift head butt to the teats of their supremely placid mothers.

Monday, 8th April. First port of call was the post office, where I despatched two parcels, laundry and souvenirs; followed in quick succession by whistle stop visits to Burn's Mausoleum in St Michael's Churchyard and the substantial stone-hewn house where the 'Heaven taught ploughman' died of 'subacute bacterial endocarditis'. And not, as a teetotal James Currie, the poet's first posthumous biographer, erroneously attributed to 'alcoholism, womanising and general debauchery'.

Having already secured the assurance of a whip-round I was promptly escorted back to the sorting office by a photo-journalist who was determined to get a picture of me being waved off by a group of postal colleagues. With the desired shot safely in the can, we strolled back to the newspaper office where we were reverently approached by a Mr Douglas, possessor of the most comprehensive autograph collection in Britain. While I appended my modest moniker, I noticed that the previous signatory was none other than the Dalai Lama.

As if to confuse the first time visitor, the 'Lowlands' beyond Dumfries are far hillier than most of England. And as the day wore on the terrain became even more undulating, with an abundance of trees thrown in for good measure. In adopting a temporary southward passage to accommodate the excesses of the deeply indented coastline, no afforested section was more impressive than the Scots pines of Shambellie Woods, planted between 1775 and 1780 when Burns was at the height of his powers. Weather-wise, wind, sun and showers remained the order of things – with the emphasis decidedly on wind.

On entering the grey-stone village of New Abbey I fulfilled a pressing engagement with the imposing mellow-stoned ruins of Sweetheart Abbey – the first recorded usage of the word 'sweetheart' in the English language. Surely one of the loveliest building in the region, the Abbey was founded by Lady Devorgilla Balliol in 1273 in memory of her beloved husband John Balliol (from whom Balliol College derives its name) and whose embalmed heart remained her 'sweet, silent companion' until her own death in 1289 – when both were buried before the high altar. Devotion personified!

From the well-maintained village of Kirkbeam I digressed shoreward to cast an eye over the modest cottage where John Paul Jones – America's first Naval Commander – was born in 1747. The following year the now disused lighthouse at Southerness Point, four kilometres to the south, was built to guide emigrant ships and coastal vessels to and from the then busy port of Dumfries.

My westerly route now carried me to land-ward of the six mile expanse of Mersehead Sands. Without my cumbersome haversack I might have risked crossing it on foot; with it I had grave reservations as to my ability to outpace the tide which sweeps in at an alarming rate of knots. On the homestretch between Caulkerbush and Sandyhills Bay, a fortuitous break in the ancient cliff-top oak-grove furnished a stupendous prospect of Lot's wife – a towering free-standing stack of igneous rock.

Tuesday, 9th April. Overlooking White Loch I received a roadside lesson in semantics from John and Huey, a pair of dignified itinerant artisans. Both clearly impervious to the continued wet and windy weather, I casually addressed them as dry stone wallers and was roundly rebuked with quasi-indigence: north of the border these highly skilled exponents of a dying craft are known as dry-stone 'dykers'. I stood corrected.

Retaining my westerly yaw, I set my sights on the Victorian sea-bathing resort of Rockcliffe where I gained access to the splendidly scenic Jubilee Path, a high-level walkway which links Rockcliffe with Kippford one mile to the north. In spite of the tattered and streaming sky, the phenomenal view across countless bays and headlands to the massif conical spires of the distant Galloway Mountains was of jaw-dropping proportion.

Unlike its law-abiding neighbour to the south, Kippford (or Scaur) has a more earthy pedigree. Now the playground of yachtsmen and windsurfers, the wooded inlets and secluded anchorages were once the realm of smugglers. From Kippford I continued upstream towards Buittle Bridge, the first feasible crossing of Urr Water. At Dalbeattie I enjoyed a first-hand encounter with quintessential small-town Caledonia: Georgian dormer-style cottages flanked the High Street on either side, some featuring the stepped-gables so indicative of lowland Scotland.

Dalbeattie Postman's Office was no less characterful. Starting life as the Postmaster's private residence (circa 1906), it retains many original features. Entering was like stepping back to the turn of the century: wire-backed wooden sorting frames, softwood 'facing' table, leather-trimmed wicker trolleys, etc. But the town had saved its principal title to fame until last. Dalbeattie Quarry provided much of the stone to make the Thames Embankment. A little piece of England that is forever Scotland.

After a daylong deviation around the shingle and sand-backed tidal flats of Rough Firth, Orchardton and Auchencairn Bays, I finally called a halt at The Rossan, an early Victorian Manse overlooking the bay towards Heston Island. As well as a wide and varied ordinary diet, my hostess, Mrs Bardsley, specialised in vegan and gluten-free meals, which gave me ample opportunity to see if I'm cut out for a vegetarian lifestyle. Verdict: absolutely delicious, if wind inducing.

Wednesday, 10th April. For the first half of a memorable day I clung possessively to the high cliffs and mysterious coves of Kirkcudbrightshire's ragged coastline. Part way to Balcary Point the seaweed-draped stake-nets of Balcary fishery zigzagged far out into the receding tide; this ancient method of fishing reaps a rich harvest of salmon and bass.

Though out of vision of much of the time, the audible presence of the Solway Firth was a reassuring companion. Lone walkers apart, here the green-mantled cliffs were the undisputed domain of myriad sea birds; fulmar, cormorant, shag and gull, while to seaward razor-bills bobbed on the rising swell.

South-west of Balcary Point a rock formation known as Adam's Chair harks back to the pre-1820s when the contraband trade was at its illegal height. For it was from this distinctive lookout place that a concealed watcher would signal with a lamp to his comrades off-shore as and when the coast was – quite literally – clear.

At Rascarrel Bay the demanding cliff path succumbed to a muddy farm track; whereupon my traitorous left ankle let me down at every turn. The sodden cliff-top pastures, meanwhile, produced a further spate of dead lambs, leaving plenty of scope for nature's dustbin men – the carrion crow. I reluctantly parted company with the coast at Orroland Lodge, eventually throwing in my lot with the A711 at Dundrennan. To the south of the village a thirteenth century Chapter House and some Norman masonry are all that remain of the Cistercian Abbey where Mary Queen of Scots reputedly spent her last night in Scotland.

The bad weather displayed not the slightest inclination to relent. But deliverance was at hand in the guise of a fond familiar face. On the stroke of 2 p.m. a car passed me in a blur of wildly waving occupants. Minutes later, the vehicle having done a rapid U-turn and disgorged one of two passengers, Ken Merrell– a 'postal pal' from Lower Edmonton – came bounding up behind me (wife Pamela and son Vince remained sensibly car-borne). For the next rain-soaked hour and a quarter we walked in tandem, lost in conversation, oblivious to the conditions. And all the while our twin footfalls echoed to the rumble of gunfire from the military testing zone to the south, without whose enforced detour our reunion wouldn't have taken place.

Thursday, 11th April. With no foreseeable let-up in the ever worsening conditions, I made tracks down the western side of Kirkcudbright Bay as fast as my gammy leg and conspiring elements would allow, hell bent on alleviating my physical discomfort at the earliest opportunity by completing the day's itinerary as far ahead of schedule as was humanly possible.

From the deserted beach-side picnic area at Gull Craig I cut across the headland to the wooded shore of Brighouse Bay. Thereafter I began a torturous cliff-top trek, culminating at the minuscule yet architecturally rich hamlet of Kirkandrews. I was particularly drawn to the elaborate castellated mausoleum of 'James Brown of Knoxbrex' and the heavily bird-limed Corseyard Tower.

Emerging from the network of waymarked paths which criss-cross Fleet Forest, Gatehouse of Fleet was nothing short of a picturesque ghost town. From here I began the final five mile slog along the west bank of Fleet Bay – past the Murray Arms Hotel, where Robbie Burns penned *Robert Bruce's March to Bannockburn*, which begins with the enduring catch-phrase 'Scots, wha hae'; past Cardoness Castle, one of the best preserved fifteenth century fortresses in Scotland – to 'High Auchenlarie', a 400 year old B&B-cum-working Beef Farm, arriving drenched and bedraggled. Located halfway up the cloud-capped Ben John and Barholm Hills, beside Auchenlarie burn, the surrounding 'pastures' were awash with the runoff from the upper slopes. I felt sorry for the floundering cattle.

Winnie Johnstone, landlady of the year (she had a Caithness Glass trophy to prove it), greeted me like one of her own. 'Her own' included not one but two gorgeous daughters. As befits the jewel in the Scottish tourist board's crown, 'High Auchenlarie' was chock-full of guests from all four corners of Great Britain. But cosy and welcoming though the place undoubtedly is, it is Winnie's traditional Scottish cuisine that steals all the plaudits. From the *hors-d'oevres* stage right through to the pudding all helpings are strictly for the larger appetite. And just as we thought our gastric juices could take a well earned rest, in she came with a late night cuppa and a tantalising selection of sweetmeats: shortbread, caramel, petite cream cakes.

Friday, 12th April. In contrast to the wild and desolate region of 'Grey Galloway' to the north, the southern half of the province is – when not in the wintry clutches of such foul weather – fertile dairy-farming country. But on all sides the terrain had long since passed saturation point. Leaden hoofed cattle trudged wearily from their pasture. For pasture read bog. If anything the rain was falling more heavily than the day before.

Thomas Carlyle once told Queen Victoria that he believed the coast road between Gatehouse of Fleet and Creetown to be the most scenic in her entire kingdom. On a fine summer's day, perhaps. On this particular godforsaken April morning the much vaunted 'commanding view' over Fleet Bay, Wigtown Bay and the Irish Sea was obliterated by a sopping grey offshore murk.

The eighteenth century 'planned' village of Creetown, overlooking the marshy estuary of the River Cree, achieved its industrial zenith in the nineteenth century as the main port for the exportation of locally quarried granite – much of which contributed to the construction of the Thames Embankment and Liverpool Docks.

From Creetown I shaped a dog-leg course for Newton Stewart – recently voted the 'Friendliest town in the UK' – upon the A75. The only reprieve from the elements and backwash from passing lorries came at Palnure, where I stopped to complement the eccentric owner of a front garden devoted entirely to gnomes and similar elfin folk.

Saturday, 13th April. One month to the day since I left Ireland. And, more significantly, my first entirely rain-free day in Scotland.

From its sheltered river valley setting, I departed Newton Stewart a little before ten expecting to rendezvous with a photographer from the *Galloway Gazette* somewhere along the coast road between ten and eleven o'clock. As it transpired, it was eleven-fifteen before she caught up with me, by which juncture the snaking course of the River Cree was way behind me and it was too late to revert to shoreline walking until I reached the other side of Wigtown. In the meantime I made a pilgrimage to the wide-spread saltings and marshland to the east of this ancient burgh and county town where stands a memorial to the 'Wigtown Martyrs' – two women covenantars, aged 18 and 65, who were tied to stakes in Wigtown Bay and left to drown by the incoming tide because they refused to conform to the English Prayer Book. As if to atone for such religious intolerance, contemporary Wigtown was ablaze with cherry blossom. But zealous observance was far from dead: Saturday afternoon and not one shop was open!

East of Kirkinner, a low-level single street village reminiscent of those of Southern Ireland, I reclaimed the tree-lined shore. Confirming the opinion of several Wigtownians that this is the wettest spring in a decade, much of the luxuriant coastal plain was under a foot or more of accumulated rain water; a glassy veneer already alive with a rich broth of microscopic life forms. After two weeks of near constant precipitation, skylarks grasped this rare opportunity to soar heavenward and deliver their distinct warbling song. A positive tonic!

Having vacated the stewartry of Kirkcudbrightshire the previous afternoon, I concluded my first complete day in Wigtownshire, Scotland's most south-westerly county and one of its quietest corners, at Garlieston. This trim, unspoilt little village of pastel-rendered houses overlooks one of the narrowest bowling greens in Scotland and a beautiful bay flanked by rocky headlands.

Sunday, 14th April. For reason of their near identical rise and fall in tide level to those of France, the twin bays of Garlieston and Rigg (or Cruggleton) came to prominence during the second world war as the secret base for the research, testing and assembly of Mulberry Harbours, which played an indispensable role in the D-day landings.

With this historic nugget in mind, I kept my eyes peeled for discarded WWII relics. Far from concealing any military hardware, the mangrove-like spinney that fringed the now sheltered and peaceful inlets, where wind-sculpted trees crept down to the very tide's edge, harboured instead a wealth of flora and fauna. Escorted the length of the waterlogged woodland trail by an attendant covey of chaffinches, swept along before me like leaves in a breeze, my observations included a grey seal – watching me in turn from the sanctuary of the water – and a startled roe buck bounding into the cover of a thicket, its powder puff white rump fluffed out in alarm. The saturated areas around the 'ponds' flourished with camps of yellow flag irises, their very presence bearing testament to the sodden terrain and warming influence of the North Atlantic drift.

Either side of the village of Isle of Whithorn, originally the port of the inland burgh of Whithorn, the coastline assumed a rugged grandeur hitherto unseen in Wigtownshire – though nowhere do the cliffs rise above 1,000 feet. Here St Ninian brought Christianity to the Southern Picts, founding a kirk or chapel in AD397. Having rounded the promontory of Burrow Head by mid afternoon, I encountered a further tangible legacy of the saint overlooking the boulder beach of Port Castle Bay. St Ninian's Cave, where Scotland's first Christian missionary spent many hours in prayer, is now a place of pilgrimage in its own right.

At the miniature landscape of Monreith, while slaking my prodigious thirst in the elevated south-facing sun-lounge of author/ecologist Marjorie Hingley, I espied the shadowy plateau of the Isle of Man, resembling a dreadnought at anchor.

Named after its founder Sir William Maxwell of Monreith, the harbour village of Port William straggles along the pebbly shore of Luce Bay at the foot of a range of low hills. I was billeted for the night with the Reids, a most amicable couple. Both spoke with a delightfully lilting accent known as 'Galloway Irish'; to such a degree that I actually thought they hailed from the Emerald Isle. After dinner – which included my introduction to Arbroath Smokies, an immediate firm favourite – I was taken on a highly profitable collection-cum-pub crawl in the light-hearted fellowship of several members of the local Lions Club. During the course of an extremely enjoyable evening I overheard one of our party order "a pint o' heavy and a low flyer" – which translates to "a pint of bitter and a *Famous Grouse* Whisky". Two countries divided by a common tongue!

Between hostelries we stood, three sheets to the wind, in object awe of the stately going down of the sun. Monopolising the entire western horizon, the Rins peninsula appeared to float on the burnished-gold waters of Luce Bay like a desert mirage...

Monday, 15th April. I awoke to a glorious God-given morning: receding into the middle-distance a sun-spangled Luce Bay rhythmically lapped a low-tide shoreline white with rime. Considering Port William's reputation for having a mild frost-free climate, courtesy of the warm air brought in by the Gulf Stream, this was a singular occurrence indeed.

As arranged, a delegation of Lions (maybe that should be a 'pride'?) called for me at 9.30 to supervise a photo-call and presentation of cheques on the quay above the curving dried-out harbour. Not that I was aware of the extent of local generosity at the time. So acute was the trajectory of the sun's rays that all present – barring the about-faced photographer – were temporarily blinded by the intense glare.

Virtually before I knew it, it was 'Good bye' and 'Good luck' as I was sent merrily on my way upon by far the loveliest stretch of Scottish coast road to date. Over the following four hours I tramped above the high tide line mesmerised by the breath-depriving scenery, the abundance of wildlife and the pseudo-midsummer climate. Throughout the walking day peacock and red admiral butterflies maintained a high profile. Though, being so early in the year, the latter were almost certainly migrants from the continent. Offshore, grey seals basked head-uppermost, like animated buoys, in the quartz-clear water. On a physical level, all aches and pains were for the present forgotten as I leapt at the opportunity to shed my shell garments. For the first time in what felt like an eternity I revelled in the liberty of shorts and wind-shirt without fear of imminent rain.

Eight kilometres along the rocky shore at Corwall Port, the rectangular ruin of the tenth century Chapel Finian looked down on a landing place used by Irish pilgrims on their way to St Ninian's Kirk, Isle of Whithorn. The further north I travelled so the rock-strewn seaboard was superseded by tracts of pliant sand. Negotiating the heathery heights of the Mull of Sinniness I descended to the all but derelict eighteenth century harbour of Stair Haven, now the haunt of picnickers and the odd die-hard lobster fishermen. Looking across Luce Bay to Torrs Warren, an M.o.D. no-go area, the metallic glint of sun-on-fuselage heralded the first of the day's bombing runs by jets of the RAF, each billowing mushroom plume followed hard on the heels by a dull thud. Sadly, in the aftermath of the Gulf conflict, a necessary inconvenience.

Set back from the coast and to one side of the narrow opening to the glen from which it takes its name, Glenluce is generally recognised as the longest village in Scotland. I was spending the night at 'Millbank', a former lint mill (circa 1860), in the convivial society of Raymond Jaques, his lady friend Ann – a newly diagnosed MS sufferer – and Blackstuff the cat.

Tuesday, 16th April. It was the second squintingly bright morning on the trot. And warm enough to begin the day as I so earnestly hoped to continue – minus my weatherproofs. The curiously shaped Rhins of Galloway, alternatively known as 'little Scotland', arced away into a hazy infinity. I set a leisurely pace, content to enjoy the benison of the morning. Such moments were meant to be savoured. Bareagle Forest was alive with the buzz of insects and the lilt of bird song. Sunshine slanted through the coniferous canopy of Sitka spruce and Monterey and Corsican pine; and the air, fragrant with scent of approaching summer, elevated my sense of oneness with the world to a new ethereal height. A metal plaque at the entrance to a cattle pasture seemed to typify my compassionate mood: 'The righteous man considereth his beasts.' And so say all of us!

As I came through Sandhead the water-borne activities of black-suited RAF divers in Luce Bay were reaching fever pitch – they still couldn't find an unexploded bomb 'misplaced' the day before. How remiss of them!

Extending from Sandhead all the way down to my evening abode near the dramatic promontory of the Mull of Galloway – the southernmost tip of Scotland – it was superlatives every step of the way. Scattered far and wide between the golden sanded beaches and quiet coves which are a prime feature of the peninsula's tranquil eastern shoreline, village post offices remained the best bet for a spot of idle gossip and much needed liquid refreshment. Ardwell postmaster Mr Wainwright, an avid yachtsman, made me pledge that I would kiss the ground when I made the North Norfolk resort of Blakeney, his all time favourite sailing haunt. A further eleven kilometres down the coast at Drummore – Scotland's southernmost village – the postmistress took me into her confidence: "Multiple Sclerosis has reached epidemic proportion in these parts".

From the precipitous multi-coloured cliffs which ring the Mull of Galloway I doubled back across the narrow isthmus to 'East Cairngaan Cottage': Scotland's most southerly Guest House.

If my calculations are correct, I've now passed the 5,900 mile mark. A major milestone in every sense of the word!

Wednesday, 17th April. Cairngaan – meaning 'Windy Hill' – was certainly living up to its name. After a grey dawn, the wind freshened by the minute. In deference to the elements I postponed picking up the cliff-girt wild West Coast until I reached Portencorkie. All the while the rolling country and sodden scrub made for laborious progress. What a contrast to yesterday's comparative breeze. In such conditions I pitied the poor Picts who by all accounts made their last defiant stand here amidst the dry-stone dykes and hawthorn field boundaries of the Rhins. But thoroughly oppressive though the weather might be, it could have been far worse. It's a sobering thought that but for the moderating influence of the Gulf Stream, whose warming currents wash this cliff-bound coast, the country would be enveloped by a new Ice Age.

And so to the picturesque holiday centre of Portpatrick – Galloway's Gretna Green. For until the Irish Steam-packet service was transferred to Stranraer in 1862, the seventeenth century parish church in the centre of Portpatrick was the destination of many an eloping couple, particularly those from the Emerald Isle.

From my window on the second floor of South Cliff House Hotel the lights of Donaghadee – just twenty-one miles away across the North Channel – could clearly be seen reflected on the underside of the ominously gathering clouds...

Thursday, 18th April. From the word go the weather seemed unable to make up its mischievous mind. Regardless of the brilliant sunshine that hastened my rising, by the time I actually got underway it was pelting down. With weatherproofs and demanding terrain a day-long fixture, I alternately broiled and froze. And though deceptively bright for long spells, the bitter cold of the near gale force head wind left me with eyes and nose in full viscous flood.

The sun burst through as I scaled the cliffs to the north of Portpatrick: St Patrick is said to have sailed to Ireland from this very port – hence the name. For the first few kilometres or so the coast path corresponds with the beginning of the Southern Upland Way, a gentle cliff-top constitutional which undulates sedately – if soggily – past a battery of radio masts, a windswept golf course and a succession of rocky coves, before abutting upon the tarmac service road to the east of Blackhead lighthouse. Fronting the hilltop beacon was an enormous foghorn – and wallowing incongruously in the surf below was the broken-backed wreck of an Irish freighter. If rumour can be given any credence, it would seem that – on putting out from Belfast Lough – the crew inexplicably put the vessel on auto-pilot before hitting in turn the bottle, the hay, and the Scottish mainland.

Thereafter my route and that of the coast-to-coast Southern Uplands Way diverged, the latter to weave its 212 mile course across country to Cockburnspath, I to complete a clockwise orbit of the northern peninsula of the Rhins of Galloway. Corsewall Point Lighthouse made a pleasant change of scene from the habitual rolling greensward, towering dark cliffs and lichen-covered rocks – all the more so for having been designed by Robert Stevenson, the grandfather of Robert Louis Stevenson. Meanwhile, Milleur Point – the northernmost tip of the Rhins – seemed as good a place as any to get stuck into my lunch-pack. On a clear day the Mull of Kintyre would have been well within my visual range. In its mist-masked absence, I made do with a grandstand view of the hill-ringed seaward end of Loch Ryan.

At Lady Bay, where local tradition asserts that Saint Columba landed on his way to Iona, I branched off from the coast, before wheeling down-country for the deserted outpost of Kirkcoln, generally accepted as being a contraction of 'The Church of St Columba'.

The wishy-washy sun was already slipping down the sky as I trudged into Kirkcolm and made directly for the Blue Peter Hotel, where a lavish meal was set before me. With my spare collection box prominently displayed on the bar – in the hope that the teams competing in that night's domino fixture would be as generous as my hosts Alice and John Mason – I made myself scarce. I was more than ready for bed.

Friday, 19th April. Less than three kilometres out of Kirkcolm, The Wig – a crescent shaped inlet – unfolded to my left. Now the home of Loch Ryan Sailing Club, Glenside Slipway was once an integral feature of The Wig Flying Boat Base. During two world wars the population of this quiet rural region was swollen to 1,800 by crews and ground staff of up to 300 Sunderland and Catalina Flying Boats. What a spectacle it must have been at its aeronautical acme!

Approaching Stranraer on a parallel course to the incoming Sealink ferry from Larne, the shortest sea passage between Ireland and Scotland, I was recognised by a fellow postie who notified me that a collection on behalf of the 'Around the Isles Campaign' was at that moment in full swing at the town's sorting office. After fulfilling my PR obligations with the press I paid a call on the staff of the Sheucan Street sorting office to thank them sincerely for their sterling effort.

From Kirkcolm to Stranraer I had benefited considerably from the chivvying assistance of a vigorous tail wind. Now, in swerving northward for Ballantrae, I felt the full head-on impact of the prevailing icy blast. Which, together with the ever steepening gradient, made for a testing conclusion to the day.

In passing through the peaceful lochside settlement of Cairnryan, the Kraken-like presence of a solitary submarine tied-up alongside the near-derelict pier recalled the village's WWII heyday as a major landing point for much needed supplies from the United States. Only the tell-tale incandescent flicker of acetylene torches gave away the area's, to my mind, traitorous development as a ship-breaker's yard.

Two kilometres short of Finnarts Bay I crossed the regional boundary. Strathclyde – whose wooded margin I now plied – boasts more coastline than the whole of France. At the seaward end of Glen App, I renounced the A77 in favour of a rough forestry track. On all sides the scenery was unmistakably Scottish: peaks and pine trees as far as the landward eye could see. To the north, an invigorating overland trail wound its way up and over Finnarts Hill towards Ballantrae fourteen kilometres distant. Considering the unremitting legwork of the last three days, I must admit to being well chuffed at my overall condition. Even my manky ankle appears to be responding slowly but surely to nightly embrocations of Deep Heat and a tight dressing. All I have to do now is steer clear of further sprains.

Looking north from the wuthering heights of Downan Hill, Ballantrae was a sharply defined island of whitewash and sandstone in a sea of rippling green, with a dramatic overview to the mountainous Isles of Ailsa Craig and Arran. I delighted in the sublime beauty and airy location. Having seen my fill I descended to Baile-an-Traigh – the 'village on the shore' – where I spent a comfortable evening amid the bijou elegance of Ardstinchar Cottage, overlooking the River Stinchar's snaking outflow of tidal creeks and lagoons and overlooked in turn by the gorse-girdled ruins of Ardstinchar Castle.

Saturday, 20th April. Despite the usual overnight application of Deep Heat and heavy strapping my wretched ankle – bor-ing! – has inexplicably reverted to square one. Anyway, sound in wind if not in limb, at least the weather was on my side. Dry and breezy, with occasional welcome glimpses of the genial sun, away from the shelter of the virtually unbroken escarpment of hills and cliffs that border the coast road to landwards it was still refreshingly nippy.

Limping pronouncedly from the outset, southern Strathclyde's flat coastal strip was as undemanding a convalescence as I could hope for, the fishing port of Girvan being my appropriately curtailed objective. Barely twenty minutes out of Ballantrae I stopped to read the inscription on a roadside memorial to one Henry Ewing Torbet (alias 'Snib'). Situated within sight of Bennane Cave, where this 'Respected and Independent' reformed chartered accountant eked out a Spartan existence until his death in 1983 at the age of 71, the rough-hewn cairn was financed and erected by the same west-coast folk in whose hearts and affections he won a place after rejecting the 'rat race' of east coast Dundee.

The other side of Bennane Head, Sawny Bean's Cave was a horse of a different colour. Credited as being Scotland's last cannibal, this demonic Charles Manson-type figure held sway over an incestuous band of cut-throats. God help the hapless traveller taking the low road between Stranraer and Ayr who fell into their grisly clutches. Those parts of the anatomy that weren't eaten there and then were literally salted away for later consumption. So incensed by their foul deeds was James I that he led a battalion of Dragoons to put an end to Sawny Bean's sordid reign once and for all. Utterly sickened by the sight which met his eyes within the cave, the King ordered it to be blown up – lest the gruesome truth emerge.

Scarcely one kilometre up the coast at Games Loop Caravan Park, having ground to virtual standstill close by the main gate, I didn't need asking twice to take tea and toast with Netta and William Fulton. From the picture window of their caravan, just shy of the shingle tide line, Ailsa Craig – nine miles to the north-west – resembled a sea-girt sugar-loaf mountain. Granite from this immense igneous outcrop, the core of a long extinct volcano, was once quarried for fashioning into curling stones. But the curler's loss is the bird world's gain. In excess of 10,000 pairs of gannets alone now breed annually on Ailsa Craig (Gaelic for 'Fairy Rock' or alternatively 'Paddy's Milestone' on account of its equidistance from Belfast and Glasgow). Closer to the shore, a crowd of white-plumaged natives of the self same gannetry were systematically patrolling and every so often plunging seaward into the crystal waters in search of sand eels, their six foot wings furling tightly just prior to impact. Seals too were more plentiful than at any time previous on my journey.

With only the high-spirited antics of a passing van-load of Celtic supporters – scarves, banners, and tribal chants trailing in their slipstream – to alleviate an otherwise excruciating afternoon's foot-slog, I hobbled into the public bar of the Ailsa Craig Hotel, Girvan, and was instantly befriended by three fishermen: Davie, John and Charlie. From then until last orders we matched each other drink for drink, yarn for yarn. Frothy pints of 'heavy' followed by chasers of Lagervulin – an Islay single malt whisky with a distinct smoky character. Not surprisingly, having eaten nothing since mid-morning, in no time at all I was totally blotto. Or in the colourful colloquialism of my Caledonian companions: "As fou as a wulk". And still we charged our glasses. Curiously, the more I drank the more I could understand what was being said. So much so, that what at first sounded like an incoherent guttural clearing of throats, with an occasional 'ye ken?' thrown in for my benefit, soon assumed an eloquence all of its own. And what I heard enraptured me. Along with the freely flowing bevvy, I drank in every nautical nuance. A swell, I learned, is a 'fair Rummel'; big waves are 'greenhouses'; a cormorant is a 'shank'. On the crustacean front: shrimps are 'lice' and prawns, which in these fertile waters can grow to the size of a respectable lobster, are known as 'crunchers'. Like seafarers the world over, they had superstition down to a fine art: 'see a seal – touch steel'; 'never take Swan Vesta matches on board'; 'never cut your nails on a Sunday'; 'never pay a bill on a Monday'; never give 'anything' away on a Monday – you'll give away your luck'. Also boding ill are whistling women – whistling raises the wind by imitative magic – and swearing aboard ship – it evokes the powers of evil. While the mere thought of 'scraggy tails' (never, never say rats!) afloat is enough to bring seamen out in a cold sweat. And I thought that I was superstitious!

As the witching hour approached John and Charlie fell by the wayside, leaving just Davie and me to uphold the bar-fly tradition. Somewhat unthinkingly, I asked him if he had known the crew of the trawler 'Antares', all of whom perished the previous November when she was dragged 500 ft to the seabed after her nets were snagged by the nuclear-powered submarine *Trenchant*. Already maudlin from a surfeit of whisky, Davie broke down in a welter of tears. I could have kicked myself for my insensitivity. One can only hazard a guess as to what morbid fears my enquiry had unleashed, fears only a fellow mariner could comprehend. Fortunately the ex-SAS man was made of strong stuff, and recovered his composure with a defiant shake of the head. By way of a diversion, developments took an unexpected twist. Would I like to see his boat, *Diaden*? Game for almost anything at this stage, we drank-up and staggered down to the lawn-fringed harbour. In the near pitch darkness I could just make out a tangle of yachts and trawlers. Anaesthetised to the cold and emboldened by the alcohol, we clambered sinuously from craft to craft like a pair of paralytic primates.

The deck of the *Diaden* was alarmingly small. Hardly room to swing a 'scraggy tail', let alone a cat. I tried to envisage the pocket-sized vessel in the white capped grip of a 'fair Rummel'. The term 'dice with death' sprang readily to mind. And it served only to redouble my admiration of all those who make their living at sea. Never again will I turn my nose up at a fish supper.

Following a wee deoch an doris at the Harbour Inn, the fisherman's local, it was time to sever our newly forged friendship. Unlike my hard-drinking partner, this legless landlubber had to be up bright and early in the morning. Well, early at any rate. In the meantime, all I had to do was find the Ailsa Craig Hotel...

Sunday, 21st April. I rose shakily at eight and, feeling like death-warmed up, put on a brave if ashen face and went down to breakfast – only to gag on the lardaceous niff of frying bacon. Apologising profusely, I plumped instead for the soothing effervescence of a glass of Andrews.

A jolt to my already shell-shocked system was the news from the cheerfully dispassionate waitress that my objective, the bustling market town of Ayr, was all of twenty-five miles away. Being in no fit state to tackle my paperwork after last night's bender, I hadn't even written up my log – let along planned today's route. This was one instance where I had no option but to play it off-the-cuff.

Continuing to hover at death's door, I took my first teetering Ayr-ward steps just under an hour later. Once abroad, the heady combination of salty tang and blustery mizzle hit me like a slap in the face. Far from sobering me up, it rekindled my inebriation. And it was in a whoozy rubber-limbed stupor that I bowed out from a desolate morning-after-the-night-before Girvan. How I kept going the Lord alone knows. Certainly I had to dig deep in my reserves – but energy, I realised, like any natural resource, is a finite commodity. I couldn't afford too many days like this.

After eight nauseous kilometres I threw myself on the mercy of Turnberry postmaster Mr Duncan. For postmaster read Good Samaritan. While his wife Helen date-stamped my witness book (albeit a Sunday), Mr Duncan prescribed a complimentary bottle of Lucozade to help me on my way. A welcome tonic. Sipping it at regular intervals throughout the day gave me a much needed shot in the arm, as well as going some way to settling my stomach. Pick-me-ups apart, the next five and a half hours shuffled by with all the urgency of a funeral procession.

Eventually, with the focus of my Herculean effort within reach, more naked tenacity was called for as I entered the south-eastern environs of Ayr – the seaport centre of Burns country – where my strength finally gave out once and for all. But bed and board were put on a back burner as I dragged myself bodily to the suburb of Alloway and the thatched cottage of Burns' birth place. Homage paid, honours seen to be done, at last I could ring down the curtain on another day.

Monday, 22nd April. After yesterday's self-inflicted handicap, it was time to make hay while the sun shone. And shine it did – be it with a raw edge to the light breeze which served only to remind one of the northerly latitude. I poodled on down to the beach-front promenade and cast an eye over Ayr's impressive two and a half miles of silver sands – all of five minutes away, followed by a more leisurely perusal of the all-dominating Town Hall: a neo-classical splendour of Cullaloe Stone from Fife. Sightseeing over for the time being, my public relations duties beckoned: namely, the inauguration of a whip-round at the town's Boswell Park Post Office and the rounds of Ayr's three newspapers. Feeling positively twice the man of the previous day, I soon got itchy feet and working on the principle that a change (of scene) is as good as a rest I shaped a determined course for pastures new.

Crossing the River Ayr via the Auld Brig – eternalised by Burns in his poem *The Brigs of Ayr* – I was presently treading the tawny coloured strand of Ayr's northerly neighbour, the ancient burgh of Prestwick. Pressing on around the sickle sweep of Ayr Bay it was high noon before I made Troon. Together with its predecessor Turnberry, that made two internationally renowned golfing centres in as many days. A pretty town of two distinct halves, Troon's south and north bays are separated by a rocky headland from which the town gains its name: Trywn – Old Welsh for 'nose'.

With particularly fine seascapes of Arran, Ailsa Craig, Kintyre and the full magnificent panoply of the Firth of Clyde to occupy me, I swung round the spacious sandy crescent of Irvine Bay for Saltcoats, one of Glasgow's favourite weekend retreats and, above all a Rangers stronghold. Red, white and blue abounded everywhere, from tri-colour graffiti to the ubiquitous replica Rangers shirts worn almost exclusively by corpulent middle-aged males. As for my digs, like many a public house, the sea-front 'Stanley Hotel' was so named in order to circumvent restrictive licensing laws. Over supper my landlord enlightened me on the subject of my walking stick. North of the border such a pilgrim's staff is known as a 'wee crommach', as mentioned in the Scottish folk song, *The Tangle of the Isles*.

Tuesday, 23rd April. The sky was pearly grey; a patch of hazy brightness betrayed the sun's latent presence. From this sombre vault an infuriating sequence of showers was swift in coming, effectively dashing all hope of shedding my weatherproofs. At twenty-eight kilometres it was a ridiculously short walking day, but I wouldn't have missed the opportunity of stopping over with old friends Tom and Mary Camp for the world.

The sea-lapped hamlet of Portencross was a martyr to quaintness possessing, for its diminutive size, more than its fair share of ancient curiosities, with a roofless fifteenth century castle, a dinky little harbour and an Iron Age vitrified fort that continues to beggar explanation.

Where habitation petered, out a barely discernible shoreway wriggled its way northward below the hump-backed eminence of Goldenberry Hill. Traversed by deep overgrown ruts and interspersed with wide belts of boulder-field, it was patently clear that in times gone by certain sections had been under the plough. But this now forsaken wild tract was quite unlike any other stretch of Glasgow's golf/water sport orientated playground coast. When not shackled by the need to watch my every step, I was able to snatch the odd brief glimpse of the cloud-veiled Cumbrae Islands. Remembering that it was St George's Day I prised a burnet rose from a sad-looking shrub. The pink-flecked bloom would serve as a makeshift buttonhole – mustn't let the Jocks think they have a monopoly on patriotism!

Where the trail transformed into a metalled slip road I took stock of my overland performance. With only a stubbed toe by way of a setback, as my first major physical test since the Ballantrae-breakdown I considered it an unmitigated success. The piebald tarmacked ribbon then swept eastward, enabling me to give Hunterston nuclear power station a suitably wide berth and to make a beeline for Largs, flanked on either side by wooded foothills and the sheltered sea-lane of Fairlie Roads.

Wednesday, 24th April. The drizzle which coincided with my Largs departure succumbed to more persistent rainfall by early afternoon. Through it all I remained strangely detached and disorientated. Having no medical expertise, formal or otherwise, I was initially at a loss as to my sudden disaffection. But salvation when it came took on unlikely shape: submarine spotting. Where previously it represented nothing more than a passing interest, I henceforth scanned the millpond waters of the Firth of Clyde with a passion verging on the obsessive. Anything to avoid acknowledging my lowly spirits. Homesickness, for that was my layman's diagnosis, was as new to me as it was unexpected. Like all potential impediments to the success of the venture, however, it was there to be overcome, conquered.

Contrary to its nuclear free zone status, the shore road which faithfully describes the north-east corner of Inverclyde District should by rights have been the ideal platform for observing my elusive quarry. I expressed as much to an elderly couple out taking the air in the pleasant waterfront town of Gourock, where the tapering River Clyde bends eastward for Glasgow, coronary capital of Europe. They confirmed my assessment. With four nuclear bases within a few miles radius it was unusual *not* to see any submarines.

A prominent feature of the tramp from Gourock to the industrial centre of Greenock was the proliferation of newly erected danger signs above the shingle beach: 'Eating shellfish from this shore may cause serious illness'. Of that I had no doubt. News of an offshore explosives dump just 'doon the watter' between Arran and the mainland had recently surfaced.

As I closed upon my Port Glasgow billet my concern rose in correlation to the reaction of those from whom I sought directions. Whenever I mentioned the 'Star Hotel' the universal response was a sympathetic shake of head, a sharp intake of breath and a chatter of tut-tuts. One kind lady in the Information Office went so far as to tell me "You're much too nice for that place", but wouldn't elaborate further. Meanwhile staff at the *Greenock Times* and town sorting office did nothing to allay my apprehension: "Ye dinna hae tae stay there?" The final straw came in the shadow of 'Goliath' – the gigantic turquoise-hued crane-centrepiece of the Scott Lithgow shipyard – where a burly docker merely muttered something about "undesirable elements" before sending me on my way with a hearty "Guid luck". Just what had walk H.Q. let me in for? I had visions of being booked into some spit-and-sawdust equivalent of a wild west saloon – with clientele to match.

As it turned out my vision wasn't appreciably wide of the mark. Within minutes of entering the public bar – wall-to-wall juiced up Jocks and still only four-thirty! – I was initiated in the fundamentals of turning back automobile milometers by a car salesman. Even those who kept themselves to themselves felt obliged to stand the stranger a drink. In no time at all the bar was lined with half-a-dozen pints of 70/- Ale – so named after the original price of a barrel – and a similar number of amber coloured shorts that smelt like Old Spice aftershave and had the kick of a mule (I'd sleep tight tonight). I wasn't really in the mood for social drinking – the memory of Girvan was still agonisingly vivid – but the genuine warmth and down-to-earth *bonhomie* exuding from all quarters won me over.

Between jars I peered through the opaque cigarette fug giving my surroundings a brisk once over. At that moment a scuffle broke out beside me. Not so much as a head turned – least of all mine. Shortly afterwards I nearly started a punch-up in my own right when I had the effrontery to offer to buy a round: "Pit that awa' – same agin, hen!"

On the evidence of today's sorry showing I clearly needed cheering up. But kindness on this scale could be seriously detrimental to one's health. If this was to be the formula for the next four months it was a toss-up what would give out first – my ankle or my liver! On the way back to my third (or was it fourth?) floor room one of my erstwhile carousing confederates – who insisted throughout on calling me Ian, Gaelic for John – was adamant that he would accompany me to Glasgow City Centre in the morning. What the Lady Provost will make of him, God only knows!

Thursday, 25th April. Several 'Star' regulars were on hand to wish me *bon voyage*. Can't get over how bright eyed and bushy tailed they looked after yesterday's binge. How do they manage it? With no sign of my pie-eyed escort (sigh of relief), I was free to hot foot the thirty-eight kilometres to Glasgow, reflecting as I did so upon the inordinate number of tantalisingly turned-out lassies who hail from the nation's unemployment black spots. There must be a perfectly simple explanation – conceivably the need to make the most of oneself in order to escape the poverty trap. Or is that too simplistic?

Other marginally less enduring distractions along the long and winding road included the shipbuilding town of Renfrew, 'Cradle of the Royal Stewarts'; Ibrox Park, home of the mighty Glasgow Rangers FC; my third sighting of the Clyde-built paddle-steamer *The Waverly*; and Harry Ramsden's famous Fish Restaurant. Any advantage to be gleaned from the dry and radiant weather-front was counteracted by a gusty head wind. But for all that I still somehow contrived to forge my way into Central Glasgow a full hour ahead of schedule.

The exciting renaissance that has taken place in Glasgow over the last few years, culminating in its recent appointment as European City of Culture, was plain for all to see. Be it the rarefied sphere of antiquarian books, designer clothing or exquisite jewellery, the quality end of Glasgow's retail outlets is now a match for any of the world's culture capitals. All large cities can bewilder and disorientate the visitor, but my initial impression of Glasgow – and first impressions are frequently the most telling – was that of a modern go-ahead metropolis peopled by a citizenry rightly renowned for their energy and amiable nature. Unlike its intemperate image would suggest, I saw only a clutch of down-and-outs knocking back the statutory 'electric soup' (Special Brew).

At the three o'clock engagement I proceeded quite literally to bend over backwards in order to accommodate the requests of the gathered press corps and battery of shutter-happy tourists. Between set-ups I was graciously received by the power-dressed Lady Provost, Susan Baird – who took an instant shine to my beard. At the ensuing reception I had the chance to socialise less formally with both Royal Mail staff and representatives of Glasgow's three MS branches, at the conclusion of which a chauffeur driven limousine conveyed me to my five star accommodation – the modernistic, smoked-glass Moat House International Hotel.

From my tenth floor suite the field of view was exquisite – likewise the room service. With the whole of north-west Scotland to tackle before the next big city shindig (Aberdeen), my kindly Royal Mail paymasters suggested I put my feet up and order whatever I desired. Having stimulated my already voracious appetite with a long lazy soak, what I desired and got was venison in port washed down with a brace of chilled Pils. *Magnifique!* This was living off the fat of the land. Pity the satellite TV didn't come up to scratch.

As darkness fell like a velvet valance, the moon hung low over the silhouette cityscape like an orange lantern. Not to be outdone by the Queen of the Night, a nebula of neon twinkled in fruitless opposition: the horizontal haemorrhage of the *Daily Record/Sunday Mail* building; the raking floodlights of Celtic Park ('the bhoys' were in training); the threesome scarlet lamps of Bell's Bridge, the last remnant of the International Garden Festival; and the lone stern light of the Falkland's veteran HMS *Plymouth*, a comforting presence... Glasgow by night.

Friday, 26th April. A day of ports, resorts and shipyards got off to a blinding start. The sky was blue and white, with fleecy clouds grazing slowly across their azure pasture. Initially paralleling the Clydeside Expressway, I made giant westward strides towards my Helensburgh goal – progress that juddered to a halt within the hour amid the urban and industrial blight of the once thriving shipbuilding centre of Clydebank.

Totally at odds with their desperate situation, the wholesale friendliness of the people ('Bankies') quite bowled me over as well as reducing me to a snail's pace. During this spell I picked-up more in the way of uncanvassed donations and pats on the back than in the rest of the day combined. Bankies are rightly proud of their peerless generosity – while decrying their Edinburgh counterparts for their: 'Short arms and deep pockets'. Bankie womenfolk, meanwhile, proved the exception to my pet 'making-the-most-of-one's-looks' theory. Even their predisposition to overdo the make-up couldn't detract from their natural beauty. As for the broader picture, the final piece of the *Lusitania* jigsaw slotted tidily into place. Beginning all those many months ago, I had now successfully duplicated the ocean liner's final fateful passage in reverse, from Davy Jones' Locker to Slipway. Beginning at Old Head of Kinsale, where she came to grief at the hands of a German U-boat, via her home-port of Liverpool, to Clydebank, where she was consummately constructed. End of story.

A further ten kilometres down stream I paused in the lee of Dumbarton Castle Crag. An area steeped in maritime tradition, it was here that the record breaking trans-world tea clipper *Cutty Sark* was built and launched in 1869. So narrow is the Clyde that, then as now, all slipways are set at an oblique angle.

After a cursory excursion to the dormitory village of Cardross, where 'Birdman' Percy Pilcher made a number of pioneering hang-glider flights in the 1890s, it was back to the dratted A814. Though hardly wider than a secondary road, it carried a volume of traffic that would do justice to a motorway. Where was it all going to? Feeling positively nauseous from the concentrated carbon monoxide fumes, exacerbated in no little part by the rising afternoon temperature, I had to endure another eight kerbside kilometres – during which I was providentially reunited with my witness books, after leaving them behind in Cardross Post Office.

The largely Victorian resort of Helensborough was bursting at the seams. Away from the jam-packed, bumper-to-bumper sea-front, a grid-pattern network of arrow-straight boulevards climbed steadily inland from the rocky bather-less beach. The over-riding impression was that of a genteel San Francisco. Predictably enough, my digs were just shy of the top of one such hill.

Saturday, 27th April. I set off into the bright blue yonder a shade after ten. Burden on back, wee crommach to the fore, this was the first day of the rest of the walk. My homesickness was now just a fading memory.

Between loch-front retreats around the patchily populated shore of Gare Loch the partially afforested lower slopes soared unhindered from the brackish waters to an all encompassing chain of wild, bare hills, in whose stately shadow I walked the day long.

Midway along the eastern bank the coast road deviated inland behind the gigantic Fort Knox-like installation of Faslane Submarine Base. Alas, I couldn't see the subs for the trees. Of the few locals I bumped into, all were completely resigned to the ominous presence of their nuclear neighbours, insisting that it was only the 'outsiders' who raised any objections. After hearing one side of the story, I made a special point of spending some time with the inhabitants of the fast dwindling Faslane Peace Camp. Now hemmed-in on all sides by M.o.D. property to prevent any future expansion of the community, it occurred to me that with nuclear disarmament off the agenda and media attention at an all-time low these idealistic gentle folk were at best beating their heads against a brick wall… at worst flogging a dead cause.

Just prior to retrieving the shoreline at Rowmore, Mr Pat Hanley – whose family was doing the accommodational honours that night – caught up with me and advised me to call into the Creggan Inn at the tip of the next peninsula, neglecting, however, to tell me what to expect when I got there.

Circling the rocky litter-strewn beach of the otherwise enchanting village of Garelochhead, I began the long trek south. Now directly opposite Faslane naval dockyard, I was overjoyed to notice a pair of red-breasted merganser cruising not far from the shore. An elation superseded almost immediately as my compact folding binoculars latched onto my first atomic submarines: two Trident class, one hunter-killer. Though too distant to photograph, I could clearly define their black pot-bellied bulk and skyward thrusting conning towers.

After an encounter with an Alfa Romeo driver who, in his eagerness to shake me by the hand, leapt from the still moving vehicle without engaging the hand-brake and came within a hair's breath of writing off his precious car, I crested the hill overlooking Kilcreggan, a prominent feature of which is the colourfully customised beach boulders, each of which is individually brought to life in a form suggested by their quirky shape, e.g. a shark and King Tutankhamun. Far below a milling throng of what appeared to comprise virtually every child on the peninsula was patently awaiting the arrival of something or someone. I was more than half way down the incline before I realised that object of their anticipation was me. Even then I couldn't bring myself to return their excited waves until I was right on top of them in case I'd jumped to the wrong conclusion. There's nothing so humbling as one's own humility.

Without further ado we repaired to the Craggan Inn, where Pat, his family, and a pride of fellow Lions Club members were already *in situ*. Following a round of introductions and a jar or two of the local brew, the children formed an orderly queue for my autograph after which we filed crocodile fashion to the neighbouring village of Cove, and to my digs for the night. An excellent evening meal was followed by an atmospheric twilight drive around the 'bonnie, bonnie banks of Loch Lomond'.

Sunday, 28th April. Any weight-saving I made from changing two day's worth of donations into notes was exactly counterbalanced by a munificent packed lunch, consisting of six cheese and ham rolls, two Pepsis and four cakes. In the interest of lightening the load on my poor shoulders and hips, I decided to devour the lot at the earliest possible moment. And while I was feeling positively revitalised, I discovered that Old Faithful II had undergone a dramatic transformation. No longer the drab down-at-tip wee crommach of old. Thanks to Pat's well intentioned handiwork it was now a riot of garish hues. But while the brass ferrule was a welcome addition, I felt that the shaft-length plastic binding in papal colours was going just slightly over the top. Suffice it to say, it wouldn't see the light of another day.

The Hanley's youngest daughters escorted me on their bicycles for the first half-dozen kilometres beside the wide sheet of Loch Long. Where the minor road corkscrewed upwards to the peninsula's spine-like central highland we parted company, waving as I went until they were out of sight. Before vacating the road to begin a strenuous overland section through the dark interior of Garelochhead forest, I trained my Pentax camera on a peculiarly local phenomenon. Set on a steep descent, the onside lay-by abruptly gave way to a shallow bunker resembling a long-jump pit filled with tiny orange nodules, the purpose of which was, in the event (God forbid!) of a brakes failure, to check the momentum of runaway nuclear warhead transporters *en route* to the nearby submarine munitions base at Coulport.

The rugged uplands eventually yielded to the B833 a mile north of Garelochhead, where the combined picnic area and dizzying viewpoint afforded the unique opportunity to eat my lunch while my eyes feasted on the mind-blowing vista of Gare Loch.

From Portincaple the road plunged to the very water's edge to begin its spectacular passage north to the head of Loch Long. Mile upon mile of ideal otter habitat. A paradise too for sub-aqua enthusiasts, the bank – and therefore the road itself – is seriously undermined with an irresistible system of underwater caves. But when the red flag is flying, frogmen beware – the upper reaches of the loch double as a Royal Navy torpedo range! Quite unperturbed by a pair of wet-suited divers, I watched a seal struggling to subdue a fish almost as big as itself. On the wooded slopes above, a cuckoo, that harbinger of summer, announced its lusty presence in the time honoured monotonous manner.

Both long in name and in nature, I concluded my end to end route march of Loch Long – or, as it's alternatively known from May onwards, 'Midge Alley' – at the lime-washed village of Arrochar, nestling beneath a sierra of snow-capped peaks. The immutable shape of things to come.

Monday, 29th April. Leaving the shelving western shore of Loch Long (not a tin fish to be seen), I penetrated the 'blanket planted' Ardgartan Forest at the foot of Glen Croe. Climbing all the while, my route corresponded initially with an old military road – part of a network constructed by General Wade after the Rebellion of 1715. Left and right the pine-clad foothills led the eye upwards to majestic grey escarpments, of which the most notable pinnacle was undoubtedly Ben Arthur (2,891 ft) or 'The Cobbler', on account of its characteristic shape. Driving onward to the giddying head of the dramatic glacial valley, a spacious amphitheatre in all but name, a Forestry Commission sign invited the weary traveller to 'Rest and be Thankful' – I did and I was.

Retaining the wooded character of the former, Glen Croe was succeeded by Gleann Mor. There the similarities ended. Where Glen Croe was a non-stop uphill grunt, Gleann Mor was a leisurely winding descent, a downward trend that continued all the way to the lush water-meadows that flank the River Goil. Towards the valley floor, where black limbed deciduous groves supplanted the omnipresent coniferous stands, I joined forces for a while with Piers, a Benedictine friar, and his soft spoken companion Frances, a nun.

Far from put out by my interrupting their Scottish Sabbatical, the angelic duo were held spellbound at the mere mention of my 'quest'. Particularly the effusive Piers who had an explanation for everything: "God cannot intervene personally on behalf of MS sufferers," he reasoned, "therefore He has empowered you to do His earthly bidding." Other startlingly significant revelations – especially to Piers – included the length of the walk, at 9,500 miles, the approximate diameter of the earth. And was it entirely coincidence that I decided to start the walk, inspired by my mother, Mary, on August 5th – which just happens to be the official birthday of Mary, Mother of Jesus! Chance occurrence or synchronisity? Whatever the case, it was certainly food for thought. With a new lease of life nothing could put a damper on my jubilation – not even the close attentions of the odd Forestry Commission 'flyer': giant timber transporters whose drivers are paid by the load – hence the Bat-out-of-Hell urgency.

Though hardly impressive from the outside, Douglas Pier Royal Naval Research Unit has an international reputation. Here the world's navies and commercial fleets come in order to establish the unique 'signature' (the sound they make on sonar) of each vessel, by which it is ostensibly possible to differentiate between friend and foe. I stress 'ostensibly' because, for purposes of subterfuge, the signature of, for example, a destroyer can be modified to that of a harmless freighter.

Tuesday, 30th April. Within an hour of my departure a hard, pelting rain shook me brusquely from my post-breakfast torpor like a cold shower. There was no 'easy' way out this morning. Before me lay an exacting two and a half hour scramble over bank and brae aboard non-existent footpaths and Forestry Commission 'green track'. Mirroring the course of Loch Goil as it wandered out of the hills to join Loch Long, I turned southward directly reversing my route of two days ago. Scenic beauty apart, if nothing else Loch-land walking is long winded.

With the worst of the terrain behind me, and my ankle bearing up surprisingly well to the heavy going and saturated underbrush, I interrupted the tea-break of a lone woodsman. Vaulting from the cab of his modified tractor or 'skidder', he openly bemoaned the scarcity of broad-leaved deciduous trees. And it was with a tinge of embarrassment that he elaborated upon the mundane end use of the three sizes of timber he is required to fell: "Paper, pallet and post". Impulsively changing the subject, he alerted my attention to the new multi-billion pound Trident submarine base – significantly omitted from my OS map – under construction on the opposite bank. Like a shore-bound iceberg, nine-tenths of the complex are concealed within the cavernous granite hillside.

Midday saw me recapture the road at Ardentinny from where I hastened south to Strone, at the junction of Loch Long and Holy Loch. Holy in name only (the high profile US Polaris depot ship, floating dock and unholy trinity of attendant submarines hold centre stage), its glass-clear waters necessitated a full twelve kilometre round trip in order to progress just two kilometres nearer my evening objective. Carved deep into the Argyll hills, the steep northern slopes of this imposing inlet are contour-planted with the variegated bands of Kilmun Arboretum, a stunning collection of specimen trees gathered from the four corners of the earth.

Across the mouth of Holy Loch at the yachting centre of Hunter's Quay (incidentally my abode for the next two nights), my haunt of last week, Gourock, was just a short ferry ride away over the Firth of Clyde. Ten minutes by boat; seven days by Shank's Mare. Two kilometres down the coast at the attractive garrison town of Dunoon I called time on the day's activities, rendezvousing with Royal Mail Delivery Office Manager Neil Watson.

That evening I had my closest encounter yet with a nuclear-powered submarine. Having extinguished my bedroom light prior to retiring, I noticed an eerie bilious glow on the curtain and proceeded to the window to investigate the source. There, silently and ominously stealing away in the dead of night, was the unmistakable coal-black profile and prominent tail fin of a present day green-eyed monster...

10   See Ben Nevis and die

He is never alone that is accompanied by noble thoughts
Beaumont & Fletcher

Wednesday, 1st May.

NEIL WATSON picked me up at 9.30 and drove me back to yesterday's termination point. My only PR duties on the day being a photo-session, by ten I was at liberty to roam as I pleased. Liberated also from all superfluous items of equipment, I was raring to go. Weather-wise I couldn't have wished for a better day. After a cloudy start the sky was now brilliantly blue and sunlit, with a massive woolpack rolling away to the west. The temperature rose by the minute.

I felt positively naked as I set off down the coast towards Toward Point – I'd omitted to bring my Pilgrim's Staff!

Stretching clear round the point to Port Lamont, where a single lane shore road snaked northward to its cul-de-sac conclusion, the A815 was a promenade in all but name. With nowhere for them to go other than back the way they came, vehicles were few and far between. And though still in a state of partial disrepair from January's storms, this minor flaw was rendered insignificant by a succession of scintillating prospects revealed by each curve in its imperceptibly meandering course.

Ahead of me the polished-glass waters of Loch Striven wandered deep into the Cowal peninsula, cradled maternally by afforested hills still garbed in their autumnal-hued finery. Following the gorse-girdled eastern shore to Inverchaolain I was in the heart of Lamont clan territory – countless generations of whom are buried at the old roadside parish church. Where the road finished I took to the hills. A year's growth and the ravages of time and weather had reduced the woodland 'footpath' to a trackless jungle. Ankle deep quagmire and the slashing sideswipes of bracken and bramble were the order of the day. Not that I didn't enjoy it, but what an inopportune moment to be without Old Faithful II!

From The Craig I looked down upon the unexpected sight of a deep-water anchorage. Currently laid-up far from the world's sea lanes were the fast-rusting oil tankers *Gastor* and *Nestor*. Of equal interest were the 'rafts' of eider duck riding the light swell. Bloodied but unbowed I emerged at Ardtaraig at exactly four-fifteen to be met by the ever dependable Neil Watson, post bus at the ready.

Thursday, 2nd May. In a re-run of the previous day's clockwork routine, Neil transported me back to Ardtaraig. A short hop round the head of Loch Striven and I was once again blazing a virgin trail. It was another bright morning with the latent promise of heat. Yet as I ran the lacerating gauntlet of bracken, heather and pine I was soon thankful for my over-trousers. Wednesday's bare-legged bravado was a lesson hard learnt. But whereas yesterday's cross country section claimed at least the semblance of a footpath, today's overland route had no such pretension. Lacking the mobility of the day before (I was once again toting a full backpack), the going was arduous in the extreme.

One continuous gruelling climb, several ankle-orientated tumbles and countless dead-end sheep trails later I found myself beside the trig-point atop the gnarled summit of Dun Mor. Thirteen-hundred feet below a cobalt-blue ribbon of sea loch meandered north and south. Lolling gently at anchor, *Nestor* and *Gastor* resembled toy boats on bath night.

Having hopefully secured one or two half decent aerial photos, I descended to the shoreline via the cataract course of a fast-flowing upland stream, pausing to take a thirst-quenching draught of the tumbling waters – my only refreshment in six solid hours afoot. Disgorged onto the shingle strand like so much flotsam, I began the long trek south to the loch's yawning mouth, passing as I went a solar powered marker buoy ripped from its moorings and deposited high and dry by the high seas of winter. A succession of natural obstacles – wave-polished boulder beach, broad tracts of slippery seaweed (both equally precarious in my treadless boots) etc. – concluded the hardest single walking stint since the switchback Pembrokeshire Coast Path.

From Strone Point, the seaward confluence of Loch Striven and the Kyles of Bute (a 'kyle' is a narrow strait or channel), I turned for home, 'home' in this instance being the Colintraive Hotel. Installed in the hotel's tastefully decorated restaurant my gaze was directed across the Kyles to the low rounded hills of the Isle of Bute and the waterfront summer residence of Sir 'Dickie' Attenborough, whose favourite window seat I was now occupying.

Friday, 3rd May. I looked out with apprehension at the low grey sky and dense curtain of rain. Whether the product of the overriding dampness or yesterday's exertions, every joint and sinew in my body was in revolt. Relatively modest though today's walking spell was (a short, sharp thirty-one kilometres), it took all my powers of self-motivation to get me up and about.

Once abroad I made short shrift of the coastal corridor between sea loch and ben, kyle and glen, each would-be glorious vista choked with a turbid bung of sea fog. A forest trail propelled me the final six kilometres to my overnight refuge. Set on a dog-leg reach of the Kyles of Bute, the cottages and villas of Tighnabruaich dotted the wooded hillside overlooking the Island of Bute.

Saturday, 4th May. In a repeat of the balmy weather of two days ago, the Cowal peninsula chose this morning to present its genial visage. Which was just as well, for with over fifty kilometres to cover before nightfall any assistance was welcome.

As hill succeeded hill, the terrain was far from short of contours. Likewise wildlife. While buzzards sailed aloft upon the rising thermals, the novelty value of eider ducks – now commonplace – was on the wane. Not so the chance sighting of a red squirrel shinning up a pine tree at Auchnaha. The first wild specimen I'd seen since childhood. But no sign of the killer whales that occasionally frequent the waters in pursuit of the big, plump Loch Fyne herrings, known locally as 'Glasgow Magistrates'.

At the lochside Strachur Activity Centre I was provided with a fish dinner (all local produce), a Radox bath and a bed for the night. After walking the final six hours with the sun behind me, the backs of my legs were cooked to a turn. Infirmities apart, an exhausting yet thoroughly rewarding day.

Latest death-toll from the Bangladesh Cyclone: 125,000 – and rising!

Sunday, 5th May. Have I really been on the go for nine months? Seems like only yesterday that I was feverishly scurrying about the West End in a last ditch effort to assemble my final items of kit. So much for the gestation period. Now for the real thing.

Ten minutes out of Strachur the icing sugar confection of Inverary swam into view across the broad reach of sea loch, its glacial symmetry set off to perfection by the verdant backdrop of forested hills.

While tramping round the head of the loch – goodbye Cowal, hello Argyll – I spent an enjoyable three-quarters of an hour in the madcap company of the 'Rudge Enthusiasts Club' whose annual get together was taking place in the otherwise sleepy hamlet of Cairndow. The last Rudge motorcycle was built in Coventry in 1939, but such was the care lavished on these pampered thoroughbreds that they looked for all the world as though they'd just rolled off the production line. Having had my fill of tea, sandwiches and biking banter I heeded the tug of the open road. But not before the combined membership had filled my collection box to the brim.

The stop-go home stretch to Inverary followed the route of another of General Wade's military roads. To the hordes of Sabbath sightseers parked at intervals along the shoreline I was 'The MS Man'. Each felt obliged to offer me sustenance of one sort or another. And even though some halts were within sight of the one before, I felt honour bound to accept all invitations. Eat, drink and be grateful!

Fronted by the sweeping inlet of Loch Shira the blue-grey proportions of Inverary Castle, ancestral home of the Dukes of Argyll and seat of the Campbell chieftains, bore a greater resemblance to a French chateau than a clan stronghold. Keeping a respectful distance from the castle, the stone-hewn hump-backed bridge on the town's north-eastern approach affords by far the best prospect of the magnificent white rendered facade of the former Royal Burgh of Inverary, of which the single most imposing element is The Great Inn – where I was fortunate enough to be spending a gratis evening. Originally built by the Third Duke to accommodate guests at the castle, the inn looked out across a manicured swathe of turf and silvery stillness of Lochs Shira and Fyne towards – despite forty-eight hours unremitting sunshine – the snow-flecked summit of Ben Bhuidhe.

Monday, 6th May. Typical Bank Holiday weather: dull, overcast and with the imminent threat of rain. Taking advantage of the intervening climatic truce, I took a look around the Georgian elegance of Inverary before the deluge set in. Benefiting no end from a lochside situation, on closer examination the uniform white livery soon began to pall. The film-set perfection put one in mind of a sterile museum piece or Hollywood mock-up – in which we the public were bit part players. Small town Scotland in aspic!

Continuing to get a favourable reaction from the many passers by who recognised me, the monotony of the A83 to Ardrishaig was relieved by a trio of waymarked (in part) forest walks along the western shore of Loch Fyne. The only wildlife of note was a slow-worm that I saved from certain extinction on the crown of a road. Half a yard of liquorice and not a grateful bone in its body!

By the middle of the afternoon the sun burst through the opaque vault with all the fervid intensity of an ultra-violet lamp. Reluctant to go through the laborious rigmarole of removing and stowing my weatherproofs, I toiled and boiled for the rest of the day in an outfit that had all the clammy, debilitating properties of a bin-liner.

The first realistic opportunity to let off steam, in the truest sense of the term (I swear my body temperature was nudging regulo-nine!), was the Lochgilphead office of the *Argyllshire Advertiser* where Nikki Thompson jotted down my story and snapped away with her Pentax. Everyone in town was so jolly friendly. A pleasant crescent of stone-built houses fanned around the top of Loch Gilp, Lochgilphead seemed to be the staging post for backpackers from all over the world.

Prising myself away, I completed the last lap to the smart little village of Ardrishaig, Knapdale, the southern end of the Crinan Canal and the end of my two-hundred and seventy-fourth consecutive day on the hoof.

Tuesday, 7th May. A day of two distinct halves: a wet, road-borne morning from Ardrishaig to Tarbert, followed by a sunny afternoon/evening's assault course from Tarbert to Claonaig Bay. Unlike the yachting fraternity and occasional Highland coaster who use the Crinan Canal as a short cut to the sound of Jura and the open Atlantic beyond, I had no desire to bypass Kintyre. It represented yet another high point of my journey, as did the unexpected quaintness of Tarbert itself. Ranged around a tiny, near-landlocked bay at the head of East Loch Tarbert, it was lust at first sight. And it came as absolutely no surprise to learn that Tarbert, indeed Kintyre as a whole, was once a Norse province. As my imagination ran riot I could envisage a high-prowed Viking long-ship, its square sail billowing, as it plied the gull-dappled waters of this fiordesque haven...

Alighting from my flight of fancy, I reported to Tarbert PO. Though impressed with my determination, no-one gave me so much as a snowball's chance in Hell of going 'over the top' to Skipness. They weren't even sure that such a route was possible since the afforestation programme of the last decade. That settled it. Nothing brings out the belligerence in me like the underestimation of others.

First taking the precaution of dropping off the bulk of my gear at my lodgings, I scaled the rising ground immediately behind the village, passing the ivy-draped ruins of Tarbert Castle in the process. Where the rudimentary track petered out into an un-navigable hillscape, cleft-deep with wooded burns, the matted tree-cover shepherded me relentlessly shore-ward. Loath to relinquish the high ground so hard-won, I stuck to my task until further penetration was impossible. Above the high-water mark dense oak-scrub formed a gnarled barrier – effectively channelling me onto the rocky margin between tree and sea.

Throughout the subsequent thirteen kilometres I bounded from boulder to boulder in a passable impression of a rock hopper penguin. But where rock hoppers have built-in crampons, my treadless boots were worse than useless. It took the painful lesson of just one grazed shin to teach me that barnacles and limpets equal traction. Even so, my necessarily near total concentration was not so singled minded as to overlook a colony of eider ducks. So tame were they that I could clearly discern the blush-pink breast and greenish-nape of the drakes with the naked eye.

As the afternoon temperature soared, along with the gradient, I removed my weatherproofs and donned a pair of Gore-Tex gloves, an invaluable asset when clambering across jagged lava. Sections where rocky outcrops barred the way required equal measure of nerve, energy and a head for heights. One slip and it was curtains. Though no matter how dangerous the situation I continued to experience the same illogical feelings of invulnerability.

The latter part of the walk – not so much a walk as a horizontal climb! – was a race against the incoming tide. With my back quite literally against an oaken wall, I had nowhere to go but forward. Driven above the barnacle-defined tide-line by the encroaching surf, the lichen-rusted rocks and tuffets of sea pink were littered with the shattered tests of common sea urchin; the debris of an alfresco banquet. Even as I resumed my staccato progress a prime suspect – in the unmistakable flat-profiled guise of a cow grey seal – surfaced just yards from shore, a young urchin in mouth. Case proven. But seals aren't the only mammals to cash-in on the rich pickings. In several secluded inlets I found mesh sacks full of marble-sized whelks ('winkles' to those hailing from south of the border), awaiting collection by small launch. Painstakingly harvested by didicoys at low tide, there is now big money to be made on the Continent from gathering these snail-like gastropods.

Still savouring my mastery over the terrain, at the abrupt termination of the rough-hewn causeway I steered a course for my penultimate port of call guided by the massive red-stone edifice of Skipness PO where, from the public telephone box, I was able to notify postman Paul Inskip of my immanent arrival at Claonaig Bay jetty. While Paul hared south in his post bus in which to transport me back to Tarbert, I pottered the final three kilometres to our common destination along the tree-flanked B8001. A crescent moon was already fast ascending the firmament, the shadows lengthening, when I had my first major set-to with an oscillating cloud of midges. Quite unlike their mammalian counterparts, the female of the species is deadlier than the male.

Wednesday, 8th May. After a fine breakfast I was back at Claonaig Bay jetty just in time to pick up some serious donations from a huddle of high-spirited holidaymakers eagerly awaiting the incoming vehicle ferry from the Island of Arran. Thus began the first of five complete days on Kintyre which, but for the isthmus, would be the innermost of the Hebridian isles. Five days that would take me the length and breadth of the semi-island – down the east coast, up the west – and encompass the full array of picturesque delights: from the jagged coastline and wild vista of the Mull of Kintyre, riven deep with sequestered glens rife with primordial ferns and ancient trees, to the wooded Kintyre Hills that roll down to the pretty little beaches and similarly pretty villages. For the most part sun, sea and solitude.

Claonaig Bay to Ballochgair. With the hot sun pulsing energy out of an azure sky I strode the 'long and winding road' south (surely the inspiration of the Paul McCartney song of the same name). With each stride I could feel the sun's radiant heat positively knitting together and mending my accumulated cuts and abrasions. Equally uplifting to the human spirit was the awesome view of Arran across Kilbrannan sound: blued by distance, the hogsback sierra formed an intermediate shade between sea and sky. A parti-coloured panorama.

As the morning reached its zenith the prevailing balmy breeze yielded to the stifling languor of high noon. Almost at once Kintyre's birds and beasts were party to an unspoken quadruped pact, an avian armistice. Hares, sheep, pheasants, buzzards – all were now as blissfully approachable as they had been before the Fall. Paradise temporarily regained...

Thursday, 9th May. *Ballochgair to Southend.* Misty morning giving way to torrential rain before the day was out. None too warm. Ailsa Craig and Ayrshire Coast lost to view.

Pulled into Campbeltown soon after mid-day. Palm trees galore. Witnessed the departure of the Sanda Island lighthouse keeper by helicopter from the broad greensward overlooking Campbeltown Loch. Fell into conversation with the officiating WPC who clearly has a soft spot for Prince Andrew, whose ship HMS *Campbeltown* spent last week in its eponymous home port. "Och, he's one o' the boys", said she with a twinkle in her eye.

In common with Tarbert's before it, the spire of Campbeltown's main church bore an uncanny resemblance to the State Crown of Scotland. Accidental or intentional? Following a protracted interview-cum-photosession with the editor of the *Campbeltown Courier*, I made tracks for Southend – breaking stride only to acknowledge the many well-wishers and to photograph Campbeltown's oriental-style art nouveau 'Picture Palace', Scotland's oldest cinema.

Beyond Kildalloig Bay the single lane Coast Road coiled away into the high, bare hills. There the climbing began in earnest. Where it ran for a while alongside a forestry plantation the notorious West Coast midges were out in droves. Local adage: 'Kill one midge and the rest come to the funeral'. Moral: Grin 'n bear it!

Not for nothing is the conical summit of the steepest climb by far known as 'The Bastard'. As Ascension Days go, today couldn't have been more apropos.

Friday, 10th May. *Southend to Machrihanish.* Another wet one. Not even the grey light of morning could diminish the stark white rock-studded strands of Dunaverty and Carskey Bays. Storm damage was rife; the view of the not so distant North Antrim coast magnificent.

Below the caves of Keil Point I stood in 'St Columba's' footsteps! Engraved into a pale slab on top of a grassy hillock, they are believed to be an exemplar of the 'Fealty Foot', in which chieftains of yore would stand to swear the oath of allegiance to his tribe or clan. Whether the imprint of Saint or Sovereign, it's just a pity the poor blighter had two right feet!

From the peninsula's southernmost extremity, the Mull of Kintyre, I forged an overland trail across a bleak upland moor, a corrugated steppe of heather, tussock-grass and amber coloured dew-pond. Ascending to the ethereal height of Corr Bhan the icy draught cut through my ineffectual shell garments like a scalpel. But with stiff climb succeeding stiff climb, I soon warmed to my task.

My forebodings of the last few days were completely unfounded. The going proving considerably easier than the trepid locals had led me to believe. Or is it simply that I'm getting fitter? A day-long hazard, however, were the electrified fences that criss-crossed the rolling hills at irregular intervals. The single major energy-outlay was the gut-wrenching grunt to the summit if Cnoc Moy. In breasting the fifteen-hundred foot brow, my backpack felt like a bag of cement – and considering the amount of rain-water it had absorbed it properly weighed as much!

Saturday, 11th May. *Machrihanish to Tayinloan.* Religiously adhering to the tide-wracked margin between dune and the lace-trimmed aquamarine surf racing in from the cloud-hung fortress of Islay, I beachcombed the entire three and a half mile length of Machrihanish Bay. In contrast to the silver sands of yesterday the bay was a ribbon of khaki. And all the better for being empty.

On a par with defiling a pristine blanket of snow, there's something sadistically satisfying in trailing one's spoor across a tract of virgin sand. Not far behind is the joy of delving among the accumulated strand-line debris. Apart from the usual man-made detritus, this morning's haul included shells, shellfish, egg cases, wave-torn seaweed, kelp fronds, the ubiquitous sand-hoppers and a number of marooned lion's mane jellyfish, fully a yard across at the bell and capable of delivering a painful sting.

But I wasn't the only one so engrossed. As if trammelled to the tide-line litter like an animated greyhound lure, a brown hare came loping towards me along the shore, nose down, eyes agoggle and completely oblivious to my presence until the last possible moment. Whereupon – while I struggled manfully to disentangle my camera – it made a bolt for the sand-dunes and sanctuary.

Sunday, 12th May. *Tayinloan to Tarbert.* The leaden cloud cover boded ill for the day ahead. Sure enough it was soon lashing down. With visibility severely restricted, my observations were limited to what was virtually under my nose. Tiny clumps of early purple orchids were a sight for sore eyes, while pockets of slender, swaying harebells – the bluebell of Scotland – had been ever-present for the last week. A welcome splash of colour on an otherwise drab and dreary day.

Bird life too continued to put in the occasional momentous appearance. Glimpsing a flourish of russet as it alighted from its perch, I stood transfixed as a cock sparrow-hawk performed a logic defying manoeuvre through a near impenetrable tangle of trees. But it was left to the tight little inlet of Ronachan Bay to provide the day's – nay, the walk's (thus far) – avian highlight. Splash landing with all the innate grace of a baby elephant was the unmistakable goose-like silhouette of a great northern diver (infinitely more evocative than its North American name – the common loon!).

Buoyed by a phenomenal afternoon's 'twitching' I returned to Tarbert following the overland route taken by Magnus Barefoot, King of Norway. In a calculated act of appeasement the Scottish King Edgar agreed that the all-powerful Viking sovereign could hold domain over any island that he and his longship could circumnavigate. In 1098 King Magnus, seated at the tiller, had his longship manhandled across the Tarbert Land Bridge thereby completing the round trip of Kintyre – which was thus ceded to the Norse nation.

Monday, 13th May. I begun my journey once more soon after first light. Apart from a few battened-down pleasure craft, Tarbert Harbour was all but deserted. The fishing fleet had slipped their cables long before dawn. Still marvelling at the bravery and iron constitution of Britain's fisherfolk, I returned to Knapdale via the headwaters of West Loch Tarbert.

The dark, sepulchral woods that bordered the sea loch's northern shore provided little in the way of shelter. Even the periodic waves of Scotch mist that filled-in between cloudbursts found their way unerringly through the scant canopy. A superabundance of lichens, mosses and hydrophytes bore testament to the overriding dampness of the region.

Beyond the tree-cover the craggy coastline was strikingly reminiscent of County Donegal. Bereft of anger and elation, I walked for the rest of the day like an automaton, programmed for the task, heedful only as I crossed marshland or bog of the need to keep to the well-worn sheep trails – sheep no more like getting their feet wet than the average hiker!

NB. 10 p.m. and the starless southern sky is a black bottomless abyss. By contrast the northern firmament is as crisp and bright as a frosty winter's morn. Roll on Cape Wrath and the land of the 'twilight' sun.

Tuesday, 14th May. A day that began grey and misty soon brightened considerably. After circumventing the wooded head of Loch Caolsiport I temporarily abandoned the beaten track in order to reverentially probe the dank interior of St Columba's Cave. Climbing steeply past sun-flecked rhododendron glades the crude footpath zigzagged through the tree-line to the spacious wind-parched plateau of A' Chrannag. Flanked on either side by towering granite crags, the graphic combination of dun coloured tableland and circling avian predators put one in mind of the African veldt. So much so that it wouldn't have surprised me one iota to see huge herds of antelopes browsing the ochre underbrush. I wasn't alone in my thinking. Quite unprompted, a pair of telescope-toting ornithologists freely referred to our uplands outpost as 'Lion Country'.

Bending away from the crofting pastures of Point of Knap, I re-engaged the coast road between Balimore and the rustic settlement of Kilmory. Marching up the eastern bank of Loch Sween my eyes were continually drawn to a triumvirate of conical-shaped mountains away to the west – the 'Paps of Jura' – from which my only distraction along the way was the brooding remains of the twelfth century Castle Sween.

Arriving at Ashfield Farm I was fêted like a king. Following dinner I savoured the sumptuous sunset over Tayvallich – my destination of the morrow – as reflected in the blush-tinted waters of Loch Sween.

Wednesday, 15th May. In accordance with Scottish tradition, 'Go oot the same door ye came in and there's a welcome for ye back', I bid a regretful farewell to the convivial atmosphere of Ashfield Farm at nine o'clock.

Resembling the aftermath of some half-drowned forest kingdom, a sequence of heavily wooded forelands projecting from the splintered head of Loch Sween led me in and out like a fiddler's elbow for upwards of three hours. On emerging from the final forest trail of the day, the Reverend David Montgomery – Tayvallich Church of Scotland – paused by the wayside to give my mission and me his full blessing.

A spate of sunny intervals towards mid afternoon brought out the day-trippers in droves, but all remained steadfastly wrapped-up. Having accepted several invitations of tea, coffee and shortcake throughout the livelong day, I was well equipped to tackle the overland return trip to Tayvallich. Considering the cloudy start, the scintillating overview to the olive-hued hills of Jura was an unexpected bonus.

Thursday, 16th May. I lit out through the mazy forestry plantation just as the first wave of showers swept in from the west, spurred on my way by a gang of Geordie builders who blithely assured me that it was possible to make it through to Crinan (the north-western terminus of the Crinan Canal) on foot – just.

Almost at once a series of topographical oversights threatened to put a spoke in my wheel: trails that radiated every which way weren't marked on my OS map; those that the map clearly defined were noticeable by their absence. Evidently Forestry Commission bridleways are as transient as the dense conifer stands that discourage plant, bird and animal life. But the single biggest obstruction by far occurred north of Dounie where the previously unbroken timberland opened-out into an immense man-made clearing resounding to a cacophony of chain saws. Faced with the unenviable choice of clambering along the precarious transitional zone between land and sea and defying the authorities, I pointedly ignored the 'No access without authority' sign and brazened it out across a no-man's-land of log-piles, mud and bemused foresters. Better to be tried by twelve than carried by six!

After a trance-like afternoon of nondescript road-walking I was brusquely jolted from my abstraction by the not so dulcet tones of Margaret Rutherford look-alike Katherine Lindsay MacDougall. "Mr Westley!!" boomed the divine Miss M in best sergeant major Britain tradition as I inadvertently overshot my loch-front billet of 'Innisaig'.

Friday, 17th May. After two so-so days weather-wise, it was great to be back in the sun's good books. Already stripped to my shorts I set off on a complete circuit of the Craignish peninsula with a pronounced spring in my step. Part way down the northern shore of Loch Craignish – an idyllic archipelago where islets outnumber mothballed yachts riding at anchor – I stopped to admire the view from the kirkyard promontory of Kirkton chapel, only to find a portly Californian recumbent upon the only bench. Though initially disgruntled by my intrusion, he nonetheless deigned to point out the island home of the tutor of China's final monarch; consummately portrayed by Peter O'Toole in the movie *The Last Emperor*.

Onward now to Craignish Point, where the seamless southerly aspect of sea and sky defied description. Doubling back on my tracks as far as Loch Beag, the extravagantly eroded western seaboard undulated northward to Craobh Haven. Underfoot the brown-clad moorland was a minefield of lichen-grown boulders and tripwire heather.

The holiday and watersport centre of Craobh (pronounced 'Croove') Haven is a comparatively recent addition to Scotland's recreational repertoire. Offshore, between the islands of Jura and Scarba, is the infamous Gulf of Corryvreckan. Though nothing much to look at from this distance, at closer quarters the seething white-water vortex of Scotland's largest whirlpool is by all accounts a fearsome sight. Not only has it claimed many lives down the years including, so legend has it, an entire Viking fleet, but when the wind's in the right direction the thunderous roar can be heard for miles around.

The track to Skiary, Loch Beag.

Having joined the A816 north-east of Craobh Haven, a sedate eight kilometre tramp beside a looking glass Loch Melfort brought me to Kilmelford and the Cuilfail Hotel, a charming old coaching inn.

Saturday, 18th May. Cup Final day north and south of the border.

I set foot into a grim morning of torrential rain and glowering sky. No sooner had I embarked for Degnish Point down the heaving northern shore of Loch Melfort than my boots and weatherproofs simultaneously gave up the ghost.

Having attained my initial goal, I turned north at the turbid, dull as ditch water confluence of Loch Melfort and Seil Sound to find what is erroneously known as 'the only bridge over the Atlantic': Thomas Telford's single arched Clachan Bridge. A somewhat grandiose title for what amounts to little more than a fifty-yard span of Seil Sound – geographically part of the Atlantic Ocean – between Seil Island and the mainland.

With zero incentive to stand and sightsee, I pressed on round the bog pitted coast. As I neared my destination of Oban, the skies darkened still further and gusts of cold rain lashed my face. Before I had time to feel sorry for myself, I was joined by the conscientious figure of Royal Mail's John Burton. Together we dodged cars and cloudbursts for the remaining few kilometres. But the day's ultimate saving grace was enacted 500 miles away at Wembley – where Tottenham Hotspur lifted the FA Cup for an unprecedented eighth time!

Sunday, 19th May. John Burton turned up at nine-thirty with Grant Nicholson of *Postscript* magazine and the *Oban Times*, both graciously foregoing their Sunday morning lie-in in order to accompany me for part of the way. At Grant's suggestion we scaled the hill for a photosession at Oban's crowning glory – the pseudo-Coliseum McCraig's Tower, from whose seaward balcony the view across the Firth of Lorn to the Island of Mull was absolutely fabulous. Though never actually completed, only non-Obanites refer to it as a folly – for its building (1890-1900) brought much needed employment to the town at a time of deep recession.

We then kicked off on a scenic circuit of the craggy headland below the creeper-cloaked ruin of Dunollie Castle, before taking to a wilderness of sombre hills beyond Ganavan Bay. Even as we bade each other farewell the murky mirror of Lochan Dubh reflected the gathering rain clouds.

Sandwiched neatly between two bold tracts of waterlogged terrain in which I picked my way through a powder keg of rank heather, slippery rocks and peat-darkened burns accompanied only by the thrum of rain on hood, the road from Connel to Benderloch was a-buzz with the bee-in-a-tin can drone of a hundred (give or take a 'mod') motor scooters. The Vespa Club of Great Britain was in town! Haven't seen so many Parkas since the sixties.

Before embarking on the day's last stretch to Barcaldine I called into the whitewashed smokery of South Ledaig Farm. From the mouth-watering array of gourmet products on offer I sent home (better to give than to receive!) a pack of sliced venison and an oak-smoked guinea fowl. Farmer's wife Margo McIntyre complimented me on my selection. She also valued my custom. The new Food and Hygiene Act which came into force in October, whereupon all comestibles must be sent in the more expensive polystyrene boxes, looks set to hit mail-order sales for six.

Monday, 20th & Tuesday, 21st May. Over the subsequent forty-eight hours it rained virtually non-stop. When it wasn't gushing from the heavens like a burst water main, it yielded to an insidious drizzle. At least that was my definition of the latter. For the purists among you I'm really informed that it falls (sic) under the category of 'smirr' – which in turn comes somewhere between mizzle and Scotch mist. So much for semantics. Whatever name it goes by it still creeps and seeps until you're soaked to the skin and chilled to the marrow. What's more it was cold enough for winter. But one fragrant compensation was the heady garlic-like odour permeating the rain-laden air from a multitude of white flowered ramsons.

Throughout day one I made remarkably good progress. Two shining lights on an otherwise gloom-ridden day were Port Appin's 'Cala Craft Shop' (superb handiwork at bargain basement prices) and a morale boasting poster on the door of Appin post office which announced: 'John Westley will be in Appin today'. But the accolade of most impressive sight goes to the island fortress of Castle Stalker. Seen through a breach in the mist wall, it called to mind an image of the phantom *Flying Dutchman* becalmed amid the seaweed-strewn mud-flats of Loch Laich...

Day two. Felt non too brilliant on rising (shivery, muzzy head, aching limbs). Little of note transpired until Kentallen Bay, a tree-girt inlet of Outer Loch Linnhe, where I espied another diver – of the bird variety – swimming low in the water. Too small for a great northern, I identified it as a black-throated on account of the conspicuous black and white ribs on its back.

Once over Ballachulish Bridge my condition took a turn for the worse. Having negotiated the climbers' Mecca of Fort William in a state of headachy delirium, gloaming saw me recuperating at the much-in-demand base camp billet of Achintee Farm, Glen Nevis. The Highlands were mine!

After four solid days of precipitation, I thought the sun had gone away for good. But soon the rain blew over and above the high curves of Ardgour to westward, threads of cirrus cloud were back-lit by a rose-fingered sunset. A 'braw' omen for tomorrow's sixth and final climb – Ben Nevis: at 4,408 feet, the highest mountain in the British Isles.

Wednesday, 22nd May. Forgive the repetition, but what a difference a day makes. The sun was up and so were my spirits. Yesterday's indisposition and horrendous weather were gone if not forgotten. The air, purified by the four day deluge, was clean and fresh. I'd never seen the country so green, the sky bluer. Hemmed by year-round white-capped mountains the beautiful valley of Glen Nevis was gilded by the early sun. Columns of vapour rose from melt-water streams as if guiding the way...

I was met at the start of the mountain path by Mary MacKenzie and Steven Mansfield of *The Scotsman*, David Campbell of the *Press and Journal,* and Inverness Royal Mail's John Park who had kindly volunteered to accompany me on the ascent. We couldn't have chosen a more excellent day for our endeavours. The one clear day in seven – we'd hit the meteorological jackpot! All the shortcomings of the previous climbs were at once put behind me. It's the here and now that counts, not the heretofore. Grasp the moment... and regret nothing!

Within no time at all the forestry plantations on the valley floor were reduced to the scale of sage-green postage stamps; cars to matchbox miniatures. Looking back down the rock-studded path the steady file of would-be mountaineers resembled a party of latter-day pilgrims – many of whom were destined to fall by the wayside. In the knowledge that more people die each year on Ben Nevis than the Eiger, it was particularly galling to see the patently inadequate footwear worn by so many. Including in one case – I kid you not – flip-flops! Such is the paradox of 'The Ben': invitingly accessible – but potentially deadly. And all the while with every zigzag twist in the convoluted trail the temperature dropped another degree.

Above the halfway point on this mineral rich massif, granite and gneiss gave way to green stone. This in turn succumbed above the three-quarter mark to a summit-wide snow-field, which grew ever deeper as we neared our lofty goal. Having dutifully added a stone to every cairn along the way, we eventually crested the flat-topped peak at 2 p.m. And what a prize! The whole experience exceeded my wildest dreams by a mile. But our triumph was hardly a solitary affair. Scattered about the southerly cambered plateau were any number of equally excited explorers.

For my part, wearing only shorts and wind-shirt, I felt all the more euphoric for being at one with the elements. Exalting in the rarefied atmosphere of our airy vantage ground, glorying in life, freedom and the sharp mountain air, we surveyed our surroundings with the wonderment of children. Except towards the south-west, mountains stretched to every horizon, the angular cone of Schiehallion prominent thirty-five miles to the east. From the sheer fifteen-hundred foot north-east face the Cairngorms were as plain as a pikestaff. Away to the west, beyond the tangle of hills on the mainland, soared the Cuillin Hills on Skye, and Askival and Allival on Rhum. To the south-west Loch Linnhe opened out into the Firth of Lorne. Closer to home at Banavie the Caledonian Canal was brilliantly showcased by Telford's virtuoso flight of eight locks – Neptune's staircase. In short, my entire route of the coming week or more was spread before me like a relief map. I'd had my sneak preview – now I had to put in the kilometres!

After reaching this pinnacle of perfection, day drifted into day; and while the burgeoning verdure of high summer fulfilled the dormant promise of spring, the remainder of Scotland's spectacular West Coast registered as a montage of phenomenal highs, near-tragic lows and many a fascinating character. Having prevailed over adversity and misfortune I considered – somewhat presumptuously as it transpired – that I had the workaday physical element well and truly licked. In the meantime I lived only for sensation...

Saturday, 25th May. *Wings over Kingairloch.* Well fortified by a rare evening I beat a reluctant retreat from the sleepy, Utopian hamlet of Camasnacroise (Bay of the Cross) – just four cottages and a chapel, each of which was tongue-and-groove panelled throughout with spruce and painted externally in the prescribed estate colours of red and white.

Once off the metalled artery of the B8043 an avenue of deer-proof fences channelled me westward to Kingairloch House and a wide delta of salt-marsh. Leaving behind the last of the estate cottages on the southern shore of Loch a' Choire I followed the coastal 'footpath' (in the loosest possible sense) through a magnificent, severe landscape of craggy hills and glowering lochs that is the embodiment of Scotland. South of Rubha a' Chiaginn the terrain deteriorated into a trackless morass. On emerging from one particularly knotty thicket of bracken and sea rush I noticed that my legs were peppered with ticks; tiny blood-sucking insects that cling on tenaciously with beak-like mouth parts. Utterly revolted though I was, I resisted the temptation to scratch them off right away as leaving the 'beak' embedded in the skin can lead to a nasty infection.

Confronted now by a swampland of bog, burn and generally miry ground, I sought the firm going of the wave-battered boulder beach. As ever, barnacles and limpets proved a real boon to rock walking; seaweed an anathema. It wasn't long before I was licking my wounds after a heavy fall. But every cloud has a silver – nay, golden – lining. While I busied myself applying a poultice of iodine-rich seaweed to my grazed forearm I sensed a movement on the skyline from the corner of my eye. Riding the up-draught above the jagged ridge of Sgurr a' Bhuic was that consummate aeronaut, the golden eagle. Even as I watched it was joined by its mate. The soaring majestic flight of these immense dark tawny-brown birds, on wings spanning seven feet, was an unforgettable experience.

Farther down Loch Linnhe's northern bank I came upon the scarred mountainside of Glensanda, Scotland's first super-quarry, which has already contributed more than a million tons of granite to the construction of the Channel Tunnel. Everything from dump trucks to bulk carriers being loaded by overhead conveyor belt was on the grand scale. The complex as a whole was buzzing with Special Branch officers in preparation for Thursday's visit by the Princess Royal.

Climbing away from the hive of shore-bound activity, the uplands quickly reverted to an empty landscape of heather moor, lichen-encrusted boulders and concealed lakes cradled by towering barren hills. Scrutinised every step of the way by a milling herd of red deer from atop the northern escarpment, I had a feeling akin to the Welsh Guards of Rorke's Drift being sized-up from on high by Zulu warriors.

Monday, 27th May. *The Longest Day.*

Bank Holiday Monday. Quite unfazed by my landlady's forebodings of today's 'tortuous' trek to Strontian (what, me worry!), I'd slept soundly in a luxury caravan serenaded overhead by a lovesick tawny owl.

Where the coast road came to an end I broke through the freezing fog bank into the full stimulating glare of the morning sun. What a stark contrast to the woolly white-out below. In between stowing my now superfluous weatherproofs and admiring the fast greening archipelago of rocky islets, peninsulas and ever-changing cloudscapes brushing the surrounding peaks, it dawned on me that my moods – and conceivably my physical condition – are directly governed by the weather. Hence my present rude health and abounding vitality.

Surrounded on three sides by sea lochs Sunart and Linnhe and the Sound of Mull, the desolate moorland region of Morvern is to all intents and purposes an island. And a place of untamed beauty for all that. Beyond the final cottage the track was no more. Picking up a host of unwanted passengers as I went, I made my way to the rugged foreshore. Bursting through the lochside scrub my legs resembled toasted teacakes – with animated currants. Talk about tick fodder! Pausing only to socialise with a startled family of six on as remote tree-fringed bay (they came in by boat thinking they'd have the place to themselves), after circuiting the foreland on a causeway of massive wave-polished basalt blocks I utilised a Forestry Commission trail which brought me out to Ardantiobairt at the head of Loch Teacuis. Flanked by wooded hills on either side, the lush pasture of Kinloch Deer Farm couldn't have had a more picturesque setting.

Failing miserably to locate the beginning of the 'fabled' highland pass of Bealach Sloc an Eich, I climbed the northern slope with the intention of breaking a trail across the formidable interior – an uphill struggle that continued clean through to the other side of Beinn Ghormaig, where the densely afforested valley of Glen Cripesdale fell sharply away to Glencripesdale Burn. Apart from the unremitting gradient, the main obstacle to my cross-country progress was a network of deer-proof fences that traversed the rolling heathland. Too long to walk round, too robust to penetrate and yet sufficiently spindly to make scaling them a precarious undertaking.

I wasted no time in driving a path through the nigh-on impenetrable plantation of Norway Spruce. A filthy business, more akin to thud and blunder than blood and thunder, accompanied all the while by the mocking duo-tone of an infernal cuckoo constantly reminding me of my mental state! With barely enough light to guide my faltering advance, I emerged some twenty-minutes later bloodied, bruised and as black as Newgate's knocker. If nothing else, at least it hid the ticks!

"Och, where'd ye come frae?" exclaimed Cameron, foreman of the 'Blasting Gang'. "Anither teen meenites an' ye'd hae fount yersel on the wrong end o' a thoosand tons o' rubble!" Cameron and Co. were engaged in dismantling an entire hillside overlooking the shingly inlet of Camas na h-Airbhe which had been the subject of a landslip – and heaven help the hapless rambler who happens along the way! Simultaneous with my first glimpse of Strontian (namesake of the rare mineral once mined in the district) across the broad turquoise reaches of Loch Sunart, a dull report and pall of dust signalled the blasting gang's belated detonation.

Soon after rounding the head of this beautiful sea loch, a natural amphitheatre of hills, I was intercepted by my anxious host who had been on the verge of alerting the Mountain Rescue Service on my behalf. Despite the lateness of the hour – it was well after nine – he assured me that both bed and board awaited my arrival. While the ticks gorged themselves on my blood I wolfed a mammoth vegetarian meal sluiced down with a litre of fruit juice. After the twelve hour, fifty-six kilometre day over some of Scotland's most demanding terrain, I couldn't wait to put spine to mattress. A full stomach, a shower and clean sweet-smelling sheets eased the pain in my limbs and transmuted it into an almost delicious ache. Exhausted but alive, I drifted off into a timeless sleep… I ache therefore I am.

Tuesday, 28th May. It was a fine summer's morning, promising a long hot day – the first in a sequence of six. Bedazzled all the way to the small fishing resort of Salen, the broken lochside canopy gave some respite from the sun's searing heat. With a narrow ribbon of sea loch my day-long companion I lacked nothing in the way of scenery. Undeterred by a steady stream of motor-tourists, the region's wildlife too were out in force. Seals basked on shore-side rocks… Loch Sunart was alive with jellyfish… blossom-dusted hawthorn thickets echoed to the chorus of bird song. To my erstwhile urban-dulled sense of smell, the sweet fragrance of may blossom truly signals the advent of summer. I inhaled with a will. Where winter is to be endured, summer is to be savoured!

Wednesday, 29th May. In a virtual re-run of yesterday's sun-kissed passage I trailed the winding, roller-coaster B8007 westward towards Point of Ardnamurchan ('Point of the Great Ocean'), mainland Britain's westernmost place. Standing proud of the Isles of Skye and Mull, the Ardnamurchan peninsula juts far into the Atlantic like a crooked finger: a *melange* of dramatic sea-shores, corrugated hillscapes, pine plantations and bald-pated mountains.

Thursday, 30th May. Another bejewelled morning. Even at seven-thirty the sun was positively roasting. Having familiarised myself with the lie of the land I climbed up and over the rim of a long extinct volcano. Above the cathedral spaciousness within hovered a crater-wide heat haze. Born of fire and ice of another age, this varicoloured Shangri-La played host to a multitude of bird and animal life. Noble red deer roamed the jagged ramparts of the surrounding hills. Strong smelling otter spraints at the waters edge of many a secluded lochan disclosed their secretive presence. Every half-hour I drank from a tracery of nectar-like tributaries – each the linear habitat of decent sized brook trout. Clegs too were out in numbers. Big Brothers of the comparatively innocuous midge, these persistent, stealthy blighters are capable of delivering an excruciating bite. Come the torrid zenith of midday and the only animate objects were myself and a waltzing confetti of butterflies; the only sounds a babbling burn and the languid trill of bird song. Drowsing sheep occupied every last vestige of shade. In my wake a cloud of dust hung in the air like talcum powder. As I walked I bathed in the hypnotic glare of the sun, with not so much as a vapour trail or penetrating wedge of aircraft noise to disturb my reverie...

I thought the sandy beach at Sanna Bay, north-east of Point of Ardnamurchan, was beautiful enough, but Camas aan Lighe had to be seen to be believed. An unspoilt sweep of gleaming white 'singing sands' with a natural awning of pine trees creeping right down to the tide's edge, it was in a class of its own. And with each gentle waft of breeze the male pine flowers dusted this golden realm with a plume of saffron-pollen...

After latching onto the B8044 west of Acharacle, the roads thereafter were swarming with the throttle-happy membership of the 'Morgan Appreciation Society'. Little did I know that eighteen months hence I would be 'appearing' on the Morgan stand at the International Motor Show ('Britain's Highest Mileage man and its most enduring production vehicle').

On the threshold of Salen I made the acquaintance of Sandra and Alistair Thomson whom I have agreed to assist in a fund-raising capacity on behalf of the 'Ann Charlton Lodge' (Cleveland), a residential home for Multiple Sclerosis sufferers.

Over the coming weeks I would cross swords with one fairly impenetrable tract of country after another. But I, like so many of the peninsula's regular visitors, had fallen madly in love with this wild, untamed land of Ardnamurchan.

Friday, 31st May. Equidistant from the cluster of cottages that is Salen and the idyllic Sylvan setting of 'Five Pines', Roshven, tonight's quarters, I fair leapt at the invitation of taking (herbal) tea with Friesian islander Bodo Clausen, who had read my article in *The Scotsman.* Bodo explained that, although a reed thatcher by trade, he is presently engaged in re-roofing the outbuildings of Mingarrypark Folk Museum with heather, a specialised craft he learnt at the hands of his grandfather. With a turf underlay, heather thatch will last fifteen years; with a felt-type underlay as specified by the local authority its life span is halved. Bureaucracy gone wild! But Bodo's expertise isn't limited to domestic use. In the late 60s he was called upon to design the hemp bindings for the papyrus hull of Thor Heyerdahl's Ra II Expedition – hemp apparently solidifies in sea water.

11   Sole destroying

He who limps is still walking.
    Stanislaw Lec

Sunday, 2nd June.

WITH swallows, midges and frequent cloudbursts for company I picked my way along the switchback northern shore of the landlocked Loch Morar – at a fearsome 1,017 ft, the deepest sheet of freshwater in Britain – keeping my eyes peeled for 'Morag', a little known relative of 'Nessie' the Loch Ness monster. West of Swordland Lodge a rough trackway filtered down to the mini-fjord of Tarbet Bay. Overtowered on either hand by the vertiginous green hills of North Morar, the blue-black inlet is as deep as the hills are high. To call Tarbet a tiny settlement is the understatement of the century. Apart from the odd outbuilding, all that remains of the once thriving herring processing station is the 'Old Post Office' – before its closure the most remote PO in the UK – and a deconsecrated Roman Catholic Chapel, currently squatted by an affable chap from Fife called Frank. At the 'Old Post Office' I was greeted by brother and sister Donald (80) and Jessie (90) MacDonald. With no electricity, gas, TV, or telephone, and their main contact with the outside world the twice weekly mail-boat from Mallaig (which stops running whenever a westerly wind blows above force seven), the local authorities were understandably trying to get them both into care. Donald won't hear of it; Jessie – oblivious to it all – was lost in a world of her own.

Over a mug of tea Donald acquainted me with the best treatment for ticks – suffocate them with butter or Vaseline. Jessie, meanwhile, stared into the log fire and sang gently to herself. When the blaze died down I earned my keep – bed, no board – by chopping a supply of fire wood.

After nightfall Donald and I were joined by Frank for a lamplight 'blether'. When the drinking mood takes them this dauntless duo row across Loch Nevis to wet their whistles at the 'Old Forge Inn', Inverie – the most isolated pub in Britain. A treacherous passage of seething cross-currents at the best of times, how they manage it after dark in a tiny skiff when three-parts soused remains one of life's little mysteries. As the perpetrators of such an extraordinary feat, Donald and Frank commanded my utmost respect. Though neither gave me so much as a cat's chance of making it to Inverie by tomorrow night. We'll see.

Monday, 3rd June. As I scaled Druim Chuilinn to the east of Tarbet Bay the rain was already tippling down. Together with the surrounding mountainscape of snow-covered peaks, such weather made an absolute mockery of the seasons. Flaming June, indeed! Alternating hail, rain and snowfall throughout the course of the day sent the temperature tumbling further and reduced my progress along the steeply cambered southern shore of Loch Nevis to that of a non-equine steeplechase, a succession of fast-flowing freshets gushing from the hillsides deputising for water-jumps. Over a six kilometre stretch of foreshore I counted as many derelict cottages – a grim legacy of the Clearances.

On the far side of a broad tract of salt-marsh I crossed the raging River Carnach on a rickety rope bridge. Looming large before me was a range of shapely mountains. Flanked left and right by the sky-scraping summits of Meall Bhasiter and Sgurr Sgeithe, I set my sights on the 2,000 ft saddle of Mam Meadail. A gut-busting grunt ensued, made more so by the freshening wind and a seeming river-bed of a track. Some gradient! Just shy of the top I sat out a particularly violent hailstorm which threatened to blow me off the mountainside. As the worst of it passed over likewise a Jaguar Jet, faithfully following the course of the glen, banked directly in front of the outcrop on which I perched. So close was it that, had I been more alert, I fancy I could have touched it with my stick. Certainly I could clearly define the helmeted pilot. But most impressive by far was the sound that hit me with an almost physical impact. Both stirred and shaken, I pressed on to the saddle from whose vantage point of the interior of the Knoydarrt Peninsula ('the last wilderness') unfolded before my very eyes. Descending the tussocky, waterlogged canyon of Gleann Meadail, I achieved my goal with daylight to spare. So much for the doubts of Donald and Frank. O ye of little faith!

With no way in or out other than by foot – or the thrice-weekly ferry – Inverie is officially recognised as the most inaccessible village in mainland Britain. And all the more appealing for its isolation. At 'Pier House' I didn't need to polish my boots to get a shine on them. A seven hour run-in with igneous and metamorphic rock had left them glistening with a lustrous sheen of mica crystals.

Tuesday, 4th June. Within minutes of departing the azure canopy clouded over and heavens split asunder – the first instalment of a nine hour sequence of sunshine and showers. Seven miles out of Inverie the single-track road petered out beside the home of Dave Smith, 'the last crofter on Knoydart'. South of Inverguseran I utilised what pass for stepping stones to cross the turbulent Abhainn Inbhir Ghuiserein – with two days provisions on my back, in addition to my pack, a risky business.

Leaving behind the cotton grass, I entered the rugged realm of Loch Hourn – the most remote and most spectacular of the western sea lochs. Classic fiord country this, where steep escarpments climb sheer from the water's edge. Though never genuinely afraid at any time during the day, my blind faith was however shaken on more than one occasion – not least when traversing the near perpendicular cliff of Creag an t-Sagairt (the 'Priest's Rock'). With no visible hand holds and my centre of gravity sent skew-whiff by the weight of my rucksack, I opted to crawl along the narrow ledge – only for my cargo to 'shift' at the worst conceivable moment, almost carrying me bag and baggage into the briny below. Had I fallen my last sight would have been that of a guano-encrusted shag's nest and cluster of swaying bluebells. Cautiously resuming the vertical, farther along the same rock-face I inched my way above a yawning wave-sculpted overhang. Chancing a downward glance, it struck me with sobering realisation that the only things preventing me from plummeting to a watery grave were a couple of clumps of heather and a tenuous foothold. Heart in the mouth time all over again!

From the sublime to the ridiculous! After the unadulterated luxury of 'Pier House', Barrisdale bothy – sleeps 16; £1.50 per night; 3 nights max. – came as a rude awakening. Spartan accommodation; but great company.While I prepared my evening meal a herd of thirty or more red deer gathered outside to graze the velvety level. With a generator that chugged on well into the small hours, whereupon the rival stags began bellowing fit to bust a blood vessel, we had nothing to do but talk the night away.

Wednesday, 5th June. Ten months on the road today. After an all but sleepless night I was up and away soon after eight. Fortunately the sun followed suit, effectively nullifying the worst of the biting cross wind. The 'footpath' to Kinloch Hourn amounted to a walk on the wild side. Strictly X-certificate stuff this. Highlands by name and by nature. All in all an exhilarating morning's legwork that was enriched no end by isolated stands of Scots pine – the last remnants of the once vast Caledonian Forest. These ancient and majestic outposts are home to such rare species as capercaillie, crested tit, pine marten and red squirrel.

Just before five I encountered the enchanting lochside hamlet of Corran, and my soft spoken hostess 'Rena' MacDonald. Such a sweet, gentle soul is she that robins, chaffinches and blackbirds feed from her hand – and reward her with their delightful song. I was immediately struck by the translucent quality of her flawless complexion which would do justice to a lassie half her age. Rena put it down to the magical properties of the local water supply, pumped from a well across the glen. Her mother, who lived to be 101, went one step further, attributing her ripe old age directly to taking the waters morning and night throughout her lifetime. Giving the longevity theory the benefit of the doubt, prior to hitting the sack I drank my fill from the tap. Better to be taken short in the night than cut short in one's prime!

Thursday, 6th June. Not for nothing is the north-west corner of the Highlands known as the 'empty country'. You can walk all day without seeing another human being, an insignificant speck amid the staggering works of nature...

Like many an avid reader before me I was paying a nostalgic pilgrimage to Sandaig – alias 'Camusfearna', where Gavin Maxwell wrote *Ring of Bright Water* among others. For the final downhill mile or so I ran the gauntlet of pestilential midge swarms, the diffused light of the forest trail being better suited to the predator than the prey. Ripe with expectation and anxious to escape the attentions of the midges, I erupted from the tree-cover into an idyllic coastal glade. It seemed all so familiar: the lush water-meadows... the pure-white quartzite sand... the causeway of jagged islets... the pale green Sound of Sleat... the purple backdrop of the Isle of Skye. Like meeting long lost friends. There too was the memorial marking the site of the author's home: 'Beneath this stone are buried the ashes of Gavin Maxwell. b 15 July 1914 – d 7th September 1969.' Not far away, in the dappled-shade of a bower of birch and ivy, I paused beside the grave of Edal '... the otter of *Ring of Bright Water*'.

In wandering away from the sun-filled clearing for the shadowy bank of the softly murmuring Allt Mor Shantaig I disturbed a red deer and her faun in the midst of suckling. As the mother fled, the speckled calf – all angular 'elbows' and 'knees' – dropped instinctively to the camouflaging undergrowth. Taking care not to touch it – for fear that the hind might reject her offspring – I took a souvenir snap before making a hasty exit.

Friday, 7th June. Following in the illustrious footsteps of Dr Johnson, before tramping the shoreline to Totaig and on to Ratagan, I hopped the ferry across the narrows of Kyle Rhea to the Isle of Skye. A ten-minute round trip, but at least I can say with all honesty that I've been 'over the sea to Skye'. In running to make the initial connection I was politely applauded aboard by the complement of cosmopolitan passengers and ferrymen – who had that very moment just finished regaling their charges with an anecdote as told them by a visiting party of geologists regarding a 'bearded giant striding the mountains'. Not only was I not charged for either crossing, but – give or take the odd pfennig and peseta – I did some healthy business donation-wise. Evidently a little hyperbole goes a long way!

Saturday, 8th June. Located on a rocky island at the concourse of Lochs Long, Duich and Alsh, the turn-of-the-century restored fortress of Eilean Donnan is today linked to the mainland by a metalled causeway. Few ancient piles have been in greater demand by the media than this former Jacobite stronghold: TV, commercials, movies (Sean Connery's *The Highlander* to name but one). I'd already exposed half a roll of film, when the skirl of bagpipes craned all heads towards one Sandy Allen – resplendent in full Highland regalia. Sandy supplements his holiday pay by playing for and posing for photographs with the snap-happy tourists. Far from charging me for the privilege, he generously put half his morning's take into my collection box – and piped me on my way to the tune of *Collin's Cattle*.

Sunday, 9th June. Beautiful landscapes, such as that of the romantic, mist-draped Isle of Skye, are being increasingly marred by a rash of kit-built bungalows. Though mercifully not as widespread as in the Republic of Ireland, they are nonetheless the scourge of Western Scotland. With the coming of the Skye toll bridge, and with it ready accessibility, who knows what architectural monstrosities will follow in its wake. Let's hope for all our sakes that the stipulations for the granting of planning permission are tightened – not relaxed!

Sheltered by a wild archipelago of islets and headlands, the lush, green, palm-fringed oasis of Plockton is the nearest thing yet to a Scottish Riviera.

Monday, 10th June. Now re-named the Applecross Scenic Route, the mountain road to Applecross is more widely known as Bealach na Bà – the pass of the cattle (if not a right cow of a pass!). From the northern bank of Loch Kishorn – where oil-rig platforms destined for the North Sea were once fabricated – the ancient drover's road, one of the UK's loftiest byways, snaked its way up the barren hillside via a series of giddying hairpins and alarming precipices to a height of 2,053 ft. The higher I climbed the chillier it became; the chillier it became the heavier the rain, the stronger the wind and the thicker the fog. By the time I reached the top I was wringing wet. From there on the going was theoretically easier. In reality the stark lunar landscape exposed me to the full demoralising impact of the elements. Several sympathetic motorists stopped me on the serpentine descent to Applecross, each of whom gladly helped themselves to an appeal card from my breast pocket as my hands were insensible with the cold. Without doubt the most severe day weatherwise since the 'Irish Hurricane'. If nothing else, such interludes are all grist to the narrative.

Wednesday, 12th June. After a hard day's legwork negotiating the red-sandstone roller-coaster of the Torridon Hills, on reaching the dinky little crofting village of Lower Diabaig I hung up my boots in the whitewashed cottage of Mr and Mrs Ross. From the sunken mountain canyon of Lower Diabaig's sheltered natural harbour, we could for all the world have been in Norway.

Scottish housewives are well known to take great pride in setting a fine table – Isabella Ross was no exception to the rule. Following a traditional suppertime spread, which in turn followed hard on the heels of an equally appetising dinner, I turned my attentions to matters of a more personal nature. Over the past week or so my midge bites have been driving me to distraction. No doubt brought on by the rise in temperature, they invariably reach their infuriating peak soon after I turn in for the night. Though curiously enough I only seem to have been bitten on my untanned 'white bits' (no need to elaborate). Before hitting the hay I lavished the effected areas with corresponding amounts of TLC and TCP.

Thursday, 13th June. One-hundred days to go!

Acquainted with the news that Mr Ross has now lost all of his hens twice over to a pine marten (though in my humble opinion the culprit is more likely a mink), I set about the steep climb out of Lower Diabaig. From the word go I fell foul of the three M's: mizzle, mud and midges. No sooner had I disparagingly dubbed the cairn-marked path to Craig a 'goat track' than a party of hardy hikers alerted me to the real thing – a herd of feral goats. With shaggy coats and splayed horns, they were virtually indistinguishable from the grey boulders between which they foraged. The most talkative of the hikers, a sun-bronzed middle-aged woman, brazenly puffed away on a Meerschaum pipe – the one sure-fire method of warding off midges.

Friday, 14th June. Due east of the automated lighthouse of Rubha Reidh (which now doubles as an exploration centre and B&B) I blazed a trail across an open moorland that swept down to a ribbon of ragged cliffs. With fatigue fast setting in, I was unable to face the long haul over the promontory, deciding instead to take a short cut along the beach of Camas Mor ('Big Bay') – which very nearly became a short cut to tragedy. Descending the moss-grown scree slope was hairy enough. But worse was yet to come. After paddling ashore I noticed with some alarm that I was in serious danger of becoming marooned by the rising tide, which comes in at a phenomenal lick in these northern climes. Wading the length of the beach, I began scaling the guano-caked cormorant terraces – only for the rain-lubricated sandstone to send me crashing to the cliff's rubble-strewn base, sustaining in the process a sprained right ankle and some damage to my outer left hamstring. Of more immediate concern was the chronic pain in my left buttock (which succinctly summed up the incident as a whole), and was probably a muscle tear. It was particularly fortunate that I hadn't climbed any higher than the twenty-feet or so I managed, otherwise the outcome might well have been fatal. Having dragged myself tooth and nail to the cliff-top by way of a less demanding route, it was quite clear that the left leg was barely able to support my paltry weight. And in compensating for it, my right leg was taking one helluva hammering. What a fine state of affairs!

Hobbling like the crock I was, I pursued the cove-indented coastline to Rubha nan Sasan. Along the way I teamed up with homeward-bound 'Roto' MacIver, a whelk fisherman and ex-regular soldier. The combination of my companion's chirpy repartee and a can of Greenmantle Border Ale kept my pecker up no end. But Roto had problems of his own. A single bag of whelks can weigh as much as four stone – hence the lumbar belt and paracetamol tablets. Roto offered me a couple of pain-killers to tide me over, but I demurred in the knowledge that the sanctuary of the metalled road was less than an hour distant.

After this latest injury crisis I settled into an automatism of limping, a daily round of mind over matter. Each faltering step required a separate act of concentration. Every sinew implored me to give in and lie down for good. A short term respite had no attraction whatsoever. The whole long winded palaver of putting my rucksack on again after going to the trouble of unhitching and removing it was too wearying a prospect to contemplate. Only as far as the next hill I deluded myself – then I'd call it a day. Having got there I set myself targets anew. The next peat-bog… the next glen… the next bothy. And so on, point to point, objective to objective, ad infinitum. As long as my gullible body was willing to be duped I was in with a fighting chance of staying the course. Blotting out all but the necessity to set one foot in front of the other I sank into a black enveloping whirlpool of pain and despondency. In this stupefied state weeks passed with the velocity of days; days like hours; hours like minutes. And still the grinding cycle gained momentum. Between ever shortening bouts of oblivion I surfaced to view the fast-forward world as a blurred procession of unrelated incidents and endearing vignettes, as if from a speeding railway carriage…

Monday, 17th June. After forty-three punishing kilometres skirting the desolate, rain-swept steppe, it came as no surprise to learn that the coast on Wester Ross is on the same latitude as Siberia. With a dearth of vacant accommodation and campsites on this side of the water, private ferry operator Mr Brown was providing me with free passage to and from the busy port of Ullapool. Seven days of unbroken downpour had swamped everything in sight – not least the pint-sized *Mother Goose*. Skipper Ross MacKay was in the process of casting off when a trio of heavily-laden German cycle tourist swept down the hillside. All three couldn't or wouldn't believe that the *Mother Goose* was the actual passenger ferry – and not the tender to a larger more robust vessel. Rather than make two trips of it the slaphappy skipper urged them aboard, bikes, panniers and all – heedless of the fact that the choppy waters of Loch Broom were already nudging the gunnels. Making the same crossing in a 'fair Rummel' didn't bare thinking about. Even when we were unceremoniously clattered by the backwash of the departing Stornoway vehicle-ferry Ross MacKay's maniacal laughter continued non-stop, much to the disquiet of the ashen-face Aryans, and hardly likely to inspire one with confidence for the return trip: "Try tae get here jist before ten in the mornin' – in case I decide no' tae wait for ye."

So much for the timetable! Though with more filthy weather in the offing it was hard not to regard it as a blessing in disguise.

Wednesday, 19th June. A right bastard of a day! With every nook and cranny in my rucksack taken up by extra provisions, I had no option but to suffocate in my shell suit from start to finish. If Thursday's leg from Lower Diabaig to Craig was a goat-track, then this afternoon's cliff-top scramble between Dun Canna and Culnacraig was nothing short of mountain goat country. At one point I inadvertently flushed a meadow pipit from the matted herbage at the side of the trail – effectively pinpointing its nest and clutch of five brown-speckled eggs. A sure sign that this overgrown right of way is seldom used. Where the path – such as it was – faithfully embraced every switchback contour of this wild coast, an unholy alliance of waterlogged terrain, deep-seated fatigue and unwieldy burden made the going synonymous with tight-rope walking. Supporting my dwindling body-weight presented no problem. But even a mountain goat wouldn't be quite so nimble with a three-stone handicap. No wonder then that in slaloming my way through an obstacle course of bramble-rambled headlands and heather-grown sheep tracks that I came a near fatal cropper for the second time in little under a week. In my impatience to cover the ground I snagged my boot in the tripwire heather and fell headlong into a briar patch. Another foot and I'd have been over the edge. *Auf wiedersehen*, Westley!

That night I dossed down at Acheninver Youth Hostel. I had now slept my way through the entire range of accommodation: from campsite to caravan; from bivouac to bothy; and from terraced house to five-star hotel. You name it, I've kipped there. After a hotchpotch of a supper I took to my cot in an attempt to complete paperwork before I finally flaked out. Even at this relatively advanced hour the 'Summer Dun', Northern Scotland's equivalent of the Arctic Circle's 'Midnight Sun', refused point blank to set. Between catnaps and fleeting bursts of ever deteriorating handwriting the soothing sound of taped fiddle music drifted up from the common room below. As I wavered on the threshold of slumber the water cistern beside my head struck-up a syncopated off-beat, dolefully augmented by the counter-melody of the north-west wind... a Coigach cradle-song.

Thursday, 20th June. Having swept out the men's dormitory (all hostellers are assigned a chore), I stretched my legs down Achitibuie's single track 'Road to the Isles' – The Summer Isles. Resembling a rocky fleet at anchor just off shore, the potent combination of seascape and archipelago provide a mercurial spectacular that changes its countenance with the weather, from Arctic to Aegean at the scud of a cloud or rise of the sun. Once seen, never forgotten.

Saturday, 22nd June. A nine hour round of sunshine, showers and stifling humidity –with a wealth of spellbinding scenery. To the few remaining crofters who scrape a living here, the remote district of Assynt – a ragged shoreline of sea, sun-bleached strand, loch and burn; half-water, half-land – is a place of work. But to the well-to-do, a playground.

Sunday, 23rd June. Following a dull and misty overture the sun broke through with a will soon after eight – whereupon the massed choirs of crickets fell silent. Back in harness by nine, Sutherland's big dipper terrain was definitely not what the doctor ordered. More hills than Cork has spires! Fat lot of good my elasticated ankle, knee and thigh supports were doing. Oh well, swings and roundabouts, I reasoned – without conviction.

My need to take the occasional breather did, however, have its compensation. During one such time-out – while sharing my rudimentary lunch with an American-born Oxford postman (a yank at Oxford!), who in attempting to cycle round Scotland had clearly bitten off more than he could masticate – I saw my first cuckoos at close quarters. Swaying precariously upon a telegraph wire, the motley duo looked like scruffy urchins in robber's jumpers. Later in the day I paused beside a freshwater lochan, yellow with the blooms of water-lilies. A vibrant hue that was echoed in the surrounding phalanxes of gorse; their sickly sweet aroma put me in mind of a certain proprietary sun-screen lotion of whose services I was in urgent need.

Monday, 24th June. Midsummer Day – with sultry weather to match. Not so elsewhere. The first day of Wimbledon and the second test against the West Indies were both rained off. Having received a new weatherproof jacket in the post, I consigned my old one to the bin. Good riddance to bad rubbish! And still the hills of Sutherland continued to rear-up before me. So engrossed in my own suffering am I that the scenery – spectacular though it is – goes largely unnoticed.

A timely warning!

Finally throwing in the sponge at the dune-hemmed hamlet of Polin, my thoughts turned immediately to the pressing matter of footwear. As a direct result of my ramrod-legged gait, I was going through my boots like a dose of salts. Only a month old and the heels of my current pair were already gaping to the elements. Purely as a stopgap measure I filled each heel cavity with 'Plastic Padding'. And though the outcome was less shock absorbing than usual, I figured that rigid and dry is preferable to flexible and porous.

Tuesday, 25th June. Yesterday's window in the weather slammed shut this morning. Monsoon conditions prevailed from the off. The boulder-studded track to Sandwood Bay was a real menace; four solid miles of slipping and sliding all over the place, during which my Wee Cromach proved invaluable as a veritable third leg, and without whose assistance I'd have bitten the mud on more than one occasion.

Sandwood Bay was certainly a sight to behold. Girdled on two sides by rabbit-cropped slopes, and by marram-knitted dunes and boiling surf on the other two, the pale pink sands stretched for more than a mile. No sign of the ghost in sailor's garb who's said to haunt the beach; nor the mermaid who was spotted by a local man in 1900. In their stead I met mountain biker Ian Jackson. Materialising from nowhere, the fact that he knew me by name only enhanced the surreal quality of it all. Two total strangers in the back of beyond linked by a common objective – Cape Wrath.

Deriving its name from the Norse hvraf, 'a turning place', Cape Wrath was still a good eight miles away across a rigorously rumpled desolation of cliffs (the highest in continental Britain), peat-bog, heath and rock – The Parbh: at 100 square miles, one of the largest uninhabited regions in the UK. What in the late summer will be a magnificent undulating carpet of purple, was now cloaked in a mantle of drab, dun coloured hues. For my part there was something intangibly eerie about this crazily concertinaed wilderness. Ian apart, I had the sneaking suspicion that I wasn't alone – but kept my thoughts to myself.

After walking the length of the beach in tandem and fording the seaward outflow of Sandwood Loch, we scaled the first cliff of the day. From thereon we set our own respective pace, the bicycle-borne Ian being the hare to my hamstrung greyhound. Formidable though the terrain was I still found time to photograph (after a fashion) a Scottish primrose. Little more than a cluster of pinkish flowers on a single stem, this tiny relative of the common primrose is unique to Sutherland, Caithness and Orkney. Soon afterwards I came within a hair's breadth of stepping on a red grouse. Rather than take to the wing, it merely cowered in the heather. Poor deluded creature. With a prominent red wattle above each eye did it really imagine that it was camouflaged? My last sighting of Ian was from the summit of Sithean na h-Iolaireich. From my aerial vantage ground I saw him freewheel down the oatmeal incline of Cnoc a Gheodha Ruaidh, two hillsides back. Lame I may be – a slouch I am not!

Long before I saw Cape Wrath lighthouse (another Robert Stevenson job; *circa* 1828, and known to all and sundry as 'Fraggle Rock'), guardian of the most north-westerly tip of mainland Scotland, I could hear the foghorn bellowing blindly into an impenetrable fog-bank which obscured all but the incongruous white stump of a sundial. The only other visitors at the lighthouse were a doctor (a rheumatologist) and his wife. According to my learned acquaintance the pain in my left buttock is a severe tear of the *gluteus maximus*. The only remedy: rest. Chance would be a fine thing!

Wednesday, 26th June. Back at Cape Wrath after a comfortable night in Durness the rain-spattered lighthouse was still in the vice-like grip of a regular pea-souper – totally blotting out the Atlantic Rollers pounding the shore almost 400 feet below; likewise obliterated, the foghorn continued to bellow forth its bellicose warning. In a fit of lunacy Kevin Clemmett, fellow patron of the grandiosely titled 'West End Hotel', volunteered to forego the comfort of the Mercedes mini-bus in order to accompany me on the eleven-mile walk back to the passenger-ferry slipway on the western shore of the Kyle of Durness. Not only one of the loneliest single-track roads in Europe, this is Cape Wrath's only link with the outside world. During the next three hours we maintained a respectable 4 mph which afforded us ample time to explore a number of abandoned cottages on the MOD bombardment range. Complete with furnishings, running water and in one case a bottle of Scotch in a cupboard, they looked for all the world as though the householders had simply vanished into thin air. Most uncanny.

On the fund-raising front John Beresford, driver of the mini-bus (originally floated over from Keodale on two boats lashed together), did his utmost to swell the campaign coffers. Our paths crossed twice during the day and on each occasion he drew to a halt in order to let me go through my appeal spiel for the captive multi-national audience on board. Despite the language barrier, I averaged £15 per bus-load. Good on you, John.

Having seen Kevin onto the ferry, I ascended the erosion-scarred foothills of Beinn an Amair. Only after slogging some thirteen kilometres around the entire landward end of the Kyle of Durness did I notice a shepherd fording his flock across an uncharted shallow. Ho-hum. I needed the exercise anyway (and pigs might fly!).

Thursday, 27th June. In contrast to yesterday's rain-lashed circuit of the Kyle of Durness, today dawned warm and dazzlingly bright. Wednesday's introduction had wetted Kevin's appetite for walking. Having endured the proverbial rough, he was determined not to miss out on the smooth. We shaped a course for Faraid Head via the broad sandy sweep of Balnakeil Bay. On such a God-given sun-kissed morn as this the headland, where hard rocks stoically resist erosion, had the palmy, isolated feel of a desert island paradise: the constant mewing and shrieking of multitudinous bird life; wedges of alabaster sand; the lush greensward; mesmeric sea vistas… No visitor could fail to be excited by the panorama or invigorated by the salty air.

But the best was yet to come. From the cliff edge there, on the turfy slopes below, were puffins galore. This was the icing on the ornithological cake. A true child of the sea, the puffin is more than at home beneath the waves than above them. Out of their watery element they cut a particularly comic figure. Huge tri-coloured beaks, squat bodies and garish red legs and feet don't exactly bridge the credibility-gap. But nonetheless a combination guaranteed to melt the heart of all who are fortunate enough to witness the puffin's scuttling land-borne antics and wing-whirring comings and goings. Timid little souls, they appeared to be in a permanent state of alarm brought about by the patrolling great black-backed gulls who, given half a chance, would make a meal of them soon as look at them. But today the butcher of the bird world was destined to be out of luck. For right in the midst of the ever vigilant 'sea parrots' and cushions of sea pink sat a coal-black rabbit. I saw it as much as a good omen for the overall outcome of the walk as for the immediate welfare of my new-found 'bottlenosed' buddies.

Friday, 28th June. A wind-tossed day; alternately cloudy and sunny. In crossing the Kyle of Tongue on both the outward and inward journey I was mobbed on each occasion by a cloud of common terns as I passed their shingle spit breeding site. Cars went unmolested; pedestrians pose a mere tangible threat. In between mobbings I completed the round-trip to Tongue by way of the towering sandstone promontory of Whiten Head. Clear of the scattered crofting community of Achininver I legged it through a barren corrugated wold of sudden cliffs and green bogs. Try though I might I was hardly setting the heather ablaze. In fact my all too obvious limitations left me fuming with frustration. Each time I upped the tempo or leapt over an age old drainage dike my gimpy leg crumpled beneath me, dumping me unceremoniously into the vegetation in a welter of pain and expletives. Taking a leaf out of Jerome Kern's song-book, I picked myself up, dusted myself off and started all over again.

In scaling the first of a series of element-scoured limestone bluffs, I froze in my tracks at the sound of 'thundering hooves' approaching swiftly from behind. Nightmare visions of a runaway bull or charging feral goat were quickly dispelled as a jack mountain hare came galloping by not an arm's length away – only to pause some twenty feet ahead as if throwing down a challenge. Catch me if you can! Just what I needed, a hare with a wry sense of humour!

Seduced by the scintillating views to seaward, due east of Whiten Head I blithely bisected what I assumed to be a regular grassy plain. Finding the going only slightly more springy than usual, it wasn't until I reached the trampoline-like epicentre of the football pitch-sized flatland that I realised I was in the middle of a quaking bog of unfathomable deepness. I tried pushing my stick down into it in order to gauge the actual depth. To my consternation, after some initial resistance it dropped away into nothingness. Like the skin of an outsize rice pudding, the only thing holding me up was a thin crust of sphagnum moss and cotton grass. Extracting my Wee Cromach with a glutinous squelch, I made a beeline for terra firma; each cautious step transmitting a wave of ripples radiating across the miry membrane. The longest walk of my life. And by the time I reached dry land the bog wasn't the only thing quaking!

12   Trading paces

A solitude is the audience-chamber of God.
   Walter Savage Landor

Tuesday, 2nd July.

AFTER a bright and promising start, a moisture-laden sea mist rolled in – where it remained rigidly entrenched for the next three days. Accompanied by the basso drone of the distant Stroma Lighthouse fog-horn, in bordering the cliff-hemmed moorland to Dunnet Head – mainland Britain's most northerly point – I penned the following ditty. In retrospect, banal; at the time, deadly earnest.

> *Dunnet Head Doggerel*
> *(to the tune of 'Morningtown Ride')*
>
> *Rocking, rolling, limping*
> *out to Dunnet Head*
> *Strewth! My poor plates of meat*
> *What a dunderhead.*
>
> *Rocking, rolling, hobbling*
> *Out to Dunnet Head*
> *If I had any sense at all*
> *I'd be tucked up in bed.*

Wednesday, 3rd July. Q: What do children and certain senior citizens have in common?
A: On occasion they can both be blunt to the point of rudeness.

There was I minding my own business, striving manfully to conceal my limp, when from of a cluster of squat cottages which constitute the seafaring community of Scarfskerry emerged a venerable old dear who tactlessly articulated:

"Have you always been lame? I'm ninety-two, you know. Are you English? I like Germans – very clean."

Charming!

Thursday, 4th July. Aided and abetted by my cousin Tamzin, and her boyfriend of the time, Mark, I pushed the boat out a little too far last night. But then such a landmark as John O'Groats – Mainland Britain's northernmost village – couldn't go uncelebrated. Now I was paying the ultimate penalty for mixing the hop with the grain. The morning after the skinfull before, so to speak. Still feeling decidedly like death warmed over, Tamzin and Mark waved me off into a swirling haar – a cold wet sea fog.

South of the lighthouse-capped Duncansby Head the fleecy haar hung low over the timeless coastscape in thick petrified waves, translating the black-soiled, treeless tundra into a scene of medieval serfdom. An image brought vividly to life in the shape and form of an elderly mother and her middle-aged son hand-hoeing an entire field of turnips. And I thought I had it rough!

Friday, 5th July. So time consuming was yesterday's highly enjoyable civic reception at Wick Town Hall, that I deferred my planned visit to Caithness General Hospital until this morning. After several days of steady improvement to my hamstring, I was mortified that something as outwardly innocuous as a stubbed toe could set me right back to square one. Hopalong Westley all over again!

Dr B – in tones reminiscent of the late Peter Sellers' 'Indian Physician' characterisation – was at a loss to my unwillingness to comply with his well intentioned instructions:

"I am telling you – no more knapsack, no more wockin'!"

Staff Nurse Evelyn Tait was more in sympathy with my catch-22 dilemma: "Just you take it easy."

With a series of public engagements, personal appearances, question and answer sessions and MS Society social evenings lined up for virtually every day from here on, above and beyond my already gruelling *wockin'* schedule, I barely had time to catch my breath let alone take it easy.

Still, it's the thought that counts.

Saturday, 6th July. As of the previous day, after an early mist the sky became abnormally clear; a seamless canopy of dunnock egg blue. Once aboard the rudimentary cliff path I was to all intents and purposes the only man alive – A latter day Alexander Selkirk (whose misadventures as a castaway inspired Daniel Defoe's *Robinson Crusoe*). To seaward, beyond the variegated tracery of drifting currents, a trio of becalmed colossi projected vertically from the stationary offshore fog bank like outsize concrete icebergs – production platforms A, B and C of the Beatrice North Sea oil field.

The sheer volume of broken serpentine bodies I've encountered since the walk began would seem to support the theory that adders, slow-worms, grass snakes and the like occasionally utilise the crown of the road as a basking place – with lethal consequences. Speaking of which, having temporarily re-engaged the A9 just north of Brora I too made a fundamental error of judgement. Espying what I assumed to be yet another hit 'n' run fatality – a female adder, or viper; Britain's only poisonous snake – I picked it up for closer examination. Whereupon it miraculously returned to life – while I died a thousand deaths!

Monday, 8th July. A pre-dawn thunderstorm was superseded by a turbid mantle of freezing fog, effectively obliterating all hope of my compiling a photographic keepsake of the pastoral paradise of Dornoch – surely Scotland's most picturesque mellow-stoned town, appearing as it does to be an almost organic extension of the surrounding countryside. Between Dornoch and the as yet unfinished Dornoch Firth Road Bridge, the Low Road was littered with the contorted corpses of innumerable rabbits, the gruesome relics of just one evening's motoring in a land where conies are once again assuming plague proportions.

Thursday, 11th July. No sooner have I congratulated myself on seeing off the last of the West Coast midges than I find I'm flavour of the month to ravenous hordes of pestilential flies. Little wonder I'd met so few locals since arriving on Black Isle (not so much an island as a bracken-rusted peninsula) – they were either ensconced in motorcars or cowering indoors!

Driven to distraction, I took a rowan switch in a vain attempt to ward off my parasitic persecutors. What a pretty picture I must have made: all garbled rantings and wildly flailing arms. Regular funny farm fodder! When their buzzing attentions became unbearable my inclination was to bury my head in the grass until they'd gone – but thought better of it. Why fuel the case for the men in white coats!

At one point I upped the tempo in a bid to shake them off my tail. It worked for a while. But when I looked back, the oscillating cloud of Satan's own creatures were gathering in greater numbers than ever. It occurred to me that they might be attracted by the darkish hues of my backpack and waterproofs (as if the flies weren't enough to put up with, it was also oppressively muggy and drizzling to boot!). Only after I experimented by holding my breath did I realise that they were in fact homing in on my exhaled carbon dioxide. A fruitless discovery, as holding one's breath while trying to outrun the little monsters was a physical impossibility. Not for the first time I had to bow to the inevitable and tough it out. The back of the flyblown Black Isle couldn't come soon enough. Give me midges any time!

Friday, 12th July. In crossing the impressive Kessock Bridge over the Beauly Firth *en route* to a media opportunity in Inverness, 'Capital of the Highlands', I revelled in the sight of a school of dolphins frolicking in the turbulent waters below – the most northerly breeding colony of bottle-nosed dolphins in the world!

By late afternoon, as the media bods began to drift away, the pallid sun made a valiant stab at breaching the anti-cyclonic gloom. Whereupon I was taken on to a sumptuous buffet-cum-reception at the exclusive Kingsmill Hotel (Rabbie Burns once stayed there) in the company of numerous local MS Society and Royal Mail dignitaries, under the auspices of John Park, my Ben Nevis climbing companion, with whose super family I was to spend the night.

Saturday, 13th July. The following evening, after a smirr besmirched round trip to Inverness via Dores on the wooded eastern shore of Loch Ness, John and I were joined by the madcap Charlie McLennan (a fellow Royal Mail employee) for a three-pronged assault on my long cherished ambition to swim across Loch Ness – the fifth most popular tourist attraction on earth!

Out of deference to the local authorities, the sub-zero water temperature and a five knot swell, we were obliged to don wet suits – without which our life expectancy was approximately thirty seconds – and to delay our attempt until after 6 p.m. when the cabin cruiser traffic was at a minimum. Other preconditions included the presence of a rescue boat – in our case a high-speed Avon inflatable.

In opting to swim from Urquhart Castle to Temple Pier we were not only crossing, at a depth of 750 ft, the deepest section on the entire loch, as well as passing over the watery tomb of Englishman John Cobb, who met his demise during a fateful world water speed record attempt on September 29th, 1952, but also the stretch where the majority of Loch Ness Monster sightings take place.

Throughout the swim I kept my mind firmly on the job at hand. Contemplating what might be lurking beneath me in the murky, peaty-tasting waters – I should know, I swallowed enough of it – simply didn't bear thinking about. I for one was perfectly happy to complete the mile wide crossing without bumping into Nessie.

Look no hands – but 750 feet (deep). Loch Ness on a cold July evening.

Thursday, 18th July. Between torrential downpours I made a bolt for the sea-front haberdashers of the golden-hearted Dorothy Newlands, wife of Sandy, President of the Buckie and District MS Society Branch. I couldn't leave without saying goodbye. As a parting gift Dorothy gave me a souvenir Buckie T-shirt and a pair of royal blue hiking socks, both of which I wear to this day with great pride. In common with many of the folk who quiz me on the origin of the T-shirt, I too had never heard of the fishing port of Buckie (now familiar as the location for much of John Byrne's *Tutti Frutti*) before last night's gala social evening. Now I would never forget it.

After some forty kilometres of empty shoreline interspersed with coastal villages and pockets of rapturous recognition – you know you've truly arrived when total strangers feel at ease to address you on first name terms – I was met at the Banff town boundary by a delegation from the Banff and District MS branch and their families. Following a few publicity shots besides the 'Royal Burgh of Banff' signpost we filed pied-piper fashion to the town sorting office where I was presented with cheques to the value of £300. Now the dosh was rolling in. According to many Glaswegians, East Coast Scots are a tight lot. Not so. Even allowing for the imbalance of population, donations on the East Coast far exceeded those of the West.

Monday, 22nd July. Starting the day at Newburgh, two o'clock saw me walking the streets of Aberdeen – 'Granite City', 'Silver City by the Sea', 'Oil Capital' (you pays your money, you takes your choice) – be it with a noticeably laboured stride. A combination of unremitting schedule and compound impediments had reduced me to an all time low ebb.

Following one or two anxious moments negotiating Aberdeen's indistinguishable grey-granite canyons, I arrived at the Mechanised Letter Office on the stroke of two-thirty and was immediately directed upstairs to a double-header cheque presentation. While I was doing a couple of radio interviews in an adjoining room it was decided, in my absence, that I should let Aberdeen FC's physiotherapist give my bad leg the once over – just to be on the safe side. Transport was duly provided. In the event the physio was on tour with the first team in Bermuda. But by way of a consolation the club's commercial manager gave me a guided tour of Pittodrie Stadium. (Pittodrie being Gaelic for, quite literally, 'Hill of Dung'.) I even got to tread the hallowed turf.

Wednesday, 24th July. An intriguing insight into the Scot's itinerant mentality is the frequency during my Caledonian constitutional with which I was asked not where I lived but where I 'stayed'. Conceivably a throwback to the accommodational uncertainties of the Clearances. Tonight I was 'staying', in the ephemeral sense of the word, at the Montrose home of Isabel Mann, octogenarian neighbour of Dave and Irene Fowler who faultlessly co-ordinated the local press and threw a dinner party on my behalf.

From three-thirty onwards I was matched stride for stride by Dave Shepherd, fund-raiser for the Montrose MS Branch. A two hour bucket collection that pushed the day's 'take' (excluding cheques) well into double figures.

Thursday, 25th July. The mist and ultra-high humidity of the past two days continued in spades, augmented by intervals of devastating sunshine. Like a drowning man who no longer has the will nor the wherewithal to put up a fight, I yielded to the inevitable and was overcome with an all encompassing lassitude. Walking, I reflected, like life itself, is one long process of getting tired.

Due south of Montrose, overlooking the majestic sun-spangled strip of sand and surf that is Lunan Bay, given perspective by the hilltop ruin of Robert the Bruce's Red Castle, the morning air was suffused with the delicious bitter-sweet tang of raspberries. Rejoicing in such evocative generic names as *Malling Jewel* and *Glen Clova*, the raspberries grown in this small corner of Scotland are the finest in the world.

Making my way to an open-air reception-cum-photo opportunity in the pedestrianized heart of Arbroath I couldn't help but notice the volume of empty retail premises, a figure which no doubt reflects the number of local people on 'the Brew' – a colloquialism for 'the dole'. Following an impromptu collection, a few of us wandered down to the 'Fit o' the toon' where, at Spink and Son, Fishmongers to HM Queen Elizabeth II, I sent home a pair of pukka Arbroath 'Smokies' ('Sea-fresh whole haddock, headed, cleaned, dry-salted, tied in pairs by the tail and hung over slow-burning, hard-wood fires of oak or beech'). As when supposedly distinguishing between edible and poisonous fungi, the criteria for determining an authentic smokie is the peelability of the skin. If it comes away like a banana skin you're onto a winner. If it doesn't, forget it. Such is the proliferation of the smokie trade, that the entire sea-front is permeated with the smell of smouldering wood. Reminiscent of the morning after Guy Fawkes night – but infinitely more appetising.

Back at my digs Julie Nevill staved off my pangs of hunger with a culinary concoction of my own choosing: Arbroath Smokie, Ambrosia Creamed Rice and locally grown raspberries – followed an hour and a bit later by a second dinner party in as many nights. The social round was beginning to take its toll with the result that – come one o'clock in the morning – I couldn't even keep my eyes open long enough to plan tomorrow's route…

Friday, 26th July. By the time I got into my stride it was already blisteringly hot, the last wispy filaments of cloud having long since vacated the azure awning. Dazzled by the sunlight I skirted the fertile crescent between Arbroath and the golfing Mecca of Carnoustie. The rich loamy soil of this coastal region is ideal for the propagation of potatoes, particularly the lucrative seed-potatoes end of the market.

Sunday, 28th July. With nothing but the mesmeric Fife coastscape and a Forfar Bridie (a cross between a Cornish Pastie and a traditional meat pie) to sustain me throughout the day, I dropped anchor at the somnolent seaside town of Anstruther Easter towards early evening. Every backpacker has their idealised billet – 'Anster', as it's known hereabouts, is mine. From the moment I crossed the well proportioned threshold until my drawn-out sun-blessed departure the following morning, never once did I feel anything other than an integral part of the household. The open-house policy of owners Trish and John Martin promoted a convivial, bohemian atmosphere *par excellence*. Mind you, the Chianti played its part…

Wednesday, 31st July. For someone with a self-professed love of heights I must admit to feeling distinctly uneasy when crossing the Forth Road Bridge. An uneasiness that manifested itself in a near neurotic aversion to treading on manhole covers – nourished by visions of falling through. I can only put it down to a lack of confidence in man-made structures. Give me terra firma any day. At the southern, Queensferry end of the Bridge I bided awhile with three members of the maintenance crew – one of whom confided that he was awaiting the results of tests to discover whether or not he himself had MS.

Having completed their shift, they accompanied me to the Administration Block where security officer Jim Flett enquired if I would care to take the service lift to the top of the bridge? My appointment with the Lord Provost of 'Auld Reekie' (Edinburgh), was put on hold. Vertigo or no, this was too unique an opportunity to decline. True to expectation the view from the gantry of the North Tower ('Brian's Bungelow' – according to the welders' graffiti) was nothing short of phenomenal. From my privileged viewpoint – 512 ft above the waves – I was moved to observe that the neighbouring Firth of Forth Railway Bridge is without doubt one of the seven wonders of Britain. Predating the Road Bridge by three-quarters of a century, it resembles a crouching prehistoric creature, its haunches raised in readiness to pounce, especially when swathed as now in a primeval mist. An extraordinary feat of engineering.

13   All the seasons round

Can two walk together
Except they be agreed?
The Bible, Amos 3:3

Saturday, 3rd August.

MONOTONOUS day; magic night. From the minute I bowled into the public bar of the Cockburnspath Hotel, Cockburnspath (like the Port: 'Don't say cock, say Co'burn'), Berwickshire, my feet didn't touch the ground. 'Jock' the lad landlord George Dutnall, a past master at fund-raising, had the entire evening mapped out. Top of the money-making agenda was a 'plain brown wrapper auction', in which the punters bid blind for miscellaneous mystery items (among the sundry 'goodies' coming under the hammer tonight included a brace of grouse, edible condoms, ladies underwear and a loo brush). The arrival of a mini-bus load of high-spirited football supporters (Newcastle United's 'Toon Army' on their way home from a pre-season friendly at Morton) transformed the already lively bar into a scene from *Auf Wiedersehen Pet*, their motto being 'Why speak – when you can chant in unison'. Thus the formula for the evening was set: community singing and synchro-clapping all the way. Once the auction was in full swing a good-humoured pandemonium broke loose as the Geordies', who appeared to have money to burn, egged each other on to outbid the locals. Watching these not-so-canny lads letting their hair down you'd never guess for one moment that they were all white-collar workers from the Newcastle Land Registry Office. Leading light among the taproom regulars was an ex-Glasgow Rangers footballer to whom I confided how far I still had to travel. His reply was typically deadpan: "Och, it's no' a long walk if you run, ken?"

With £75 already in the campaign kitty, the successful, if paralytic bidder of lot number three, a matching bra and panty set, gamely volunteered to model them if everyone present would put a pound in the pint-pot – thereby single-handedly doubling our money. Even when I accidentally-on-purpose let it slip that I was a Spurs fan during my brief thank you speech the worst I came in for was some light-hearted heckling. I was in grand company all right.

When at long last the 'Toon Army' finally hit the road, getting on for twelve, the festivities were as good as over. But of all the Newcastle contingent I made a special point of personally thanking the show-stopping 'drag artiste' for his gutsy performance. To which he modestly demurred:

"Anything for charity, man."

And so say all of us.

Sunday, 4th August. Eyemouth. My last night in bonnie Scotland.

Looking out upon a sliver of white moon suspended like a claymore in the blue-black sky, I reflected with favour on my first excursion north of the border. Seduced as much by the Scots themselves – unfailingly warm and courteous – as by the stupendous scenery, you can add my name to the growing ranks of Caledonophiles. As to the immortal cry: 'Will ye no' come back again?' – just you try and stop me!

Monday, 5th August. One year on the road. Bank Holiday in Scotland.

With nothing worse than a drizzle of thunderbugs to contend with, I tramped the clifftops – a superb, convoluted wall of red sandstone – from Eyemouth to Hilton Bay, where I joined the A1 for the short hop to the English border. Waiting to welcome me 'home' and to outline my exciting but exacting itinerary for the coming few days, was Tom Brown, Royal Mail PR Manager for Newcastle Upon Tyne, complete with chauffeur driven limousine. Not that

I was touting for a lift. The object of my purposely abbreviated walking day – Berwick Holiday Centre – was less than five kilometres away. This was my third in a string of mutually beneficial holiday camp engagements (the previous two being 'Silver Sands Leisure Centre', Lossiemouth, and 'Kinkell Braes Holiday Park', St Andrews).

At the main gates I was received by merry band of camp red/gold coats and hordes of balloon-popping children – the boisterous offspring of upwards of two-thousand paying guests, the vast bulk of whom hailed from north of the Border. Summer holiday periods in Scotland are known as trade fairs and are staggered so that the inhabitants of all the major cities aren't on vacation at the same time. An eminently sensible practice. At present we were into the second week of Dundee fairs fortnight, which was preceded by Glasgow and Aberdeen respectively.

That evening in the camp night-club I was mercifully spared the ordeal of addressing the assembled throng by the timely intervention of fate – in the unlikely shape of a torrential downpour. Having taken the stage, heart going ten-to-the-dozen, the roof of the ladies powder room took it upon itself to cave in, whereby flushing a tide of caterwauling women into the main hall. Soaked to the skin and hyper-hysterical, the resulting pandemonium resembled a cross between a wet T-shirt contest and Beatlemania. Now that's how to put a damper on the proceedings *and* bring the house down in one fell swoop!

Thursday, 8th August. No sooner had I wended my way through the labyrinthine back streets of the attractive little resort of Amble-by-the-Sea *en route* to the harbour than I saw Freddy the Amble dolphin captured in all his majesty, as if in freeze-frame, at the apex of his arcing leap. What a thrill! Many natives of Northumberland's self-proclaimed 'friendliest port' have never seen Freddy in all the years he's been in residence. And here was I spotting him on my very first visit. How lucky can one get. This more than made-up for missing-out on Fungi the Dingle dolphin.

N.B. A matter of weeks after my fortuitous sighting, Freddy was in collision with a police launch. For many months it was feared that Amble's one-mammal tourist attraction had died as a result of his injuries. But by March of the following year ('92), in true fairy tale ending fashion, he made a dramatic reappearance. Yes, we could all breath a sigh of relief, Freddy the bottle-nosed dolphin was alive and flipping!

Friday, 9th August. After just five hours shut eye, I was thrown headlong into another hectic day's programme. Little did I realise on waking that that was the last sleep I'd get until Saturday night. First stop was Morpeth sorting office for the handing over of the staff whip round for the benefit of the local press – not to mention the campaign fund. Then, at the end of a full morning's walking, there was a lively reception at Newbiggin Sports Centre on behalf of Wansbeck district council and the Morpeth MS Branch.

By late afternoon, with an additional fifteen kilometres on the clock, I checked into the Steamboat Inn, Blyth. Even at such an early hour the place was throbbing with life. It came as no surprise to learn that in a previous incarnation the Steamboat had topless waitresses! All things considered the day had gone remarkably well. Seven weeks had now elapsed since my Rubha Rehidh 'setback' and the after-effects of the hamstring were slowly but surely subsiding. Physically shattered though I was, I still had one more task to perform – to make a collection at Newcastle's state of the art MLO (Mechanised Letter Office). Apart from the financial aspect, this was well worth the effort for the sheer novelty of seeing one's name illuminated on the office's mobile light show.

Eight-thirty found me back at the Steamboat and longing for a good blow-out and my pit. In that order. Not having eaten properly all day, my stomach thought my throat had been cut. Enter co-proprietor Jack Wright, who was generously standing me both bed and board (though in hindsight 'bawd' would have been more appropriate), and at whose instruction the best part of a roast chicken was set before me. Let me at it! While polishing off my repast word filtered down that I was invited to the stag night do of local-boy-made-good Steve

Moss. Already crammed into the high-ceilinged chamber (directly opposite the neighbourhood copshop!) in vacant-eyed, slack-jawed anticipation were many of the north-east's wealthiest fisherman. Still decked-out in my walking togs of T-shirt and shorts I felt distinctly underdressed. Until, that is, the cabaret started: two strippers and a comedian with a small 'c' (black, white and blue respectively). When the 'Gateshead Lass' finished her WPC routine I was in two minds whether to sterilise my right elbow or preserve it in aspic. (Maybe she was short-sighted, poor thing, and mistook it for a bar stool?) Whatever the case, the fragrance of Johnson's Baby Oil will never again have quite the same connotation.

Even when the hijinks came to an end I was unable to get my head down. With no access to an alarm clock or early morning call, I daren't go to sleep for fear of missing my six-thirty appointment at Blyth sub-district office. Instead I opted to work through the night (or what was left of it) on bringing my paperwork up to date. Tom Brown and my Royal Mail Paymasters were certainly getting their money's-worth out of me.

Saturday, 10th August. Feeling remarkably sprightly after last night's excesses, I was on the hoof again by eight-fifty, having earlier received a sizeable contribution from Blyth SDO. By ten-thirty I put in an appearance at Whitley Bay Holiday Park for a scheduled cheque presentation and get-together with some of the mirthful members of North Tyneside MS Branch. Barely had we exchanged pleasantries than my presence was required for a photo-opportunity in front of the nearby St Mary's Lighthouse. It's all go in the GPO!

In lining up his namesake Tom Delaney – fund raising officer for Newcastle upon Tyne MS branch – to accompany me to Newcastle, Tom Brown did me a great service. Our stride patterns meshed to perfection. An incompatible walking partner is tantamount to marching against the beat – a right pain in the butt. But Tom was a joy to trade paces with.

As we veered westward from Tynemouth the overcast morning transmuted to a sultry afternoon. But for our hell-for-leather tempo, it was ideal sightseeing weather. Among the local landmarks I glimpsed in passing included the prize winning 'Byker Wall' Estate, Tyne Bridge, and the New Criminal Court, the latter's pseudo neo-classic lines being right up Prince Charles' street, so to speak. Delayed primarily by the over-zealous commitments of the PR Department, we were slightly late in arriving for the reception at Royal Mail House. It was a crying shame that we had to eat and run (particularly as the buffet was the most exquisite to date: smoked salmon, canapés… the works), but St James' Park beckoned. It's not every day that one gets the chance to watch a game of football from the unadulterated luxury of an executive box.

Try though I may, I couldn't make out the lads from the Land Registry Office at their favourite Gallowgate end, though I fancy I heard their familiar tones at the forefront of every chant and barrack. At the end of the match my host wangled a meet with the then Newcastle manager Ossie Ardiles. I recall blurting out something about being at White Heart Lane on the day that he and fellow Argentinian Ricky Villa arrived from Buenos Aires. Still wet-haired and steaming from the post-match shower, his smile was genuine enough but his glazed eyes disclosed that his mind was still very much on the game. I felt intrusive. The following spring Ossie was given the managerial kiss of death – a vote of confidence. Three days later he was sacked. Ossie's dream had become a nightmare.

Even now my fund-raising activities were far from over: I was required for a personal appearance at the Asda Superstore, Gosforth – the culmination of a three day MS collection – where I made many new friends and a good deal in the way of contributions. For the remainder of the day I functioned in automaton-mode. It seemed like an age since I'd put spine to mattress. Man that is born of woman has but a short time to live – it only feels like an eternity.

Sunday, 11th August. Any hope of a leisurely day after my whirlwind stopover in Newcastle was dashed by a one-thirty engagement in South Shields beside the *Marsden*

John's dream: receiving a donation from Ossie Ardiles,
then the Newcastle United manager.

Rattler (a Pullman railway coach mounted on the sea-front). To make matters worse my blistered heels were in a critical condition. Serves me right for not heeding my own golden rule: in hot weather change socks twice a day.

'Catherine Cookson Country', proclaimed every sign. Not that I had time for anything other than a perfunctory recce. My urgent seaward shuffle left no avenue for rubbernecking. One-thirty came and went. Finally, after four hours excruciating footslog, I hobbled onto the front at South Shields – albeit twenty-minutes adrift of my deadline. I was going through a bad patch punctuality-wise – though you'd never have guessed as much from the cheery dispositions of my reception committee. Most of the menfolk were ex-bobbies and knew all about spending all day on their feet. Following an alfresco bite to eat (what with the sun, sea and acres of white sand it looked more like Tenerife than Tyneside) my heels were patched up by members of St John's Ambulance Service, none of whom could actually believe that I'd walked all the way from Newcastle on such dodgy dogs. On emerging from the first aid trailer my good companions announced that they'd arranged a photo-call with singer-songwriter Alan Price and the Mayor and Mayoress of South Shields. What a turn-up for the book. Ushered backstage, I sensed that Alan, like Ossie Ardiles before him, was with us in body only. Physically he was in our midst; mentally he was going over the running order of the second half of the show. Abstracted or not, it couldn't diminish the thrill of meeting a childhood hero.

All too soon it was time to head off for Seaburn along the grassy margin which borders the crumbling limestone cliffs. But not before expressing my heart-felt appreciation to the lovely people of South Tyneside MS Branch for making my day.

Wednesday, 14th August. Hottest morning in recent memory. Positively blistering. The galvanised flair stacks of Wilton (ICI) Chemical Works teetered drunkenly in the heat haze.

Welcome to South Shields.
Mayor, Mayoress and singer Alan Price (second right).

Intermittent alarm sirens rent the arid air, fuelling images of the Flixborough disaster. I lengthened my stride accordingly.

I was due to rendezvous at Ann Charlton Lodge, due south of Redcar Race Course, at eleven o'clock – which I did to the minute. Back to my old punctual self. A pleasant forty-minutes ensued during which I was taken on a hard-hatted tour of the soon to be completed MS treatment and respite centre.

Fortified by a sachet of Lucozade Sport I made tracks for Redcar Sorting Office where I enjoyed a cuppa and a chat before completing the day's schedule to Saltburn-by-the-Sea. After the last couple of days near billiard-table flat terrain, Redcar's paved promenade provided an unhindered aspect of the red-grey cliffs rising beyond Saltburn to the south – the beginning of the coastal section of the Cleveland Way. It was Victorian Week in Saltburn with the locals parading in their authentic Victorian finery. A superb tradition.

Friday, 16th August. Who should I bump into as I prepared to depart from Whitby but good ol' Tom Brown; he was in the process of setting up the Royal Mail exhibition trailer on the greensward near the famous whalebone arch – a poignant reminder of Whitby's history as a whaling port. Tom had both good and bad news for me. The good news was that he could spare the time – just – to take my photo beneath the arch and beside the statue of Captain

Cook, whose ships *Endeavour, Resolution* and *Adventure* were all Whitby built. The bad news was that this afternoon's Scarborough reception and PR Exercise were off. Scarborough Council wanted an extortionate £750 for permission to park the Royal Mail trailer. Scarborough fair (not).

From the airy promontory of West Cliff I followed Cook's vacant gaze over the russet roofscape below. Falling away at my feet, the huddled terraces and pantiled cottages tumbled towards the harbour like waves of terracotta lava. I followed suit. Having crossed the swing-bridge to the Old Town, I called into the office of the *Whitby Gazette* who gobbled up my offer of a story. Scant compensation for the Scarborough farrago. Before tackling the spectacular 199-step stone flight which leads to the jagged ruins of Whitby Abbey (as in the tradition, I lost count half-way up), I decided to post home two pairs of oak smoked kippers. Easier said than done. EC regulations now forbid the sending of kippers through the mail, a regulation to which Arbroath Smokies are curiously exempt. A few discreet enquiries, however, led me to one of 'noble' birth who was willing to bend the rules. Every man has his price – and every fishmonger likewise.

Saturday, 17th August. Ten kilometres north of the white chalk cliffs of Flamborough Head, I crossed the county boundary from North Yorkshire into Humberside. But don't tell the natives. To them the 'Historic East Riding' has always been and will always be Yorkshire through and through. The few Humberside sign-posts still standing were summarily defaced. With only one eye and one lung, Eric Lount, of Westfield Farm, Flamborough, exemplified the Yorkshire tyke's intransigent approach to life. A published dialect poet and accomplished musician, to this day he still plays the melodeon, a type of small accordion, in defiance of his late father who cut his original instrument in half "wi' a bread-saw" to see "where t' notes cam from".

Tuesday, 20th August. The third of four complete days coasting the gigantic golden prairie of the East Riding (from the Scandinavian *thriding,* a 'third part'), my nostrils assailed all the way by the unmistakable carboniferous niff of stubble fires, a forest of pallid mushroom plumes to landward highlighting this widespread practice. Agricultural methods die hard in this ancient land.

From the scattered community of Kilnsea I trekked out to Spurn Head, a recurved spit of shingle and sand that swept some three and a half miles into a sun-burnished Humber Estuary. As narrow as fifty-yards in places, the Yorkshire TV crew who met me in the lighthouse carpark confirmed my suspicions that all it needs is one 'really big sea' for Spurn Head to become Spurn Island.

Wednesday, 21st August. The Met Bureau predicted another sweltering day. For once they were as good as their word. From the outset it was a race against time. Perspiration and sun-bleached crew-cut crop-stubble all the way to an open-air reception in the newly gentrified docklands area of 'Old Town' Kingston upon Hull. A busy port noted for its unique white phone boxes, the user-friendly hardware of the UK's first independent telephone service. My one delay occurred within sight of my goal at the confluence of the River Hull and the Humber Estuary in the shape of the rotating mid-section of Myton Bridge, a necessary concession to shipping traffic.

Try as we might, the reception, already a low-key affair, never really recovered from an incident involving a young lad – poor little mite – who gave his napper a nasty rap on the pavement when falling from his perch on the pier wall. Fortunately no bones were broken – though it dealt the event a mortal blow. Nothing puts a damper on a social gathering like a child's tears!

Friday, 23rd August. A seven-hour buffeting by gale force head winds left me with streaming eyes and a soaring temperature. Awaiting my clammy arrival at Cleethorpes Pier ('Smiles more fun', so the sign read), with her congenial cohorts from the Grimsby MS Society, was ex-nurse Bryony Chapman (a regular Florence Nightingale) who drove me back to her home in Grimsby ('Europe's Food Town') for a taste of South Humberside hospitality.

Tuesday, 27th August. Suffering a slight reaction to yesterday's protracted stint of shore walking (the soft going plays merry hell with my naff left knee), I was met by Eileen and Dennis Allen, part of the Boston MS delegation who made last night's arrival such a memorable one (Ansell's mild – highly recommended!). Over the next two hours – in true tourist parlance – 'we did' St Botolph's Church (The 'Boston Stump'), a landmark for miles around and one of the largest churches in England, and the medieval Guildhall Museum, as well as gaining extensive campaign coverage in the tabloid pages of the *Boston Standard* and *Boston News*, Boston being a contraction of 'Botolph's Town'.

After the dramatic cliffs and wooded 'wykes' of North Yorkshire and Cleveland, the flat polder of Lincolnshire – some of the most productive agricultural land in Britain – was a striking contrast. That night, with a further forty kilometres behind me, I booked into the Crown Hotel, Holbeach. Not so much a listed building as a building with a list, compared to which Southend's Crooked House was perfectly perpendicular.

Wednesday, 28th August. Walk co-ordinator John Mole's radio broadcast went out this morning. Created quite a buzz. Everyone appears to have heard it. A star is born!

Following a day skirting the broad sun-baked horizons of Lincolnshire and latterly (from twelve-forty onwards) Norfolk, I was intercepted on the threshold of King's Lynn by a TV crew from *Anglia News.* They'd been on my trail since first light and were on the verge of calling it a day. With a voice-over already recorded, they filmed a tracking shot from the car's sunroof. Brilliant in theory. In practice a disaster. I had to walk so slow to keep in frame that I wound up resembling a geriatric duck. So much for my street cred!

Saturday, 31st August. It was a breathless morning of filigree cloud and searing sun. What air there was, was succulent with the fructose smack of ripening blackberries. On making my exit from the delightful flint-and-brick village of Burnham Overy Staithe via the dappled-shade of the first convenient 'loke' – colloquial Norfolk for alley or pathway – I realised with unbridled relief that I was no longer limping. Wonders will never cease! My already buoyant mood lightened accordingly – if not my backpack. At the loke's shoreward conclusion I paused to admire the wide sandy creek where the future Viscount Horatio Nelson learnt to sail (he was born two miles or so inland at Burnham Thorpe). Though Nelson isn't the village's only claim to maritime fame: Richard Woodget, Master of the *Cutty Sark,* lived here between 1899 and 1926.

Over the ensuing couple of walking days, blessed as they were by some of the sultriest weather since last year's Indian summer, my route faithfully embraced the spellbinding North Norfolk Coast Path – an ever shifting shoreline of sand flats backed by high dunes, shingle banks, saltings and flint-walled villages. Only where the long distance footpath deviated from the coast did our ways diverge. Then, as ever, I religiously held my seaward tack.

Due north of Wells-next-to-the-Sea, where the sea-wall terminates at the lifeboat station, 'Norfolk Dumpling' John Milestone (now there's a name to conjure with) single-handedly atoned for the monosyllabic holiday-makers: "Bet you've covered a foo moil?" Give the man a cigar! As we were going in the same direction I was pleased to accept his invitation to meet his wife and to slake my thirst on a glass of Greene King. Welcome to the real Norfolk!

In compliance with the wishes of Mr Wainwright (16th April) I got down on all fours and kissed the friable topsoil of Morston Marshes – just west of my objective and his favourite sailing village, Blakeney. No mean feat with forty-plus-pounds of purgatory on one's back. Here my cousin Tim Mole came out to greet and escort me back to the village for a family reunion and where there was a Stilton Ploughman's and a pint of Charles Wells with my name on it.

14   **Homeward bound**

It is not the going out of port,
But the coming in,
That determines the success of a voyage.
Henry Ward Beecher.

Sunday, 1st September.

TRAILING the parched sea embankment to Blakeney Eye, the wide, flat salt marshes stretched into a shimmering infinity. With no rain to speak of in East Anglia for upwards of nine weeks, the crazed and fissured sod underfoot resembled the bed of a long dried-up river. A buff coloured river-bed that was reflected in the tinder-dry herbage.

After three hours walking, and ten minutes putting a particularly persistent stoat to flight that was worrying a moorhen, the plaintive toot-toot of a steam-hauled train heralded my arrival in Sheringham, headquarters of the North Norfolk Railway ('The Poppyland Express' as immortalised by the pen of Clement Scott).

A further six kilometres along the coast I teamed-up with a party of fancy-dressed Cromer postal staff all of whom gave up their Sunday afternoon to help boost the campaign. With balloon festooned Royal Mail vans fore and aft we made a complete circuit of Cromer, accumulating £112 in little over an hour and in the process putting the noses of the Fire Brigade, who were also collecting, well out of joint.

I learned that two members of the postal staff party – as if walking the streets in all weathers wasn't enough – are both regular crew members of Cromer lifeboat. For a citizen of Cromer – home town of Henry Blogg, the most successful lifeboat coxswain of all time, with 450 lives saved between 1909 and 1947 – there is no higher calling.

Tuesday, 3rd September. There was a distinct, almost autumnal nip in the air this morning. For the initial twelve kilometres south of Sea Palling – a contradiction in terms if ever there was one – I retained the snaking B1159 to rendezvous with Dick Hutchinson of *Radio Broadland* and Malcolm Colman, Ipswich Area Delivery Manager, who was to be my escort to Great Yarmouth. Parked at the scenic waterside setting of Horsey Windmill the enormous telescopic aerial on Dick's radio car vied for prominence with the white-sailed whirligig.

Outside broadcast complete, we engaged the coast-proper at Winterton-on-Sea. The fervour of midday felt all the more torrid for the cold night that preceded it. Ten kilometres of stupendous beach walking ensued, marred only by the RNLI flag which flew at half-mast above Caister lifeboat station out of respect for the coxswain who died on Sunday while sending up a maroon for what turned out to be a false alarm.

Towards Great Yarmouth the compacted sand and shingle succumbed to exhausting tracts of sinking sand. Malcolm and I plumped for the parallel shore road. After a swift pint of Whitbread Mild (not a Patch on M & B or Ansells!), we reported to the assembly point for the Royal Mail cavalcade. Heading the colourful crocodile was a brand new eight-foot by three-foot banner (*John Westley: Around the Isles Campaign*) followed by a full-scale motorised mock-up of Postman Pat's mail van complete with Jess the Cat and a postie in a Postman Pat suit. For once the whole shebang – media, general public, weather – came together in perfect harmony. After a lengthy round of speeches, photos, presentations – a cheque from the secretary of Great Yarmouth MS group and a civic plaque from the chairman of the local council – and still more photos, we trooped out to the end of the Pier ('almost the most easterly point in Britain') to mark the occasion with a celebratory snifter and a rundown on forthcoming events. This is the way every day should end. Not with a whimper but a bang. Bring on the dancing girls!

Wednesday, 4th September. Bordered by limitless sea and sky, at the northern end of the fifty mile Suffolk coast path I descended to the shoreline. The sheer euphoria of tramping the deserted crowd-forsaken beaches at dusk will live with me forever. The exhilarating synthesis of ozone rush, grasping fingers of spume, the harsh twittering call of legion sand-martins flitting above their crumbling colony, the maritime melody of jingling-shingle and the tumult of waves cleared my head of everything save the joy of being alive. Everybody should be at liberty to consummate their day with a leisurely stroll along the beach – in a rational world it would be obligatory.

Thursday, 5th September. Ten minutes out of Southwold I purchased a chilled can of authentic Texan Root Beer at Jim's Beach Hut Cafe, Gun Hill. Tasted for all the world like liquefied Euthymol toothpaste. So enthralled was I with Southwold – shy, secretive, virtually unspoilt – that I clean forgot to take any photographs. More fool me.

Two miles down the coast at Walberswick, by way of the sluice at the landward end of Southwold harbour, I paid a visit to Molly's Tea Room for a cinnamon-dusted custard tart and a pot of char – a time-honoured ritual for walkers on this stretch of the Suffolk Coast Path.

Top of the Walberswick Social Calendar is the annual British Crabbing Federation Championships. Unfortunately – or otherwise – I missed out on the frivolities by a matter of weeks and with it the dubious distinction of qualifying to wear an 'I caught crabs in Walberswick' T-shirt.

Monday, 9th September. I was partnered over the subsequent two days by my Lower Edmonton colleague Ken Merrell (last seen on April 10th), two days in which Ken acted as my self-appointed PR man. With the current good weather forecast to see the week out, he couldn't have chosen a better spell to join me.

We departed Felixstowe at nine-thirty for a 2 p.m. reception at Ipswich Town Hall. And though we set the most dilatory pace imaginable, we still contrived to arrive well over a hour early – time to grab a bite to eat and sample the regional tipple, of which Adnams Broadside (a Southwold brew) and Tolly Mild came out on top.

Assembling outside Suffolk College, everyone present was furnished with a pristine Royal Mail T-shirt and, accompanied by Round-the-World yachtsman Josh Hall and banner-wielding post office employees, we proceeded to a civic welcome. Unfortunately a group of wheelchair-bound MS sufferers were unable to join us for refreshments in the Mayor's Chamber as the handsome Town Hall is without a ramp.

Tuesday, 10th September. With the sun still gloriously in the ascendance, we mirrored the tidal waters of the River Orwell to Shotley Gate, then, after admiring a fine view of Harwich Harbour, hugged the much indented shoreline of the River Stour as far as Holbrook Bay, before cutting through the extensive grounds of the Royal Hospital School, taking our bearings from the school's imposing ivory tower.

Just over the River Stour – the natural border between Suffolk and Essex – an egg launched from a passing car occupied by two cackling youths caught me in the meat of my right calf. Within the hour it was all the colours of the rainbow and as stiff as a poker. So much for my 'peak condition'. Welcome to the Home Counties!

Wednesday, 11th September. By the time I got started a red wintry sun was already peeping through the cloud-laden sky and there were flurries of light rain in the air. A modified foretaste of things to come. For the initial half-mile I plied the tree-lined thoroughfare known as The Wall which runs alongside the turbid River Stour between Manningtree – burial place and onetime headquarters of Matthew 'Witch Finder General' Hopkins – and Mistley. Even the ubiquitous mute swans appeared a depressing donkey-grey. Beyond Mistley's flourishing port area I trod the featureless foreshore to Copperas Bay, a joyless yomp alleviated in part by the curiously comforting presence of infrequent passing trains. Good job I was on the home straight.

At long last I came to the ship-spotters paradise of Harwich – from the omnipresent fly-posters and graffiti seemingly a hot-bed of the ultra-left. But after an altogether grim walking day my hosts for the night, Lila and Steve Hammond, restored my sense of well-being with an absolutely orgasmic *spaghetti alla bolognese* "justa likka mama used to make" … in bowls. Only restaurateurs who don't know chalk from cacetta would dream of serving it on plates. Lila should know – her Mama *is* Italian!

Thursday, 12th September. Enveloped by lush vegetation still saturated from yesterday's downpour, I navigated the tranquil wilderness of Walton backwater bathed in sunshine and serenaded by the glissando peal of church bells (wedding? campanology practice? invasion?). The still air was charged with the acrid residue of myriad stubble fires and the unmistakable odour of newly harvested onions. A potent combination.

What should have been an idyllic conclusion to the day was relegated to the realm of monumental drudge by a superabundance of insect life. Throughout every one of the ten sea-front kilometres between Walton-on-the-Naze and Clacton-on-Sea I was frontally assaulted by wave after pestilential wave of hover-flies, gnats, lady-birds and some curious little beetle-like creatures. When I wasn't dazzled by the strobe-like effect of sun on sea, I was blinded by the airborne onslaught. And when they weren't getting in my eyes, they found their way unerringly into my ears, mouth and up my nose. You name an orifice – they wheedled their way in. Every so often I was obliged to give the accumulated winged-debris the brush off. On occasion it felt as though I were bring pelted with rice – without the solace of an evening's connubial bliss to look forward to. For once I couldn't wait to relinquish the coastline.

Just short of Clacton Pier I met up with Vera Andrews – or as she's better known 'Granny Vera'. This was a momentous occasion. Only last year Vera set a record for the longest walk in mainland Britain when she covered a distance of 7,318 miles, taking in each of Britain's Gas Showrooms and raising £50,000 in the process. Having, in my own right, already overhauled the previous men's record for the longest continuous solo walk around Britain, we were the Nation's reigning Endurance Walking Champions. Everyone in Clacton is rightly proud of Vera's fantastic fund-raising feats on behalf of the Help the Hospices Movement since her husband's untimely death. I wasn't the first person to wear my 'I met Granny Vera' badge with pride, but I am perhaps one of the select few who fully appreciate the enormity of her undertakings.

Tuesday, 17th September. Following a triumphal arrival at Southend Mechanised Letter Office at the head of a banner-waving column of postal staff, we continued on to Southend Pier – the longest in the country – where a pleasant surprise awaited me. My presence in Southend coincided with the issue of a new set of Royal Mail Stamps which paid tribute to 200 years of map making by Ordnance Survey, Britain's official mapping agency. And what better publicity tie-in than myself – a Royal Mail employee – and Ordnance Survey, without the aid of whose maps I would no doubt have lost my way on countless occasions. The PR department's dream scenario! Southend Mails Manager Graham Syrett presented me with a permanent reminder of the town in the form of a specially hand-stamped first day cover bearing all four of the maps stamps (inside the envelope was a more tangible tribute – a cheque for the campaign fund as a parting gift from PO colleagues in Essex). And Kerry Barrett, Chief Surveyor of Ordnance Survey, exchanged my dog-eared maps of the Essex coastline for the latest 1991 edition. On an otherwise rainy day, Southend was a veritable ray of sunshine.

Friday, 20th September. The dawn came in grey and misty. Despite a touch of last-day butterflies, the condemned man ate a hearty breakfast. Still in a daze from yesterday's tumultuous welcome (the Press-corps alone got through enough film to keep Kodak on overtime for a week) and a rollicking good evening at the Phoenix public house, Rainham – so named after the number of times its risen from the ashes of conflagration over the past 300 years – it was once again time for my boot heels (or what was left of them) to go wanderin'.

By the time I was ready for action the sun was back at its scorching best. To coin Pop Larkin's quaint catch phrase, the weather was absolutely perfick! As indeed it had been this time last year. Last year? How callow I was then, how green. And how much I've wised-up in the meantime. Fourteen months of outdoor action had honed my senses to the nth degree; fourteen-months that had passed in a trice. As I strode the East Thames corridor towards London nothing escaped my vagrant's eye. Glinting in the morning sunlight, the giant Ford motorworks at Dagenham looked positively picturesque. As did the chromium-plated Thames Barrier, strung-out across the river like a collection of scaled-down Sydney Opera Houses. And always there to guide me that phallic landmark – Canary Wharf – Dockland's answer to the Colossus of Rhodes. Another of the seven wonders of modern Britain.

As Silvertown Way was under reconstruction, I cut across acre upon dust-bowl acre of building site to East India Dock Road. The only person to challenge me was a genial Irish navvy who offered me some apples – the succulent spoils of an earlier scrumping expedition. With a full circuit of the Isle of Dogs behind me, I paused to gather my thoughts in a handkerchief-sized public garden off Wapping High Street overlooking the stately gliding Thames. From a sun-steeped bench I surveyed the beaming tourists aboard countless pleasure craft and the occasional commuter-crammed river bus. Despite its grimy visage, my love for London, *The Smoke*, was undiminished. As the final moments of the walk ticked away I broke my journey yet again and nipped into The Town of Ramsgate for a last minute stiffener. John Mole's instructions were imprinted upon my memory: Never arrive early.

Back where it began (Tower Bridge) and a resounding welcome
from postal pals Ray, Randy, Roy, Ivan and Brian.

Zac Macaulay

By 2.35 (better five minutes late than never) three shots of vodka-and-orange had done their stuff, I was ready to face the mob. 412 days after setting out, I returned to the forecourt of the Tower Thistle Hotel via St Katherine's Way. What more evocative backdrop to the ensuing proceedings than Tower Bridge, still gleaming from its recent refurbishment? So disorientated was I by the overwhelming reception awaiting me (or was it the Stolichnaya?) that I didn't know if I was coming or going. As I breasted the General Portfolio finishing tape – the bounteous acclaim of family, friends, work-mates, neighbours and well-wishers reverberating about me – my feelings were mixed. Glad to complete the task; sad in many respects to see its end. The end of an era. The last few weeks since overcoming the hamstring injury were so easy in comparison with what had gone before that my immediate sense of achievement was non-existent. Only when the clamour died down and the congratulatory speeches began – notably by John Walford, General Secretary of the MS Society, and Mark Lamb, head of Royal Mail Personnel London North-East – did the full implications of it all strike home. Against all the odds I had walked the seasons round, averaging twenty-two miles per day in winter and summer, rain or shine. Seen the first primrose and daffodil; heard the first cuckoo; witnessed the migrating swallows and sand-martins. Seen the British Isles – the most mapped and documented islands on earth – in good mood and in bad, in fair weather and in foul. I exalted in my accomplishment. No one could steal my thunder as the first person to have circumnavigated the world's eighth and twentieth largest islands (Great Britain and Ireland) as a single continuous walk. A distance of 15,239 kilometres (9,469 miles).

Whether through the lives of our offspring or by some futile gesture, legal of otherwise, we all make a bid for immortality – this is mine. That, as they say, was that. A lifetime's ambition fulfilled. The end of my epic journey... a 22-million pace odyssey.

The ultimate accolade – Guiness Book of Records status at last!
John with founding editor Norris McWhirter (left) and the late Roy Castle.

Epilogue
but not quite...

THE following morning, after an evening of celebration and re-acquaintance in the plush surroundings of the Tower Thistle Hotel, I returned to my Cheshunt home, completing the final few sun-kissed kilometres on foot in full walking regalia. Little did I know what was in store.

"Watch his face as turns the corner", whispered the youthful vanguard of the Local Reception Committee.

Lying in wait to escort me to a rousing yellow-ribbon homecoming-cum-street party were a scarlet-liveried marching band (the high-stepping 'Winchester Twirlettes') and a host of balloon-waving well-wishers. You could have knocked me down with a feather. Taking my place at the rear of the colourful column, the lead vehicle struck-up a highly appropriate canned medley (including): 'Congratulations', 'Spurs are on their way to Wembley' (Cheshunt being a traditional hotbed of Tottenham allegiance) and 'When Johnny Comes Marching Home'. Never had I seen the community so united. Not even the Queen's Silver Jubilee celebrations achieved as much. Family, friends, neighbours and total strangers lined the bunting-draped route. I was overcome with emotion and gratitude – but retained my composure. Only when the bubbly flowed and the agony and the ecstasy of the past fourteen months came flooding back, washing over me in a tide of remembrance, did the true significance of it all strike home. I'd finally crossed my personal Rubicon; broken out of my rut. For better or worse, life would never be quite the same again.

For a period of some several weeks after the walk's completion I underwent what might only be termed 'Post-perambulatory depression'. Such was the diversity and intensity of experience during the preceding 412 days that my return to 'civvy street' was inevitably mundane by comparison. Fourteen-months of media attention, public acclaim and red carpet treatment would unsettle the most level-headed individual – let alone a gullible traveller such as I. The walk therefore was a double-edged sword. At once providing a tantalising glimpse of a totally different way of life – without furnishing the wherewithal to make it my own. Thus the conclusion of the walk left a yawning chasm of dissatisfaction and guilt. In the words of the old anthem to discontent: 'How you gonna keep 'em down on the farm after they've seen Paree?' How indeed?

But not every after effect was of a negative nature. Such was the watershed significance of the walk upon my workaday existence that not only is it the fount and focus of continued reference, but also the yardstick by which I measure all aspects of life: fellowship, elation, solitude, privation, *et al*. For example, prior to setting off that sultry August morning my definition of adversity was to endure the cut-throat belligerence of a Friday night shopping expedition to Tesco; on the blizzard-gripped summit of Mount Carrantuohill I discovered an altogether more cogent definition. Another lasting legacy is that I seldom feel the cold any more. After the marrow-numbing chill of the West Coast of Ireland, south-east England is positively balmy by comparison.

On the charitable front, despite the valiant efforts of all parties, we regrettably failed to reach what was in hindsight a patently unrealistic fiscal objective (a quarter of a million pounds) in view of the ongoing recession. Notwithstanding the unfavourable economic climate, the eventual sum total realised – well into five figures: five figures that wouldn't have otherwise found their way into MS Society coffers – was far from insubstantial. (Let us hope the revenue from the sale of this volume will go some way towards offsetting the shortfall.) I can, however, derive some consolation from the fact that our campaign raised public awareness to the plight of Britain's 100,000-plus Multiple Sclerosis sufferers. No mean feat in itself.

Though daunting at the outset, when broken down into manageable daily portions (I averaged 22 miles per day throughout) the walk-load wasn't half as intimidating. Don't look beyond your immediate target – that's the secret. German poet, playwright and novelist Johann Wolfgang on Goethe hit the nail on the head when he said: "It is not enough to take steps which may some day lead to a goal; each step must be itself a goal and a step likewise." The backpacker's watchword! Certainly my experiences as a London Postie – putting up with all manner of weather; dealing with the general public, etc. – stood me in good stead. Even before I met Piers Grant-Ferris (29-4-91) I had a strange conviction that it was all pre-ordained. And now, at the Journey's End, I can rest secure in the belief that I accurately interpreted the call of my maker...

On frequent occasions, when provisions had fallen precariously low, I functioned on nought but the adrenaline-high borne of the awe-inspiring panoramic splendour. Suffice it to say, never did I want for sustenance. The seascape spectacular provided all. I only hope that my modest word-pictures conveyed some of the visual grandeur, some of the euphoria, some of the anguish. Only towards the end, when I knew I had it licked, did I become a little blasé in regards the scenery. After all, a beach is a beach is a beach. The one constant source of amazement, however, was the people I met along the way who gave so selflessly of their time and energy. And whose unstinting kindness and warmth has convinced me beyond doubt that the world, more so than at any time in the past, is now a global village – and we are all but far-flung members of an extended global family. Certainly we have more in common than we have differences. For regardless of race and culture – with the obvious exception of the lunatic fringe – do we not share the same hopes, the same aspirations? Among the many fallacies debunked and myths exploded during the course of my grand tour were such old chestnuts as: the Welsh are morose; Scots are thrifty; Irish are dullards... and all are united by a common loathing of the English. In all cases my findings were quite the reverse. Now if we can only put aside out petty grievances and live in harmony with each other, ourselves and our planet. Gloria Mundi!

It will therefore come as no surprise to the reader to learn that long after my press-cuttings have curled and yellowed with age and my short-lived celebrity is but a faint recollection, that the walk's one abiding feature, etched indelibly upon my heart and mind, will undoubtedly be the inherent goodness and innate generosity of the fair folk of these equally fair Isles.

To whom it may concern – thanks for the memories.

Appendix

Daily Schedule

i) It was arbitrarily decided to calibrate the walk in kilometres from the off. This was in no way due to a strident anti-imperial/pro-metric stance on my part. Merely that my twin measuring devices (map measurer and pedometer), as stipulated by the *Guiness Book of Records*, were both of continental manufacture — kilometres thus being the standard calibration.

ii) Slí na Mara nights: <u>underlining</u> denotes location of evening stopover.

iii) Where location of evening stopover and termination point of day's walk do not concur, the former is additionally shown in (parenthesis).

iv) Denotes acquisition and chronology of New Boots. Though termed 'new', each pair had in fact been thoroughly broken in.

v) Kilometreage: My figures, if anything, err on the conservative side. Indeed, they fall well short of the highly erroneous claims of certain ultra-distance walkers (no names, no pack drill). The sum total is arrived at via the following formula: aggregate map measurer plus pedometer readings divided by two.

vi) Apart from those instances where extreme weather conditions, MOD/Private property, injury or PR duties dictated otherwise, I invariably undertook the longest possible coastal route.

Date	Route	Kilometres Daily	Cumulative
5.8.90	Tower Bridge-Dartford	32	32
6.8.90	Dartford-All Hallows Marshes	48	80
7.8.90	All Hallows Marshes-Hoo St Werburgh	26	106
8.8.90	Hoo St Werburgh-Funton	27	133
9.8.90	Funton-Teynham	31	164
10.8.90	Teynham-Whitstable	34	198
11.8.90	Whitstable-Ramsgate	37	235
12.8.90	Ramsgate-Dover	35	270
13.8.90	Dover-Dymchurch	30	300
14.8.90	Dymchurch-Rye	33	333
15.8.90	Rye-Bexhill	30	363
16.8.90	Bexhill-Seaford	39	402
17.8.90	Seaford-Hove	25	427
18.8.90	Hove-Worthing	23	450
19.8.90	Worthing-Bognor Regis	24	474
20.8.90	Bognor Regis-Birdham	39	513
21.9.90	Birdham-Portsmouth	33	546
22.8.90	Portsmouth-Gosport	28	574
23.8.90	Gosport-Southampton	33	607
24.8.90	Southampton-East Boldre	32	639
25.8.90	East Boldre-Mudeford-(Bournemouth)	27	666
26.8.90	Mudeford-Poole	24	690
27.8.90	Poole-Studland	38	728
28.8.90	Studland-West Lulworth	46	774
29.8.90	West Lulworth-Fortuneswell	35	809
30.8.90	Fortuneswell-Burton Bradstock	50	859
31.8.90	Burton Bradstock-Seaton-(Chard)	39	898
1.9.90	Seaton-Budleigh Salterton	34	932
2.9.90	Budleigh Salterton-Dawlish	45	977
3.9.90	Dawlish-Brixham	34	1,011
4.9.90	Brixham-Totnes	42	1,053
5.9.90	Totnes-Hallsands	40	1,093
6.8.90	Hallsands-Salcombe	44	1,137
7.9.90	Salcombe-Kingston	41	1,178
8.9.90	Kingston-Brixton	41	1,219
9.9.90	Brixton-Saltash	42	1,261
10.9.90	Saltash-Millbrook	45	1,306
11.9.90	Millbrook-Downderry	37	1,343
12.9.90	Downderry-Polruan	37	1,380
13.9.90	Polruan-Par	45	1,425
14.9.90	Par-Portloe	45	1,470
15.9.90	Portloe-St Mawes	43	1,513
16.9.90	St Mawes-Truro	34	1,547
17.9.90	Truro-Mawnan Smith	35	1,582
18.9.90	Mawnan Smith-Coverack	42	1,624
19.9.90	Coverack-Mullion	32	1,656
20.9.90	Mullion-Penzance	38	1,694
21.9.90	Penzance-Land's End	31	1,725
22.9.90	Land's End-St Ives	40	1,765
23.9.90	St Ives-Portreath	38	1,803
24.9.90	Portreath-Perranporth	27	1,830
25.9.90	Perranporth-Mawgan Porth	43	1,873
26.9.90	Mawgan Porth-Padstow	40	1,913
27.9.90	Padstow-Polzeath	31	1,944
28.9.90	Polzeath-Boscastle	42	1,986
29.9.90	Boscastle-Bude	35	2,021
30.9.90	Bude-Clovelly	48	2,069
1.10.90	Clovelly-Bideford	34	2,103
2.10.90	Bideford-Croyde	39	2,142
3.10.90	Croyde-Combe Martin	36	2,178
4.10.90	Combe Martin-Lynton	36	2,214
5.10.90	Lynton-Bossington	27	2,241
6.10.90	Bossington-Watchet	34	2,275
7.10.90	Watchet-Bridgewater	39	2,314

Date	Route	Miles	Total	Date	Route	Miles	Total
10.90	Bridgewater-Uphill	42	2,356	15.12.90	Glenbeigh-Boolteens	33	4,966
.10.90	Uphill-Clevedon	33	2,389	16.12.90	Boolteens-Anascaul	28	4,994
0.10.90	Clevedon-Avonmouth	23	2,412	17.12.90	Anascaul-Ballyferriter	50	5,044
1.10.90	Avonmouth-Newport	46	2,458	18.12.90	Ballyferriter-Dingle	37	5,081
2.10.90	Newport-Cardiff	27	2,485	19.12.90	Dingle-Stradbally	27	5,108
3.10.90	Cardiff-Font-y-Gary-(Rhoose)	34	2,519	20.12.90	Stradbally-Tralee	34	5,142
4.10.90	Rhoose-Ogmore-by-Sea	31	2,550	21.12.90	Tralee-Ballyheige	28	5,170
5.10.90	Ogmore-by-Sea-Margam	31	2,581	22.12.90	Ballyheige-Ballynaskreena	31	5,201
6.10.90	Margam-Southgate	47	2,628	23.12.90	Ballynaskreena-Sallowglen	40	5,241
7.10.90	Southgate-Llanmadoc	44	2,672	24.12.90	Sallowglen-Kilcoran	46	5,287
8.10.90	Llanmadoc-Burry Port	40	2,712	25.12.90	Kilcoran-Limerick	30	5,317
9.10.90	Burry Port-St Clears	45	2,757	26.12.90	Limerick-Ennis	37	5,354
0.10.90	St Clears-Tenby	40	2,797	27.12.90	Ennis-Kilrush	43	5,397
1.10.90	Tenby-Bosherton	37	2,834	28.12.90	Kilrush-Kilbaha	37	5,434
2.10.90	Bosherton-Rhoscrowther	40	2,874	29.12.90	Kilbaha-Kilkee	33	5,467
3.10.90	Rhoscrowther-Sandy Haven	41	2,915	30.12.90	Kilkee-Spanish Point	38	5,505
4.10.90	Sandy Haven-St Brides	43	2,958	31.12.90	Spanish Point-Lisdoonvarna	45	5,550
5.10.90	St Brides-St Davids	38	2,996	1.1.91	Lisdoonvarna-Ballyvaghan-(Leagh South)	39	5,589
6.10.90	St Davids-Mathry	38	3,034	2.1.91	Ballvaghan-Kinvarra	26	5,615
7.10.90	Mathry-Newport	41	3,075	3.1.91	Kinvarra-Galway	40	5,655
8.10.90	Newport-Mwnt	40	3,115	4.1.91	Galway-Spiddle	21	5,676
9.10.90	Mwnt-New Quay	36	3,151	5.1.91	Spiddle-Kinvarra-(Turlough)	32	5,708
0.10.90	New Quay-Aberystwyth	46	3,197	6.1.91	Kinvarra-Glinsk	41	5,749
1.10.90	Aberystwyth-Machynlleth -(Aberdovey)	42	3,239	7.1.91	Glinsk-Ballyconneely	39	5,788
.11.90	Machynlleth-Llwngwril	38	3,277	8.1.91	Ballyconneely-Cleggan	45	5,833
.11.90	Llwyngwril-Llanfair	30	3,307	9.1.91	Cleggan-Kylemore	39	5,872
.11.90	Llanfair-Pwllheli	45	3,352	10.1.91	Kylemore-Leenaun	29	5,901
.11.90	Pwllheli-Meillionydd Bach	37	3,389	11.1.91	Leenaun-Thallabawn	40	5,941
.11.90	Meillionydd Bach-Llangwnnadl	28	3,417	12.1.91	Thallabawn-Louisburgh	30	5,971
.11.90	Llangwnnadl-Clynnog-Fawr	39	3,456	13.1.91	Louisburgh-Croagh Patrick-Westport	35	6,006
.11.90	Clynnog-Fawr-Llanberis	37	3,493	14.1.91	Westport-Mullaranny	39	6,045
.11.90	Llanberis-Snowdon-Caernarfon	49	3,542	15.1.91	Mullaranny-Achill-Mullaranny	40	6,085
.11.90	Caernarfon-Valley	41	3,583	16.1.91	Mullaranny-Bangor	40	6,125
0.11.90	Valley-B & I Ferry-Central Dublin	16	3,599	17.1.91	Bangor-Gweesalia	33	6,158
1.11.90	Dublin-Greystones	36	3,635	18.1.91	Gweesalia-Belmullet	27	6,185
2.11.90	Greystones-Arklow	52	3,687	19.1.91	Belmullet-Fallmore	30	6,215
3.11.90	Arklow-Blackwater	50	3,737	20.1.91	Fallmore-Belmullet	36	6,251
4.11.90	Blackwater-Rosslare Harbour	41	3,778	21.1.91	Belmullet-Pollatomish	28	6,279
5.11.90	Rosslare Harbour-Grange	39	3,817	22.1.91	Pollatomish-Stonefield	37	6,316
6.11.90	Grange-Fethard	46	3,863	23.1.91	Stonefield-Carrowmore	48	6,364
7.11.90	Fethard-Whitechurch	42	3,905	24.1.91	Carrowmore-Ross	40	6,404
8.11.90	Whitechurch-Waterford	36	3,941	25.1.91	Ross-Inishcrone	36	6,440
9.11.90	Waterford-Tramore	42	3,983	26.1.91	Inishcrone-Ardanglass	37	6,477
0.11.90	Tramore-Dungarvan	42	4,025	27.1.91	Ardnaglass-Strandhill	35	6,512
1.11.90	Dungarvan-Grange	36	4,061	28.1.91	Strandhill-Rathcormack	28	6,540
2.11.90	Grange-Garryvoe	43	4,104	29.1.91	Rathcormack-Mount Edward	26	6,566
3.11.90	Garryvoe-Cahermore	42	4,146	30.1.91	Mount Edward-Ballyshannon	41	6,607
4.11.90	Cahermore-Weaver Point	53	4,199	31.1.91	Ballyshannon-Donegal	30	6,637
5.11.90	Weaver Point-Kinsale	36	4,235	1.2.91	Donegal-Dunkineely	36	6,673
6.11.90	Kinsale-Timoleague-(Upton)	39	4,274	2.2.91	Dunkineely-Kilcar	32	6,705
7.11.90	Timoleague-Clonakilty	38	4,312	3.2.91	Kilcar-Doonalt	33	6,738
8.11.90	Clonakilty-Glandore	36	4,348	4.2.91	Doonalt-Ardara	35	6,773
9.11.90	Glandore-Rathmore	43	4,391	5.2.91	Ardara-Naran	38	6,811
0.11.90	Rathmore-Schull	36	4,427	6.2.91	Naran-Dunglow	45	6,856
1.12.90	Schull-Callaros	40	4,467	7.2.91	Dunglow-Bunbeg	40	6,896
2.12.90	Callaros-Kilcrohane	44	4,511	8.2.91	Bunbeg-Gortahork	31	6,927
3.12.90	Kilcrohane-Bantry	39	4,550	9.2.91	Gortahork-Carrickart	44	6,971
4.12.90	Bantry-Trafrask	38	4,588	10.2.91	Carrickart-Milford	40	7,011
5.12.90	Trafrask-Allihies	40	4,628	11.2.91	Milford-Ballynashannagh	35	7,046
6.12.90	Allihies-Coolounig	37	4,665	12.2.91	Ballynashannagh-Ards	38	7,084
7.12.90	Coolounig-Kenmare	33	4,698	13.2.91	Ards-Letterkenny	32	7,116
8.12.90	Kenmare-Black Valley	26	4,724	14.2.91	Letterkenny-Buncrana	50	7,166
9.12.90	Black Valley-Carrauntoohil -Black Valley	21	4,745	15.2.91	Buncrana-Ballyliffin	34	7,200
10.12.90	Black Valley-Killowen	27	4,772	16.2.91	Ballyliffin-Malin Head	41	7,241
11.12.90	Killowen-Caherdaniel	55	4,827	17.2.91	Malin Head-Moville	43	7,284
12.12.90	Caherdaniel-Dungeagan	31	4,858	18.2.91	Moville-Derry	30	7,314
13.12.90	Dungeagan-Cahersiveen	44	4,902	19.2.91	Derry-Limavady	31	7,345
14.12.90	Cahersiveen-Glenbeigh	31	4,933	20.2.91	Limavady-Coleraine	38	7,383

Date	Route	Miles	Total
21.2.91	Coleraine-Portballintrae-(Coleraine)	26	7,409
22.2.91	Bushmills-Portballintrae-Ballycastle	37	7,446
23.2.91	Ballycastle-Cushendun	34	7,480
24.2.91	Cushendun-Aughagash	49	7,529
25.2.91	Aughagash-Ballystrudder	47	7,576
26.2.91	Ballystrudder-Brown's Bay-Ballystrudder	26	7,602
27.2.91	Ballystrudder-Belfast-(Newtownabbey)	32	7,634
28.2.91	Belfast-Donaghadee	31	7,665
1.3.91	Donaghadee-Cloghy	44	7,709
2.3.91	Cloghy-Greyabbey	43	7,752
3.3.91	Greyabbey-Killyleagh	41	7,793
4.3.91	Killyleagh-Strand	38	7,831
5.3.91	Strand-Newcastle	37	7,868
6.3.91	Newcastle-Slieve Donard-Annalong	32	7,900
7.3.91	Annalong-Warrenpoint	26	7,926
8.3.91	Warrenpoint-Carlingford	32	7,958
9.3.91	Carlingford-Dundalk	37	7,995
10.3.91	Dundalk-Ganderstown	42	8,037
11.3.91	Ganderstown-Rush	47	8,084
12.3.91	Rush-Malahide	33	8,117
13.3.91	Malahide-Dublin 1	30	8,147
14.3.91	Dublin-Manchester Airport-Valley	27	8,174
15.3.91	Valley-Bull Bay	38	8,212
16.3.91	Bull Bay-Llangoed	48	8,260
17.3.91	Llangoed-Conwy	41	8,301
18.3.91	Conwy-Rhyl	49	8,350
19.3.91	Rhyl-Connahs Quay	38	8,388
20.3.91	Connahs Quay-New Brighton	48	8,436
21.3.91	New Brighton-Runcorn	46	6,482
22.3.91	Runcorn-Central Liverpool	29	8,511
23.3.91	Liverpool-Southport	35	8,546
24.3.91	Southport-Warton-(Lea)	42	8,588
25.3.91	Warton-Sower Carr	47	8,635
26.3.91	Sower Carr-Lancaster	30	8,665
27.3.91	Lancaster-Silverdale	41	8,706
28.3.91	Silverdale-Cark	43	8,749
29.3.91	Cark-Barrow in Furness	44	8,793
30.3.91	Barrow in Furness-Millom	48	8,841
31.3.91	Millom-Boot	43	8,884
1.4.91	Boot-Scafell-Boot	31	8,915
2.4.91	Boot-Whitehaven	43	8,958
3.4.91	Whitehaven-Silloth	53	9,011
4.4.91	Silloth-Bowness on Solway	36	9,047
5.4.91	Bowness on Solway-Carlisle	25	9,072
6.4.91	Carlisle-Annan	36	9,108
7.4.91	Annan-Dumfries	38	9,146
8.4.91	Dunfries-Thorniehill	41	9,187
9.4.91	Thorniehill-Auchencairn	29	9,216
10.4.91	Auchencairn-Kirkudbright	33	9,249
11.4.91	Kirkudbright-High Auchenlarie	38	9,287
12.4.91	High Auchenlarie-Newton Stewart	26	9,313
13.4.91	Newton Stewart-Garlieston	27	9,340
14.4.91	Garlieston-Port William	39	9,379
15.4.91	Port William-Glenluce	26	9,405
16.4.91	Glenluce-Cairngaan	40	9,445
17.4.91	Cairngaan-Portpatrick	43	9,488
18.4.91	Portpatrick-Kirkcolm	35	9,523
19.4.91	Kirkcolm-Ballantrae	42	9,565
20.4.91	Ballantrae-Girvan	23	9,588
21.4.91	Girvan-Ayr	42	9,630
22.4.91	Ayr-Saltcoats	40	9,670
23.4.91	Saltcoats-Largs	28	9,698
24.4.91	Largs-Port Glasgow	36	9,734
25.4.91	Port Glasgow-Central Glasgow	38	9,772
26.4.91	Glasgow-Helensburgh	40	9,812
27.4.91	Helensburgh-Cove	33	9,845
28.4.91	Cove-Arrochar	38	9,883
29.4.91	Arrochar-Carrick Castle	37	9,920

Date	Route	Miles	Total
30.4.91	Carrick Castle-Dunoon-(Hunter's Quay)	38	9,9
1.5.91	Dunoon-Ardtaraig-(Hunter's Quay)	38	9,9
2.5.91	Ardtaraig-Colintraive	27	10,0
3.5.91	Colintraive-Tighnabruaich	31	10,0
4.5.91	Tighnabruaich-Strachur	55	10,1
5.5.91	Strachur-Inverary	38	10,1
6.5.91	Inverary-Ardrishaig	51	10,1
7.5.91	Ardrishaig-Claonaig Bay Jetty-(Tarbert)	46	10,2
8.5.91	Claonaig Bay-Ballochgair	47	10,2
9.5.91	Ballochgair-Southend	43	10,3
10.5.91	Southend-Machrihanish	41	10,3
11.5.91	Machrihanish-Tayinloan	32	10,4
12.5.91	Tayinloan-Tarbert	37	10,4
13.5.91	Tarbert-Coulaghailtro	33	10,4
14.5.91	Coulaghailtro-Ashfield	45	10,5
15.5.91	Ashfield-Tayvallich	50	10,5
16.5.91	Tayvallich-Ardfern	43	10,6
17.5.91	Ardfern-Kilmelford	39	10,6
18.5.91	Kilmelford-Oban	41	10,6
19.5.91	Oban-Bercaldine	37	10,7
20.5.91	Bercaldine-Duror	37	10,7
21.5.91	Duror-Achintee Farm	43	10,8
22.5.91	Achintee Farm-Ben Nevis-Fort William	33	10,8
23.5.91	Fort William-Camusnagaul-(Fort William)	44	10,8
24.5.91	Camusnagaul-Camasnacroise	37	10,9
25.5.91	Camasnacroise-Lochaline	40	10,9
26.5.91	Lochaline-Drimnin	22	10,9
27.5.91	Drimnin-Strontian	56	11,0
28.5.91	Strontian-Salen	17	11,0
29.5.91	Salen-Achnaha	46	11,1
30.5.91	Achnaha-Salen	44	11,1
31.5.91	Salen-Roshven	34	11,1
1.6.91	Roshven-Mallaig	46	11,2
2.6.91	Mallaig-Tarbet	25	11,2
3.6.91	Tarbet-Inverie	37	11,2
4.6.91	Inverie-Barrisdale Bothy	41	11,3
5.6.91	Barrisdale-Corran	30	11,3
6.6.91	Corran-Glenelg	29	11,3
7.6.91	Glenelg-Ratagan	25	11,4
8.6.91	Ratagan-Kyle of Lochalsh	34	11,4
9.6.91	Kyle of Lochalsh-Lochcarron	43	11,4
10.6.91	Lochcarron-Applecross	37	11,5
11.6.91	Applecross-Sheildaig	49	11,5
12.6.91	Sheildaig-Lower Diabaig	35	11,6
13.6.91	Lower Diabaig-Gairloch	33	11,6
14.6.91	Gairloch-Pool Crofts	48	11,6
15.6.91	Pool Crofts-Laide	29	11,7
16.6.91	Laide-Camusnagaul	35	11,7
17.6.91	Camusnagaul-Allt na h-Airbhe-(Ullapool)	43	11,7
18.6.91	Allt na h-Airbhe-Ullapool	25	11,8
19.6.91	Ullapool-Achininver Youth Hostel	28	11,8
20.6.91	Achininver-Laide of Reiff	30	11,8
21.6.91	Laide of Reiff-Lochinver-(Badnaban)	47	11,9
22.6.91	Lochinver-Glenleraig	44	11,9
23.6.91	Glenleraig-Scourie More	37	12,0
24.6.91	Scourie More-Polin	46	12,0
25.6.91	Polin-Cape Wrath-(Durness)	23	12,0
26.6.91	Cape Wrath-Durness	37	12,1
27.6.91	Durness-Hope-(Tongue)	50	12,1
28.6.91	Tongue-Whiten Head-Tongue	55	12,2
29.6.91	Tongue-Farr	37	12,2
30.6.91	Farr-Melvich	43	12,2
1.7.91	Melvich-Thurso	44	12,3
2.7.91	Thurso-Dunnet Head-Dunnet	46	12,3
3.7.91	Dunnet-John O'Groats	28	12,4
4.7.91	John O'Groats-Wick	34	12,4
5.7.91	Wick-Dunbeath	38	12,4
6.7.91	Dunbeath-Brora	53	12,

Date	Route	Miles	Total
7.7.91	Brora-Dornoch	37	12,576
8.7.91	Dornoch-Portmahomack	42	12,618
9.7.91	Portmahomack-Saltburn	53	12,671
10.7.91	Saltburn-Cromarty	50	12,721
11.7.91	Cromarty-Fortrose	25	12,746
12.7.91	Fortrose-Inverness	28	12,774
13.7.91	Inverness-Dores-Inverness	38	12,812
14.7.91	Inverness-Nairn	36	12,848
15.7.91	Nairn-Findhorn	42	12,890
16.7.91	Findhorn-Lossiemouth	35	12,925
17.7.91	Lossiemouth-Buckie	34	12,959
18.7.91	Buckie-Banff	44	13,003
19.7.91	Banff-Rosehearty	42	13,045
20.7.91	Rosehearty-Peterhead	44	13,089
21.7.91	Peterhead-Newburgh	38	13,127
22.7.91	Newburgh-Aberdeen	25	13,152
23.7.91	Aberdeen-Stonehaven	33	13,185
24.7.91	Stonehaven-Montrose	44	13,229
25.7.91	Montrose-Arbroath	32	13,261
26.7.91	Arbroath-Dundee	36	13,297
27.7.91	Dundee-St Andrews	36	13,333
28.7.91	St Andrews-Anstruther	36	13,369
29.7.91	Anstruther-Methil	32	13,401
30.7.91	Methil-Inverkeithing	41	13,442
31.7.91	Inverkeithing-Central Edinburgh	26	13,468
1.8.91	Edinburgh-Gullane	38	13,506
2.8.91	Gullane-East Linton	34	13,540
3.8.91	East Linton-Cockburnspath	31	13,571
4.8.91	Cockburnspath-Eyemouth	38	13,609
5.8.91	Eyemouth-Berwick upon Tweed	14	13,623
6.8.91	Berwick-Bamburgh	37	13,660
7.8.91	Bamburgh-Alnmouth	45	13,705
8.8.91	Alnmouth-Ellington	35	13,740
9.8.91	Ellington-Blyth	29	13,769
10.8.91	Blyth-Newcastle upon Tyne	30	13,799
11.8.91	Newcastle-Seaburn	33	13,832
12.8.91	Seaburn-Horden	34	13,866
13.8.91	Horden-Eston	41	13,907
14.8.91	Eston-Salthburn by the Sea	22	13,929
15.8.91	Saltburn-Whitby	37	13,966
16.8.91	Whitby-Scarborough	41	14,007
17.8.91	Scarborough-Flamborough	43	14,050
18.8.91	Flamborough-Hornsea	35	14,085
19.8.91	Hornsea-Withernsea	32	14,117
20.8.91	Withernsea-Spurn Head-Easington	39	14,156
21.8.91	Easington-Kingston upon Hull	39	14,195
22.8.91	Hull-Barrow Haven	25	14,220
23.8.91	Barrow Haven-Cleethorpes-(Grimsby)	39	14,259
24.8.91	Cleethorpes-Mablethorpe	48	14,307
25.8.91	Mablethorpe-Skegness	27	14,334
26.8.91	Skegness-Boston	40	14,374
27.8.91	Boston-Holbeach	40	14,414
28.8.91	Holbeach-King's Lynn	47	14,461
29.8.91	Kings Lynn-Hunstanton	33	14,494
30.8.91	Hunstanton-Burnham Overy Staith	27	14,521
31.8.91	Burnham Overy Staith-Blakeney	28	14,549
1.9.91	Blakeney-Cromer	29	14,578
2.9.91	Cromer-Sea Palling	33	14,611
3.9.91	Sea Palling-Great Yarmouth	30	14,641
4.9.91	Great Yarmouth-Kessingland	37	14,678
5.9.91	Kessingland-Dunwich	24	14,702
6.9.91	Dunwich-Snape	27	14,729
7.9.91	Snape-Bawdsey	42	14,771
8.9.91	Bawdsey-Felixstowe	39	14,810
9.9.91	Felixstowe-Central Ipswich	23	14,833
10.9.91	Ipswich-Manningtree	40	14,873
11.9.91	Manningtree-Harwich	22	14,895
12.9.91	Harwich-Great Clacton	40	14,935
13.9.91	Great Clacton-Shrub End	44	14,979
14.9.91	Shrub End-Maylandsea	44	15,023
15.9.91	Maylandsea-Cherry Garden	43	15,066
16.9.91	Cherry Garden-Doggetts Farm	44	15,110
17.9.91	Doggetts Farm-Southend on Sea	25	15,135
18.9.91	Southend-Stanford-Le-Hope	39	15,174
19.9.91	Stanford-Le-Hope-Rainham	32	15,206
20.9.91	Rainham-Tower Bridge	33	15,239
Total	Kilometres		15,239
Total	Miles		9,469

Weather

In the interests of simplification, a day's weather is solely determined by the predominant meteorological feature. Thus, for example, where rain persisted for the greater part of a given walking day (my least favourite element), with perhaps sporadic sunny intervals, Rain will be the official designation.

With a view to avoiding the climatic excesses of the Scottish winter, I opted to walk round Ireland first – and walked slap bang into Ireland's worst run of weather in living memory. The 'Hurricane' of January 5th 1991 far exceeded the ferocity of the Great Storm of October 16th 1987, both of which I experienced first hand. Meanwhile,Scotland basked in its mildest winter in years...

| Date | Rain Free | | | | Fog/ Sea- mist | Snow | Hail | Rain | Hurri- cane | Total days |
	Sun- shine	Mild	Cold	Gales						
1990 5-31 August	20	2						5		26
September	15	8						7		30
October	3	11	1					16		31
November		15						14		30
December		10	1		1	1	8	10		31
1991 January		1	11	1		2		15	1	31
February		5	6		1	3		13		28
March		10	2	1	1			17		31
April		6	4	1				19		30
May	13	1	1	1	1			14		31
June	9	1		1				19		30
July	9	5			5			12		31
August	23	1		1				6		31
1-20 September	16	1						3		20
Total Days	108	77	26	6	10	6	8	170	1	412

Total Precipitation dominated days (Rain, Snow, Hail, etc) : 195.
Total Precipitation free days (dry) : 217

Footnote: Winds above 34 mph are deemed Galeforce; storm winds above 75 mph constitute a Hurricane.